D1373316

Creative Rhythmic Movement

Boys and Girls Dancing

GLADYS ANDREWS FLEMING

School of Education
Virginia Commonwealth University

PRENTICE-HALL, INC., Englewood Cliffs, New Jersey

Library of Congress Cataloging in Publication Data

Fleming, Gladys Andrews.
    Creative rhythmic movement.

    1. Dancing—Children's dances. I. Title.
GV1799.F57   793.3   75-2087
ISBN 0-13-191114-7
ISBN 0-13-191106-6 pbk.

Printed in the United States of America

10   9   8   7   6   5   4   3   2   1

Prentice-Hall International, Inc., London
Prentice-Hall of Australia, Pty. Ltd., Sydney
Prentice-Hall of Canada, Ltd., Toronto
Prentice-Hall of India Private Limited, New Delhi
Prentice-Hall of Japan, Inc., Tokyo
Prentice-Hall of Southeast Asia (Pte.) Ltd., Singapore

Acknowledgments

Words are inadequate to express my gratitude and respect for all the boys and girls who have participated over the years with me in creative rhythmic movement and dance. The children who make up this edition of *Creative Rhythmic Movement* are but representative of the throngs of children in this and other countries whose zest for movement and creative spirit and desire for expression have touched my life. Also I wish to acknowledge the role of the chidren's principals and teachers, who have welcomed me into their schools and have contributed in unique ways. I am particularly indebted to the following persons for their participation in this edition: Mrs. Elizabeth Wall (Principal, Maury and Blackwell Schools, Richmond, Virginia) and many of her teachers, specifically DeNette Garber Steverson, Hallibeth Judd, and Loretta Woolard Blanks. They made it possible for me to work with them in intensive ways and to extend the experiences with the same group of children for five years. I am also grateful to Mrs. Katherine Sevedge (Principal, Sherwood School, Memphis, Tennessee) and her fine group of teachers, specifically Mary Ann Watson. They have helped in a variety of ways. Special recognition is given to Joan Oates and Clifford Miller III for their help in working with me with the staff and children of Collegiate Schools (Lower School), Richmond, Virginia.

What a joy it has been working with good friends: Joyce Eldredge Brown, Florence Burns, Clark W. Graves, Judy Hogan, and Alonah Stith. Reference is made throughout this book to their contribution by their recording, arranging, or composing music with the boys and girls as it spontaneously happened.

I am grateful to many people who have been involved in *Creative Rhythmic Movement* in special ways:

My colleagues Judy Schwartz and Richard Bull for their expertise and constant prodding and encouragement;

My former teachers, Isabel Cranes, Katherine Cronin, and Margaret H'Doubler for their persisting influence;

The many graduate and undergraduate students on many campuses whose enthusiasm has challenged me;

Marguerite Hogan and Elaine Quinn for working on the manuscript;

iii

Linda Raines for the sketches and Phyllis Borucki and James Raines for sharing of their time;

Robert Grey, Pete Hobson, Helen Stahl, and Michael Pearlstein for their willingness to share their hobby of photography and their perseverance in trying to "catch us" in action;

Jamie Fuller and Martin Behan of Prentice-Hall for their painstaking efforts in the production of this publication;

And finally my husband Bob, who in a very real sense became my catalyst in preparing this new edition. His enthusiasm, tolerance, gentle humor, penetrating understanding, and Socratic questioning helped to clarify and focus my thinking. A constant source of stimulation has been his respect for my work with boys and girls.

GLADYS ANDREWS FLEMING

Contents

III

Initiating Movement
and Dance

7

Getting Started, 125

8

Chants, 140

9

Dance Songs, 163

10

Helping Children to Relax, 187

IV

Elements of Dance

11

Conquering Space, 194

12

Time and Force, 218

13

Sound, 241

V

Boys and Girls Dancing

14

Fun with Folk and Social Dance, 275

15

Putting It All Together:
Making Dances, 302

Resources, 345

Index, 349

Foreword

Creative rhythmic movement has a unique and vital place in today's schools. The potential of this area is unlimited in efforts to help children feel good about themselves, find zest and excitement in learning, and relate to others in meaningful ways. Opportunities for individualization occur in settings that are secure and yet stretch and extend learning and group relationships.

The author continues to work with children and teachers over the country. The materials included come from active work with many schools and thousands of children. There is a fresh quality which generates enthusiasm and reflects sensitivity to children and their world. The author worked with a group of inner city children for five consecutive years. Their growth and development has contributed to the vitality of the book.

The organization emphasizes creativity, movement, and rhythm as major components. These forces are constant and are treated in a thorough and developmental manner. Much attention is given to ways of getting started and to creative uses of the materials in making dances which reflect children's understandings, concepts, and communication skills. The approaches employed are practical and can be used in any type of school situation.

It is refreshing to view children's creative rhythmic movement as an integral part of the total curriculum. No effort is made to develop dance as an end point; instead, the dance compositions described in the last chapter reflect a total curriculum focus. The arts including the dance experience become clearly a dynamic and essential ingredient in the total curriculum design.

The music used throughout the book is unique; it was developed as teachers and children worked together. It came from them in expressive ways as meaningful movement and creative activities were carried out.

Children need opportunities to develop and release their rhythmic and creative qualities. This is the underlying premise. Hence, it should be of interest and help to many audiences—to physical education teachers and specialists for its developmental qualities reflecting the power and importance of movement and creative dance; to teachers of dance, since it brings together components essential for dance competence; to classroom teachers for the practical help and insight it provides; to music and art teachers, since rhythm is basic; to administrators, since it communicates the importance of the arts in children's growth and learning. College students looking forward to teaching should find great help in understanding rhythm and dance in the lives of children.

A lifetime of persistent and active work and dedication is reflected throughout the book. The author has lived creative rhythmic movement; she knows children and teachers and demonstrates leadership and vitality in fostering movement—dance and creative expression.

Robert S. Fleming

Preface

Our book is *of*, rather than *about*, boys and girls. It is of actual experiences, understandings and unforgettable creative moments. The glimpses of boys and girls in action through photography, dialogue, materials, and "creative gems" have been initiated by us. They are set forth as they actually happened with many children, and sometimes their teachers, in diversified situations in various parts of this country. *The boys and girls are real* as are the *experiences and situations!* We have tried to share with you some of the conversations, understandings of our movement and its language, and samples of our discoveries and creative work as we moved and danced, chanted and sang our way through this expressive realm of human experience. We call this creative rhythmic movement—boys and girls dancing.

We—the boys and girls who make up this book, and this teacher—invite you to join us as we explore, communicate, and interact in this exciting adventure in creative rhythmic movement. For us it has been a total integrated experience. We have come to feel good about ourselves and about one another. Something important has happened to us as we have invented and solved problems, moved and danced together. It is our hope that as you follow us through the pages of our book, you too will become involved and encouraged to transmit opportunities to other boys and girls.

Our book is for *you*! It is for teachers working with children, who may or may not have a background in creative rhythmic movement. It is for the teacher of physical education, or movement. It is also for the teacher of dance who may not have had background with children or with elementary education. Classroom teachers who wish to help children with active ways of learning will find many cues and suggestions for enhancing their programs. Teachers of special education, music, or art will find it useful, as will teachers of reading and science or librarians. In addition it is for administrators, supervisors, and curriculum workers who want to "pep up" their school. Parents might find in these pages approaches to aiding or understanding their children. Our book is also geared to serving students preparing to teach as well as teachers in colleges and universities offering professional courses.

This new edition of *Creative Rhythmic Movement* has been prepared for those seeking more effective ways of working with boys and girls in creative areas. The materials, music, movement, dance progressions, dance studies, and compositions presented have been developed in actual teaching-learning situations. Some occurred over short periods of time, while others extended over longer periods of time. The content has been refined and used with college students in preservice classes, with teachers in workshops, and with groups of educators in professional conferences. The materials used in this book have been sifted from numerous records of children's responses, from recordings and products of their work, from photographs and sketches of children in action, and from carefully developed plans for initiating and carrying out activities in creativity—rhythm—movement and dance. Since 1954, when *Creative Rhythmic Movement* was first published, individuals and groups have indicated features they liked and suggested areas they would like extended. These suggestions were valued and have been used extensively in an effort to make this book as helpful as possible. The extensive use of dialogue has resulted from requests of users of *Creative Rhythmic Movement*. We have also responded to requests for:

Ways of initiating a program in creative rhythmic movement, or how to start a program of dance with children;

Ideas for planning a developmental program K—6th grade;

Spurs to those who are hesitant to use experiences in creative rhythmic movement;

Helps for those lacking background in movement and dance;

Encouragement, particularly for the men in physical education, and others whose professional programs may not have included creative rhythmic movement or children's dance;

Aids to classroom teachers;

Nudges to those fearful of rhythmical activities or who have had unsuccessful previous experiences in dance;

Clues to those trying to understand more about the physical child;

Insights to grown-ups who want to better understand and help boys and girls.

GLADYS ANDREWS FLEMING

I

The Meaning of Creative Rhythmic Movement: Children's Dance

1

Creative Rhythmic Movement: Dance For Every Boy and Girl

Bill of Rights

Let me grow as I be
And try to understand why I want to grow like
  me;
Not like my Mom wants me to be,
Nor like my Dad hopes I'll be
Or my teacher thinks I should be.
Please try to understand and help me grow
Just like me!

Gladys Andrews Fleming

This Bill of Rights may be thought of as the child's quest to be an individual—a somebody. Is it too much for any boy or girl to say to adults, "Let me be myself"? Everyone has a right to be uniquely himself in how he feels, what he likes, what he thinks, what he can learn, what he can accomplish, and what he can become. The Bill of Rights may be considered the child's plea for understanding and help in the process of molding and becoming his own particular self. There is no telling to what heights boys and girls might soar if given the chance to fulfill themselves. Let us give them their chance!

This does not just happen. There is no one way, no blueprint, but there are clues. These clues are given to us by boys and girls themselves as they search for individualism.

3

Their zest for aliveness, for movement, for communication and expression, are urgent ever-present clues. Are we wise enough to recognize that their need to *move* is an indicator of individual uniqueness which needs understanding, nurturing, and encouraging?

In a way movement and children are synonymous—it is difficult to think about one without the other. Movement is a universal language of boys and girls, who use it to express reactions to us, to each other, to their world, to situations, and to things. Through their zest to move and to express themselves they communicate their very personal ideas, thoughts, feelings, and aspirations—what they prize as well as what hurts them. These movements can tell us how we can help them in their process of growing. Such clues give purpose and challenge, direction and excitement to teachers, parents, and adults privileged to share in the development of a unique, creative human being —a *somebody*.

One way we help boys and girls is to offer meaningful opportunities to move. We can provide purposeful, developmental programs through creative rhythmic movement and dance for all boys and girls. This book is dedicated to that end. It is about boys and girls and first-hand experiences in creative rhythmic movement in the elementary school. It is about boys and girls in diverse situations and in various parts of this country and abroad. It is about bringing these experiences to more and more children.

THE MEANING OF CREATIVE RHYTHMIC MOVEMENT:
Children's Dance

Children tell us how much movement means to them in their own language.

"I have something inside me. I'll show it to you. Watch me move." *This is dance.*

"I have something to say to you. I'll dance it." *This is dance.*

"It's sort of like a different language which everyone in the world can speak and understand." *This is dance.*

When we have something to "say" we sometimes talk with our bodies and muscles instead of our mouths. We have to think about things like the movements we put together, what comes first, the space, the music. *This is dance.*

Creative rhythmic movement is the communication of one's thoughts and feelings expressed through the instrument of one's body. A child, who is often limited in the experience and ability to communicate verbally, explores and uses movement to express and interpret, in his own way, in tangible form, that which is within his experience. Creative rhythmic movement, with guidance and encouragement, gives the child the ability to produce and control the movements he, as an individual, wishes to use so that he can "say" to others what he wishes to say. It is an opportunity for children to respond to others and to the world. Through exploration of movement, the child also gains an understanding of his body. He becomes able not only to express that which is within his immediate experience but to expand himself. He is given the opportunity to select his actions with thought and understanding and purpose. He is helped to *grow*.

The Importance of Creative Rhythmic Movement

In creative rhythmic movement there are no failures. Children are innately endowed with the ability to move, with creativity and rhythm. All that is needed is to bring these to the surface. This enables sensing and responding to occur as the body and mind are freed, and brings about acceptance of self, respect for self, and some understanding of self. Awareness of self in relation to space, to others, to things, to the world—all are part of the sensitizing process so important for children.

A child being himself—a somebody—often reveals through movement many personal characteristics which might not otherwise be evident. In addition, his self-concept, self-image, and self-confidence is bolstered as he is actively involved in experiences directly related to him. Inhibitions are overcome and a good feeling about self emerges as *discovering, identifying,* and *accepting* are encouraged. Michael finds that he can leap across the room in a different way than anyone else. He is himself and good.

As children gain in self-respect, they have the conviction that what they discover for themselves or work out for themselves is worthwhile. They grow in stature when they lose the fear of presenting their creation to a group, or of sharing their creation with a younger or older group. Their eyes light up when their creations are genuinely accepted, because of their sincerity of purpose, ability to organize an experience, or to establish a logical arrangement of ideas expressed in a form others can understand. Their verbal outbursts of "Let's do it again" are recognizable expressions of achievement. The glow mirrored on their faces is another manifestation of the good feeling which children have about their accomplishments. Seeing Tom grow "inches in height and degrees in personality" when directing a group in a square dance he has written, is a satisfying experience which teachers and children share. This recognition, resulting from accomplishment, helps children to "let go" and to shake loose from strains of cramped quarters, periods of mental concentration, tensions, or from "inside" hurts.

"Gee, That Was Fun!" "Look What I Can Do!" "It Worked Out!" "We Need More Time!" Fun, happiness, satisfaction, and growth take place when children can "let go" and use creative rhythmic movement to express that which is within their own experience. When they interpret an idea, feeling, picture, or sound through the use of movement so that others can understand what they are trying to say or to portray, they realize satisfaction in accomplishment. Children grow as individuals and as members of a group when they are not ashamed to let their feelings come out, or when they are not afraid to express what is within them. They gain confidence in themselves when they are able to give expression to an interpretation they have worked out. Realizing that each person "says it" differently, they take pride in the satisfaction they receive from an accomplishment or when another group members says, "That's really neat, Carl. That's great!"

Creative rhythmic movement allows teachers to recognize and respect the physical child. For too long education has placed marked attention upon the intellectual development of children with too little emphasis on the physical aspects of growth. Our work with urban schools reinforces the often untapped phenomenon of the physical self. Recognition and use of physical factors provides a comfortable, meaningful, and nonthreatening setting for working with children. Emphasis on the physical may for many children provide a new key to cognitive development, self-esteem, and ultimate human renewal.

CHILDREN'S DANCE ACTIVITIES

Creative rhythmic movement reflects the way the individual uses movement involving elements of space, time, and force for the purpose of expression, communication, or personal pleasure. There are varying opportunities for creative expression, and yet they all require a movement and rhythmic base.

A national survey concerning the status of children's dance was recently conducted by the Task Force on Children's Dance of the Dance Division of American Association of Health, Physical Education and Recreation. A summary of its findings follows:*

SUMMARY OF QUESTIONNAIRE RETURNS

The Status of Dance and Rhythmic Activities

THE DATA reveal that some dance and/or rhythmic activities are a part of most elementary programs with a wide variety of activities categorized in this area ranging from fundamental movements to various dance forms, ball bouncing, and tumbling to music.

NO CLEAR-CUT DESIGN or framework is indicated. . . .

EMPHASIS ON DANCE seems to be somewhat stronger for the early childhood period than in later years of the elementary school, with a concentration on fundamental movement, rhythmical activities, folk dance and singing games, and some creative dance in nursery through third grade. . . .

VERY LITTLE creative activity or creative dance is provided for children of any age.

LIMITED EMPHASIS is given the relationship of rhythmic activity and dance to literature, creative dramatics, science, and social studies.

CURRICULUM LEADERS in elementary education do not appear to have a clear-cut rationale or design in which rhythmic activity and dance can make their unique contributions to the total development of children. . . .

* Report: Task Force—Children's Dance, *Journal of Health, Physical Education and Recreation*, 42 (June 1971), 19.

Preparation for Teaching Dance in Elementary School

DANCE PREPARATION (dance courses) has been primarily designed for secondary level. . . .

DANCE COURSES in college, many said, consisted of learning the dance or participating in a dance rather than learning how to relate, present, teach, and create dance for children. . . .

ONLY A SMALL PERCENTAGE of the preparation time of some respondents was devoted to dance. . . .

MEANINGFUL DANCE EXPERIENCES for many tended to come after graduation through workshops, clinics, brush-up courses, private dance studio experiences, summer programs, and graduate work.

TEACHERS by and large seem to feel unprepared to work on dance at the elementary level. . . .

Problems Encountered in the Teaching of Dance in the Elementary School

The problems most often encountered were mentioned as follows:

LACK of adequate undergraduate preparation.

LACK of understanding regarding nature of dance and its contribution.

LACK of space, resource materials, and time; large classes with little help; and lack of administrative support.

THE FEELING of inadequacy on the part of men teachers.

COMMUNITY ATTITUDE (centering around religion and integration).

TERMINOLOGY (that is, the failure to standardize terms in dance and rhythmic activities).

Help Needed to Improve Dance in Elementary Education

The kinds of help needed are a direct reflection of the problems outlined. Suggestions include the following:

BETTER undergraduate preparation.

IMPROVED communication and dissemination procedures for information pertinent to the area.

HELP to understand relationships with other curriculum areas.

IMPROVED administrative support and aid from competent personnel, e.g., demonstration lessons and help in developing curriculum.

MEANINGFUL in-service education—workshops, clinics, conferences and extension courses; more men conducting workshops.

RESOURCE MATERIALS—records, books, films, rhythm instruments.

THE TERM *CREATIVE RHYTHMIC MOVEMENT:* DANCE

The status of children's dance, however, is often confusing because of the many terms that are used relating to it—such as "creative movement," "rhythms," "creative rhythms," and "dancing." These terms are often used interchangeably. To most teachers they mean the same thing: They are the expressions of children in the use of movement, rhythm, and creativity. But tradition, religion, stereotypes, association with physical education and music programs, previous experiences of teachers, and adult forms of dance all are responsible for some degree of confusion in understanding dancing activities for children. Additional misunderstandings have been caused by the way in which rhythmic movement or dance experiences for children have been provided.

Recent activities in acceptance of movement and emphasis on the arts and humanities are important aspects of children's learning that have led to greater clarification of terms. It is the *meaning* and purpose of these experiences in education which is

important, rather than the terminology used, however. When movement becomes fully recognized as fundamental in children's learning, and becomes a recognized part of the total educational program, perhaps, schools and communities will be ready to give this area of experiences a standardized term, such as "dance" or "children's dance." *It is the meaning of the underlying concept that is important.*

In this book, "creative rhythmic movement" and "dance" are used interchangeably. When movement competence is developed it may become channeled into dance. Although the three components of children's dance—creativity, rhythm, and movement—are dealt with in depth in Chapter 3, they are briefly defined here so as to form a better understanding of the subject within the context of this book.

Movement is an organized change in the location, place, or position of the body or some of its parts using time, force, and space. Movement *is not dance*, but all dance involves movement. *Dance* is a comprehensive term which requires a movement ingredient—yet it includes much more. Dance includes moving through and in space with varying degrees of time and force. It must have expressive and esthetic qualities.

By *rhythm* is meant the regular recurrence of patterns of movement in dance and patterns of sound in music. Every child has a rhythm and a body language that is unique to him. Dance helps boys and girls to discover and "feel" the rhythm in their movements. Young children particularly benefit from the rhythmical opportunities this type of work provides. They *feel, hear,* and *respond* to rhythm as they participate in such activities as dance, songs, and chants. Children discover rhythmical relationships when they move at different rates of speed, with different combinations of strong and weak accents, and to the accompaniment of different patterns of sounds. As they are able to respond to a sound, they can adjust their own rhythmical response to the rhythm of another, or to the rhythm of a group. When they can clap out a beat, walk out a pattern of their own making, or dance with others they feel good.

The term *creativity* bears mention here as it is used in relation to movement. Creativity concerns inventiveness and productivity. We want children to recognize their power to produce, to make, to build, to do. One of the most dynamic ingredients of a program in children's dance is the creative emphasis. Children must have first-hand experiences in order to express themselves creatively. These experiences include the recognition of new relationships in doing, thinking, responding, and communicating ideas, attitudes, and feelings.

Creative opportunity is provided in dance activities for problem solving, experimentation, discovery, taking chances, designing, taking clues, making choices and judgments, sharing relationships, and projections. Through creative movement, boys and girls can express more of themselves than is possible with words. They can respond to questions of why and how things happen. Dance invites boys and girls to use movement in unique creative ways in order to communicate—this leads to esthetic development. First-hand experiences of creating a dance, taking part in a dance experience, or sharing dance with others makes for better understanding of the art form and its components. Children tend to trust themselves and each other as they become involved in

creative activity. They also tend not to be afraid of their world. This, then, is another dimension of creative rhythmic movement.

CREATIVE RHYTHMIC MOVEMENT:
Its Contribution to the
Elementary School Curriculum

Creative rhythmic movement can contribute to every facet of the curriculum in the school. Though it is a part of the total physical education program, it is also basic in all learning. The uses of movement as an integral part of other areas of the curriculum is almost limitless. Classroom activities such as language arts, science, and social studies give impetus to movement activities. Practical examples will be used extensively in future chapters. At this point let us briefly consider the importance of movement both as an independent part and as an integral part of the curriculum areas offered in our schools today.

Listening and following directions, vital prerequisites to learning, are stressed throughout movement activities. Movement provides numerous opportunities to enhance and intensify learning by aiding the ability to perceive, identify, and solve problems. Evaluating, understanding, sensing relationships, organizing, and conceptualizing all flow from movement activities learned within the classroom and gymnasium.

"We've Got an Idea!" "Guess What we Are!" "Let's Find Out!" Children take responsibilities for their own learning when situations and opportunities are provided for them to solve problems. They grow in their ability to find things out for themselves by working with movement problems or responding to experience from their classroom, neighborhood, or community. Moreover, as children discover things for themselves, they are less apt to be afraid to tackle new problems and to work them out to completion. They can share their findings

with a group and thereby gain in knowledge, appreciation, respect, and judgment concerning themselves and others.

Movement experiences are an integral part of holidays, field trips, or even experimentation with the effects of words, sounds, colors, and feelings. Relating chants or folk or social dancing to studies of cultural, national, or geographic backgrounds provides opportunities to include rhythmic movement as a part of the school program. Language development comes naturally as boys and girls develop vocabulary and make associations with movement. Mathematical concepts are also clarified as individuals relate movement to quantitative relationships.

In our schools today there is an emphasis on the broad area of the humanities. Children learn about human relations, sensing and responding by talking, reading, and participating with other boys, girls, and adults. What better opportunities than

through creative rhythmic movement and dance?

Education today places new importance on art forms. Children's movement and dance activities are now beginning to occupy a prominent position in the arts as well as in elementary education in general. Opportunities which provide for responding to color, sound, space, movement, people, places, and things assist in learning development. As boys and girls interpret and portray their feelings and experiences through movement and dance, learning and appreciating is enhanced. During just such a marvelous music and movement experience Jane said, "I never dreamed I could write a song we would dance to." We hear good music, we move to it, we move and find *good* music to accompany, and we make our own music. Assembly programs, parent programs, and sharing with other classes are but a few of the school activities to which creative rhythmic movement—dance—can contribute.

Endless possibilities for children lie in the area of creative rhythmic movement and dance. Serving as releasing agents allowing boys and girls to be alive and active, to sense and respond, to learn and create, to express themselves uniquely, to become participants in the curriculum, movement opens to us as teachers many diverse opportunities for working with children.

"Please try to understand and help me grow just like me!"

The child's Bill of Rights—his quest to be himself—is understood in more depth with a fuller understanding of the meaning of creative rhythmic movement. If everyone had the experience of participating in these activities with children making a "case" for children's dance would be unnecessary. It becomes clear in actuality that this is an important emphasis, a dynamic way of bringing vitality, meaning, humanism, and creativity into the growth and learning of boys and girls. It will provide for them their fulfillment as human beings.

2

Children Are People

Childhood is characterized by phenomenal energy and an enormous enthusiasm for activity. This knowledge is the basis for creative expression through rhythmic movement. And yet there is much more that we know about children that supports the need for creative rhythmic movement as a part of their lives. Movement activities provide a wide variety of meaningful situations in which many kinds of learning and growth can take place. Researchers have told us much about children and their growth and development patterns. The progression of experiences described throughout this book should contribute to our knowledge of the relationship of physical and creative movement to other forms of growth and learning.

We must know and understand children. We must know why they act the way they do, and why individual differences among children are so important in the educative process. *There are many ways of thinking about children that are essential to understanding them as people.* Children cannot be thought of as a number of separate entities; bodies to be nourished and kept in repair; minds with brains to be kept active and alert; or bundles of emotions to be kept from exploding. From the time he is born, the child has a body, mind, and emotions

which are interrelated and interactive. Anything happening to one part affects the whole. Determination of childish reactions and how a child is going to behave, develop, and make use of his potentialities is an intriguing problem. Impinging upon these endowed potentialities are multitudinous environmental factors. A friendly, cooperative, and sympathetic environment will determine, to a large degree, how well the child makes use of his potentialities.

No two children are exactly alike: Despite these important individual differences, they are children; they grow, talk, react, and progress through marked stages of development. All children follow a general basic growth pattern, but at their *own individual rates.* No two children are likely to arrive at the same growth stage at the same time or in the same way. It is important, then, that teachers recognize these stages of growth, and realize that one stage does not suddenly terminate and the next then begin. Children of any given chronological age will express varying levels of maturity and various stages of growth.

Children crave to belong to a social group. They constantly seek approval from others. They crave love and affection and a chance to display their feelings. They are eager to establish their worth through accomplishment. They are extremely curious about their surroundings. They have a desire to know how and why, and an urge to be active, to do something about a discovery.

EARLY CHILDHOOD: THE "I" PERIOD

Children in this group are generally in kindergarten through grade three. They range normally from age five through eight. This is the "I" period; an age in which the child generally thinks he is the center of the universe. It is commonly referred to as the "egotistical" period, and the most striking characteristics are exemplified by such outbursts as: "I did this." "See what I did." "Look at me." "When I grow up, I am going to be a . . . ." "I want to . . . ." It is an age of constant chatter and self-expression; an age which demands a stage and an audience for the star performer! It is the time of the "toothless wonder."

Healthy children of this age are in constant motion and find it almost impossible to stand or sit still. They bounce when they sit, run instead of walk, scuffle their feet, and jitter from one foot to the other. This need for activity expresses itself not only in dance and games, but in all kinds of complex skills and random locomotor movements. They are constantly jumping puddles, climbing over and under everything, tugging, pushing, squeezing, hunching their shoulders, and slapping their heads. They love to move because it is fun. It is the time when motor abilities flourish.

Activity is all-important. This period is in some respects unpredictable. The approach to activity is most frequently with abandon; at other times it is with serious determination. A child of this age requires boisterous, vigorous play; noise and boundless energy are co-existent. Strenuous play contributes best to growth if it is geared to the individual child. The child is the best guide of the amount and kind of activity he needs. Adults must take the cue from the child. Movement and dance, directed by the child's activity needs, provide the opportunity for self-regulation. Not all can "take" the same amount.

Doing—Learning

Early childhood is the time when large muscles are better developed than small ones. In general, muscle development is uneven and incomplete, and the large-muscle groups cry for action. Greatest concentration should be on the development of such basic locomotor movements as walks, jumps, and hops, and on such body movements as swinging, twisting and turning, pushing and pulling, bending, and stretching. Basic movements serve as the foundation for a program in creative rhythmic movement. Childhood experiences in locomotor and body movements serve as a framework for the development of expression and understandings.

When children enter school, they have limited vocabularies. Increased ability to communicate with others develops from constant conversation about happenings of the moment, day, or week.

This is likewise the period in which most children learn to read and acquire other new skills, such as writing, spelling, and telling time. It is the time when skills that require the use of the smaller muscles and eye-hand coordinations are attempted. Many skills can be developed if varied opportunities to learn and practice at this age are provided.

It is important that all children have the chance to experiment; to use and master newly acquired skills at their own rate. Recognition of a child's readiness to learn a skill precludes a single standard of achievement or set pattern of action.

Children like to plan their daily programs in practical, realistic detail. They take delight in planning with the teacher what they will do from day to day. Creative rhythmic movement provides ample and endless opportunities for planning by children and teachers. For example, a social studies unit can be reinforced and vitalized through dance. A group of seven-year-olds are interested in going to the store, the fire-

house, the post office, and other places that offer community services. They want to know where things come from. After they visit a grocery store, the story of milk may take them on a visit to a farm where they see how the cows are milked and the milk is prepared for the dairy. They can follow the milk to the dairy and watch its processing to the point where it is ready for delivery. All this can be later demonstrated through movement. Opportunities for planning can be provided as the children interpret their understanding of milk and its delivery.

Development of Concepts

There is a steady increase in children's ability to think. Concepts concerning objects and human relationships develop gradually, change with repeated experiences, and very gradually become logical and fully serviceable. Children's concepts of time, space, largeness, smallness, fastness, slowness, highness, lowness, heaviness, or lightness develop out of their own experiences. Such concepts cannot be acquired through mere verbal learning, so creative movement is used as a medium of expression to help develop them. Boys and girls are principally interested in here-and-now experiences; those they can see, hear, or feel, and which directly touch their lives. First-hand experiences are all-important.

Feelings

Children enter school with many well-established, emotional patterns, bringing with them all their feelings of "having lived five years." Children of this age exhibit actions that can be described by such labels as "fresh," "smart-aleck," "demanding," "sensitive," "sulky," "withdrawn," "affectionate," "shy," "pensive," or "possessive." Often they want their own way. It is the age when children begin to show in their eyes the "I dare you" look. They assert their authority and insist upon knowing who is boss. They frequently explore a situation to determine the lengths to which they will be permitted to go. There is a reason for being this way— the same reason for being six, seven, or eight years old. The child who is the "most" of all these things needs the most love and understanding. Actions of this sort must be accepted as right for children five through eight and there should be no penalties for being this way. Unless the expressions of the "I" drive are accepted as an important part of growth at this stage, they are apt to emerge later in much less desirable forms.

Strange new school experiences fill young children with uncertainties and apprehensions, until they learn what to expect and what to do about them. They ask adults for help and security by wanting to hold their hands and standing next to them. However, there are days when the entire group erupts like a volcano at the slightest provocation. During the early part of this period some difficulty may be encountered in adjusting to new and sudden changes. At first, some routine and repetition of tasks is necessary, accounting for demands for the same story or activity over and over again. When change is thrust upon them, it should be gradual; if they can understand the reason for change, they accept it more readily.

The many intense inner feelings of children—their needs, frustrations, excitements, and pleasures—make them feel and act as they do. Opportunities should be provided for children to talk, write, draw, sing, play, work, move, and dance out their feelings.

Children early become sensitive to praise. They seek praise or approval and need opportunity to accomplish things in their own right. They begin to want adults to pay attention to them. As they mature, they increasingly desire prestige and individual distinction. They become particularly interested in activities in which they can excel.

Nurturing Children's Curiosity

Because children have vivid imaginations, they dramatize life around them. At times they may confuse imagination and memory. They enjoy here-and-now things and places. Being curious about the physical world, they are constantly asking "What's this?" "What's that?" They often do not wait for answers but find out for themselves by poking or smelling or crawling over, under, or about the world around them. Time is of little consequence. Life takes on meaning with every new experience and association.

Early years in school should provide

many opportunities for children to say, "I am a Somebody. I can do things, and I want to show you." These years can be filled with activities that give adventure, and vitality to their lives. Moving creatively contributes to this process of learning and living.

OLDER BOYS AND GIRLS: "I AND WE"

The group referred to in this book as "older boys and girls" (roughly nine through twelve) are usually in grades four, five, and six. As a group they show an increasing tendency to leave behind "me" and "my" and adopt an "our" and "we" philosophy. This is the period when it is most important that children belong to a group, and to be recognized and accepted by peers. It is the age when distinction is made between "our world" and "your world"; the world of boys and girls and the world of adults. Parents and teachers are generally regarded as "oldsters" or "has-beens." This is the age of unpredictable actions.

Growing Up

This is definitely a growing-up period. Children no longer want to be called children but demand to be recognized as older boys and girls. Growth is continuous, each child having his own unique and distinctive pattern. The tempo of growth and the patterns of acceleration and deceleration of social, mental, and physical development are highly individualistic. This age presents a notably wide range of individual differences and physical maturity. While the slow growers are trying to leave early childhood behind, the fast growers may be approaching preadolescence.

This is the period in which nicknames flourish. "Beanpole," "Fatso," "Shorty," "Slim," and "Peewee" seem to represent physical growth types. As boys and girls start their preadolescent growth spurt, growth may be taking place so rapidly that organic strength and vitality are at a low ebb, with tiredness and lack of ambition clearly apparent. They boy or girl whose growth spurt starts early may be easily fatigued and generally stands out in marked contrast to others of the same age group whose spurts have not yet begun. Caution must be taken with youngsters who have suddenly become heavy, tall, or lanky and who may consequently feel distressed or out of place. Excessive height or weight loom large in importance in the way children feel about themselves, particularly in activity situations.

Maturation is rapid, with girls usually maturing a year or two earlier than boys. Because of the rapidity of growth, many boys and girls appear to lack coordination. They seem to be all hands and feet. They find the gymnasium and the out-of-doors better places in which to move than apartments, classrooms, or restricted living quarters. They find they do not know how big their hands are or how long their legs are and need time to adjust to this lengthening. Creative movement and folk dancing provide excellent experiences in movement congenial to them at this time.

Helping boys and girls understand and respect these differences in individual structures is essential. In creative movement and dance programs differences in size need not be emphasized. When boys and girls are square dancing, height makes no difference. Unless attention is called to it, the boy who has not yet started to "shoot up" will swing his tall partner with no concern about his size.

Learning

Usually children are avid and enthusiastic learners when well-motivated. They seek rich and meaningful experiences which afford them opportunity to see, hear, touch, taste, smell, and react. Because of the depth and range of their interests, their desire for information, and their concern with details, they can be ready and eager for varied learning experiences. Unfortunately many children have already been "turned off" because of unrelated and drab experiences.

During this period most children become more and more proficient in the use of the *written and spoken word.* They carry on many lengthy telephone conversations, and enjoy "putting on" shows of all kinds—talent shows and broadcasts or television shows and assemblies. They will describe in detail things that are important to them—batting averages, the story of the lives of baseball players, astronauts, or the recent movie or television show. It is a good time to help students become efficient listeners as well as contributors.

As a group, the interests of older children have broadened, but as individuals they are very keen about certain people and things. Interests take on a more permanent form. These include art, music, plays that interpret adult life, sports of all kinds, woodworking, doing things with their hands, hobbies, science, and research. They seem particularly interested in those activities—science, space, electronics, oceanography, dance, and sports—which help them to better understand themselves. A capacity for more accurate thinking makes its appearance, stemming in part from their transfer from fantasy to reality and a growing ability to see causal relations.

Children of this age often like to experiment with their environment, trying out things and people more intensively than in early childhood. They absorb information and accumulate ideas concerning the origin and function of sun, moon, space, earth, water, plants, animals, and mechanical and scientific devices. Their desire to know about the physical world in which they live and things and people around them offers a rich source of ideas for creative rhythmic experiences.

Language may become a tool for immediate use in reasoning and problem solving. When encouraged to write about ex-

periences of their own choosing, they do so vividly and in detail, although in somewhat less dramatic terms than in early childhood. Their writing is likely to be full of horror, fighting, humor, or desires. Animals frequently play leading roles in their writing and songs. When they use factual material, they include much detail and action. Individually or in groups, they write project reports, dance themes, perform songs, music, stories, and dramatic skits. Poetry of this period seems to have lost some of the free, personal expression that was characteristic of early childhood.

Active Participation

Development of the large-muscle groups, together with increased motor coordination and endurance, makes participation in vigorous, rhythmic activities possible. During this period girls and boys usually cannot get enough vigorous activity. This is the time when they want to develop and improve their skills. They will practice an activity of their own choosing for hours at a time. It is during this period that one often hears parents exclaim, "If only he would stop playing that guitar or walking on his hands or shooting that basketball and do something worthwhile." Too often, adults are apt to forget what *is* worthwhile, according to the standards of boys and girls. At this age they are generally confident of their ability, engrossed with their own strength, and interested in making comparisons with others. Their play is noisy and boisterous; the larger the gang, the louder the noise.

This is an age when motor skills are essential; they are important tools by means of which boys and girls gain and maintain a place in the peer group. Children who have not had experiences in play, games, and dance often feel uncomfortable with their group. (In many of our inner-city schools this is an important force that needs to be recognized.) This is one of the reasons they frequently withdraw and find substitute activities which may not be desirable. The

feeling that they are not like the rest can be so strong that they will play the role of the spectators rather than be active participants. Vigorous forms of dance are experiences that can help them take a more active part in the important social activities of their group.

It is often stated that many young people are bored. The dropout situation, as well as many problems of juveniles, are actually efforts in which youth is searching for involvement, for identity and for a "cause." They require situations in which there is action, excitement, and an opportunity to participate. Many require an opportunity to exploit their physical selves. Without this, they often keep their problems inside and anxiety, pressure, or frustration occur. Anxious parents and academic demands often intensify the problem.

Feelings

The emotional needs of older boys and girls must be met. If deprived of deserved praise and recognition, they are not likely to continue to make adequate progress. As in early childhood, boys and girls of this age need a variety of opportunities to provide for achievement and a chance to excel and to develop confidence in self. They seem to desire to be dealt with directly and individually.

This is the age when feelings of insecurity are often dominant. Physical growth, expanding interests in people and things, the great drive to "do," the anxiety to measure up to group expectations, the effort to belong, and the need for independence all engender feelings of uncertainty. The tensions produced by these feelings are expressed in many different ways. Some may revert to infantile ways of showing tension—nail biting, daydreaming, and stuttering. Others, at times, appear shy or bold. The "big shot," "nobody likes me," and "I don't care" attitudes are ways they express what is happening to them. Adults often say to them, "You don't act the way you used to." They are as unpredictable in their actions as seven-year-olds, but the twelve-year-olds have their own reasons for being this way.

It is during this period that they display stormy feelings of anticipation. They are anxious to know what is coming next, and how it is going to affect them. This is a major problem in many large schools.

Belonging

Children of this age are primarily interested in themselves as persons and secondarily in their relation to others. Learning to be one of a group, to enjoy games and sports, to win friends, and to make a place for oneself outside the home is a gradual process. This soon merges into readiness for organized group experiences. They begin to show a desire to play and work in small groups and to assume responsibilities and minor group leadership but this leadership is generally short-lived and changes frequently.

Boys and girls find security in their peers —in the feeling of "belongingness." The loyalty and support they give each other has the effect of making them "gang up." This is a time when they continually think up things to do that will bring them together as a group. Family affairs become quite secondary, and a delayed mealtime often ends in "verbal eruptions" because it interferes with the business at hand.

The feeling of "we can do" is so strong that adult interference is apt to bring forth words and actions that may be interpreted as defiance or as a polite invitation to "let us take care of our own affairs." Acceptance or disapproval by one's friends is very important at this time.

"We and Us"

Because of cultural patterns, there seems to be some drawing apart of the sexes during this period. This is recognizable in different cultural and ethnic interests, playing, social activities, conversation, and reading

selections. In many neighborhoods in which girls and boys of different cultural backgrounds have grown up together, there is evidence of cooperation rather than antagonism or separation of the sexes. In such instances boys and girls of different cultural backgrounds continue to get along amicably.

There is no doubt that the customs and habits which influenced the growth of certain attitudes in parents continue to have a direct bearing upon the relationship between parents and children. Many of these parental attitudes in relation to sex may possibly have caused the feeling, in some areas, that dance and rhythmic creative movement are activities more appropriate for girls than for boys. The nature of folk, square, tap, fad, and social dancing provides for fun experiences and a chance to participate in wholesome, vital, vigorous boy-girl activities. This would support the contention that more should be done in our school programs in the direction of helping boys and girls grow up together more under their own standards rather than according to complete adult dictates and prejudices. In schools where activities are meaningful, where the interests of boys and girls are challenged, where cultural differences are appreciated, and where cooperation rather than separation of the sexes is stressed, greater respect for the roles they play may follow.

Accomplishments of boys as compared with those of girls may be another determining factor in widening the breach between the two sexes when emphasis is placed on all reaching the same level of achievement. It has been recognized that girls of this age mature before boys. Thus, many differences between the performance of boys and girls can be explained in terms of rate of maturation. Boys, at a given age, continue to achieve and behave in a manner consistent with those of somewhat younger girls. Similarly, because of different rates of muscle and motor maturation, as well as social drives, girls perform some activities less well than boys at a given age. As boys and girls work together in small groups, particularly in such activities as dance (where the emphasis is upon a sharing of mutual and cooperative effort), they tend to break down some of this competitive animosity between the sexes instead of striving to "beat" the other fellow.

Children's dance experiences can substantially assist in the socialization process at this age by offering group and leadership opportunities. A group of forty boys and girls were busy explaining, in movement, their ideas of different forms of transportation. They were boats, trains, airplanes, automobiles, motorcycles, horse-drawn carts and rickshaws. Some were working alone, some with another child, and many were working in groups of three and four. Chip had the idea of a train, but he needed three other children. Susan could do her train alone. Billy wanted to be a rickshaw because his daddy told him when he was a little boy in China he used to go to school in one of those vehicles. He needed two other boys to be the rickshaw, while he was the rickshaw-boy. All participated in the social group structure best suited to their way of working. They shared with others, they contributed to group action; even though a child worked alone, he was part of the larger group activity.

At no time do any children ever behave entirely typically for a given age in all phases of their growth. At all times they represent what they were, what they are, and what they will be. Transition from age to age is continuous. Time, experiences, and having lived through early childhood (five to eight years) gives older boys and girls (nine to twelve years) opportunities for quality and maturity.

THE CHILD'S INSTRUMENT
OF EXPRESSION: HIS BODY

It is a wondrous discovery for the child to find that in his body he has an instrument through which he can express his ideas, thoughts, and feelings. Discovery and exploration of body parts by a child, and his use of them to express or interpret in *his own way* that which is within *his* experience, constitute *creative rhythmic movement*. The opportunity to use movement is as expressive for the child as it was for primitive man. Through this medium the child can react to the world about him, use it as a means of communication, and express the thoughts and feelings that are deep within him.

Dance experiences, carefully selected according to the varying needs of boys and girls, contribute to growth if emphasis is on *children* and their development, rather than on *activity*. Because children are different, their expressions of movement are different. Therefore, no one standard or pattern can apply. When they are given the opportunity to express themselves through dance, the results must be considered in terms of continual self-improvement. In this area of expression teachers are concerned with the education of all children. We should see that opportunity is provided for all children to participate in a program of creative rhythmic movement, rather than for producing star performers. It is exciting to watch children discover the wide variety of movement of which their own bodies are capable and the pleasure that comes from using these movements in patterns and relationships to interpret feelings and express thoughts and ideas.

As children become familiar with their bodies they discover they can manipulate them in many ways. As they have opportunities to know about what their bodies can do, they begin to raise questions. They want to know what makes certain parts of their bodies stretch and bend, twist and swing, and what enables other parts to bounce, push, or pull. Such questions lead to the recognition of human hinges (joints) and levers within the body, as well as an appreciation of bones, muscles, nerves, and ten-

dons. As boys and girls develop varied progressive sequential movement experiences, they gain more and more control over their bodies. They can begin to transfer body weights up, down, over, and under, transferring large and small weights *through space, in time, with degrees of force.* As they practice and are given extended opportunities to use and handle their bodies, they sense their ability to maintain balance, to defy gravity, to sense degrees of speed, to adjust and even control space and force. When boys and girls feel that they are at the controls they can stop and start and set many parts in motion at once. It is then that they feel they are in tune with and at home in their bodies. They are now developing power, flexibility, endurance, strength, agility, and coordination. They are actually understanding the construction of that which makes them uniquely human: their own bodies. They find out that there is no end to inventing movement combinations. As boys and girls achieve this appreciation for the physical aspects of their bodies, they begin to realize that they have other controls which also set them into motion, including both affective and cognitive aspects, which we refer to as psychomotor abilities.

When boys and girls gain respect for their instrument and their medium of expression (movement potential) they have opportunities to express themselves, to make judgments, to experience through trial and error, to make decisions, to coordinate, to anticipate, to take chances, to communicate, to make comparisons, to invent, to observe, to relate to others, to describe and to symbolize through movement deep feelings, attitudes, and perceptions. Regardless of age, body structure, size, sex, race, or religion, young people need help in understanding and keeping their bodies in tune.

We need to see that every child is provided opportunities to gain respect and appreciation for his instrument of expression through experiences in creative rhythmic movement, and dancing is an ideal way to effect this goal.

WORKING WITH CHILDREN

Several fundamental generalizations about growth can be recognized as a *basis for relating to each individual child*.

Putting ourselves in the child's place. How does it feel to be five years old? What would we do if we had a mother like Joe's? Sue is the oldest child in her family. Jack's report card caused the family concern.

The sensitive teacher seeks to identify with the individual child, regardless of number in class. There seems no better way than to attempt to put oneself in the child's place. In this way it is possible to anticipate concerns, questions, and problems. The more experience we have in asking such questions as "What does this child hear? What worries him? Does he understand? Is he a part of things?", the more we are helped to establish a meaningful role for him.

Establishing a climate of acceptance, "at-homeness," security, trust. Before children can say "I can't," "I don't know how," "The teacher doesn't like me," "She doesn't know I'm here," the climate should be one of acceptance.

Making it possible for each child to be successful in something. As children experience success they are revealing themselves. We can identify their status. Praise, recognition, and group success tend to create positive feelings.

Taking cues from children themselves. Through careful observational techniques we can get many important leads. "Today is my birthday." "I like to move with music." "This is fun!" "Joe has a new brother!" Such comments are often of great value in identifying interests, motivating next steps, identifying "fatigue points," and discovering anxieties or pressures.

Growing in many ways. We cannot work with a group of boys and girls without careful attention to the multiple factors that relate to total growth. The interdisciplinary approach to development is essential. Health records, attendance, nutrition, home factors, out-of-school experiences, maturity, and relationship with others illustrate the interrelationships that must be observed.

Observations of children in movement also give us an opportunity to look for such things as physical development and coordination, and relationships with boys and girls and adults.

Active involvement with children—including the deprived, gifted, or handicapped —tends to provide for multiple learnings. Experiences in movement and children's dance and other art forms are vital for dynamic and creative involvement of children in the school program and as a means of facilitating a richer life.

Modern living makes it all the more necessary that boys and girls have room to play, move, and work. Observations of classroom settings indicate that problems can result when boys and girls are required to sit and listen for long periods of time with restricted movement. Only as we understand the child in relationship to the growth process will we be able to help him learn and later to be a part of the adult world. A program of dance activities based on the needs and interests of boys and girls can assist in this growing-up process. Children are people with great activity needs.

3

Creativity – Rhythm – Movement

Creativity, rhythm, and movement are the three major components of children's dance. These elements are intertwined significantly, yet each makes a unique contribution in programs of dance activities for boys and girls.

CREATIVITY

Creative Potential

All boys and girls have creative potential. Creative potential is the dynamic quality of a "unique me"—of becoming a singular and special "somebody." To be human is to be creative. The self is the focal point and remains as such throughout the process of creating. It is what the individual *thinks, feels, sees,* and *expresses* in terms of himself and in his own way.

All children are endowed with creativity in varying degrees. Any creative sparks that ignite can cause a person to tingle with ideas, take off on "flights of fancy" until he finally reaches his "moon." The extent to which creativity can be motivated and developed is dependent upon experiences to which children are exposed and opportunities they are given for expression.

Boys and girls differ in their creative potential just as they differ in their rate of growth, movement quotient, rhythmic response, and aptitude for learning. Regardless of age or maturity, creative potential can be encouraged when children are given opportunities to express themselves through media of their own choice—construction, science, art, writing, or physical activity. Creative potential can lead certain of them to eventually build bridges, write symphonies, choreograph dances, explore Mars, conceive plans for bringing about peace, or design formats for eradicating world hunger. It can enable others to simply achieve lives of self-fulfillment and happiness. There is no limit to what boys and girls can aspire to if their creative powers are unleashed, influenced, and encouraged. Not all creative efforts will lead to major discoveries or the solution of profound problems, but the release of creative powers can bring about fuller and more meaningful lives. Children can be helped *to see more, feel more, be more of all that the world has to offer because they dare to be givers as well as receivers—to find and do their "own things."* How exciting to bring something of one's own into being—to be encouraged to find one's own way!

Creativity is that quality of living which helps in the discovery of new possibilities,

23

new associations, new relationships, new experiments. Creativity keeps "me" central in the action of inventing and expressing. This creative power within each of us, regardless of the extent of our development, seems to contribute to our attitudes about living. It is an active rather than passive, exciting rather than dull way of looking at things. It is a way of thinking, a way of seeing, a way of behaving. It is a way of communicating. The creative process is "turning oneself on" and generating unique personal responses to external experiences, stimuli, or motivations.

It is the imagination at work and an inner urge that stimulates or triggers one to action. This involves making choices and taking chances, *not knowing the outcome*. Creativity extends the imagination by generating ideas, insights, and hunches that are selected and organized into forms of expression. Creativity is deeply personal. Personal involvement and emerging action—sensing what others may not—evolve from creativity as it influences attitudes and actions.

Creative Expression

The basis for creative expression is to be found in experiences. These consist of things a child does for the first time, in a way that is *new* to him. They include recognition and interpretation of new relationships in thinking, learning, and doing. For example, a third-grade group became interested in the kinds of boats that might be found on a lake. The children were asked to imagine the room was a lake and each child some sort of a boat. They were asked to form small groups to represent the larger boats, or they were encouraged to work alone and be small boats. Not only did these eight-year-olds have to decide on the kinds of boats they were going to be, but they also had to figure out how they could use movement to navigate on the lake and then "dock up." The sail, sloop, Indian canoe, small canoes, rowboat, kayak,

speedboat, and raft were *original interpretations*. The children devised their own methods of moving so that others could recognize what they were. Many of these interpretations were indeed unique, and there were obviously as many ways to interpret a sailboat as there were children in the class.

Creating is exciting because children never say anything in the same way. The creative aspect is the *uniqueness* of the experience of the individual concerned. This process is affected by something from one's own *experience* that is modified, re-

assembled, or given an original twist, and outwardly is manifested as an *ongoing* experience. This is the process by which new life comes into being and by which living things continue to grow and to reach maturity. This is progress, growth, and development.

Creative power, the dynamic element within each child, develops with discovery and exploration. The result is creative expression. Children at work, children who are experiencing this process of creativity, reflect in their faces the thrill of vibrant expenditure of energy, the elation of complete satisfaction, and the harmony within themselves. One can actually feel them "think" and can share with them in the enjoyment that comes from expression.

In creative expression the emphasis is on what is happening to children rather than on what they may produce. Teachers gain an insight into their developing personalities by observing them when they are free to express themselves in an encouraging, understanding environment. It is a common error to suppose that creative activity starts by itself. The act of expressing original thoughts, feelings, and ideas in tangible form has its beginnings in experiences of everyday life and flourishes best in a normal, natural atmosphere.

Experiences surround children! However, they need to be selected, channeled, and arranged according to specific needs and stages of development. It is not enough merely to expose children to experiences; they need to interpret them in their own way. For example, a school was preparing children for the local appearance of the Boston Pops Orchestra. There was much evidence of the "big affair" in the decorations, in the halls, and in some of the rooms. In the music room, children were being given first-hand experiences with various instruments that make up an orchestra. Sixth-graders were seriously demonstrating their instruments to a group of seven-year-olds. Kim was taking his horn

apart, showing what it was made of, and how sound came out of its various parts. The potential musicians announced the original selections they played for their second-grade audience. A cello, violin, French horn, and flute were never more appreciated by any group of listeners. After the applause had ceased, the music teacher announced that the performers had another surprise. Every youngster was given an opportunity to play the instrument of his choice. The seven-year-olds were asked to think about the instrument which they most wanted to play and then to go to the spot in the room where a sixth-grader would help each one. Not only was this an experience in sharing, but the tremendous concentration and joy registered on faces when a sound was produced gave thirty second-graders and four sixth-graders a happy learning experience. The genuine appreciation evidenced by Kim when he said "Good" as he looked down at the child trying to make sound come forth was memorable. Each sixth-grader handled his pupils in his own particular way, determined to give each of the smaller children a successful experience. Thirty children left that room as potential musicians—each an artist in his own realm.

This experience was intensified by the opportunity of moving the way the different instruments made them feel; different qualities of movement suggested by the instruments were explored by each child. Creativity had started.

As children use their creative powers they develop a greater awareness of the world around them. They respond more perceptively to what they see, feel, hear, and touch and react to qualities of color, sound, movement, and space. Hence new alternatives or relationships are formed as they reconstruct the old. Creativity is going beyond what is known or sensed at the moment.

Days are full of opportunities for children to "run" with their thoughts, impressions, and ideas rather than suppressing them. This can only happen when adults *free* rather than *capture, bolster* rather than *criticize, encourage* rather than *deter,* and *uncork* rather than *bottle up.* It happens when children are opened up—and when adults are willing to be open and flexible themselves. When we put a premium on children's curiosity, sense of wonder, and questioning, and respect diversified ways of expressing, creativity is released. Children must be given opportunities to express with their whole beings, rather than just one part; with the whole self—body, emotions, sensitivities—not just the head, and expressed in terms of things and acts, not necessarily words.

Creative potentialities in children frequently remain blocked, unnurtured, and untouched. In observing kindergarten or first-grade children, one is impressed with their individuality, their utter abandon, and especially their desire to discover and explore new things. Their wholehearted interest in various forms of expression, such as songs, plays, drawing, conversation, and rhythmic movement, is evident. In their need to explore the world around them they vibrate like young butterflies emerging from cocoons. There is in them a freedom of thinking that demands expression in terms of their everyday experiences— expression that is spontaneous, meaningful, and direct. It seems appalling that much of this vibrant, natural zest may be lost or submerged, when children grow older. Frequently, from the second grade upward, children are apt to appear hesitant, self-conscious, inhibited, bored, and uninspired. When this is true something tragic has happened to their way of learning and to their urge to explore new realms and tell about them. Can it be that natural activities of children are too often upset and disturbed by adult conditioning? Have joyous, natural, creative expressions of children been suppressed by adult-imposed patterns of how children should act and move as

they grow older? Have creative activities been outranked by academic pursuits? If so, perhaps this may be attributed to the lack of understanding, direction, guidance, and variety of experiences and opportunities provided by parents and teachers. Perhaps they have either failed to realize or have been denied the importance of expressing their own creative potentialities.

If children are to develop creatively, they must be provided chances to experiment with a variety of media. When the expressions of creative effort are given form, they need to be received with understanding, encouragement, and appreciation. The tremendous air of concentration, pulsating output of energy, and enjoyment that emerges from expression are symptomatic aspects of growth, development, and change through the creative process.

That important changes do take place cannot be questioned! Everyone who has worked with children over a period of time knows this to be true. One can actually see such changes taking place and can observe that the children have important contributions to make to their world.

One cannot share a creative experience with children without realizing that something important has happened. This reaction is visible in the eyes and on the faces of the creators; something important is manifested in the genuine pride in individual or group effort. Children express their satisfaction when they say, "Look what we did!" "Bet you can't guess what we are?" or "I did it all myself." This is the basis of respect for self and others working in a cooperative endeavor.

Helping to release the creativity in young people adds zest to teaching, and enthusiasm and richness to the efforts to individualize, personalize, and humanize our schools. Creativity denotes action—it involves trying, seeking, extending, thinking, learning, identifying, risking, choosing, judging; it includes imagining, discovering, originating, organizing, and evaluating. It

denotes progressing—going ahead, going beyond, trying another way, becoming more aware, looking for alternatives. Creativity also involves feelings—of satisfaction, accomplishment, disappointment, frustration, spontaneity, and enthusiasm.

The Creative Process

The creative process starts with the individual, is directed by the experiences he has had, and ends in the form of a new expression. The creative process utilizes conscious effort. The child deals with both feelings and concepts that must be "said" by him in a form of expression that is his very own.

It seems as if the creative process expands like a snowball gathering momentum as it rolls downhill. As creative power is set into action by an experience—seeing, hearing, feeling, thinking, or doing—the child responds with his own feelings, ideas, asso-

ciations, and concepts in some tangible form of expression. Experience initiates the action; it becomes the raw material of self-expression. Only what a child is aware of through first-hand experiences can be readily expressed in tangible forms.

The creative process requires an immersion or complete involvement of the individual. The teacher confronts a group with a specific situation, object, or problem to be considered in a variety of ways; an open setting is essential. The situation is "mulled over" and new relationships begin to emerge. The group is encouraged to organize some of these new relationships. Often individuals have a "flash" of an idea which reflects reshuffling and rearranging of ingredients. A chain of inner reactions often occur, suggesting inner turmoil and personalization as crystallization occurs. Then some of these new relations begin to be organized, internalized, and a new form or statement begins to develop. With the selection of media or materials the product is a tangible one that can be communicated to others in a unique way.

To reconstruct the crucial elements in the process, the following items are important:

1. Confront children with something to think about.
2. Encourage and facilitate personalization and internalization of the idea.
3. Consider alternatives before development and reorganization occur. Make choices.
4. Express inquiry, product, in individual ways.

Exploration and Creative Expression

Exploration is an essential part of the creative process—no discoveries can be made, no creative products emerge without it. Exploration does not occur in a vacuum; both things and ideas are essential. The teacher's job is to keep an eye on the activities and to help by questioning, encouraging, respecting, and reacting. In many cases the teacher's role is one of nondirected activity (facilitator or expeditor) in which he asks leading questions such as, "Where will this take you?" "What will you do next?" "Who could help?" What other materials could you use?"

The process of creating rather than the product itself is the vital implication for us in our consideration of children's dance. This does not minimize the importance of the product, but it tends to free students to "let themselves create." Participating in creative experiences does not have to terminate in an outcome that is entirely new or original—rather it consists of new insights, new relationships, new conceptions, new possibilities, and new choices. The individual may not even realize he is engaged in a creative act. Creativity puts emphasis on becoming inwardly involved and personally a part of an ongoing experi-

ence. The individual finds numerous ways of using himself and of expressing his ideas, hunches, insights, and experiences.

What can we do to foster the creative process?

Encourage creativity—do not be afraid of it.

Start with the children as they are—assume that they are creative.

Open doors, initiate discussion, and encourage ideas—do not seek a blueprint.

Anticipate success, not failure or confusion.

Invade the child's world—do not drag him into the adult (your) world.

Help children lift themselves out of the ordinary—do not do it for them.

Help children to feel by seeing and hearing —do not "tell" them.

Help children sense depth and importance to their aspirations—do not ridicule or take them lightly.

Seek ways of providing opportunities for experiencing—do not employ vicarious experiences.

Help boys and girls in their discovery of their own experiences—do not minimize or reorganize.

Help children to appreciate and become aware of the uniqueness of others—do not undersell or underestimate the power of the group.

Help children make effective choices—do not settle for only the expedient.

Help children to respond in a variety of ways —do not limit responses to verbal ones.

Encourage and work toward high standards— do not accept any product of work.

Build trust in a child in his own natural creative ability—do not allow him to become overdependent upon the adult or group.

Measure or describe a child's progress according to his own scale—do not use adult scales.

Allow the teacher's creativity to show and flow out to the group—do not reflect attitudes or lack of imagination or ingenuity.

All children possess creative potential. A developmental program in children's dance is replete with opportunities for children to express their creativeness.

RHYTHM

Feel your pulse with your fingers. *Feel* your pulse as you *listen* to the pulsations. *This is rhythm.*

Listen to your breathing. Respond to the steady in and out or up and down that goes on constantly with each breath. *This is rhythm.*

Pause at the street corner and watch the regular recurrence of the red—yellow—green light. *This is rhythm.*

Stand in the sand at the edge of a sea-

shore and feel, see, hear and respond to the *Surwishhhhhhh Surwishhhhhhh* of the waves as they rise and fall. *This is rhythm.*

Stop! Beware of the flashing lights and penetrating sirens as the firetruck tears down the street. The whirrrr whirrrr and bupppp—t bupppp—t sounds signify a dramatic pattern that causes one to halt, caution, observe. *This is rhythm.*

Rhythm is a vital, potent, dynamic, exciting, and joyful force in the lives of children. It is an important part of every child's life. *All children possess rhythm—* their own individual rhythm conditioned by both physiological and psychological factors. Children experience rhythm as they move, because rhythm and movement are inseparable. Children feel rhythm in and with their bodies, and recognize rhythm because they experience and sense it with their bodies. Their internal rhythm responds actively to their external world.

Boys and girls are rhythmical beings living in a rhythmical world. They respond alertly to the change of seasons, wonderingly to sunrise and sunset, reluctantly to bedtime and wakeup time, and eagerly to playtime and vacation time. They respond with their ears, eyes, and sometimes with their whole self to the rhythmic sounds of birds at the light of day and insects in the dark of night, to the mechanical sounds of machines—sucking, roaring, growling, whirring, whining—and the natural sounds of the open fields—whistling, calling, chirping, mooing—the roaring of the jet plane high in the sky, and the blip-blop of their bicycles on the sidewalk. They respond to the rhythm of lines in bridges, rows of houses in the development, shelves of books in the library, repetitive designs of fabrics of clothing.

The world is full of rhythm to be *felt*, to be *seen*, to be *heard*, to be *touched*, to be *appreciated*—to be used. As Judy remarked after experiencing the rhythm of Spring "bursting out"—buds popping, greenness everywhere, lines and shapes in and of the trees themselves—"Everywhere we walk I feel bubbly seeing outside myself —most of the time we walk around inside us."

Rhythmic Potential

Rhythm is an integral part of movement —it is the internal organization of time and force. As children have varied opportunities to explore movement they develop a kinesthetic awareness of rhythmic structure. And just as movement and rhythm go together, so do sound and rhythm. Sounds are varied, and help us to sense rhythm, to respond and to hear many muted rhythmic qualities.

Dance comes from the combination of rhythm and movement; music comes from rhythm and sound. It is natural and important to explore these forms at the same time as they complement, enhance, and reinforce each other. This is especially true when working with young children.

Rhythm as used in creative rhythmic movement contributes to one's personal growth as well as to various art forms. To be understood in this context one must recognize the function of rhythm in music, dance, and in everyday living. It may be characterized as follows:

Regular recurrence of pulse

Regular recurrence of beat

Regular recurrence and developmental patterns of strong and weak, of long and short, of even and uneven

Ordered sequence and groupings

Balance and harmony

Symmetry and opposition

Cycles of work and rest

The various rhythmic elements of time and force—duration, accent, underlying pulse, rhythmic pattern, intensity, tempo, phrasing, measures—which affect, stim-

ulate, or influence movement are to be developed in Part IV, which deals with rhythmic elements of dance. There also we will discuss the effect of spatial elements of lines, shapes, paths, levels, direction, and range.

Rhythmic Expression

All children have a sense of rhythm. This sense of rhythm or an ability to respond to a built-in time structure is evident in very young children as they bounce on Dad's knee, gurgle, roll or thump in their cribs, teeter back and forth as locomotion becomes a way of getting somewhere, bouncing up and down on a bed, and swing on play equipment—to say nothing of the chatter, chanting, rhyming, and repetition of sounds in early speech. This sense of rhythm needs to be aided, for not all children are endowed with the same degree or extent of the sense of rhythm. This probably reflects both age and quality of experience. No two children have a like sense of rhythm. That of young children varies depending on such factors as physical condition, nutrition, and the presence of other children and adults who provide both experiences and opportunities to listen and to participate in moving and sound experiences.

Planned experiences should be provided for chanting, for dancing and moving, for listening to music, for listening to poetry. Here children sense rhythm and respond through movement. Children should be given many early moving, verbalizing, and listening experiences to help develop their sense of rhythm.

Sensing One's Rhythm

All children should experience the joy and fascination of sensing their own rhythm. Opportunities for children to "let go" are essential for developing spontaneous movement. A feeling of being "in tune" with oneself can be experienced while moving rhythmically and being able to respond kinesthetically. Teachers can observe the rhythmical development of boys and girls by their responses, facial expressions, and often by what they say. "I never felt so good—I'm all together—wow!" says Patti, who was moving rhythmically, in command; she felt balance and harmony—she flowed.

Others in the same group needed more time and more experience. Some of Jackie's movements were still tense and choppy. His leg and arm parts were not moving together easily and he was having trouble with transfer of weight. His whole countenance showed he was laboring—he wasn't ready for the rhythmical tasks he was attempting—he was not in tune.

Rhythmic Readiness

Children need to move easily, freely, and to handle their bodies with confidence before they can be expected to adapt their movements to a specific time sequence in music or percussion accompaniment. Children must be able to feel pulse and sense time relationships in their movements—they need opportunities to explore rhythm. As they experiment and invent their movements they sense rhythmic structure (varying speed, duration, and force) even though at the time they are not aware of a rhythmic vocabulary. They do realize, however, that any movement they invent takes time—it is fast or slow, continues for a period before it stops, has a feeling of evenness or unevenness, is heavy or light—and that they move in or through space. At first their concentration is in the *moving*, not in the establishment of specific movement qualities.

During this stage of rhythmic development, sound accompanies the group rather than the group accompanying the sound.

Boys and girls must be given the chance to move freely before they can be expected to keep in precise time to a specific piece of music or rhythmic pattern. Some children are just not ready—yet—to "keep in time" with the rest in the group. In order to have a relationship between movement and a specific accompaniment, a child must be able to listen, adjust his rhythm to that of the music, and move accordingly. This takes experience. Children need to respond to their own rhythm *before* they can be expected to adapt to another or to a group movement. For instance, if a child has not yet developed the skip pattern, or cannot skip easily—if he is having trouble handling his body in the rhythm of the skip—it is folly to expect him to skip with the group, or even with another boy or girl. This child needs more time with skip experiences. When children can readily relate their rhythm to their movements we say they are moving rhythmically—they have developed skill and they can move to external rhythms of music, percussion, words, and with another individual or with the group.

It is for this reason that rhythmic experiences must be carefully selected. One cannot afford to place boys and girls in structured dance forms before they have developed effective movement and rhythmic skills. Older children can, however, engage in fascinating rhythmic activities such as current "fad" dance forms. They are able to do this as a response to their rhythmic sensitivity.

In all of this the teacher plays an important role. She needs to be able to feel pulse and to be able to pick up the rhythm of individuals or of a group rather than set her own rhythm. When a class of children develops the skill to perform as a group, a sense of pleasure and accomplishment is felt—not only by the teacher, but by the children as well. This occurs when rhythm is recognized as a natural force in the lives of children.

MOVEMENT

Children say "Movement is me" when they are on the go, trying out, finding out, getting out of the way, getting somewhere, sharing with their friends. Movement is the alive part of them and helps them to show everybody that they are "somebodies" and they can do something, maybe something better than anybody else.

Movement is Jeff galloping all alone around and around the playground. It is Ann jumping up and down because we remembered her birthday. It is Joe portraying his feelings of being sassy or silly or of being mad, important, proud, or scared. Or it is Jason leaping higher and higher just for the fun of testing to see how long he can stay up in the air. It is Adrienne and Paul promenading around the square. Or it is the fifth grade depicting a hurricane through dance because that was the only way they feel they can show their understandings.

A world without moving children—what a dull world it would be! What is your world like with children who can and do move? What does movement mean to you? Is it motion? release of energy? play? just running around? noise? boisterous, yelling kids? *Yes, but much more.* How can one who has had a lifetime of meaningful relationships with children in movement relate the magnificent scintillating world of children moving? Moving at times as if their life seemed to depend upon it— moving for the great joy of being alive, and because they have important things to move about—moving because they want to say "I'm somebody." Movement has many meanings for children. That is why such a form of learning and living is so exciting.

In order to understand a theory of movement, which is a basic component of dance, we need to ask ourselves some questions. Why are children almost always in motion? What is motion? Why do children want and need to move? Why do some children

appear not to want to move? How do Jeff, Sammy, and Andrea really move? Why do they move differently? What is there about these children and about their movement that causes them to perceive differently, even though they are exploring with the same movement? Why do Cindy and Philip continually say, "My feet just won't go with the rest of me," or Winston complains that "I can't get my arms and feet going together?" What does movement really mean to Glen, Michael, and Winfred when they dance on their hands rather than their feet? How does Deborah feel about her movements in relation to the rest of the class? Why did the fifth grade plan its all-school assembly program using movement and dance? How did the fourth grade feel when new students were added to their class who lacked the movement-dance experiences their group had had?

Characterizing Movement

In working with children, *movement* is characterized in the following ways:

Movement is activity, action, motion.

Basic movements are either locomotor or non-locomotor.

Movement skills are combinations and extensions of basic movements.

Movement patterns may be developed from complicated movement skills, many of which become dance patterns.

Movement skills develop dance skills.

Basic movements have a precise vocabulary for children.

Movement is conditioned by spatial elements because there is an important interrelationship between space and movement.

Movement is conditioned by elements of time and force.

Movement is affected by many tangible external factors—equipment, sound (music), and elements in the physical environment.

Movement is affected by ideas, thoughts, and

feelings coming from acceptance of peers, adults, audiences, and the emotional environment.

The movement environment is of great significance. Awareness and perceptions of self are directly related to self-expression, communication, and relationships with peers. This environment is also affected by the opportunities available for exploration and discovery of movement, for the uses of these discoveries, and for opportunities to perfect skills to increase efficiency and effectiveness.

Movement for All

Children like to move! They respond to opportunities to move, and this becomes a powerful asset in helping children develop the underlying ingredient for self-understanding—creative rhythmic movement.

Movement becomes a self-motivating force for each child. It means getting oneself into action. It is the activity of propelling oneself in and through space, adjusting one's body to various dimensions of space with large movements or small movements. It is being kinesthetically aware and sensing the shape one makes while moving alone and with others. Movement means action —going sometimes fast, sometimes slow, employing specific qualities of motion such as heavy or light, smooth or jerky.

Children in movement transfer body or body parts through space using energy, timing, and pacing and adjusting weight. Adapting the body or body parts to external factors requires perception, control, and co-ordination whether moving with a partner in the polka or moving to the sound of percussison instruments or the rhythmic patterns of a popular dance.

Movement has design in space. This is not to be thought of as a series of steps, but rather a series of movements organized with elements of time, force, and space to take on a definite form—this is dance.

Learning how to control one's energy, to conquer space, to control one's movements at will, to stop and start—these denote one's power and eventually contribute to efficient movement. Effective and efficient movement is the substance of dance.

Movement: A Form of Communication

Movement is a universal language of boys and girls, a nonverbal dynamic form of expression and communication. Movement serves as children's direct, personal, and expressive language. It is communicating through the whole body—questioning, transacting, sensing, responding, experimenting, and using discoveries in esthetic ways. Boys and girls tell us about themselves, what they know, what they are learning, how they feel about what they know, what they can do, what they do not know, and what they cannot do. They tell us also how they feel about themselves in relation to others and to their environment.

Movement: A Way of Learning

Movement can be a child's way of expressing his impressions and understanding. Through movement-related procedures children engage in indentification, building vocabulary, making associations, and clarifying ideas. It is a way of sharing what one knows. It involves conceptualizing, problem solving, organizing, analyzing, and making judgments. It is a way of exploring ideas and using findings for making decisions, taking responsibility, making adjustments and adaptions, and testing alternatives. It implies trying and trying again. Out of such efforts comes qualitative learning.

Sensing and responding are essential qualities to be fostered in boys and girls through creative rhythmic movement. Included is creating a setting for "letting go" and releasing tensions, for controlling actions. It involves listening, following directions, participating and contributing, getting out of the way of moving objects, and projecting self. All of this involves the ability to "feel" and outwardly respond to situations, perceive relationships, and interact to and with people and things. Movement that involves sensing and responding manifests itself in both the work and play of boys and girls. It is the ability to communicate through movement the quality and depth one feels that makes possible an esthetic form such as dance.

Regardless of how movement is viewed—as activity or motion, catalyst for sensing and responding, a way of learning, or a dimension of growth—movement is purposeful. Whether large or small, spontaneous or contrived, random or directed, discovered alone or with others, awkward or perfected, exploratory or repetitive, friendly or hostile (having varying degrees of force and aspects of time and space), all movements are used purposefully. Extensive, varied movement experiences help boys and girls to deal with their world and with themselves in ways that have meaning for them.

Movement does not serve the same purposes at the same time for all, however. Careful observation—watching and listening—often reveals an individual's purpose.

"Look at me! Watch me!"

"I'm a rocket—see me go way up."

"Boy, me and Nancy can turn ourselves into the best turtles."

"Jake's calling too fast for me."

"Man, that was a chant!"

"Benny keeps messing us up!"

"Let Deborah read her story again for us."

"How many flips do you think it would take us to go around this room?"

In an open environment movement signifies how boys and girls feel, what they understand, what they like, and what they want to communicate to others. This is an effective way of identifying purpose and serves as an important beginning place. To be sure, purposes change, but they are valid when revealed by the learner.

Summary

From all we know about children and their growth and from the extensive experiences presented in this book, we can present the following operational factors as having special emphasis in creative rhythmic movement:

Children like to move.

Children respond to appropriate challenges in movement.

Children have a type of "movement quotient" or "movement intelligence."

One's status in movement reflects *experiences in movement* as well as health, social, and emotional factors.

Boys and girls differ in movement status, interest, and response; sex differences play an important role at times in determining movement experiences.

Movement of an individual is affected by height, weight, overall health, strength, handedness, feelings of self, peer relationships, achievement, and previous satisfying movement experiences.

Motor skills are not isolated from other areas of skill development.

Movement experiences are developmental and sequential.

Progression of movement experiences is determined by readiness.

Movement experiences must be planned.

Movement skills are not uniform for all children of a given age group, but skill development is continuous.

Children need to identify themselves "in space."

Movement contributes to cognitive, social, and emotional development.

Leadership, cooperation, initiative, and imagination are often observed through movement.

Exploration in movement takes many forms; it may even be structured for a particular purpose.

Movement is extended as concepts are developed and appropriate applications are made.

Efficient movement involves thinking.

Through movement activities many children clarify values, think critically, develop esthetically, and are helped in both physical and mental health. They accomplish these things as skills are being developed or perfected.

Efficient and effective movement "depends upon the effective application of the physical laws of the universe and the relationship of time, force and space." *

Much interest is being given today to motor activity and perceptual development. Researchers in this field hope to achieve more adequate perceptual functioning for children by improving their sense of *directionality, spatial orientation,* and *visual perception* of objects and events through sensorimotor *experiences.* Increasingly it is recognized that such development is related to total development, including academic skills. Although much attention in this field is given to children with *learning problems,* it appears to be a fundamental area that has unlimited implications for creative movement and dance for all children. The child, through his growth and learning, provides us with many opportunities for assessment and planning. The central bases for programs of children's movement and dance are multidimensional and draw from human development, creativity, rhythm, and movement.

* Marion R. Broer, "Movement Education: Wherein the Disagreement?" *Quest.* April 1964; pp. 22–23. A Publication of The National Association for Physical Education of College Women and The National College Physical Education Association for Men.

II

Movement: The Universal
Language of Children

4

The Content of Movement

In any area of the curriculum there is content that reflects the principles of the field and the major ideas to be studied. There is a design, a logic, and a development of these principles. This may be thought of as the underlying conceptual theory; without this the content is shallow and the activities do not have a framework to hold them together.

In the content of the area of creative rhythmic movement and dance we have a core of basic ideas upon which the theoretical base rests. Because *creative movement and dance represent the child's thoughts and feelings as they are communicated by the use of his body,* the content of the area grows *out of the nature of human movement—the body in movement, or the body "speaking" with movement.* This is the foundation of the structure of the discipline.

Adults frequently take basic movement symbols for granted. If two people were asked to describe in words a jump, hop, swing, leap, or push, rarely would two answer the same way. Yet these are some of the basic movements children must experience if they are to have a progressive developmental program in dance activities. A teacher must not only be able to demonstrate these basic symbols and to differentiate between them, but he or she must also

be able to talk about them, describe them in varying ways, and use each as a part of movement "talk and do" vocabulary with children.

BASIC MOVEMENT SYMBOLS

The following list enumerates movements basic to all of dance.

Locomotor:
   Walking
   Jumping
   Hopping
   Running and Leaping
Nonlocomotor:
   Bending and stretching
   Swinging
   Pushing and pulling
   Twisting and turning
   Bouncing
   Shaking

Developing a movement vocabulary may require the teacher to learn or relearn a vocabulary with children. As movements are experienced and discovered and are understood and communicated, more complex movement patterns emerge and skill becomes automatic.

What is the basis of the dance program? We might ask the same question of other areas of the school program. What is the basis for skills in arithmetic or reading? Each of these disciplines is unique. In the area of writing, for example, many specific skills must be developed before a story can be written. In the process words, sentences, and combinations of sentences are involved. Through experiences a child is led to expand and combine and relate these symbols. From basic words come sentences; from sentences paragraphs; from paragraphs come compositions or stories. Just as is true in various content fields, there are basic understandings and movements that must be experienced in creative movement and dance.

Why an analysis of movement? Many teachers are working with children in a variety of areas. They should become familiar with movement terminology. When working with young children it seems appropriate to put labels on things, attaching meaning to movements. Vocabulary helps in communication about movement experiences and skill problems.

ANALYSIS OF MOVEMENT

There is no one accepted classification of movement. Neither is there a particular sequence for presenting or developing the basic movements, because if there were, creative expression and creative teaching would be stifled.

The analysis of movement presented herein has emerged over the years from the author's work with children. To help clarify meanings of the various movement elements the terminology of children is used. Their illustrations have been taken from recordings of stenographic notes and from work with many groups of children and teachers in various locations throughout the country. The material has been constantly refined, evaluated, and used in work with children.

Table I, "Basic Movements" consists of an explanation or description of each movement. Actually this is a type of "definition." Each movement is also defined or described by boys and girls as perceived by them. The fourth column includes comments children make regarding meanings or associations. Such material illustrates the clarity that comes from children.

These Basic Movements are usually classified by children according to the movement task involved as *nonlocomotor (or body), locomotor,* and as *combinations of basic movement* (making movement skills and dance patterns). As children have quality experiences with movement and continuing opportunities to explore and extend movement they recognize that there is overlapping and interdependency of basic movements.

NONLOCOMOTOR MOVEMENTS

Nonlocomotor movements are those the body is capable of performing from a fixed base of sitting, standing, lying, or kneeling. Children think of body or nonlocomotor movements as those they do "without going any place"—i.e., the way they can move their body while staying in one spot. Body movements are *swinging, bending, stretching, pushing, pulling, twisting, turning, shaking, and bouncing.*

Certain of these basic nonlocomotor movements are of prime importance, such as the push and pull, bend and stretch, swing and twist. Adults would probably not list the additional ones of turn, bounce, and shake. We do realize, of course, that everything that starts or moves has a pushing and pulling force and involves in some way these two basic movements. When young people work with the push and the pull, develop more complex movements, and use their explorations in specific ways, they often discover a striking and dodging kind of movement which seems more like a pulling away and a pushing toward some object.

Therefore, we are considering the strike and dodge as a type of movement in pushing and pulling.

As children work with a twist, they invariably consider it as being accompanied by a turn. A turn does seem to be a movement which for them has its own structure, "feel," quality, and association. A twisting movement often terminates in a turn, the body has been twisted as far as it can go around. A turn is really a combination of basic movements including a *walk* (step) or a roll—starting prone on the floor or starting from a twisting movement adding a *push and stretch*—depending on the kind of movement pattern desired. At any rate, the *turn* has real meaning for children and is used most often in connection with a *twisting motion*.

When working with young children the bounce and shake have been thought of as basic nonlocomotor movements. True, the bounce involves a pushing and pulling force, but the "feel" of the movement seems different and again the meaning for children has been taken into consideration. For the same reason the shaking-type movement has a distinct "feel" for children. It is realized that this movement includes a rapid, continual, successive pushing and pulling and probably it would be more correct mechanically to call this a type of pushing and pulling movement. We have included the turn, bounce, and shake in our movement vocabulary because each has meaning to children.

LOCOMOTOR MOVEMENTS

Basic locomotor movements are those which propel the body through space. They are the large, free movements to which the legs give impetus. Children think of the movements in terms of "going some place" and how to get from "here" to "there." The basic movements which provide for locomotion include *walking, jumping, hopping, running,* and *leaping.* The first four are primary and the movements most frequently used by children. The *leap* may be thought of as an extended run because it is executed in a similar manner to the run and developed usually from the run. The "feel" of the leap, the complexity of the skills involved, and the body coordination required are factors that make children consider this a separate movement. In the leap one must hold himself in space and apply force. Hence, we have thought of it as having a structure all of its own and have included it as one of the five basic movements which involve locomotion.

Older boys and girls have often discussed the analysis and execution of the leap. It does not seem difficult when combined with walks or runs, but when executed by itself we find it to be the most difficult of basic movements to perfect. The *basic movements which involve locomotion* also include some of the other *nonlocomotor movements such as the push and swing involved in walking.* But when working with children on a movement that involves locomotion, the emphasis in the *beginning* is on the walk, jump, hop, run, or leap.

When older boys and girls become more perceptive and skilled in discovering, performing, analyzing, and observing movement and when they become aware of the body and force and transfer of weight in a movement, then we have extended discussions of the movements involved in some tasks. When exploring movements, some children feel that they can start with a hop and end with a jump; they raise the question of what to call this. Such questions represent dealing with description, formulating assumptions, and making projections.

All other locomotor movements that propel the body through space, such as skipping, sliding, galloping, and traditional dance patterns, are variations or combinations of these five basic locomotor movements. They are also basic in organized activities of games, sports, stunts, and swimming, as well as dance.

BASIC MOVEMENTS*

CLARIFICATION OF BASIC MOVEMENTS

Basic Movement Symbols	Description	What Boys and Girls Say	Meaning for Children
Walking	Transferring weight from one foot to the other. One foot is on the floor at all times.	"Going 'some place' from one foot to the other or from one foot to the other 'right here.'" "Stepping on one foot, then on the other."	Walking like giraffes, my daddy, with new shoes, on tight rope, in mud, fog, leaves, funny walks. "My Feet Went Walking." Promenading in a square dance.
Jumping	Distributing the body weight on two feet; elevate one's self by pushing completely off the floor; landing on floor with both feet simultaneously. (Sometimes the propelling force of lifting the body off the floor is with one foot. This happens when locomotion such as a run precedes the jump.)	"With two feet take off into space and come back to floor on two feet." "Going fast off the floor one foot feeling the jump."	Jumping like my dog, frogs, kangaroos. Salmon going upstream. Like grasshoppers (Why aren't they called grassjumpers because they jump with their back legs?) Jumping beans, "Seven Jumps"—"Jump and Jiggle."
Hopping	Putting weight on one foot; elevate by pushing oneself off of the floor; landing back on floor on same foot.	"On one foot go up in the air and back to floor on same foot."	Hopping like a flamingo, puppet on a string. Hopping mad. Sounds like rain. Hop Scotch. Indian Dance.

* Adapted from original work. Gladys Andrews, *Creative Rhythmic Movement for Children* (Englewood Cliffs, N.J.: Prentice-Hall, Inc., 1954), pp. 37–43. Extended in Robert Fleming's *Curriculum for Today's Boys and Girls* (Columbus, Ohio: Merrill, 1963) pp. 226–28.

Basic Movement Symbols	Description	What Boys and Girls Say	Meaning for Children
Running	Transferring weight from one foot to the other while the body is momentarily suspended in air.	"Being in a hurry in the air."	Running like mice, greyhounds, horses, moles underground. Fireman when the siren blows. Running to get on the school bus, running for your life, Marathon race.
Leaping	Transferring weight from one leg to other involving elevation and suspension while in the air. Uses more space and force than in running and more coordination.	"Going away up in the air, stretch out from one leg to the other."	Leaping like a dog, a deer, a gazelle. Leaping over puddles, sidewalks, hurdles, across the room. Leap year.
Swinging	Suspended, pendular, arc-like movement executed by the arms, legs, or whole body.	"Going side to side or up and down, or back and forth like swaying." "Moving part of a circle or 'whole' circle."	Swinging like clock pendulum, cow's tail, monkeys in zoo. Makes me think of a rainbow, Christmas bells, cranes digging, trees in bad storm, suspending bridge, tennis racket. Swinging my partner.
Bouncing*	Back and forth or up and down motion in quick rhythmic sequences. Rebounding.	"Jiggling." "Going up and down in a hurry." "Bumpy."	Bouncing like a ball, clown in circus, or giggly bubbles in drinks. Bouncing on bedsprings, water skis, pogo sticks, astronauts on the moon. Like popcorn. Atoms bouncing off each other. Rain on an umbrella. Makes me think of flowers on my aunt's hat. Story of "The Red Balloon."

* Bouncing and shaking are really qualities of pushing and pulling and other basic movements. However, small children have identified these as specific movements. Therefore, they are included here as individual basic movements.

43

Basic Movement Symbols	Description	What Boys and Girls Say	Meaning for Children
Stretching	Extending and expanding one or more body parts.	"Reaching." "Growing tall or wide."	*Stretching* like my kite string, a rubber band, inchworms, chewing gum, my daddy's suspenders. When I yawn.
and			*Bending and stretching* like playing the trombone, accordion, caterpillar. The policeman telling me to cross the road. Cherokee Indians when they dance.
Bending	Contracting, flexing one or more body parts.	"Getting little." "Pulling in real small." "Humping up."	*Bending* as in zig-zag lines, bending like my granddaddy, Licorice sticks. Sitting Indian style and Okinawan style.
Pushing	Shoving and thrusting away from the body, using force (pushing also involves a stretch and bend). Exerting force against something that pushes back.	"Getting something out of my way." "Starting the revolving door."	*Pushing* like animals that use their heads (goats, elephants, and buffalo). Rockets going off the pad, crowds of people in subways, Christmas shoppers, off ski slope, pushing against the floor when we jump.
and			*Pushing and pulling.* Vacuum cleaner. Sawing wood. Rowing a boat.
Pulling	Drawing or attracting toward a fixed base (the body) using force.	"Bring something toward me that might not want to come."	*Pulling* like a tug-of-war, train pulling a red caboose, in the anchor, my dog on a leash, on my boots.

Basic Movement Symbols	Description	What Boys and Girls Say	Meaning for Children
Twisting	Changing position using some rotation around an axis or center.	"As far as you can go around without moving feet or seat. Head toward you, rest of me away from you."	*Twisting* like pretzels, corkscrew, vines, cyclones, tornado, washing machine. Twisting when I bat a ball, when I mess up my fishing line.
and			*Turning and twisting* like a rope, my ankle, door knob.
Turning	Revolving completely around a center or base.	"All the way around." "All the way over."	*Turning* over and under, upside down. Over-forward roll. A screw with a screwdriver. Turning like bicycle wheels, planets, mobiles, windmills. Fashion models.
*Shaking**	Short, rapid, successive vibrating motion.	"Wiggly." "Quivering." "Shivering movement."	*Shaking* like jello, dog when he comes out of water, stuff in my pocket, my loose tooth. I shake when I'm scared. Makes me think of milkshakes, harp strings, birds fluffing feathers, my mom shakes the can before she squirts the bugs.

* Bouncing and shaking are really qualities of pushing and pulling and other basic movements. However, small children have identified these as specific movements. Therefore, they are included here as individual basic movements.

45

COMBINATIONS OF BASIC MOVEMENTS

Combinations of movements may be either a series of locomotor movements (walking and leaping), a series of nonlocomotor (body) movements (bending and stretching), or a series of locomotor and nonlocomotor movements (jumping and bouncing). As boys and girls gain freedom in using their bodies and develop understanding and more efficient and effective ways of using their basic movements, it is natural for them to discover combinations which then become movement skills. To skip (walk and hop), to gallop (walk and run and/or leap), and to slide (walk and run and/or leap) brings great satisfaction and enhances quality movement. Other illustrations of combinations include skipping and swinging, sliding and pushing, galloping while bending, as well as such movement patterns as are found in traditional dance steps. Movement patterns are often referred to as dance-step patterns involving combinations of basic symbols related to aspects of time, force, and space—such as the schottische, polka, two-step, waltz, and tango.

Both acquisition of these movement skills and awareness of them as tools (techniques) are essential for a program of creative rhythmic movement. As these basic movements are combined into innumerable complex skills and patterns, they can readily be analyzed by older boys and girls. Children should be encouraged to think "movement-wise," and to be able to describe and to dissect movements. This gives them the thrill of feeling and analyzing their movement discoveries, problems, and accomplishments. But just as it takes time to grow and develop, it takes time to learn to use one's body in meaningful ways through movement. If movement experiences are planned progressively and sequentially according to the specific capabilities and interests of boys and girls, they then acquire a storehouse of movement skills which can be used in even more complex creative rhythmic movement activities.

To be specific, in order for a child to *hop* he must be able to maintain himself in space, using enough force to take off from the floor on one foot and stay up in space momentarily, and land on the floor on the same foot. He needs to be able to perform this basic movement (hop) equally as well with the right foot as with the left before he can be expected to combine a hop with other basic movements. When he feels comfortable with his hop he can then combine it with a walk. The way these two basic movements are combined and the rhythmic relation involved is what makes the movement skill pattern of the *skip*. The skip, when combined with the slide or gallop, becomes the more complex dance pattern of the polka.

The following is an example of movement relationships:

Basic Movement .... Hop
Combination of Movements .... Walk and Hop
Movement skill pattern .... Skip (Walk and Hop)
Movement skill pattern .... Slide (Walk and Leap)
Dance pattern .... Polka (Slide and Skip)
                                                                                             or
                                                                                     (Gallop and Skip)

or, shown another way: Walk + Leap = (Slide)   Slide
                                                                              Then   +   = Polka
                                        Walk + Hop = (Skip)   Skip

THE DEVELOPMENT AND INTERRELATEDNESS
OF MOVEMENT AND ELEMENTS AFFECTING MOVEMENT

Locomotor	*Nonlocomotor (Body)*	
Walking	Swinging	Twisting
Jumping	Bending	Turning
Hopping	Stretching	Shaking*
Running	Pushing	Bouncing*
Leaping	Pulling	

MOVEMENT SKILLS

Combinations† of Locomotor and Nonlocomotor Basic Movements

Locomotor Combinations	*Nonlocomotor Combinations‡ (Body)*
Walk and Hop (Skip)	Stretch and Bend
Walk and Leap (Gallop)	Push and Pull
Walk and Leap (Slide)	Swing and Stretch
Jump and Hop	Twist and Turn
Run and Leap	Shake and Bend

Locomotor	and	*Nonlocomotor Combinations*
Hopping and Swinging		Walking and Shaking
Bouncing and Jumping		Walking, Bending, and Stretching
Skipping and Swinging		Galloping and Bouncing

DANCE-STEP PATTERNS

Complex or complicated movement skills—combination of movement sequences
to make special patterns

Combination of Movement Skills

Slide and Skip	} Polka	Walks and Hops or Runs and Hops	} Schottische
Gallop and Skip			

* Bouncing and shaking are really qualities of pushing and pulling and other basic movements. However, small children have identified these as special movements; therefore, they are included here as individual basic movements.

† Children often refer to movement skills as combinations.

‡ Young children often associate the term *body* with nonlocomotor movement.

It is not just the movement combination but the inherent rhythmic elements in the combinations that makes the skip a skip, the slide a slide, or the polka a polka.

ELEMENTS OF SPACE, TIME, FORCE RELATED TO MOVEMENT

Previously it was stated that no basic movement could be considered in isolation. In addition, movement cannot be considered as isolated from the related elements of *space, time,* and *force.* As we begin to work with young children in the area of dance, we soon realize that these elements are related to one another as well as to movement. In working on the basic movement of *walk,* for example, these elements are "felt" and observable. When children move or walk in an area, they become aware of space by moving *through* space, by going in a certain *direction,* by traveling in a "high" or "low" *level* in space, and by using specific *amounts* of space. As they progress with their walk, *timing* is involved. They are moving in space at a certain rate of speed or with varying speeds, using time in their movement. Often they may respond to a specific pulse, which is simply a way of saying that their time is organized. In addition a third element, that of *force,* must be considered. Force both initiates the walk movement and determines its "quality"; amount of strength or intensity of the energy used can make a strong, hard walk or a soft, easy, flowing walk.

Space

Space is the area *in which* and *through which* we move. Space is the area around a person as well as the specific area a person covers on the floor or in the air. Children may be thought of as shapes and lines in space, changing shapes and lines as they move. When working with young children, the interdependence of space and move-

ment may be readily detected because of the difficulty some boys and girls have in relating to and handling themselves in space. Awareness of self moving *in* and *through* space as well as recognition of where one is *in space* at any given time has to do with the area that his movement covers and the direction(s) one's moving takes.

Children analyze by saying, "We are going backward using big jumps to cover a lot of space." "We can jump right here in this *one space.*" "This is my space." The elements of space that relate to movement include: *direction* (forward, backward, sideward, and "around");[1] *levels* (high or low, in horizontal, vertical, or diagonal planes); *range* (small or large amount); and *floor pattern* the picture, path, or design on the floor that is made while moving). *Focus* must also be considered as an aspect of space. It is the attention of movement toward a specific spot, point, or area in space.

As children discover and understand these terms, they are able to extend their movement vocabulary. They become aware of themselves moving in space, aware of adjusting their movements to certain amounts of space, and they become adept in handling themselves in and through space. Spatial awareness lends excitement and variety to movement. (See Part IV, Chapter 11 for a comprehensive development of space.)

Time and Force

It takes time and energy to move. The arrangement of time and force in movement is what we know as rhythm. Movement cannot occur without rhythm. As children continue to create and use their movements, they become cognizant of

---

[1] Young children often perceive "around" as a direction. Later they realize that around is backward, forward, or sideward.

ELEMENTS AFFECTING MOVEMENT

Spatial Elements

Direction	Levels
Range	Focus
Floor Patterns	

Rhythmic Elements (Time and Force)

Tempo	Accent
Duration	Intensity
Pulse (Underlying Pulse)	Rhythmic Pattern
Measure	Phrase

Additional Elements Affecting Movement

Ideas	Hearing	People	Amount of space
Thoughts	Seeing	Music	Scenery, Props
Feelings	Touching	Percussion	Costumes

various rhythmic elements. These rhythmic elements which relate to time include: *duration* (the amount of time it takes to do the movement—long or short); *tempo* (the speed at which movement occurs—fast or slow); *basic pulse* (the constant, steady evenness in time and force, giving a feeling of regularity, which seems to characterize movements); *rhythmic movement pattern* (unevenness or irregular aspects of time and force sensed in a series of movements, sometimes called rhythms). (See Part IV, Chapter 12.)

Closely related to the idea of time as a factor that conditions and characterizes movement is the idea of force or energy, which includes: *accent* (emphasis or stress —strong or weak) and *intensity* (amount or degree of energy expended in a movement or movements). These rhythmic elements which have to do with force and movement are often referred to as *dynamics*. The children with whom I have worked prefer the word *force*, however, so that term will be used in this book.

Another aspect we consider because of its relationship to time, force, and movement is that of *sound*. To illustrate: we *hop* at certain rates of speed with certain intensity, and each hop makes a sound. The sound heard relates to the time and force used. Again, all components—movement, space, time, and force—are related and as we respond to sound (or as sound in the form of accompaniment is added) we feel the rhythm in movement we are making and we can also hear rhythm in sound.

Aspects of sound which we use include: *beat* (the unit of time similar to the movement basic pulse); *measure* (grouping of beats—meter); *phrase* or *phrasing* (natural grouping of measures, rhythmic pattern— the components of the melody).

As indicated in Chapter 3 of Part I, rhythm and movement are related to dance as rhythm and sound are related to music, and throughout this book we will see that there is a fusing of rhythm in movement and sound. Here most of a child's senses are at work. (See Part IV, Chapter 13.)

Additional Elements Affecting Movement

As children have varied opportunities to (1) explore, use, and understand basic movement; (2) use their bodies in effective ways and become more efficient in their use of movement combinations; (3) discover and comprehend numerous movement patterns; and (4) become aware of the relationship of space, time, force, and sound and how these elements affect their movements, they begin to realize that they have acquired a *media for expression*. They can concentrate on the spirit and fun of using these movement combinations in meaningful, organized patterns of expression. They are now ready to cope with additional perceptual, affective, and external factors that affect their movements in many ways.

When children are helped to develop movement tools for expression, they are more deeply influenced by additional experiences growing out of their own surroundings—including those things they apprehend with their senses. These perceptions may be translated into movement or they may simply modify movement. For example, yellow usually makes children feel light and happy; almost without exception, it makes them want to take high, light skips. The *sound* of a drum may make them want to march; and the *feeling* of a light breeze may inspire them to sway.

Movement may be further modified by the ever-present *feelings or emotions* children possess. These are the experiences which come from within and give added meaning and expression to movement. The changing *ideas* and *thoughts* of children may be consciously translated into movement or serve as the stimulus for movement expression. Movement is also affected by the necessity to relate to another person in movement tasks, and having to work in small and large groups on movement and dance problems.

THE DANCE CONTINUUM

Children progress unevenly; they do not learn at the same rate. Nevertheless, we hope that progress in movement in general and in dance specifically will be in positive directions. A chart has been developed to show a movement continuum that has been helpful in working with children. This chart diagrams the structure of children's dance from its beginning to its most progressed form; creative movement and dance must be conceived in terms of successive items in the continuum.

DANCE CONTINUUM

Exploring oneself and one's body

Identifying body parts

Determining ways one can move

Moving the body in space

Moving through space

Moving rhythmically

Moving with others rhythmically in space

Moving with others in space recognizing time and force factors

Moving to express ideas, thoughts, concepts, perceptions

Developing movement skills

Discovering some movement and dance patterns

Sensing and responding through movement

Refining and improving movement skills (rhythmical and spatial)

Moving expressively with quality movement

Perfecting movement skills with deeper sensitivities to time, force, space, and other factors

Communicating through movement and dance in structured situations (folk)

Creating and communicating in the form of dance

Developing dance perceptions and concepts

Feeling secure in expressing thoughts, feelings, and ideas through dance (alone and with others)

Composing, perfecting, performing, and receiving dance

The items in the continuum are cumulative because each one is built upon all those listed previously. In a way, the process of developing dance competence is an evaluative one. Individuals develop skills, evaluate status, identify areas needing further development, and refine and extend skills. This leads to the assumption that expressive movement follows exploration. The earliest form is exploring oneself and finding out how one can move. The final progression results in a level of dance competence that includes performance and choreography. Each step between the extremes is of great importance.

It should be borne in mind that many of the items in the continuum are interrelated and that perceptive teachers will find no sharp boundary lines between items. For example, time, force, space, and perceptions are continuous threads. However, there are times when we must consciously work on them and develop greater skill in handling them.

Such a continuum serves to dramatize the point that there is a gradual building on dance skills and competencies; unless one starts early, a high level of competence will probably not emerge. It also demonstrates the importance of each level on the continuum.

The assumption is made that the school, through its program and staff, build opportunities for children to progress as far and as rapidly as they can. We desire to release the individual to realize his highest intellectual interest and creative competencies. It is interesting to note that this assumption was supported by the Developmental Conference on Dance, sponsored by the United States Office of Education, held at the University of California in 1967 and attended by leaders in the dance field. The report of the Conference stated that "each individual should have a broad range of movement experiences resulting in greater awareness of the total movement possibilities of the body, progress in the mastering of the body, and the development of perceptions and concepts relating to these movement experiences." [2]

The work of the Task Force on Children's Dance sponsored by the Dance Division of the Association for Health, Physical Education and Recreation has applied itself to the business of (1) determining what kind of dance is being taught in the schools of the country; (2) establishing guidelines that describe a comprehensive dance program; and (3) determining ways of implementing these guidelines.

GUIDELINES FOR CHILDREN'S DANCE

The guidelines formulated indicate content that is both movement-centered and audience-centered. "The latter aspect is included because dance is an art of communication and needs understanding and appreciation from an audience. By viewing dance performance in a variety of ways, as well as participating in it himself, the child broadens his knowledge of and sensitivity to the art of dance." [3]

"As listed, the guidelines attempt to cover recommended dance activities for children from the ages of 3 to 12 years. This span of years is divided into two—those of early childhood (3 to 7 years) and those of middle childhood (8 to 12 years). It is recognized that although many activities are appropriate for all ages, providing there is adaptation by the teacher to the level of development, there are a few that serve their purposes best with either younger or older children.

The method used in providing dance experiences is of utmost importance. The contributions of dance, and its significance

[2] Marion Van Tuyl, *Dance, a Projection for the Future* (San Francisco: Impulse Publications, 1968) .

[3] *Children's Dance*, AAHPER, Washington, D.C., Fall, 1973, p. 6.

that can only be realized by creative teaching methods.

The problem solving method, with its related activities of guided exploration, discovery, and selection, and other experiences in invented and improvised movement, is used in most of the movement-centered dance activities.

The teacher's first task is to plan the situation. Through exploration and discovery, in an open-ended approach, are unlimited possible experiences.

Next comes a period of refinement so that the dance is carried out more effectively.

"The learning principles of discovery, perception, and actualization are thus applied to the child's increasingly discerning use and mastery of his own body's movement. Such a method requires that the teacher produce an environment where the child is free to discover how his own movement feels. He needs to sense what it is that is communicated to him when he responds to or resists gravity: when his body expands or contracts; when he can take himself through open space or must move in a limited space; when he moves alone or with one or many others; when he can support himself on a single small base; when movement and stillness, or high and low, or heavy and light, or fast and slow are juxtaposed.

The key to joy in movement lies in such self-discovery." [4]

Movement-Centered Dance Activities

The following movement-centered activities[5] are basic to children's dance development and, when adapted to age level, should form the major part of the dance curriculum from early through middle

[4] *Ibid.*, p. 7.
[5] From the guidelines established by the Task Force on Children's Dance in their publication *Children's Dance*, AAHPER, Washington, D.C., Fall 1973, pp. 8–9.

childhood and beyond. It is upon the success of these experiences, especially the first four, that satisfactory and satisfying dance learnings will depend.

1. *Experiencing Movement Elements*
2. *Providing for Exploration*
3. *Relating to Rhythm*
4. *Experimenting with Basic Movements*
5. *Making Dances*
6. *Relating to Curriculum*
7. *Singing Movement Songs*
8. *Using Folk Dances*
9. *Increasing Physical Power*
10. *Relating to the Present Culture*
11. *Performing for Others*

Audience-Centered Dance Activities

The following audience-centered experiences should expose the child to dance as a performing art, helping him to understand and appreciate its ramifications. Children of all ages can participate as an audience to their esthetic and artistic advantage.

1. *Sharing* and responding to other children's dances.
2. *Seeing pictures and slides* of dance.
3. *Seeing films of concert dance* artists.
4. *Seeing and discussing lecture-demonstrations* by professional and semiprofessional dancers, with active participation when possible.
5. *Seeing concert or theater dance programs appropriate to age level* and experience.
6. *Participating in other enriching experiences,* such as dramatic performances, music concerts, museum exhibits, or book and science fairs.

The work of the Task Force on Children's Dance supports our theories on movement presented in this chapter. The interpretation and implementation of the guidelines set forth by this group are reflected in the content and philosophy of this book.

Movement, then, is the basis for all dance. It must be understood and its uniqueness respected and used. There is a high degree of specificity and precision in the identification and analysis of movement. There is a type of universality about it which places it on a highly objective, scientific, and artistic level.

Movement, then, is indeed the universal language of all children. Properly understood and used by the child, movement experience can relate to many other areas and result in not only greater awareness of the body and self but also in developing perceptions and concepts enhancing personal growth and fulfillment.

5

Working With Basic Movements

Earlier chapters have attempted to clarify the nature of movement and have placed major emphasis on the need for creative movement for boys and girls. The relationship of movement to creativity and rhythm has also been stressed. This chapter will focus on the development and uses of movement to enable boys and girls to become aware of themselves moving. As this happens they begin to experience qualities of freedom, control, and independent thinking.

Let us look at some of the ways movement may be approached and developed. An attempt will be made to show progression in the execution of increasingly difficult movements. The approach employed is in no way an attempt to standardize a procedure —it is used as an illustration of actual accounts of the author's work with children in school settings.

WAYS OF DEVELOPING BASIC MOVEMENTS

Several suggestions are given for various age groups as illustrations for getting movement started; they might well serve as an introduction to nonlocomotor movements.

Starting To Explore with a Kindergarten Group

Teacher: Let's find out about—*me!*
Look (moving my nose)! I have a nose. Do you have a nose? Show me.
Show me by moving your nose—see what it can do. (I am moving my nose in various ways as I talk and pose questions.) Try moving your nose another way—and another. Look at the wonderful way Brad is moving his nose! Brad, try moving your nose still another way. Look at Brad!
Carla: See *me*—mine can go fast!
Joey: Hey, my nose feels funny!
(Exploration has started—it's that simple.)
Teacher: Now what am I moving—(shoulders)? Look and see if you can move your shoulders. (No verbalization, just movement.) What do we call what we are moving?
Carla: This part of me. (shoulders) Hey Jill— look, I can go up to my head—I don't have a part here (moving shoulders up and pointing to the disappearance of her neck).
Teacher: Great, Jill—see if you can make your shoulders go up higher. Lets all try with Jill. (Much trying and chatting.) Suppose we try to move our shoulders very slowly ... slower. (Slow does not mean the same to all kindergarten children.) Now faster ... faster. ... Who can find still another way? (Some do while others are still exploring going fast and slow.)
Carla: I can squeeze mine up together—watch

me! (Many start trying to squeeze their shoulders and move them up and down).

Teacher: This time think about this—who can find still another part of me or of you that will move—a magic part? (Class moves heads, tongues, feet, an eye—and others keep on moving their shoulders.)

Teacher: What do we call that part Johnny is moving? (Johnny starts moving his head as though he were shaking it off.)

Brad: Look at mine go!

Teacher: Let's all move our heads and find many, many things we can do as we move them.

(There is a chorus of "Look!" "See *me!*")

Teacher: How can you move your head very, very slowly? Now a little faster, but not as fast as Brad was because I'm afraid you will all shake them off, and wouldn't we look funny with no heads! Can we move our heads up... down ... 'way down. ...

Jill: I've lost this part of me again, again (pointing to her neck)!

(This is what we are after—awareness!)

Teacher: Can we make our heads feel as though they are going around? What other things can you do with your heads?

Betty: Look, I can make mine go to sleep (moves to the side and some others follow).

Teacher: Sure, Betty's head can go from side to side as though it's going to sleep. Can we try Betty's way?

Mike: Hey, look! I got a toe (holding up and moving)!

Teacher: Yes, Mike discovered his toe and foot too. Can we all find out what we can do with

our feet and toes? (Off come some of the shoes and more exploration has started.)

Now forget about your toes; can you find a big—very, very big part of you that you can move?

(Different perceptions of "big" emerge. Most move their heads, and Brad finds his back while Judy rocks back and forth. Some still worked with a foot.)

Teacher: Let's see what big parts are moving.

(Much talking—"It feels funny." "Look at me." "Butch is so big he's going to bust.")

Teacher: Let's see if everybody can close their eyes just for a minute and very quietly move a part, still keeping your eyes closed. My, I see all kinds of parts moving.

I have a song that we can sing, it's about "Moving Me"—just what we have been doing today. (Young children respond readily to movement and dance songs.)

(Here is exploration of movement and identification of moving parts as we relate it to a song.)

> Look at me,
> Look at me.
> Here's my nose,
> Here's my nose.
> Look at me,
> Look at me.
> See my nose!

This became a favorite song of these children and they were able to include many moving parts as they sang. We have used this same tune for identifying people, making them "special," or creating the feeling of "I'm somebody."

> Where is Pat?
> Where is Pat?
> Here I am.
> Here I am.
> Where is Pat?
> Where is Pat?
> *THERE SHE IS!*

An Initial Meeting With a Second Grade

Teacher: Right here where you are sitting, can you pull your whole self "in" so that no part of you touches anyone else? Try. (Teacher tries with the group.) Freeze! Stay as you are and let's see if I can find space around each of us. (Spatial awareness, sensory perception.) It is hard for some of us—why?

Billy: Patti's too close to me.

Teacher: Many of us are too close; what will we have to do? I can't move at all—if I do I'll touch you, Donny, and Eddie and Sandra —so what will I have to do? (Shrugs from some.)

LOOK AT ME

Arr. *Clark W. Graves*

Child: Oh, you go over there away from Eddie (pointing to a space away from the group).

Teacher: O.K., what do you call "over there"? Where am I going?

(Some cries of Over there. Away from me. Away from us. The rest of the class just looks.)

Teacher: Now I am over here Eddie, where you suggested I go. I'll call this "my space." It's space that belongs to me. Eddie, where might you go to find a space that belongs just to you? Careful not to bump into anyone else as you go to find your special space. (Eddie very slowly and carefully moves himself through and away from the group into another space. Many in the group respond "Pull in" as he moves, helping him not to touch them.)

Teacher: Curtis you go. Vernon, do you think that you could, also? Find another space that would belong to you away from the rest and away from each other? Let's try. (Children run, anxious to find a space.) (Curtis and Vernon are selected because they are sitting a good distance away from each other, so they won't bump as they start. Also note that they are not called together. By this time most of the group wants to move to a space. This is evident by their actions. This is helping children establish controls.)

Teacher: Eddie, Curtis, and Vernon—each of you stay right in "your space" and I'll stay in "my space." I'll call my space a launching pad. Let's see if everyone can find a special space that's all his. Careful—some of us are still too close—take a place that's all yours. (Some move as far away as the room allows—three just sit where they are.)

Teacher: Sherri, suppose you move just a little bit away from Ginny so each of you will have a special space. Now everybody show me your space stations—"special space," or what ever you want to call where you are. (Some just stay put, but others start stretching out, and a few start moving around in their spaces.)

Teacher: Find a way to show me where your space is and how big it is. Can you walk around your space? Can you move around in your space another way? Can you go up and down in your space? Can you turn around in your space? See if you can find another way to turn around in your space. (Exploration is underway—some sitting, some on stomachs, some on feet, and two skipping and turning.) Can you put your knee in the middle of your special space? Now, how far away from your knee can you stretch your arms? Can you stretch any other part of you far away from your knee too? My, you all look different— what shapes you are making! Can you freeze in these shapes? From where you are now, can you very carefully and very, very slowly move so that you are standing up in the middle of your space? (We quickly discuss some of our observations—"My knee won't stay still." "It is hard to go slow.")

Teacher: Right where you are in the middle of your "space station," let's play the "Can You" game.

Can you shake your hands ... your shoulders ... your heads ... all over ... Freeze!

Can you hop on one foot right where you are? ... Can you stop? Freeze? Can you hop moving around in "your space," careful not to go out of your own "space station"? Freeze!

(Some have trouble stopping on the freeze, some fall over. We are working on listening and establishing controls.)

Can you find a way to swing one part of you —just one? Swing another part. Swing two parts together. Can you swing your whole self? Swing, swing, swing ... and can you freeeeeeze? (Lowering voice almost to a whisper. This is sensing and responding).

Teacher: (Still almost whispering) Can you make yourselves invisible and come from your special space station to my big station here in this corner so that you will have space around you all the way? Careful when you find a spot on my space station—stay invisible so no one will know you are there—careful!

(The majority follow directions; some are anxious to get there in a hurry. The group has been reading a story about an invisible penny so the word *invisible* is meaningful to them. We are now making associations.)

Helping Older Boys and Girls Move in Groups

Teacher: Let's all move out and take a little space. Now let's see if we can go way down as low as we can in our spaces. How low can we go? Lower yet? From *where you are,* low down and from whatever position you are in, how high can you go? How far out can you go from where you are? Can you stretch even further?

Can you start to bounce from where ever you are? Bounce your head; shoulders. Bounce from your feet. Bounce yourself up in the air. Higher, higher—feel that bounce all through your body even though you are still in a strange position.

(Various reactions and remarks are made as exploration starts.)

Teacher: Let's all start bouncing with just our feet ... with heels. Now feel the bounce up through your body. Bounce with your knees ... your sitter ... your shoulders ... all of you. This time keep bouncing so hard that you push yourself off the floor ... Try again.

Peter: Boy, I could really feel that jump. Let's do it again!

Teacher: While we are resting let's watch Peter jump. See him push himself from the floor. Good for you, Peter! You bounced yourselves into a jump. Let's start again with a bounce. Bounce bounce bounce bounce and push push push. How high can you go? Sherri, how high can you go? And Jean? Still higher? What would make you go even higher?

Frank: Jump harder and use our arms.

Teacher: Let's go way up. What would help us to go high?

Frank: Jump and push.

Teacher: What do we mean by push?

Margie: Use your arms.

Teacher: Let's try that jump and move our arms. Jump, jump. While resting, let's clap our hands and make them say jump. Do we jump with one foot or two?

Children: Two.

Teacher: What other way could you jump besides straight up?

Deborah: Like this (forward), and this (side to side), and like this (crossing and uncrossing her feet as she jumps).

Teacher: Start to jump and find all kinds of ways you can jump. Good, some of you are trying turns as you jump. Let's watch Frank and Mapes and Bud—they are trying to jump and turn. What would make them go higher as they turn? What do you think Frank needs to do?

Sandra: Maybe twist first to send him up. (Discussion follows about different kinds of jumps and what we need to do with our bodies—particularly our heels—in the process.)

Teacher: How many corners in this room?

Children: Four.

Teacher: Suppose this group goes to one corner (designates a portion of the class), this group goes to that corner, and this third group goes to that corner. O.K., we have groups in how many corners?

Children: Three.

Teacher: And what could we call that corner (pointing)?

Children: Empty—free—unoccupied.

Teacher: We have three groups—group *one, two, three* (designating each group.) Let's see if we can move as one group, doing the same type of movement when I call your group. But ... no group can move the way another group moves. You must move to the empty corner. Any questions?

Children: You mean we all have to do the same thing? How will we know? You mean we have to go to the corner where no one is?

Teacher: Let's try. *Group Two*—(someone in the group calls "jump" and they all start to jump, but doing different kinds of jumps. They stop) Let's go back to your corner and try again. What did we say about all going the same way?

Children: We were jumping. Oh, I get it. Some of us were jumping with big jumps and some with forward jumps. O.K.

Teacher: *Same group.* (This time almost immediately they all start jumping backwards to the empty corner. *Group One* skips. Then *Group One* skips backwards and are surprised to be called again. *Group Three* does long, low jumps.)

(Exploration has started in various ways of moving as a group with leadership emerging. The groups quickly begin moving as a single group—at times some members of the groups became so involved with the movement that they forgot where the empty corner is.)

These illustrations suggest that there is no such thing as isolating a specific movement because of the interrelatedness of what goes on within us. But with young children, as a point of departure, we start finding out about some of our most basic ways of moving. Even though, in the beginning, a teacher's initial emphasis might be on helping boys and girls to identify a bend and stretch, the emphasis is on becoming more and more aware of movement possibilities and using these in various expressive ways for specific purposes. A movement is not as important as ways of developing it, for out of discoveries of bends and stretches, for example, come other sensitivities to movement, movement combinations, and the recognition of one's power to extend movements. With the bend and stretch one will note other movements being employed. Actually this chapter begins with basic nonlocomotor movements such as the bend and stretch and ultimately goes into dance patterns. Reference is again made to the continuum, because the basic assumption is made that growth in dance competencies becomes increasingly complex.

Setting Controls

At the outset controls are necessary to insure successful and pleasant experiences for all those participating in dance. Children understand why controls are necessary and it becomes a learning experience for them when they have a part in establishing their controls. The children and one teacher worked out in chart form certain realistic controls which they "lived up to" when they came to the play room for dance. Occasionally reminders were necessary, but these were most often given by the children themselves. The following listing resulted from a specific discussion of Miss Garber and her fourth grade about the necessity of responding instantly to the word "stop" or "freeze." The children preferred the term "freeze," and in the words of this fourth grade, freeze in movement meant:

Stay just like you are.
Stop!
Don't move.
Stop right then and there.
Stay in your position.
Stop real quick.
Hold your balance.
Stay where you are.

Be still.
Stay in your place.
Don't even let your eyes move.
Don't move even one muscle.
Stand still.
Hold it!
Keep your same position.

THE DEVELOPMENT OF NONLOCOMOTOR MOVEMENTS

The way each child is constructed and the kind of body he has determines *his* kind of movement. The basic fundamental movements are natural to a child; he can explore them in many ways, talk about them, and analyze and use them to express that which is within his experience. Basic movements have been defined in general terms, but this chapter is concerned with specifics. No attempt will be made here to indicate the extent of development of any one nonlocomotor or body movement. Instead, samples will be presented to indicate how children have considered them, how they have explored and developed them, and how movement has been used to express experiences.

It is difficult, if not impossible, to portray through the written word a true picture of the spontaneity, intense concentration, exhilaration, electric atmosphere, and the give and take that is evident when children are exploring, expressing, and *creating*. One large factor contributing to this difficulty is the fact that children move and think very quickly. The samples recorded here are the kinds of things that have been done with children in the various aspects of creative rhythmic movement. *The examples, suggestions, teaching hints, ideas, and descriptions of experiences are related as they have actually been developed and recorded from accounts of the author's work with teachers and children.*

Nonlocomotor (body) movements are different from the locomotor movements; as children say, "They are the movements that may not take us any place," or "... the way I can move while staying right here." Body movements may apply to the body as a whole or to specific parts. *One* body movement can never be entirely divorced from the other body movements. For instance, it is difficult to think of a bend without thinking of a stretch; therefore, the body movements which children have explored together and which logically go together will be considered.

An Illustration of Bending and Stretching with Younger Boys and Girls

The following account of bending and stretching is an attempt to illustrate a composite of these two movements and might apply to any nonlocomotor (body) movement. This account is a combination of discovery and use with some attempts to make application. The following account is suggestive of ways by which children have been led to comprehend, analyze, and use these movements. All boys and girls in given classes will not respond uniformly.

Bending may be thought of as flexing (contracting) and *stretching* as extending (reaching). When we bend we flex; when we extend we stretch. Children consider themselves bending when they "squeeze up" or see how small they can make themselves. They consider themselves stretching when

they "reach up or out" all the way or when they see how tall, how big, or how wide they can become.

They say bending and stretching is like being an accordion, rubber band, alligator, snake, crepe paper, gum, smoke, midget, or stilt man. The impetus to bend and stretch comes from within; these movements can be developed in the same manner as any of the other movements. Here are a few suggestions from recordings of groups working on stretching and bending. Not all these items were developed at the same time, but are presented simply to show examples of what has been done. Note the role of the teacher and the way of using children's responses. (Later, attention will be given to ways of working with older boys and girls on the bend and stretch.) Exploration is begun in a secure environment in a meaningful way.

Teacher: Right where you are sitting, show how tall you can make yourself. Try making yourself even taller. How far out can you stretch? How wide? Wider! See if you can feel tallness as you go up higher and higher ... think about a puppet, and see if you can think of your back (backbone) having a string going through it. Your sitter is where the string is attached and that is heavy, but the string goes up through you and comes out your head. I have that end of the string. I have all of your strings and I start to strrrrrettttttchhhhhh your backbone by stretching your string up ... up. Feel it coming right up through your head ...

BENDING AND STRETCHING

Arr. *Alonah Stith*

I *let go!* What happens to all of you?

Children: Flop, Flop, like this.

Teacher: Well I'll let the strings really go and now let's see you flop even more. Let's try again—I have you all as my puppets (holding up hands as though containing strings). Where else can we see strings that are attached? I see arms, legs—I even see Richie's shoulder. Again I'm going to start to stretch the strings ... this time the backbone string. I'm going to leave your head right up there.... I'll secure the string and this time I'm going to stretch up the two arm strings. I guess I'll stretch them up as far as your two shoulders ... whoops! I let go of the strings!

(The children really "feel" the stretching and then flop into complete relaxation. Continuing as a sitting puppet, with the strings attached at the waist, we try the strings stretching our legs and going through the hips, the legs, ankles, and finally through the toes. We stretch our legs as far as we can trying to balance ourselves as we are stretching our toes. We find that different things happen to us as we stretch our arms, or stretch our legs and toes.)

Teacher: Suppose we are in control of our own strings now. Find other parts we can stretch. Yes, you are supersonic self-propelled puppets. So if you are self-starters, your strings will begin stretching and then you turn them off any time and just let the strings go ... but they will start right up again. Find many ways that you can move as puppets with strings.

This time let's try stretching our strings very slowly, making our strings stretch as long as we can possibly go, and then letting go of them suddenly! What would you call what we were just doing?

Children: I was a Martian puppet. I was a red one from Mars. I thought I was like Charlie Brown. I was just me.

Making Associations—Developing Concepts

Here is an approach to informal evaluation.

Teacher: What might we call what we were doing when we extended our string and made ourselves taller and taller? (Stretching, going farther and farther up ... and out ... holding on as I was going away up.) Could you feel yourself stretching from inside you? When you let go and flopped, what happened?

Children: I squeezed up, curled up. Got smaller —shorter.

Teacher: Could we say that when we reached up all the way we were stretching and when we squeezed up we were bending some parts of us? Let's see you bend your arm. Find another part to bend. What else can you think of other than puppets on strings which seem to stretch and bend?

(After a little time associations emerge—"I stretch like Miss Arnold's accordion—that stretches out and then squeezes up or bends," "I am a rubber band" "my gum," "bedsprings," "supersonic," "magic shoes," "snakes." Making many applications helps to reinforce understandings.)

Teacher: "How tall can we make ourselves ... taller ... still taller? And how wide ... still wider? Can we reach with our hands and arms, too? Esther is even reaching out with her legs and feet. What do we call what we are doing?

Children: Reaching. Stretching.

Teacher: Sure, now let's see if we can stretch every part of us, starting from our feet up ... way, way up to our very fingertips.

Hold on to your stretches and let them go. How could you stretch yourself even higher or wider or in another way?

(This is keeping students challenged. Malcolm immediately starts stretching upward, at the same time bending his knees until he maneuvers himself into position so that he can get up to his feet ... still stretching up through his back, through his head, and out through his arms.)

Malcolm: See, I'm higher. I'm all stretched out!

(Ronald watches with amazement, sensing Malcolm's stretch every inch of the way.)

Ronald: Ouch! Ouch! Malcolm's really all stretched out. Careful—if you stretch toooo far, tooo farrr, you'll snap! And break awwwwway, and no more Malcolm.

(At this point the group is finding other ways of developing stretches, going from their seat to their feet and making various designs of shapes in space. "Ffffflllllop!" This is the cue to get the group back from its world of finding out more and more—and back to a position on the floor listening to what's next.)

Teacher: This last time suppose you try to find ways of getting into a full stretch without using hands. In other words, do not put hands on the floor to help you get up—instead, start feeling yourself stretching from inside and keep on until that stretch carries you onto your feet ... slooooowly ... slooooowly stretch ... strrrretch (verbal guidance from the teacher)—keep stretching until you can't any more. ("Ouch" was the chorus now, indicating a feeling of accomplishment.)

Teacher: Bobby was even trying to make parts of his face stretch! Do you suppose we could discover all the different parts of our faces that we could stretch? Now, see how different it feels to bend those same parts of your face.

Children discover things they can do with noses, forehead, ears, and eyes. They have fun, too, sharing these discoveries with others. "Look at Johnnie." "See Peggy. Wonder if I could do that?" (Thus awareness begins in finding another way of moving us.)

Teacher: Shall we forget all about stretching ourselves for a minute, and see how small we can make ourselves ... still smaller ... every part of you make smaller? What would you call what we are doing as we make ourselves smaller and smaller?

Children: We are making a little ball, curling up, stooping down, bending every bit of us. (Here is the teacher's cue.)

Teacher: Suppose we call what we have been doing "bending." Let's try to bend our fingers and hands ... now our arms, wrists, elbows. Find more parts to bend. How does it make you feel when you bend each part of yourself?

Children: I feel shriveled up, old, awful, or tiny. Hey, look I'm a haystack! I feel crooked. So we all decide that we will be haystacks and then bend in crooked ways.

Teacher: Now, let's see if we can bend, bend, bend, and then stretch, stretch, stretch. (This is repeated several times.) Do you know what we call the tall man in the circus?

Children: The man on stilts? The stilt man? The skinny man? (Discussion follows about stilts, walking on stilts, and so on.)

Teacher: What do we call the tiny man at the circus?

Children: Midgets. I saw a circus with Tom Thumb.

Teacher: Do you suppose we can stretch up like the stilt man; then bend way down low like a midget? In your own space make yourself like you think a midget might be and feel. Now what can you say about "you"?

Tad: Now I'm like a midget.

Teacher: Yes Tad, you convince me that you are different from the way Tad usually looks. Let's watch Tad. What do you see?

Lois: He's a proud little midget.

(After some discussion and analysis of Tad's impression of a midget, the group decides that he seems proud because he has made himself small, but he has a nice stretchy back right up to his head and he is able to be little without wobbling or tipping over. So he is stretching and bending at the same time. He can control himself.)

Tad: Look, when I put my knees this way ... and then I put my back on top of here (pointing to base of his spine) and then put my head up on top of my back—well, see, I could stay here all day.

(This is body awareness. These children are beginning to be aware of body alignment, finding that part of them which helps them control movement. They do this as experiences are progressive and as they have the strength to cope with new movements they discover.)

Communicating Ideas and Feelings

Teacher: How do you suppose it would feel to be like a stilt man?

Willie: I tried to walk on stilts once, and I kept falling off. It didn't feel good. I was way up there!

Teacher: Without getting on stilts, see if you can feel yourself stretching a long, long stretch straight up. Stretch every part of you, stretttttch. How do you feel like a stilt man might feel up there? What would be the difference in the way you moved your bodies if you tried to become a stilt man or you felt like you were becoming a tiny midget? Let me watch you—show me which you are trying to become by what you do with yourself.

I know a song about the stilt man. Would you like to hear it and try it?

(This is just one example of the ways words, music, or songs can be written to assist in the exploration of movement. Sometimes, the songs come from the children as they are working; at other times, teachers compose songs as a result of working with children. Sometimes, teachers and children work them out together; at other times, the music is original, or the

THE STILT MAN

Arr. *Florence Burns*

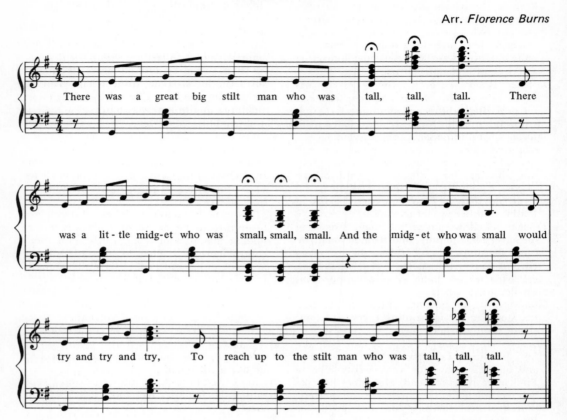

There was a great big stilt man who was tall, tall, tall. There
was a lit-tle midg-et who was small, small, small. And the midg-et who was small would
try and try and try, To reach up to the stilt man who was tall, tall, tall.

songs are adapted to appropriate music. "The Stilt Man" is an illustration.)

Teacher: In relation to the stilt man, where was the midget in space? Down! "There was a tiny midget who was down, down, down." What's a word for tiny? How does it feel to be tiny? How does it feel to be wide? Way out as far as you can go. How does it feel to be in? Go out, out, out. Pull yourself in. What does it feel like to be tall?

Children: Big, important, noticed, happy.

Teacher: What is it like to be down?

Children: Flat like a pancake.

Teacher: We can go *up* in our space—what can we be?

Children: High, big, gigantic, huge, tall. How

does it feel to be *way out? Stretch … Stretch stretch!* How does it feel to be *"in"*? Shrink yourself into a long, thin package—a flower box. Stretch to the ends of the box.

The question of how it feels to stretch and bend has brought forth movement qualities, concepts, and verbal expressions such as:

High as the sky
Low as a toad
Wide as the ocean
Round as a globe

Proud as a peacock
  strutting here
Proud as a peacock
  strutting there

Like a seaweed all crinkled up
Like a seagull off on a flight.

Occasionally the teacher needs to give hints like, "What else can you think of that bends and stretches besides the stilt man and midget or a proud peacock?" "I know," says Warren, "crepe paper." "Suppose we all make ourselves into crepe paper like Warren. Now, make your paper bend and stretch out and make it go somewhere." Often we inject humor and warmth into any lesson by such comments as, "I see Joan as red crepe paper and Sammy as brown and white stripe" (suggestive of the color of the clothes that they are wearing). "Suppose you try to think of something that bends or stretches, then we'll see if we can all guess what you are." Again all kinds of purposeful ideas and movement execution follow. If some children can't get started, a casual hint or some "drawing out" helps. It is easy to say, "Henry, what's that attached to the top of your pants that helps to hold them up?" or "Does your father ever wear anything to help hold his trousers up?"

The following suggestions lend themselves well to two or more children working together to figure out bending and stretching ideas. One could start with: "Do you two suppose you could bend or stretch any *one* part of your body while you are lying or sitting on the floor? Let's try. What part shall we start with?" In another position they try bending their trunks, legs, and so on. They may get on their knees, stomachs, or sides to try other ways of bending and stretching. Sometimes, with chalk they draw their bends and stretches on the blackboard or on newsprint, at other times, they translate movement with finger painting.

Poetry and stories help us to become more aware of such movements as bending and

stretching. Hilda Conkling's poem "The Old Bridge" is an example.

One of the most delightful studies to come from a group started with the idea of bending and stretching. The children were bending in such a fashion that they looked like turtles. "Do you know what you make me think of while I watch you?" (Vachel Lindsay's poem was most appropriate and enhanced the experience).

There was a little turtle.
He lived in a box.
He swam in a puddle.
He climbed on the rocks.[1]

The poem was repeated as most of the children started their version of moving like turtles. They found a space they called their box and moved as the poem was repeated ("And then these little turtles went back in the box"). All went back into their space. Here was control—a space to come from and go back to. This started the group off on "turtle" discussion. We talked about turtles we had seen. We found a turtle story in the library which the teacher read, extending the ideas. Sammy brought a turtle to school. All could then actually observe turtle movements. We talked about how we might feel if we were turtles and what we might do.

We snapped at flies
We snapped at you
We tucked in our heads
And slept in the sun.

Varied stretching and bending movements came about as the boys and girls became snapping turtles. Responding to their

[1] Vachel Lindsay, "The Little Turtle," from *Johnny Appleseed and Other Poems* (New York: The Macmillan Company 1925). Used by permission of The Macmillan Company.

turtle poem, being turtles, feeling like turtles moving, discovering more about turtles caused several of the children to write other turtle poems. We particularly enjoyed this one from Karen, which later became this group's turtle song.

> There was a turtle in my way,
> She was so slow, she took all day
> To see her close I bent down low
> And there she walked so slow, so slow.

More discussion about turtles coming from exploration of bending and stretching resulted in a class study, with the music consultant helping the children write their own music to fit the poem.

Another way in which interest has been stimulated in bending and stretching has been through a conversation, such as "Can you imagine you are in a very long box, such as a long flower box? You have to stretch and stretch tall to fit into it. Make yourself very, very skinny. Now, put your-

I MET A TURTLE

Karen Hill

I met a tur-tle on my way. She was so slow she took all day.
To see her close I bent down low, And there she walk'd so slow, so slow.

This led us to *where's* and *why's*, and the following resulted:

Question: Where—why?

Where, oh where, is the turtle's house?
Where, oh where, is the turtle's house?
Where, oh where, is the turtle's house?
Right on his back.

Why, oh why, does he go so slow?
Why, oh why, does he go so slow?
Why, oh why, does he go so slow?
Because his little feet won't go.

Why, oh why, is the turtle green?
Why, oh why, is the turtle green?
Why, oh why, is the turtle green?
'Cause when he's in the grass he won't be seen.

All of this was translated through movement. Such concepts have led to ideas for dance compositions.

self in a tiny, tiny box so that you have to be very little. Can you put yourself in the long box first, and then very quickly put yourself in the small one?" Reva said that it made her want to be a Jack-in-the-Box. (Again, this is a cue for the teacher.) "Let's see if we can make ourselves into some kind of a Jack-in-the-Box. When you hear the tom-tom, stretch out any way you think your Jack would go." This particular experience of the Jack-in-the-Box ended with Reva playing the wood-block. She went around to two and three of the Jack-in-the-Boxes and had them pop up when she gave them the signal.

"Find how many different ways you can pop out of the box. What kind of a Jack are you? Wonder what it would feel like to be closed up in a box? How far out of your box can you stretch yourself without losing your balance or going out of the box completely?" "Sammy, can you think of a new

way of bending and stretching your body?"
A leading question like this caused the exploration of the day to include forward, backward, and sideward rolls. The children discovered many different ways of handling their bodies. The stretch and bend was a start of the more difficult skills of "tip-ups," standing on hands, flips, and cartwheels.

Sometimes brown paper is rolled out on the floor, and crayon or chalk is selected by everyone. Then bends and stretches (or other movement factors) are drawn the way children perceive them. Other times this can be done on the blackboard. One day, while graphically representing bends and stretches, Rita was "feeling" and saying "bends and stretches," movement and other words then came which were recorded:

> To roll and stretch, to roll and stretch
> Makes me think of the sea;
> The ocean with its great big waves
> Goes on and on and on.
>
> How I would like to be a wave
> That comes to meet the shore
> I'd roll and stretch,
> And roll and stretch,
> And roll and stretch some more.

Having a tape recorder handy helps to capture some of these fleeting creative moments. The following was recorded as Sue Ann was stretching and bending:

> Wiggly, wiggly, wiggly,
> Crawly, crawly, crawly,
> Squishy, squishy, squishy,
> Slippery, slippery, slippery,
> Stretchy, stretchy, stretchy,
> Earthworm—That's me!

This was put to music which seemed readily to come from the class as they picked up her words.

There are infinite combinations of movement emanating from bending and stretching. In answer to a question, "Could you combine a bend and stretch with some other movements?" The following have been recorded. *Bends and jumps; bends and stretches; bends and runs; skip and stretch, skip and bend;* and *bend and gallop.* Other groups found it was fun to *hop and stretch;* they ended with the children portraying wooden puppets. They worked this into a script which they developed into a dance

composition. (This was a more sophisticated form of puppet than designated earlier using more highly developed forms of movement than in the version of puppets used in the beginning of this chapter.)

As boys and girls get the "feel" of bending and stretching in all parts of their bodies, develop a repertoire of movement possibilities, and feel the difference in these movements from other movements, it is easy to help them analyze complicated combinations of movements. They may be asked to try to get more stretch in their toes. Do you suppose you are bending over too much? Feel the stretch in your back as you hold yourself in the air.

Even though numerous suggestions for developing the bend and stretch have been given, it does not mean that we are just working on the bend and stretch—we work with many movements at the same time. We review constantly and go back and pick up as well as go on to find more and more movement discoveries.

As boys and girls learn to handle their own bodies, such feats as cartwheels, headstands, walking on hands, and various other complicated movements come readily. These combinations involve bends and stretches as well as other movements and elements that affect movement. They also

provide a way of helping and communicating with boys and girls. Glen, trying to do a better handstand, is guided by: "Try not to bend your knees—stretch your toes, feel the stretch in your arms—check what's happening to your elbows."

As boys and girls develop movement possibilities they have the means of organizing, expressing, and communicating their ideas and feelings. Dance studies and compositions have spontaneously emerged from work with bending and stretching—the following are illustrations:

Winfred's Cookies

"Those were yummy cookies Winfred's mother made for his birthday. Rather than telling—could you show us the cookies you had? (A variety of human cookie shapes emerged all over the floor.) Try to make

yourself into another cookie shape you have seen. This time let's start from the dough part of the cookie before it is baked—stretch yourself, every part of you, until you are flat, flat dough on the floor. How do you suppose it would feel to be cookie dough?" "Thin, not heavy, sticky" were some of the responses. "Stretch your dough out even more, until the whole floor is covered with cookie dough. Can you think about the cookie shape you would like to move yourself into? Start to move, and keep on until you are a cookie shape ready for baking." (Here was concentration, cookie construction with one's own body and as we watched we could almost feel the texture of the cookie dough taking shape. Some of the children flattened and stretched themselves out on the floor several times before they were satisfied with their shape for baking.) "You know what?" said Felicia. "There's something wrong." "What's wrong?" "Wellllllllllllll—Winfred's mother had to roll the dough out before she could make cookies—so we have to do that." "O.K. Felicia—suppose you get us all into a big lump of dough and then you roll us out." Felicia started with exaggerated stretching and bending kinds of movements as though using a huge rolling pin. She then decided to put the rolling pin down and gathered together all the children close to her in "inner space" which she called "her bowl." Again she started rolling the group away from her as though it was dough. (No verbalization was necessary.) Cookie shapes finally emerged from the flat, stretchy, rolled-out dough. Felicia made the group wait (hold their shapes for what seemed like a long, long time) until they had finished baking!

Something Strange

It was one of those rare winter wonderland mornings—unusual for the South. The group had been reviewing basic movements including the bend and stretch, and Miss Wollard said, "Something strange happened last night while I was asleep." (That was the motivation). "It snowed. Everything turned to ice. I fell down three times, I slipped and slid all the way to school, and clothes were frozen stretchy stiff on the clothes line. Allan, how did your clothes look on the line?" "They were stiff, awful stiff—they were all stretchy." "Can you show us? Good! What else looked stretchy frozen this morning?" "Icy telephone poles, wires dripping with icycles. Tree branches were pretty." "How did all the things you saw make you feel?" "Real freezy, cold and pretty, sorta, curvy, like shiny pictures, still and quiet, like they were going to break and fall down, maybe crack and fall."

Trying to turn themselves into something that was *icy, stiff, stretchy* resulted in a different quality of movement for this group in their dance. The following account was developed and danced with the title "Something Strange Happened While I Was Asleep Last Night."

All of the trees are covered with ice;
They look very beautiful.
All of the trees glistened like glass;
They are so beautiful.
Icycles, icycles everywhere.
Icycles, icycles everywhere.
All of the trees are covered with ice—
   Because
Something strange happened last night.

Curtis' Trees

In response to reviewing possibilities of stretching and bending with a third grade, associations were made with trees and parts of the trees that seem to stretch and bend as well as swing and twist. The next day Curtis said he wanted us to dance to his poem about his trees (this came completely unsolicited).

Trees are very nice,
They fill up the sky;
They stretch and stretch;
They grow by the river;
They live on the hill;
They stretch and stretch.
Trees make our woods;
Trees are very nice.

What has developed here can be applied to any of the basic movements; even though we are concentrating on understanding a specific movement, others are bound to be involved. Notice some of the differences in language and perceptions of older boys and girls as they use their bodies in bending and stretching ways.

An Approach to Stretching and Bending with Older Boys and Girls

The approach is quite different with older children because of their interest, feelings about self, and feelings about movement. If they have had little or no previous experience with creative rhythmic movement and dance movement we need to start gradually so that they get immediate satisfaction in the challenge within the movement itself, *rather than how they look to others while moving.* (It is necessary to adapt to each particular group of children.) Sometimes we almost need to "trap" older boys and girls (or adults) into becoming involved because they may not be secure with just themselves. Too often they develop dependence on a ball, or something to hold onto. With the group described here we avoided starting with an idea as such, but emphasized the movement itself in an attempt to keep it appropriate for the age. Older children are often self-conscious with "ideas" in the beginning but are challenged with movement.

Teacher: Can you get to your feet without touching your hands to the floor? Let's try. Try going back down to the floor without using your hands. Now see how quickly you can get up to your feet from where you are on the floor, and how slowly you can go back down—no hands. Try another way and this time I'll challenge you to be up onto your feet by the time I count to *five!* Join with another person and find ways of getting yourselves up and down. What helps you to get up now? What starts you?

(Kenneth thinks that he gives himself a push to get started and then he pushes against Newton on the way up. We ask Kenneth and Newton to show us their pattern of getting to their feet and back down. We decide that they both give themselves a push to start and this creates the force to carry them up.)

Teacher: This is the last time—try to get up once more and this time find out what seems to be happening to your knees ... your back ... your head."

Billy: I did a push and a swing of my arms to help me start.

Teacher: What happened to your knees?

(With some discussion about knees and more trying out, they decided that they had to bend their knees and then stretch them, and that the stretch continued through their bodies. We talked about this and discussed why it was easier in most cases to do this movement with a partner, particularly when each coordinated his movement and seemed to work together, rather than pulling apart.)

Teacher: Work with just one elbow—bend that elbow; bend it as though you really mean it. Keeping the elbow in that kind of a bend, see what you can do with just the elbow ... make it strong—even stronger. Keep the elbow moving. Concentrate on your elbow but make this move other parts ... (exploration continues) keep going until you seem not to be able to move another part. Remember, the elbow really seems to be taking the lead for you.

Decide upon another part you can bend. Let that part take the lead, put your attention on that particular part and feel it moving other parts of your body. Try taking a position on your back, on your side, sitting, any way—you find a way and start stretching from some part of you leading ... keep on stretching while I play the sticks and when they stop, "freeze." Let's see a stretch in another part of your body. Forget about a specific part leading this time and concentrate on finding opposite parts that stretch. Start by stretching one part and then start stretching an opposite part (an arm and then a leg). Think about what you are doing—Let your stretching take you up to your feet.

While you are standing, try stretching one of your legs gradually up off the floor and let that leg continue, continue to stretch in many different ways. Now what is happening to you?

Billy: I lost my balance; I couldn't keep my leg up any more. I started to twist around.

Teacher: What else could we call what you are doing? Any other terms for stretching?

Children: Extending, raising, elongating. (Analyzing movement.)

Teacher: This time let our stretch be as smooth and controlled as we can make it—let it start from inside of us. Feel a point of control, a point where we seem to be holding on. Try again but this time start with stretching and then let our stretching develop into bending, but still control our movements. Feel the importance of our back in this procedure.

(Here were evidences of consciously trying to refine movements as well as sensing quality of the invented movements.)

Teacher: Bend your knees lower and lower and streeeeetch up from your toes, trying to go to a full extension with one continuous stretch. Try to control these movements and, going from your full stretch, feel that every part of you is stretching, and when you cannot stretch another part go back down to your original position of bending knees ... slow ... slow ... even slower. Face another person right where you are and do the same with this person—see how slowly you two can stretch yourselves. Try doing it in opposition—one of you start from an extreme feeling of stretching and the other start from complete feeling of bending your whole body ... decide when you will start moving and keep on going holding onto your movements, controlling all of the time.

As older boys and girls experience bending and stretching movements, invariably head- and handstands develop; so we work on activities that include balance. As bends and stretches are combined with other movements, twists, pushes and pulls, walks, runs, jumps, cartwheels, and various skills of holding oneself in the air result. The composition "Feet Talk" in Part V, Chapter 15 ("Making Dances") resulted from initial work with bending and stretching.

The picture that Geital painted of cartwheels (see page 68) was the result of working with stretching and bending activity. She put her feelings about this body movement into action on paper.

The Bounce as a "Special" Bend and Stretch

In order to further explore the bend and stretch, other basic movements have been introduced.

"Let's start to *bounce* some part of you just where you are standing ... bounce, bounce, bounce your knees, get that feeling of bouncing all through your body. Keep bouncing and make yourself go higher and higher—push harder against the floor as you try to bounce yourself up. Now what are you doing?" "*Jumping!*" was the chorus.

"Let's try this again and get some good bouncing going so hard that it takes you into a jump. As you do this notice the force you are using to get you up into your jumping. Where does the force come from, Pete?" "I was just thinking about that—I guess it is between me and the floor. I seem to push against the floor and then it seems to push against me and sends me back up." (This movement analysis initiated a conversation about force—what it did to us trying to jump and where the force was exerted.) "Try to determine where we are placing our energy as we start bouncing at the knees, hips, whole self, and then take ourself into a jump, the fullest extended jump we can make. As we began bouncing this time, what other movements were involved?" (Another discussion and trying out movement disclosed the bend, stretch, swing, and push. Some felt that as they reached a full jump they felt some twisting. Here the group was analyzing movement and clarifying what was happening. Note: the *teacher challenges*.)

"Yes, of course you cannot jump without many of the other basic movements being involved, but this time try to concentrate on the stretch and see if you can find five different kinds of stretchy jumps." (Exploration continues.) "Invent some new jumps that involve real stretching. Can you jump by stretching your legs out in front of you and also stretching your arms or hands and touching your legs or toes while you are in the air?" "On TV, I saw the Russian dancers use this kind of a stretch. I also saw them do something like this," said Willard, bending knees, stretching legs, shifting weight from one leg to the other using the leap. "Let's all see if we can do the Russian Folk form that Willard found." (Folkdance patterns come naturally as children discover movement skills.)

"Let's watch Pam and Willard. What are they both doing with their heads?" "Pam is looking out and Willard is looking up, really stretching all the time they are jump-

ing." "Yes, that's a good observation, because the head helps to take us up. What would happen if they both looked down? Try your patterns again, Pam and Willard, and this time look down. Suppose the rest of us watch what happens to them. What do you see?" Willard says, "It feels awful." (Bending the head pulls Pam down—they can't go as high because they are bending their heads down. This is the beginning of understanding mechanical principles. The question of "why" started a discussion about gravity and the force it takes within the body. This led to more discovery and then putting into use what was found. Encourage the group to continuously think about what they are doing, and work with it.)

Vigorous movements such as jumps and leaps involving stretches and bends are helpful for getting older children, particularly boys, involved with movement. Working with percussion to relate the movements in sound, or intensifying the movements by accompaniment, adds another dimension of interest. Often children have favorite records; identifying movement possibilities associated with a favorite recording adds to their interest in movement.

Other Uses of Stretch with Older Boys and Girls

"We are going to need all the space we can find this time, so look around and find a place where we can streeetch ourself into one long line—make another long streeeeetchy line. Find various ways of stretching your bodies into *long straight lines*. Suppose we have about four of us on the drums. Volunteers? Mattie, Jake, Chan, and Red will watch us and try to accompany our stretches, so start stretching as far out as we can go and even farther. Try the same thing on your back, or from various body positions. After we have invented many stretches, assume the body positions that seemed most comfortable and the one for which you think you could get the greatest feeling of stretching. This time let the drums take the lead. As they start to play sounds that seem like stretching, we will follow and continue stretching or holding on to our stretches until the drums stop playing. Mattie—suppose you be the conductor so that the drums start and stop at the same time." (Paula, lying on her front, remarks that she has gone beyond what she thought she could stretch because her whole insides were stretching too. Other comments lead to a good discussion of sensing and responding.)

"With another person about the same height, join together, attaching yourselves at some point ... now see how far your stretches can go. Try other ways, see how long, how wide you two can stretch. Careful that you do not interfere with another grouping. Our room isn't large enough for all of us to extend our stretches while we are standing, so some of you will have to find other ways of working." (Relating stretch to space.) "Careful, some of you are getting yourselves into almost impossible stretching ways—control them so that you don't fall over, and remember—you are working with another person." (Several headstands emerge. Bill is standing and facing Joel, who is sitting and gripping Bill's ankles with his feet; Margie and Joy are stride sitting, with one hand joined; Mark is standing legs apart and Willard is lying prone holding Mark's left ankle with his two hands.) "Keep developing more and more stretchy kinds of ways of moving; make some of them long, powerful ones."

"When you find that you get into impossible positions, stop and start again. Instead of talking so much about what we are doing, see if we can communicate through the ways we move.

"Let's try to complicate this situation. Do you think you could stretch in such a way that this whole room looks like one continuous connected stretch?" (One thing leads to another.)

This took some discussion and then we

started from two partners—gradually they connected with two others. The excitement of this overshadowed the idea of stretching, and the children became concerned about the connecting. Some also were in such impossible positions that they could not hold onto their movements until all were connected. We had to attempt this idea several times. Finally, by controlling our movements, planning an appropriate place to connect with one another's stretches, and moving at a slower tempo, all boys and girls were connected. We decided to do it again, adding music from the record of the Warsaw Concerto. This gave us more continuity and the class began to really put feeling into purposefully stretching and extending movements.

The important factor in working with older boys and girls is to involve them quickly in finding interesting ways that they can move and challenge themselves. In the beginning, it seems important to start with specific ways of working with the basic movements such as has been presented above. This makes it possible for students to readily identify with each movement. We help them by verbal encouragement and suggestion and by posing problems and situations, to become aware of themselves moving within the space available to them and to feel the tensions and release involved in moving. Expressive forms of movement often emerges into improvisations, dance studies, and compositions.

A group of forty-six fifth-graders was exploring bending and stretching combinations. They divided into groups taking twelve minutes (which they had agreed upon) to work out combinations of bending and stretching with jumps. The following compositions resulted, and were entitled: "Piano Keyboard" (to which they sang an accompaniment of "Three Blind Mice"); "Tennis Match" (two boys as players and one boy the ball); "Kangaroos Go Dancing"; and The "Story of the Kangaroo" (one boy narrated a story which they wrote on the spot to accompany their movement). Another group interpreted the "Fight Between the Grasshopper and the Worm."

Swinging

Swinging consists of a pendular, arc-like movement executed by the arm or the leg, or the body as a whole. Children think of this in terms of back and forth or side to side, like a pendulum on a clock, and say "swinging like" a camel, boat, monkey, railroad signal, lantern, trees, leaves, rainbow, tennis forearm, windshield wiper, elephant's trunk, cow's tail, lasso, and the way some people walk. Sometimes they say, "We can swing over like this ⌒, or under like this ⌣, or we can swing up and down."

Swinging seems to be a basic movement that has a real "freeing" affect on individuals. If we can get people to "let go" by *feeling themselves swinging* we have cut

through some tendency to "hold back" or to resist using oneself in moving ways.

Our purpose is toward eventually helping people move as total beings and helping individuals develop a storehouse from which to select and use any type or combination of movements.

At this particular time let us put our emphasis on the *swing*. For this we need *space* —the kind of space that allows for "moving out" from confinement. Probably the greatest emphasis in the development of movement with children should be on the swing. If for no other reason, the swing is used because it is so conspicuous in the child's world. It is an essential part of the games—skills children love including throwing, batting, kicking, and serving balls.

As a fourth-grader Bo said, "I feel like music's in my arms and in all of me" (as he "just let go" swinging). Watching his experience, one could not help but wish that adults could feel such freedom. Through swinging we feel harmonizing, orchestrating, and conducting of the whole inner being.

Developing the Swinging Movement

Because the swing is so important in movement, a variety of suggestions for developing and motivating the swing are given. Depending on the group the language would vary, and the ideational, affective, and external factors would be different, but the approach and suggestions would be much the same. Refinement of specific swinging skill patterns comes as a result of children's increased understanding of this movement. Patterns they find as they are given opportunities to develop the swing should be worked on to improve the skill and to make the swing do just what they want it to do.

In exploring the swing children can sit, stand, or take any position. For example, "Just let your head go and then let it swing

SWINGING

Arr. *Alonah Stith*

SWING

Alonah Stith

from side to side. Let it swing just as easily as it will go. Think of your head as suspended or hanging there, going back and forth, side to side. Try just one arm swinging, going side to side. Try swinging different parts —hands, wrists, the whole arm." (Teacher chants "swing," "swing," going gradually slower and then changing the tempo. The children should be helped to feel the quality of the smoothness, the rise and fall involved in the use of the voice.) "Try swinging a leg. Can you swing another way? Try standing, swinging the leg forward and back, but keep it smooth. Try the other leg. This time try swinging your leg and add your two arms. Keep all of your insides swinging with you—make the swinging movement start from the inside. Feel as though your legs and arms swing from the inside and are not just something attached.

"Put your two hands together and start swinging with them that way. Keep them swinging but make different designs in space.

"Where you are standing, start swinging one arm; swing it harder, but keep the smoothness there. Be careful not to stop the movement, and keep swinging your arm in various ways. Find out all you can do with the swing." (The momentum of the swing can carry children through all dimensions of space. For instance, bending their knees they can swing high to low, or around in arc-like patterns. Challenge the group.)

"This time start with any part of you just swinging. Let another part come in and swing that part, and another part, and still another—bigger and bigger and bigger until you are one complete swing."

Verbal chanting by the teacher helps, and piano accompaniment or good records aid in the process of swinging. Repeating this idea of starting from one part, adding others, and increasing the range of the swings, making them bigger and bigger until the whole body is involved, helps a child to "feel" the excitement and the momentum of the swing. There is no holding back here and children will just let the swinging movement take them through space. "Now, *go* somewhere when you swing." (This is why space is needed if one is to develop the true feeling that can come from swinging. The whole body seems in tune.)

"Try swinging various parts while sitting down. Try various ways of swinging while on one side and then another side, and also try swinging while lying on the floor. Start with one arm just swinging in front of you in a circular motion and then increase the range, making the swing larger and larger until the entire body is involved." (By analyzing the use of the swing we find that different things happen to the knees. We find if we have a broader base, our feet apart, our swing increases. We find that if

we really get a good swing going our head and finally our whole body is carried with the swing even to the point of lifting us off the floor.) "Try the same on the other side. Then start swinging two parts together in a circular way. If we start with our head and knees and arms all swinging at the same time we get bigger swings." (At other times the children can say "swing" as they move, increasing and decreasing the tempo and interest.)

"Try figure eights, slicing the space with an arm swinging a figure eight first and then getting the hips and all parts swinging. Try this on your other side, concentrating on large swings." (As we are developing these swings we are constantly analyzing what makes them different, why some of them seem easy, others hard. Also we think about why it seems as though we cover more space if we go from side to side swinging across the body rather than swinging two arms just in front of us, or by swinging figure eights with our two arms in front of our body rather than going across our body.) "Keep swinging and when you find a pattern that feels good, repeat it many times." (We analyze the swing and discuss the force or energy involved in the control of the swing in the language of the group. We discuss the swinging we have experienced and how it makes us feel—smooth, loose, happy, big, as though we had no bones, or strings. We also discuss and try out the different swings involved in various sport skills, and we analyze them. Sometimes with an adult group this is the way we start movement exploration.)

"Start swinging one arm forward as the other starts swinging backwards (swinging alternate arms forward and back). As you feel comfortable swinging, start bending your knees a little and feel as though you have springs on your feet which bounce you up and down as you are swinging your arms. Work on short, fast swings of arms still going back and forth, gradually getting longer and longer and slower and slower swings."

(We discuss this as we are doing it and have all kinds of words for this—short fast swings make us feel bumpy, stiffer swings, "not good"—broken, jagged; the slow long swings make us feel smooth, "out," open, long—from an older group we get words like *sustained, expanded.*)

Importance of Swinging Movements

A teacher can readily evaluate progress and detect when children have found the swing; because it seems so much a part of their way of moving, they have control of it and it is natural. The reason that time needs to be given to the development of the swing is that it helps children in performing other kinds of movements. It is an integral part of an easy walk; it helps with the jump, and it contributes to many interesting jump patterns. The swing is an integral part of the leap, and again, it is the swing of the upper part of the body as well as the "feeling" of the swing from within the body that helps in the execution of leaps. If children do not have control of their swings and have not had an opportunity to sufficiently develop their many kinds of swings then the leaps may look and seem like uncoordinated movements of the arms and legs. This is noticeable when the arms do not go with the legs.

To extend our comprehension and perception of the swing and the swinging movement we can listen to music that involves this quality. We use percussion and swing with sticks, often chanting as we swing the sticks together. We get full swings beating the tom-tom. We write dance songs with swings. We look for things that swing in nature, in the city, in mechanical things. We make many applications—talk about clocks, swinging bridges, lanterns, things in the circus and at the fair, rainbows, mobiles, windshield wipers, electric fans, yo-yos, lassos, the way some people walk, swinging from girders, skating, bicycling. We listen for this quality in words and poetry. We rep-resent the swings graphically. We find pictures or art work with "swings" and sometimes translate these through our movement impressions. As Tom said, "Ours is a swinging world."

Older children are encouraged to look for swinging movement skill patterns in television programs of sports and to find, try out, and list all the kinds of swings in various sport skills. In fact, they may find that there is hardly a sport without swinging movements. Children can particularly watch their favorite baseball or football player and look for swings in his playing. They are also encouraged to look for swings in various types of dance.

An illustration follows of a class of young children who had been introduced to the swing at an earlier session. This is a sample of how visual perception can assist some children.

Using Chalk To Intensify the Feeling of the Swing

Teacher: Can you think of another way of moving your arms?

Child: This way (swinging).

Teacher: What are you doing with your arms?

Child: Swinging them back and forth.

Teacher: Let's all do it. See if you can swing your bodies too. Now let's try swinging just one arm, and now the other. Can you do great big swings and then very small ones? Maybe the music can help you. What do very small swings make you think of?

Children: Me. My dog's tail. Jungle gym. My tongue.

Teacher: What else can you think of that would suggest a swinging movement?

Children: A camel. Boat. Yo-Yo. Monkey. Clocks. Trees. Bells.

Teacher: Can you swing your arms any other way besides across your body?

Children: Forward and back, like our swing goes.

Teacher: How would you like to swing with the pendulum of the clock up there on the wall? How does that swing? Listen, can you hear what it says? Let's see if we can swing with it (swinging motion both arms and body). Can you reach out and do a big stretchy swing? (*Elspeth discovers that with a wide base she can get a huge swing and tells the group about it.*) Let's watch and try Elspeth's.

Let's try something different—see if you can *draw* the swing. How would you do it? With this piece of chalk? (*Brown wrapping paper is rolled out on the floor and boys and girls have their choice of colored chalk.*) Just keep one arm swinging, only have a piece of chalk in your hand. When you draw it, do you have to make your swing any smaller?

Children: No, because we have lots of room on our paper.

Teacher: How would you draw this kind of swing?

Children: Up and over this way ... we're making designs.

Teacher: Can you say "swing" or "sway" while you draw? Some of us are drawing so fast. Let's slow the swings down so that we can make them bigger. What else could we do about it?

Children: Make ourselves swing as we chalk.

Teacher: What other ways could you swing with your chalk? Try them.

Let's put our chalk down for a few minutes and just swing with the scarves. Make all kinds of scarf swinging patterns.

Betty: Whoops. They're bigger swings—look!

Teacher: Now try chalking the way the scarf swings make you feel. Keep on swinging and make many swinging designs. I see Joel and Ralph getting huge swings using chalk in both hands.

(The children are feeling swings as they graphically represent their idea of this movement. As Joel so aptly remarks, "Golly, the whole paper is swinging. This is what I call a swinging room.")

When boys and girls feel comfortable with the swing—when it has become a natural part of them—then they can forget it and direct their attention to other things that make use of combinations of movements, such as swinging walks. They can find a variety of swinging walks that have all kinds of styles and characteristics because they can now concentrate on different movement patterns and refine the patterns. They swing so hard that they take themselves up into space and find *they are swinging and hopping.* This leads to enjoyable *ways of combining movements and discovering many folk dance patterns*—"hop swings," as some children call this combination. The fourth graders' dance composition "Christmas Bells" was based on just such a movement discovery.

The swing was so important to Mike that in analyzing its use one day he said, "How could I really skip or polka without the swing?" Swinging combined with various other movements have sent boys and girls into space spinning, pushing, turning, leaping and twisting like rockets, space labs, geese in flight, cyclones, and kites. One day as children discovered many ways of swinging themselves they began inventing a variety of swinging patterns; the classroom teacher used this experience and helped the group identify many things that swing. This was combined into reading and vocabulary charts. The experience terminated in a song and dance that had remained a favorite of the group. (See Part V, Chapter 15— "Things Are Swinging All Over Town.")

The acquisition of swinging movements and the many discovered patterns contribute to children's participation in folk dances, as well as their response to fad dance music, Rock and Roll, Ragtime, and favorite records as well as the composition of dance studies based on the swinging movement.

Other Nonlocomotor Movements

Space does not permit developing all basic movements but the suggestions and procedures as applied to the *Bend, Stretch* and *Swing* are also appropriate with *Pushing and Pulling, Twisting and Turning, Bouncing and Shaking.* These are the Basic Nonlocomotor (Body) Movements which we can do sitting, lying, or standing here in "my space."

PUSHING AND PULLING

Arr. *Joyce Eldridge*

TWISTING AND TURNING

Arr. *Florence Burns*

Twist and twist and turn a-round, Twist and turn down near the ground.

Twist and twist and turn up high, Let's twist up to the sky._____

Pushing and *pulling* occur when we impel toward or shove away from our fixed base. If we draw toward our fixed base, we are pulling. If we shove or thrust away from a fixed base we are pushing. Pushing reminds children of a car, doll carriage, being in a subway, animals that push with their heads (buffalo, elephant, goat, bull), wheelbarrows, lawn mowers, doors, crowds of people, and Christmas time. Pulling is connected with wagons, taffy candy, oars, gum, dogs on leash, swimming, little brother, rocks, anchor, sled, and curtains. Pushing and pulling include the movement of bending and stretching, but the force exerted against or toward an object makes the pushing and pulling movement different in quality from the bending and stretching. (For instance, in pushing a lawn mower, our arms bend and stretch, but we are applying force to the object, and we call this "pushing.")

We experiment and find that whenever we pull anything, that thing pulls back or when we push on or against something, that something pushes back. This is what *force* means to us as we work specifically with pushing and pulling movements. We realize that everything, ourselves included, moves because of pushing and pulling forces, and whenever we work on jumps, we feel the push against the floor as we take off and the

pull of gravity pulling us back.

Some of the mysterious complex forces—gravity, energy, centrifugal forces, friction, weights—can be better understood when boys and girls discover movements involving pushing and pulling.

The original edition of this book included striking and dodging, but as children work with these terms they feel that they are performing pushing and pulling, bending and stretching, and turning and twisting kinds of movements. Therefore, we have eliminated striking and dodging from the classification in this edition.

Twisting results when the upper part of the body is rotated around and the lower part of the body remains stationary. *Turning* results when the body completely revolves. Children say, "... twisting as far as you can go without moving your feet or your seat." Twisting is like corkscrews, pretzels, eggs, ice cream cones, trees, hurricanes, tornadoes, currents, and fishing lines. Turning is like tops, fans, swinging doors, and egg beaters. Turning is going around using a locomotor movement; it is a rolling form of movement. We find that vigorous twists help us with turning jumps or "jump turns"—a challenging movement for older boys and girls.

Shaking is caused by quick, successive tensions of muscles. Children think of this

SHAKING

Arr. *Florence Burns*

as shivering, the chattering of teeth, the vibrations of a refrigerator, and the quiver of jelly, the jiggling of riveters, and the agitation of mechanical toys, windows, dust mops, milkshakes, and rockets taking off.

As indicated earlier (Part II, Chapter 4), shaking and bouncing may not be true forms of basic movements but rather qualities of movement, as far as the adult world is concerned, but in the child's world these are two distinct movements with meaning and feeling.

Bouncing occurs when children make themselves go up and down or back and forth, in quick rhythmical sequence. Children associate this movement with bouncing a ball, bobbing for apples, bouncing on the bed and on chairs, the occasionally wavy lines on a television screen, divers on a springboard, and the bouncing of clowns, trapeze artists, and tightrope walkers.

BOUNCING

Arr. *Joyce Eldridge*

As children develop the nonlocomotor movements, they come to realize that they can move just an arm or leg forward or back or sideward, or they can move their whole body. They can start shaking their toes, then their heels, knees, middles, shoulders, heads, and then every part of them. They work with the many ways they can push with their shoulders, their heads, feet, knees, and their whole selves. They realize that they can pull toward their middles, and that they then can pull down or pull up. They identify the smallest part of their bodies that they can twist, and then the largest part that can be twisted, or the different parts they can twist and turn. They find that bouncy walks feel different from shaky walks. They come to realize that some body movements can go together easily and others cannot. Often they sing about what they are doing. Children realize also that some body and locomotor movements feel good together, such as the bounce and the jump, and that others, such as the leap and the shake, are hard to do together. They soon associate body movements with other things. All nonlocomotor movements are greatly enhanced when children have enough control of locomotor movements to coordinate the two. As nine- and ten-year-olds often say, "I feel like I am polka-ing all over," or "My leap makes me feel like I'm flying." Usually, twelve-year-olds discover the rhumba and other dance forms by combining nonlocomotor movements with locomotor movements.

As soon as we want to go somewhere, from my space to another space, or across or around the room, or through empty spaces, then one or more of the locomotor movements are included.

THE DEVELOPMENT OF LOCOMOTOR MOVEMENTS

The way children are constructed and the opportunities they have had for moving determine to a large degree their performance of locomotor movements. Because we have only two legs we can do only so many kinds of locomotor movements. Of the basic locomotor movements (walking, jumping, hopping, running, and leaping) the most common is walking.

Walking is basic to many skill and dance patterns (such as the skip, slide, gallop, polka, schottische, folk and social dance patterns). In other words, movement skills and dances using locomotion—"going somewhere," as the children say—are combinations of two or more of these basic movements.

The walk progression in this chapter was recorded from work done primarily with children of early childhood, while the jump progression, which follows, was taken from notes concerning older boys and girls. It cannot be too strongly emphasized that, although certain age groups were kept in mind relating these progressions, they may be used for any age group by making certain adaptations. (These adaptations are largely concerned with readiness in terms of language, coordination, and movement experience.) Our discoveries about the walk have been applicable to all locomotor movements. Many of the same questions and cues for motivation have been applied effectively to the other movements. When a child explores a movement element, such as the walk, he is usually not aware of any related motor activities until they are pointed out to him or until he discovers them after a period of working with the one movement.

Walk Progression

Walking is a transfer of weight from one foot to the other, or stepping from one foot to the other. Children say, "...on one foot and then on the other." One foot is on the floor at all times during walking.

It is important that each child be encouraged to develop the kind of walk that is best for him. This should be a free, easy walk—his kind of walk, rather than a stylization of someone else's. Restrictions and stiffness, such as those frequently result-

ing from marching, should be avoided. The music that accompanies walking should likewise avoid stylization and should have an easy, natural quality with tempo appropriate to the particular group of children.

A teacher can have the group start with an easy walk, going around the room toward the door. The music or two sticks will pick up their walks as they move. With the walk (hop, jump, run, or leap) the children discover that they can go high, low, or somewhere in between. They have short, long, fast, slow, hard, soft, heavy, and light walks. They can walk quickly and then slowly, up high and then down low, or they can walk and then stop, and then walk again. They can walk, turn around, and walk in other directions. With this exploration plenty of room is needed to avoid bumping; this often necessitates a discussion of what is meant by controlling our walks so that we will not bump into one another.

In answer to the question "What other ways could we walk?" children discover all sorts of variations. They walk on heels, peg-legged, with a goose step, on the outside or inside of the feet, with the toes turned in or out, with the knees in or out, or they may

WALKING

Arr. *Alonah Stith*

just lumber along or be crooked all over. Using exploration such as this often gives us a cue for finding out about animal walks. "Look at Red; he reminds me of a duck, the way he is walking." "Nat looks just like a penguin."

Pets which children have in their classroom or at home or see in a visit to the zoo, circus, or museum may initiate discussions about animal walks. A group of five-year-old children were concerned with their setting hen. They became interested in the way Henny Penny walked. This instigated finding out *how* Henny Penny walked. A lively discussion resulted, which called for investigating by looking, seeing, and doing or trying out.

Other discussions have centered around which animals do walk and how and why they walk. Children can become walking ducks, penguins, hens, lobsters, tigers, dinosaurs, and turtles. They may all be the same kind of an animal, or different ones. In one class we decided that because Jeannie looked like a cute, little, lively monkey who toddled along with her walk we all wanted to walk like monkeys. From just such an exploration among seven-year-olds, the following verse resulted:

> We're all monkeys, we're in the zoo
> I'm a monkey, so are you
> We can do all kinds of things
> Watch us close . . .
> Now aren't we funny?

We found out that we had to use many other movements to make our monkey funny.

Other approaches to walking have developed from discussions about people. "Look at the way Ralph is walking; he makes me think of my mailman." Such questions as these follow: "Today, whom did you meet on the street? What kind of a walk did he have? Could you walk like

someone you know—like an astronaut, lifeguard, bus driver, or principal? Will you let me guess who you might be? Can we show the difference in these walks?"

Ginny says, "You know what? This is the way my Granddaddy walks!" This cue starts us exploring the way baby walks, Mom and Dad walk, and the way we walk. We try to find out what helps us develop various kinds of walks and what we do with our heads, arms, and other body parts. Sometimes the way we walk affects the way we feel, and we find we have certain individual qualities in our walking. Our walks can be *smooth* like a skier, *jerky* like a robot, *bumpy* like a cowboy, *stiff* like a stilt man, and *loose* like Raggedy Ann. We walk the way we feel—proud, angry, silly, sad, or funny.

The following dance song came about as we were saying that our feet went walking down the street and then they stopped. We discussed how different it would feel and look if we were barefoot or if we had boots, swimming flippers, or skis on. Our skis wouldn't go down the street but where? Down the hill—on the snow. This is using controls— it also involves imagining movement, problem solving.

We learn that we can walk in various directions. Sometimes recognition of various types of walks occurs as we experience various walking relationships—different things happen to us as we change direction, going sideward, forward, or backward. We find as we start to back up that sometimes we have collisions. This elicits a discussion about the ways we can avoid bumping into one another. We explore many items in connection with direction of movement. We find that as we walk sideward different things happen to our legs, and that we can walk sideward with our legs crossing over in front or in back, or with our legs going side by side. We find it hard to walk backwards—we have to balance ourselves.

After this discovery we might divide into small groups (about two to three in a group for seven-year-olds, but larger groupings for

MY FEET WENT WALKING

Arr. *Clark W. Graves*

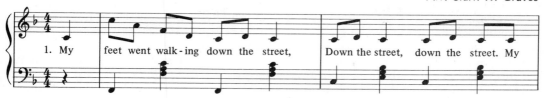

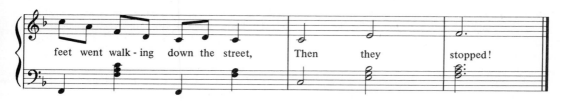

2. My roller skates went rolling on the sidewalk,
   On the sidewalk, on the sidewalk.
   My roller skates went rolling on the sidewalk,
   And then they stopped!

older children) and make a walking study by combining different directions in which each group moves. We can come from the different corners of the room to our opposite corner (the backward walkers, then the sideward, and then the around walkers). All this walking movement makes a design and leads easily to more discoveries of walking in larger and larger space and finding other movements that look and feel right.

Another approach to walking might be discovered by asking the question, "Can you walk so we can hardly hear you? What does this make you think of? Does walking lightly make you think of anything?" The answers usually come tumbling out. Walter starts, "Yeah, snow or quiet rain." Others follow: "Tick of a clock, baby asleep, airplane 'way in the distance, sailboat, the desert, soft breeze, candlelight, walking in outer space, church, ghosts." To deepen the problem-solving experience we can ask, "How can we walk so that we could hear every step?"

"... heavy with both feet making loud sounds." "Do you feel any different when you walk lightly or heavily? Let's watch and see if we look any different when we walk heavily or lightly. What do we have to do with the rest of our body? Can we think of anything that seems like a heavy walk?" "Sure, hailstones, squeaky shoes, riveters, steam rollers, rubber boots, horses." It is here that the teacher has to know how far to let the discussion go, when to channel it, and when to change the topic. This allows children to "loosen up" in their discussion and discoveries about walking movements.

Playing a walk on a tom-tom starts endless opportunities for incidentally bringing in elements of rhythm. Using percussion frequently helps us discover more ways of responding to a walk. We say to a child who is playing a tom-tom, "Do you suppose you could listen while we walk, and then, try to play our sounds?" To encourage children to think more about their movement, and to help them get the rhythm of the walk, we pose the question, "Can you clap the walk? Let's try to keep our claps as steady as we can."

We also find we can make other parts of our bodies "go like a walk." We say we are walking with our heads, eyes, tongues, fingers, knees, and so on. This way children get the "feel" of the walk throughout their bodies. They find that they can make certain rhythmic movement patterns and often say in sort of chant form what they are doing. They can accent the first walk of a series of walks as WALK walk walk. They can change the tempo of their walks and feel and look different when they walk slowly rather than fast.

For the most part, the children should set their own tempo rather than having the teacher or accompanist do it for them. As a group moves, it establishes a tempo to which most of the children can respond. It is the teacher's job to be sensitive to the group's tempo.

Stories and poetry have provided us with walking experience. We have responded to poetry such as Elinor Wylie's "Velvet Shoes":

> Let us walk in the white snow
> In a soundless space;
> With footsteps quiet and slow . . .[1]

or Vachel Lindsay's "The Mysterious Cat":

> I saw a proud, mysterious cat,
> I saw a proud, mysterious cat . . .[2]

By participating in varied experiences using walking, elements in space are easily

[1] From *Collected Poems of Elinor Wylie.* Copyright, 1921, 1932, by Alfred A. Knopf, Inc.
[2] From *Johnny Appleseed and Other Poems* (New York: The Macmillan Company, 1925). Used by permission of The Macmillan Company.

recognized. Children recognize, or it may be pointed out to them, that as they walk they make certain patterns or designs. This may be a good time to start working on floor patterns. (Full development of floor patterns will be discussed in Part IV, Chapter II). We include rangy walks, walks that have focus to them, and those concerned with different levels.

When given opportunity children find various kinds of combinations of movement based on the walk—walk and leap, walk and jump, walk with a twist, walk with push and pull, walk with a bounce. Discovering the combination of the *walk-hop* is fun, because children find out that it sometimes becomes the *skip.*

Children come to know the walk as their most fundamental movement. It is basic to folk and social dancing, which they should experience when they are ready. *This discussion on the development and progression of the walk is directly applicable to any of the other locomotor movements.*

Jumping

Jumping is performed on two feet. If we have our weight on two feet and elevate ourselves by taking off from the floor and landing on the floor again with both feet simultaneously, we have jumped.

Older boys and girls can accomplish fantastic movement discoveries while developing the jump. Six- and seven-year-olds have as much fun discovering and exploring this movement as do older children.

In any approach to the jump we need space. Children should spread out so they will have space to go up and down and out. First of all, they should spread out so they have plenty of room to themselves in order to really move, because that is exactly what they are going to do.

The jump calls for distributing the weight evenly and using force. Boys and girls need to apply force against the floor and feel it through their bodies in order to push themselves off the floor. There are

JUMPING

Arr. *Alonah Stith*

times when children are in locomotion (running, leaping) before adding a jump. When this happens sometimes they may take off from the floor with one foot. We call this a "one-foot takeoff"; however, the "feel" of the true jump is maintained. At other times when locomotion is applied after the act of jumping, children may come out of the jump or seem to land on one foot and continue in locomotion. (Again the "feel" of the jump is maintained.) Our initial purpose is to have children recognize *the structure and feel of the jump by taking off and landing on two feet.*

Illustration of Development of Jumping

Teacher: Can you start bouncing just with your knees, letting your hips and shoulders bounce too? Let's try feeling bouncy all over. Can you keep bouncing as the sticks bounce, and then when the sticks stop you stop? Let's try again. This time as the sticks sound louder you increase your bounces and make them go higher and higher. Good! Keep on getting higher, and swing your arms, too. What are you doing?

Joyce: I turned right into a jump!

Teacher: Suppose we try that again, starting from a jump, and gradually push ourself off the floor—yes, swinging our arms at the same time. Now we are jummmmmping ... more push, higher and higher ... rest a minute. When you are ready, all jump again. How could you go higher? Could you go faster, then slower and slower until you are not jumping any more, but just sort of bouncing? What makes you go up in the air? Thinking about that will help you to get a good jump.

(Children discover that if they use their arms, keep their heads up, bend their knees to get started, and land on the balls of their feet, they can spring right back up. We discuss this; we watch demonstrations; and we all try. We talk about the mechanical principles involved. Then we work on the "springy" feeling. While we rest we talk about what really sends us into the air. David tells us that it is the force in our bodies contacting the

floor. We push against the floor, and the floor pushes against us, and that pulls us up into a jump.)

Teacher: David, that sounds pretty complicated. Show us what you mean. Where does the push really come from?

(Often this turns into an involved discussion about gravity and relates to many of the stories youngsters are reading. Plans can be made to secure more information before the next time you are to meet.)

Children: It's pushing off the floor with our two feet.

Teacher: And then what? Do you just stay up there off the floor?

Len: I push myself off the floor, my two feet go up in the air off the floor, and then I'm pulled back down to the floor on my two feet.

Teacher: Suppose we all try. This time jump as high as you can possibly go, away, away up there. Let your swings help you.

Bill: This is like blasting off like a supersonic rocket.

Teacher: Yes—only really blast off the floor! Bernadette, suppose you clap a jump for us. Now, let's all clap and really make it say "jump." What would we clap if we wanted a sound to help us get ready to jump?

(As the children jump they discover how different it feels to do it with something that suggests "blasting off." The blasting off soon turns into "count-downs." This experience helps their jumps and the children increase in their development of handling themselves in space, utilizing the swing and expenditure of energy in pushing themselves off the floor. This becomes a challenge to see how low they can start and how high they can go. They start from their count-downs, blasting off and then zooming into space. They try to see how many "zoom's" they can say while in space.)

Teacher: Count down—10-9-8-7-6-5-4-3-2——— Blasssssst Offf! Zoooom!

This experience and its subsequent discussion resulted, in one class, in the following poem:

Rockets Rockets
Shooting up up
up to the sky
Rockets Rockets
Jetting up up
Through space
Supersonic
ZOOOOOOOOOM! SHHHHHHHH!

Children discover they can jump sideward, backward, and around and that they can jump in straight lines and in curves. All these forms take skill and coordination. Control of the arms and upper body is needed to help them turn in the air. Trying these things often leads to a good discussion of the body as a whole or in parts and of what particular parts help us to jump. Boys, particularly, have a wonderful time trying to spin in the air on "around" jumps. This brings forth images of an electric fan, a pinwheel, and a half-gainer. "Lets try" becomes the challenge of the day.

Things happen to children's legs when they jump; they find that they can jump with their legs crossed, apart (one foot forward and the other back), or astride, weight on one side and then on the other side. With their jumps they can touch their hands with their feet, bend their knees up in front, or in back, and many more combinations. Time needs to be given to develop the different ways of jumping. Not all children within a group can explore jumps with the same speed or have developed enough force or ability to handle themselves easily in the air. At a slower tempo sometimes more complicated explorations result.

Jumping and walking is different from jumping and hopping, as the following illustration shows.

Teacher: What could we put with a jump?

Clark: We could hop and jump.

Teacher: Why don't we try this? Hop-jump, hop-jump. (The children go up and down and sideways, circling.) What does it say? Can you clap it?

George: "One foot, two feet" is what it says.

Teacher: Shall we try it? (Music followed the group, and was used for the first time.) Why don't you really let go? See how much space you can cover. Let's clap it again while you catch your breath. Now, shall we do it narrow and then wide? Think of being back in that box and then springing out. See if we can go farther out if we use the upper parts of our bodies, too.

What would help to remind us to jump and hop?

Dave: We can say to ourselves as we do it, "Jump and hop," or, "Two feet and then one foot."

Teacher: That's a good suggestion. Let's try ... Some of us aren't quite doing it. What do you suppose is wrong?

Clark: It's because we are jumping too far to the side.

Sheran: Maybe we are forgetting to hop and just jumping all the time.

George: Yes, but do we want to move just up and down or out to the side?

Teacher: Maybe we should try both—jump and hop in place, and then in space out to the side, and then in place again. Now let's move out every time we hop—that's it, jump where you are and then move out on your hops. Maybe if we say what we are doing, it will help.

George: Golly, I didn't hop because my jump carried me too far. I kept forgetting to hop.

Teacher: Suppose we watch George and all say "Jump, hop," while he does it. Is he covering space?

Children: Oh yes, just look at him go!

Teacher: Let's think of another way to cover space, using first a little kind of movement and then a big one, changing our range as we move. While you are resting, think of ways, and then we'll try them.

Some patterns with the jump that have been worked out by children include the following:

> Jump, jump, leap, leap
> Jump, hop, jump, hop, jump
> Walk, walk, walk, jump
> Run, run, run, run, jump
> Gallop, gallop, jump, jump

Groups have fun with parts of songs, whole songs, or jingles which they make up on the spot. For example, one day when a group of eleven-year-olds were working on jump patterns, they were asked to think of the first few lines of favorite songs and work out jump patterns as they sang. (Some included jazz, others soul music.) The following samples were given:

> Jump, jump, jump like a pogo stick!

Six boys and girls working together in a group completed an entire song; the following accompanied their jumping pattern:

> I'm a little jumping bean,
> I'm happy as can be.
> I jump and bounce and jump and bounce
> Like a funny jumping bean.

Another group started their jump pattern this way:

> Jumping up and bending down ...
> And skipping in a circle
> Jumping up and bending down . . .

For accompaniment they used a tune of a popular song. These jump patterns and songs to accompany movement give added meaning and inspire many new variations on the jump.

To such questions as "How does a jump make you feel?" or "When you jump what does it make you think of?" the following responses have been recorded from a group of ten-year-olds: roller coaster, ferris wheel stop, going over gutters, football passer, high jumper, space cadet, frogs, fireflies, jumping horses, cheerleaders, the occasionally wavy lines of television channels, neon signs, balloons bursting, firecrackers, soda fizz, square dancing, sky diver, parachuters, folk dancers, or square dancers.

"I jump when something frightens me—scares me—yes, I sure jumped out of the way the other day when I saw a snake." "Sometimes I jump up and down when I'm mad, my sister makes me so mad." "When I feel happy about a surprise, like when it snowed the other day or when I just feel good all over, I jump and jump." Many of these feelings and ideas have been used for dance studies and compositions. Note that emotions often provide powerful and meaningful opportunities for expression of feelings through movement.

Children find that they enjoy jumping with accent. They identify accents from the piano, records, drum, or wood-block beat. They also identify accents in songs they can sing. They may move accordingly with one group jumping on the first accent, the second group on the second accent, and so forth.

The use of groups in exploring the jump is particularly helpful with older children.

A group of boys and girls can be asked to form groups according to colors and then to work out some kind of "color" pattern using the locomotor movement of the jump, for example. Other movement, space, or rhythmic element can be added to their study, just as long as the pattern is predominantly jumps. This is setting the situation or posing the framework of the problem. One group may work on a square dance—here is the result of one such effort:

All join hands
And circle the track,
Keep on going
'Til you get back,
When you get home
All *jump* the track,
And swing that girl like thunder.

There goes first couple
Jumping the track,
Others circle left
Around the track,
Keep on going,
'Til they *jump* back,
Keep on going
Around the track.

A teacher can set the situation by asking the children to select three elements to combine with the jump pattern—one from space, one from rhythm, and one from the body movements. Then, as the groups start to work, it may be necessary to probe further. The teacher may say, "Consider using different directions to give interest to your patterns. Can you start from different positions or levels? Would accent help your movements? Have you thought of doing part of your pattern slow and ending up with a fast tempo?" Sometimes, however, boys and girls prefer to set their own movement problems. Frequently groups set problems for other groups to work out. It helps to clarify the problems if we record them on written form on brown wrapping paper or large pieces of newsprint. Children must learn how to share not only their movement ideas but their accomplishments; this takes time. Teachers must see that the patterns do not become so complicated that some members of the group cannot achieve. Children should also be given opportunities to become members of the audience to deepen their observations and learn to appreciate the efforts of others.

Hopping

Hopping is executed on one foot. If we put our weight on *one foot* and elevate ourselves by pushing off the floor and landing on the *same foot,* it is hopping. Children say, "... up in the air and back down again on just one foot, the same foot, like a puppet on a string."

Hopping involves balance in leaving the ground or the floor on one foot and coming back on the *same foot* without falling over. It is much easier to jump than to hop. Jumping helps hopping. Many children have to be *helped to hop.* Both jumping and hopping involve leaving the ground, holding oneself "up there." Some children may be afraid of this. Often they push down into the ground rather than pushing themselves upward.

One way to get youngsters secure in trying a hop is to have them jump first. Once this is achieved, the realization that they can leave the floor encourages them to continue. The hop is one of the keys to enabling children to enjoy creative rhythmic activities and later the dance; it is involved in such things as the skip, polka, the jig, the schottische, etc.

The hop must be taught or encouraged in such a way that children will be able to *hop on either foot.* For most children the hop has to be accomplished long before skipping, but there are some children for whom skipping seems to be natural. Following is an illustration of class activities involving teaching the hop.

HOPPING

Arr. *Joyce Eldridge*

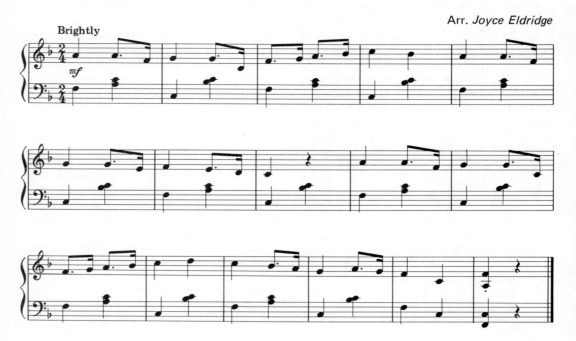

Teacher: Let's start to jump very fast. Can you jump even faster, turn yourself around as you jump? Now could we start to bounce—bounce like a rubber ball, higher and higher, bounce up into the air. Look—we are jumping! Keep your heads up, look at me as you are jumping. Can we try something very, very hard! Can we stand on just one foot, just for a second? Try. Take hold of the table or the desk or I'll help you if you need me. Careful, not the chair, that might fall over. Everyone on one foot— now start to bounce fast, bounce higher and higher, make yourself go up, up, up, up, up. (Teacher uses pitch in voice to help group get up. Usually when children first start to hop they bend over with their eyes on the ground. This pulls them down and keeps them from getting up.) Look at me. Look up at the ceiling. Now try to bounce and see if you can get up to the ceiling. Remember, you can't get up there unless you look up there. (When young children first sense that feeling of "look what I can do" they go very fast and often turn

around and around trying to keep their balance.)

See if you can hop without turning around. Make your back real stretchy and let your arms help you hop. (When boys and girls once have the feeling of the hop, then we play a "can you" game.) Can you hop—keep hopping —and *stop!* Stop just as though I cast a magic spell on you. Put on your magic boot with the springs in it and now hop, higher and higher. Keep going and STTTOOOP! Hop someplace, over here, over there, and stooooooop.

Can you clap a hop? Clap your hop here on your legs; make your shoulders feel as though they are hopping, make your head hop . . . and stooooop. Find another part of you to hop. (As children gain in skill of handling themselves on one side, start them on the other, using the same procedure. Some children may need the help of the teacher or parent to support them.)

Try swinging your arms and elbows and it

might help you *hop*. Look at this red ball. As I bounce it, see how it goes off the floor. Can you try to make yourself hop like the ball is doing? Look at Tyrone hop—let's watch him. How does it feel, Tyrone? Did you see what Tyrone was doing with the other foot or leg? *Often in the third grade or even in graduate classes we find some who have never developed the hop on both sides. We find this in "one-footed skippers," those who skip on the "good side,"* walking on the other. If this situation is observed with older children, rather than embarrass them or make them conscious of their differences, we try many, many experiences with hopping.

Can we all swing the other leg? Now change to the other foot, and hop and swing your other leg and arm. Just see if you can balance yourself on this foot and hop. I'll bet you can't bounce and stay in one place on that foot! I'll bet you can't stretch way up high while you are still on one foot. Can you stand on your foot and put your hands around the other knee? Now see if you can turn around on that foot you are standing on.

Try something new, that you have never tried before—hop forward on one foot. Can you hop toward the stage?

When hopping is achieved, there are various challenges, such as the hopping game suggested in Chapter 7. Children can be asked to hop and swing; hop, bend, and stretch; hop higher and lower; faster and slower; hop to the drum accompaniment; hop while chanting; hop to get across lines on the floor; hop over to the door, around the room, around each other, and through empty spaces.

Teacher: How many think that they could make up a hop that is all their own? If you care to work with a partner, that's O.K.

Today when you go home and the sun is out, try watching your shadow while you hop. See if your shadow will hop with you. Try making your hopping shadow do all kinds of things. Maybe you can draw us some pictures of your shadow hopping—it will be fun to see them. A hopping shadow mural can be made and then danced.

Suppose we close our eyes and listen to this record. Try to hear the hopping music. Maybe it says many other things to you, but try to hear some hopping too. Maybe we could try to hop while the music is playing—let's try.

(Elizabeth and Judy think of a hopping helicopter, so all watching first-graders become helicopters, ending up with this helicopter story: "Helicopter high in the sky ... propeller on my head goes round and round and round and then lands down on the ground.")

There is a feeling of wonder and power in being able to do what one wants with his body. "It's me, look at me! See—I can hop!" For many children this takes time and encouraging help, but the feeling of accomplishment and the increased body skills and intellectual knowledge that accompanies such an achievement are valuable to every child.

Running

Running is a faster movement than the walk and includes more elevation. If we do a faster step, pushing a little harder against the floor, suspending the body in the air for just a moment, so that we transfer weight while getting some elevation, it becomes a run. According to children, this is "being in a hurry in the air just a little."

Some of the locomotor movements seem easier for children to perform than others. For instance, in working with six- to nine-year-olds, if the run is developed before they know how to manage movement or before they have had many opportunities to move freely and handle themselves in relation to space, a group may get out of hand. The very nature of the run, with its accompanying exhilaration, often makes children "let loose" like exploding firecrackers. *As in anything else with children, their readiness for an activity is an important consideration.*

Children find that they can run in various directions in their own spaces, and this feels and looks different than when they run

RUNNING

Arr. *Alonah Stith*

through a lot of space. They can make variations of these runs and as they combine these variations with body movements, they experience different qualities of movement. For instance, they can do just about all the things they did with the walk and more—but the run serves a different purpose and has its own "feeling." But as with any other form of activity, to present it to first- or second-graders who have not acquired the necessary coordination and control may cause discouragement. There are, of course, some first-graders who can execute beautiful locomotor movements without exception. The group members must learn to handle themselves in space and interact and respond to individual and group tempo before any new activity can be introduced. This is particularly true of the leap.

Leaping

Leaping is the elevation, or suspension, of the run, which is held in the air for a longer period of time, with a transfer of weight from one leg to the other. Actually there is little difference between the run and the leap, except in range of the movement. Children analyze the leap as "going away up in the air, stretching out from one leg to the other—like going over a big puddle."

Boys and girls usually discover the leaping way of moving from working on running movements. For instance, when they slow down their runs, but at the same time go higher up in space or farther out in space (using more force), they find that this is a different kind of run. It looks different, feels different, and demands stretching out their legs. In the leap there is more distance between each contact with the floor and one is suspended in the air longer than with the run. It is this ability to hold oneself "up" in space that challenges older children who have achieved movement competencies.

Remaining in one spot, we find many kinds of leaping patterns; these look quite different than when we are leaping through considerable space. We feel the momentum as we shift our weight from side to side or from front to back. These movements demand body manipulation. Combining leaping and running challenges the ingenuity of older boys and girls and numerous com-

LEAPING

Slow   8va -   Arr. *Joyce Eldridge*

plicated movement skills are added to their movement repertoire. Experiencing leaping and running forms of movement often provoke analysis and discussion concerning the space and time involved. *It seems that the higher we leap, the farther off the floor we go and, therefore, the more space we consume, the slower the tempo; the closer to the floor we go, the less space we use, the faster we go or the faster the tempo.* This

feature is particularly important as far as accompaniment of movement is concerned. Our accompaniments—percussion, two sticks, mouth, or other sounds—take on accuracy when we can kinesthetically sense movement and follow specific ways of moving.

Children use a variety of leaps in their dance compositions. As they master the leaping movement and its many complications, it often becomes their favorite way of moving. It has been interesting to note that favorite ways of moving for younger children include the *swing* and the *skip;* and for older boys and girls the *leap* is preferred.

The walk, jump, hop, run, and leap are the five basic locomotor movements. When presenting and developing particular locomotor movements, our concentration at the moment may be on one particular movement such as the run. Nevertheless, we recognize that basic nonlocomotor movements enter into each of these activities. For instance, we cannot leap or run without swinging or bending or pushing with various parts of our bodies. In addition, we cannot perform locomotor movements without some of the body movements.

Other movement skills and dance patterns (dance steps) are combinations of two or more of these basic movements. As these are combined and organized within time and space elements, different kinds of movements emerge. It is out of this combination of basic movements with spatial and rhyth-

mic elements that the more complicated movement skills, such as the skip, slide, and gallop, are developed.

RELATING NONLOCOMOTOR AND LOCOMOTOR MOVEMENTS

A single class period would rarely concentrate on exploring or developing only one of the basic movements (as presented in the progression write-ups). Teachers plan each day according to their own specific purposes, situations, and the particular group of children. They also plan in terms of variety, review, and specific *purposes of the session.* This is approached in numerous ways. The following class session is an example.

Development of Movement Experiences with a Second Grade

The following account illustrates how movement experiences were developed with a second-grade group. These children were working with the author for the first time, therefore it was necessary to become familiar with them and their knowledge of movement. (After a time it became obvious that they had a good background.) The lesson was given for elementary school teachers. It was developed and stenographically recorded as it appears below. The use of questions, cues, and reactions of the boys and girls and the creative rhythmic movement progression within the lesson should be noticed.

Teacher: Find a place that's all yours away from anyone else—your space station. Now let's see if we can go down as low as we can. Down ... down. How low can we go? Lower yet— what will you have to do with yourself to get all of you as close to the floor as possible? What are you doing to yourselves?
Children: Getting flat. I'm holding my breath!

Teacher: What prevents us from going down more?
Children: The floor.
Teacher: While you are as close to the floor as you can get, find *one part* of you to move ... find another part ... now move the two parts at the same time. Can you move yourself into a sitting position? What's the biggest part you can move while you are *sitting up?*
Children: (The first individual verbal responses) Head, back, my legs.
Paul: My whole legs *(stretching* his legs up and out wide and balancing on his sitter).
Teacher: Look at the *stretch* Paul is getting in his legs! Can we all find a part of us that will stretch? Let's see.
This time find *five* parts that you can stretch *all* at once.
(Exploration had begun and gradually all of the group became involved.)
Teacher: Could you stretch two parts? Try ... now *add* three more parts. How many parts are stretching?
Children: Five. Hey, we were doing this on the board this morning!
Teacher: Doing what, Thelma?
Thelma: Addition, putting numbers together, like 2 and 5.
Teacher: Suppose you show us. (Thelma stretched two legs and five fingers, all of which started "Look at this!" There was a room full of various combinations of stretching 7 parts.) What other ways can you move besides stretching?
Betty: We can shake—look, like this.
Carol: I'm shaking my head and my feet and my sitter all at once.
Teacher: Let's see if we can shake our toes, heels, knees, hips, shoulders, our heads, and all over. Try again ... what is it that shakes all over?
Bobby: (in the most serious and grave tone of voice) Well, I would say that I was one of those little toy trucks—self-propelled.
Peter: I'm a top.
Teacher: Everyone start shaking until you get yourself to your feet. That was not easy, was it? Now that you are up on your feet, try moving about the room but still shaking ... freeze! From wherever you are, will you come back over here with a very shaky walk?

When I saw you this morning you told me that you liked to skip. Let's see your skips ... try a shaky skip ... How did that feel?

Children: Terrible, awful, yuk!

Teacher: Suppose you try skipping while swinging some part of you—see if that feels better. Can you stop and clap a skip?

Frank: Look, I can make my fingers skip.

Teacher: Can you make your tongues skip? Let's clap a skip on our knees. This time make every part of us skip ... now that you have the feeling of the skip, let's move, skipping in all the space. Now see what you can do with your skip that feels good ... freeze! That was very good; I saw all kinds of skipping. Bobby, that was different, the way you were skipping —please do it again. (He crossed his legs over each other as he skipped, following with a swing with the rest of the body.)
Think about this for a moment—what is another way you could move through empty space in this room?

Margie: Gallop and gallop.

Charlie: Yes, gallop like this—gallop, gallop, gallop (and he took off, galloping even faster than he spoke).

Teacher: Charlie, I'm afraid that we would have trouble making our feet go as fast as you say. Suppose we all gallop—Whoa! While you are catching your breath just make your hands and shoulders gallop ... let's really let go and gallop with all the different parts of you that you can find. Frank, please show us how you can gallop through this open space, and the rest of us will clap your gallop.

Charlie: Why doesn't Frank do it again? I want to make my mouth go the way he is galloping.

Teacher: What was good about the way Frank was galloping?

Laurie: His feet.

Carol: He really looked like a horse—that's what he made me think about.

Teacher: What kind of a horse did you think he was?

Stephanie: A pony—a frisky pony.

Teacher: Good! Let's be frisky ponies ... now gallop slower—slower—and now faster and faster and then slow down.

Children: Whew!

Teacher: Carol—when we were working with shakes you said you thought of horses. Could you show us your idea of a horse doing shakes and gallops (combining movement)?

Children: That looked like fun—can we?

Teacher: Yes. Whoa—but first do you remember the space station you started working from at the beginning of our session? Well, suppose you all try to be really shaky—galloping ponies or horses, and when the music stops and we call *Whoa!* you end up in *your* own space station. (Most remembered, but two children had to be reminded about their space areas.) Tired, tired horses. So tired no more shakes. You're so, so tired you can hardly stand up on your feeeeeet—so your head gives way, your middles "give in," your knees "give way," poor tired horses (relaxation); and very tired second graders can't stand up any more so you went "plop" right there in your stalls. While you are tired horses, or ponies lying in your stalls, how heavy can you make yourself? What's the heaviest thing you can think of? Feel heavy. In about one minute decide what is the heaviest thing you could be.

Joan: I'm just heavy in my feet.

Teacher: Can you all be heavy in your middles? your shoulders? your head and feet? Watch Peter, and see how even his fingers are heavy. I can't lift him, he's so heavy.

Mapes: Well I can lift him; well, anyway I can lift one foot just a little.

Teacher: I'm coming around to those who really look heavy and you tell us what you are—be the heaviest thing in the world.

Children: Alligators. A train. An elephant. My Daddy's truck.

Bobby: Look—try to lift me—I'm the iron part of the train.

Teacher: Now turn on your backs and see what the lightest thing is that you can be. Oh, so light! (At this point there was much wiggling and waving of fingers, toes, and arms.) Think about the lightest thing in the whole world. Show us.

Philip: A breeze.

Barbara: A pillow.

Vicki: I guess I don't know, air.

Mapes: Toilet paper.

Teacher: When I first met you today, what did you tell me you were studying about?

Ginger: We've been studying about turtles, and we've been studying about dinosaurs.

Teacher: What's the difference between a turtle and a dinosaur? And how would they move?

Mapes: Turtles are funnier and dinosaurs real bigger. Look, I'm a turtle.

Teacher: Shall we see this group over here move like dinosaurs? We will watch (designating a part of the class). Could we see other groups move like dinosaurs? What was the difference? (Much conversation.)

Teacher: What other animals could you be?

Stassie: Monkeys.

Teacher: What does a monkey do?

Suzie: Tricks; he can hang by his tail, but we can't do that.

Teacher: What are some other animals?

Mapes: Cavemen.

John: Cavemen? That's not an animal. How about a deer?

Teacher: What does a deer do?

Frank: He runs and leaps.

Teacher: How would you like to have a zoo? (They were divided into seven groups and given about three minutes to work out what they were going to be.) Stay in your spots and decide on your animals, and then you can come back to the zoo in your little groups. Where shall we start?

Frank's group

Teacher: What are you?

Carol: I'm an elephant.

Teacher: Oh, you're all elephants.

Carol: No, I'm the elephant, the only elephant.

Frank: I'm a deer. (He ran lightly and swiftly and softly and was beautiful in motion.)

Nina: I'm a horse, and I can prance.

Peter's group

Children: We're great big dinosaurs.

Gene: I'm a wild one.

Vicki's group

Children: We're kangaroos.

A group of four boys

Children: We're monkeys.

A group of two boys

Child: Bet you can't guess what we are. (They were gazelles.)

A group of one boy and two girls

Children: We're birds.

Teacher: What kind?

Child: Cardinals, I guess.

A group of four girls

Teacher: What are you—turtles?

Mapes: I'm not—I'm a big gorilla. (Her arms were dragging all over the floor.)

Teacher: Of course, you know the gorilla got to the zoo before the turtle. Now that all the animals are back in the zoo, that's all we can do today, but maybe you could write a dance story about the turtles and dinosaurs and I'll bet Miss Kelly will help you. After you have your story written, why not dance your story?

Combining Movements

At times, we just work on combining movements. For instance, fifth- and sixth-graders can be put to work on combinations of locomotor movements in groups to work out a pattern of movement or studies of combination of movements. When studies have been worked out, usually it is important that they be shared. If time should run out, it is the teacher's job to see that those groups that have not presented their particular studies have a chance at the next opportunity to share other accomplishments. When studies are presented for a group, the presentations are usually followed by a discussion and evaluation. These are some of the points discussed: *"Did we stick to the problem? How could we improve it? What did you particularly like about the study? What did the group combine with (for example) the jump pattern? Did you notice a definite beginning and end?"*

Helping children explore movement by using their bodies is the starting point. How we initiate these movements—how we include different elements which affect movement—depends on the teacher and the group of children. We select questions, cues, and experiences that motivate a particular group. We start a group with a simple suggestion or question concerning a fundamental movement (such as a hop), build on this locomotor movement, and then continue to the other movements (jump, walk, and so on). We may start with a body movement (swing) or with a combination of movements (push and pull). We discover many possibilities concerning the movement selected: how we do it, what we are doing, how we can do it better, what it reminds us of, how it feels, and how it looks. These are but a few of the ways we start to work and become familiar with basic movements.

6

Combinations of Movements

MOVEMENT SKILLS

Movement skills and dance patterns develop as children are given opportunities to use various combinations of basic movements in meaningful ways. But "a movement pattern does not just appear, fully ripened. Some appear in infancy, some at age two or three, some later. A few appear "in toto" or nearly so, others develop over a period of several months or even years. The neuromuscular complex is there and the nerve-net may be built-in, but how and when the child is motivated to use it will depend on the appearance of pattern and his later achievement." [1]

As children start to school, many seem to perform certain movements fairly naturally, while others need to develop coordination. Because no two children are alike, they differ in the way they perform any movement skills. The way a boy or girl is constructed—the length of legs, ability to coordinate legs and arms, ability to lift off the floor and sustain elevation—as well as ability to hear and respond to rhythmic

[1] Caroline B. Sinclair, *Movement of the Young Child* (Columbus, Ohio: Charles E. Merrill Publishing Co., 1973), p. 34.

elements, determines the way in which specific movement skills are performed. We are constantly reminded of this as we observe children's varying abilities with such movement combinations as the gallop and skip.

But *all normal, healthy children can acquire movement skills and find joy and freedom that come with them.* As they gain movement experience and become aware of their capacities, they can be helped in developing and refining movements and in combining several movements. The important factor is that teachers can recognize new ways of moving when they emerge, or have knowledge about these "special" ways of moving to help particular groups of children. It is hoped that the individual movement patterns are already developed *before* they are used in formalized dance forms. The emphasis is on discovering, understanding, and using each movement combination and having fun with it at the moment; later it can be used as needed in skills and dance patterns.

The skip, gallop, and slide are similar in that all three have two sounds of an uneven duration and are a combination of locomotor movements involving elevation. They are different in that the *gallop* and

slide are made up of a *walk and leap* but the *skip* is a *walk and hop*. In the gallop and in the slide the same foot is always in the lead and the walk comes on the lead foot. In the skip the leading foot changes from one foot to the other.

The following items should help to clarify the uniqueness of each to these movements:

The skip, gallop, and slide are each formed in combination with two basic locomotor movements and therefore have two sounds.

skip .... walk and hop
gallop .... walk and leap
slide .... walk and leap

The two sounds are of uneven duration or length of time. The division of time is long-short. It is this uneven rhythmic relationship which makes these movements unique (See Part IV, Chapter 12 for explanation of rhythmic analysis used in this book.)

skip	walk	hop
gallop	walk	leap
slide	walk	leap

The direction of the movements are different.

skip .... any direction
gallop ...... forward and backward
slide .... sideward

In the three movement skills there is some elevation off the floor, but in varying degrees. The level may be high or low and the range of the movement large or small.

The movements skills vary in distribution of body weight.

skip—weight is distributed with alternate feet leading taking the walk part of the combination.

gallop and slide—weight is on one side with same foot leading taking the walk part of the combination each time.

All three movements employ force and a push off the floor.

The qualities of movement usually differ.

skip and slide—seems smooth.
gallop—seems bumpy, jerky, and more forceful than a skip or slide.

Although the combinations of locomotor movements differ in the gallop and skip, the similar rhythmic patterns make it possible to change from one movement skill to the other. All can be varied in tempo, intensity, range, and level, and can be related to feelings, ideas, and experiences boys and girls are having. The same accompaniment can be used for all three but with greater accent on the gallop. Finding unusual ways to combine these three movement skills provides new patterns from which some dances are made. (In a class of thirty, one day we had twenty-seven different combinations of the skip, gallop, and slide.)

The way the basic movements are combined and the way in which they are specifically affected by space, force, and time provide the uniqueness of these particular movement skills. It is their interrelationships and the emphasis on each that makes the slide a *slide*, the skip a *skip*, or the gallop a *gallop*.

The Gallop

Because of the way we are constructed, it seems as though we can do more with ourselves going in a forward and backward direction than going in a sideward direction. Children seem to readily "take to" the gallop. As with any other skill pattern, if it isn't used it might have to be relearned, but it doesn't take long for children to recall the gallop kinesthetically. Some adults take longer to develop or recall gallop. Of all the locomotor combinations, the gallop is usually found before the slide or skip in early childhood. This combination is often accomplished before they "feel good" running or leaping.

The gallop is made up of a combination of the *walk* and *leap*; we hear two sounds of

GALLOP

Arr. *Joyce Eldridge*

uneven duration as the feet contact the floor. The walk takes a longer amount of time than the leap, and we say that the walk is the long sound and the leap is the short sound. It sounds like Gaallll-op-Gaallll-op, or dummm da dummm da. The gallop is taken in a forward direction (later with more skill in galloping we find that we can also go in a backward direction). In the forward direction the same foot is always in front, or takes the lead with the walk, and the other foot "tries to catch up" with the leap. We start with our weight on our "front" foot or on the walk (this carries the accent that is pronounced in the gallop). The spatial and rhythmic elements affect the combination of the *walk-leap* and this makes the gallop a gallop.

Movement Combination	walk leap	walk leap
Rhythmic Pattern	—— —	—— —
Underlying Pulse	————	————
Direction	forward or backward	

The *galloping* movement combination is similar to the sliding movement combination, and the rhythmic pattern is similar, but the gallop differs because of the direction in space, the tremendous amount of force that can be put into it, and the exaggerated accent on the walk part of the gallop. Children seem to favor the gallop over the slide, saying, "It's faster, bumpier, higher, and more fun."

Rarely does one have to teach the gallop. To introduce this movement combination one has only to mention ponies, and this sets a group in motion. "Put one foot out in front of you and let's gallop around the room—make yourself go higher and higher and push with your arms." We work on refinement and quality in the "feeling" of the gallop.

"Timmy, that was a terrific gallop. Show us how you did it. Why do you think Timmy gallops so high? How could we gallop higher and higher?" (This does not mean that the teacher necessarily has to gallop continually around the room with the children. If she wants to, all the better—however, it is possible to participate actively by playing a gallop on the drum or clapping a gallop rhythm with her hands or with two sticks.) "Listen to the sound of these two sticks. Can you clap the sound of the gallop while I am playing on the sticks? Now try galloping on the other side with the other foot in the lead—the foot we did not start to gallop with before." (This poses a problem for some children.) "Push really hard to take off. Let's try galloping in place and really pull your knees way up, bending them up as far as you can. Hear our feet making the gallop sound?" We analyze the sound as "galllllop, galllllop" and often say or chant it as we move. We make the sound of the gallop with our hands on our thighs, clapping, snapping our fingers, clacking with tongues, gallllloping with many parts. Sometimes we make the sound on the floor with our feet, and get into varied positions as we do this. We try to get the feeling of the gallop in our bodies all through ourselves, not just in the feet, by sensing galloping with our shoulders, our arms, our heads, and then taking off with our feet. Working on increasing speed (tempo), some notice that the leap part turns into a run, because the faster we go the shorter our movements, and we cannot go off the floor very far. We work on decreasing and increasing tempo and adjusting our gallops accordingly. Adapting to space and changing directions and levels, galloping over all kinds of obstacles, galloping with and around other people at various tempos, help to develop this step just for the fun of it at the moment and later for use in a variety of combinations in dance studies.

We are not afraid to make up "gallopy" patterns and we never cease to wonder at the many, many ways we can gallop. When we watch other classes giving assemblies, we even see different kinds of gallops—we find it interesting to combine our particular gallops with those created by others. Many of the dance compositions created by young children have come from the gallop and its association with horses and ponies.

The Slide

The *slide* is made up of a combination of the walk and leap; therefore it is made up of two parts and we hear two sounds as the feet contact the floor. These sounds are of uneven duration, the walk takes a longer amount of time than the leap and therefore the walk is a long sound and the leap a shorter sound. The slide is taken in a *sideward direction*, with the same foot (the lead foot) always taking the walk part of the combination. It is the spatial and rhythmic elements (direction and duration or the uneven rhythmic pattern) affecting the combination of walk leap which makes the *slide* a *slide*.

Movement Combination	walk leap	walk leap
Rhythmic Pattern	⸺ ⸻	⸺ ⸻
Underlying Pulse	⸻	⸻
Direction	sideward	

At times children discover the slide when they are exploring walking in various directions. As they are going sideward they sometimes find that they can push themselves off the floor and that something different has happened to them while they are moving. ("It doesn't feel like a walk any more.") Analysis shows that they are combining a walk with the leap and this makes it different from just walking—the sideward leap takes them off the floor. At times developing the slide is presented as a movement problem, and at other times a group or a member of the group finds the slide as he is refining his gallop. But the most fun of all comes when a youngster says, "Look! I just found something new!" We watch that "something new," discuss it, give it a name (*the slide*), and start to work with it. We listen to the sounds our feet are making as they go in a sideward direction and we realize that the sounds are not the same. We discuss this and often help the sliders by saying "waalllllk leap, waalllllk leap" or "slideeeee, slideeeee." As they slide, moving in a sideward direction, they are encouraged to go higher and higher. Sometimes some of us have been working so hard with our feet that we forget about the rest of our body. "Maybe holding your arms out to the side will help you go sideward—also, keep your

SLIDE or SKIP

Arr. *Joyce Eldridge*

back, chest, and head up; maybe this will help you go up in the air when you slide."

As boys and girls are able to do this they realize that the amount of energy (force) they use helps to make them go up and keeps them momentarily in space. The walk is always on the same foot and as one child said, "The leap never catches up to the walk." We work on smoothness and control by the way we use our arms and upper part of our bodies. We feel smoothness and lightness as we get up higher and higher. The slide feels very different as the tempo changes. *The higher we go, the slower the tempo and the larger our movements; the faster we go, the shorter our combination of walk-leaps and the lower to the floor. We work to keep our heads up, and to let go with the knees as we come down from the leap so that we won't feel stiffness in our slides.*

Joining two hands, with partners facing each other, one starting to slide on left foot, the other on right, often helps get greater height. Sliding together with another person helps children to sense smoothness and lightness.

As children gain in their ability to move with a slide and understand what they are doing, they can combine other basic movements. Swings make them feel one way, and shaky, bouncy slides feel different. Soon they have made up new and different movement patterns based on the slide. Frequently the problem is set to find an entirely new way to use the slide—"What can two of us do together with the slide?" or "Make up a new dance pattern combining the slide with other movements." Often children become so aware of themselves moving that they realize that still another movement has been added—this is independent thinking.

The Skip

Skipping comes from the basic movement of *walking* and *hopping* while *swinging* (and feeling the inner push involved). The other ingredient, duration of time, *makes a skip a skip.* We hope that the day will come when adults will be as elated over a child discovering skipping as they were over that same child walking or talking for the first time. Perhaps this recognition is even more important because now the child knows and understands that something important has happened to him! He has done it with his whole body; he has discovered a new

SKIP

Arr. *Alonah Stith*

way of conquering space, of putting himself up there and staying just a little while, coming back down just to send himself up again—every part of him is up there! It is an extraordinary power he has found. His new conquest of interrelationships—movement, time, energy, and space—gives him a new sense of exhilaration and abandonment which he wants to tell the world about —"Look at me!" This will happen when a child is *ready*—when his inner communication system is all in tune and he is at the controls.

Movement Combination	walk hop	walk hop
Rhythmic Pattern	—— —	—— —
Underlying Pulse	———	———
Direction		
any: forward, backward, sideward, "around"		

Skipping is probably the most loved of all the movement skills or combinations of basic movements. It isn't often that the skip needs to be taught to children if they have had progressive movement experiences. It does need to be taught to many adults and to many teachers who have lost the skipping pattern.

Often teachers ask, "What can I do to help a child skip?" There is no formula except that the youngsters must have had some previous opportunities to take off, to go, to let loose, to respond, *by hopping on one side and then hopping on the other side.* Although some first-graders and younger children have already acquired the skipping skill, this is when they have lived in a moving world that prized rather than restricted their moving, or when teachers have provided opportunities for "moving out."

Discovering the combination of the walk-hop is fun, because children find out that it sometimes becomes the skip. As they go faster in this combination, and pull their knees up—first one and then the other— and change their rhythm from even to un-

even, the walk-hop combination becomes the skip. This is something they can figure out for themselves, especially if we make it a game or a problem to solve. It is not too difficult for them to learn about the uneven rhythm; the hop seems shorter than the walk and they hear the two different sounds that their feet make. Joel says, "It doesn't sound like a walk any more; it sounds like two different sounds and they say skiiiiip, skiiiiip, dummmmm da, dummmmm da."

In every class there usually are some one-footed skippers for a period of time. This makes such children look as though they are uncoordinated. These children need more time to develop unilaterally—to be given many opportunities to work on the *hop* and feel the shifting of weight from one side to the other side. Teachers need to be concerned when they discover an older child who is a one-footed skipper. This is the time when peer relationships mean so much; how one looks to others is primary. An older one-footed skipper becomes conscious that he is different, that he can't keep up with the others. This may cause him to make excuses to avoid participation. To avoid this, we can go back to hopping ways of moving with the entire class involved, using a variety of approaches. Another help is to have the children pull up first one knee and then the other, and to decrease the rhythmic tempo as well; in these ways a child is encouraged to analyze his own movement difficulty. *Sometimes we find that children have difficulty skipping because of their balance—they cannot seem to get their legs and arms going together. Working with swinging movements of the arms and the whole body, "feeling" the swing and then combining this with the walk-hop combination may be what is needed.* Some children need to be reminded to keep their heads up, which aids them in getting their bodies in the air. Encouragement and a relaxed atmosphere contribute to overcoming skipping problems.

We find it fun to sharpen our wits by

listening to the sounds our feet make. We try to clap the sounds we think our feet make and then we clap the sounds we hear others make. "Close your eyes and listen— can we hear Joan skipping? Can we tell when she is just walking? Listen to the drum—is it skipping or is it walking? What is the piano saying? Look at Butch's skip— is he going fast or slow? Why do you suppose he goes up in the air so high? Look how he seems to be pushing against the floor. Look at the way he is swinging his arms and how they help his skip."

Children often realize their own difficulties by observing others. Depending on the atmosphere within the class, children may help each other. It may be that a child needs a few minutes with the teacher alone, or with an adult or an older child to help him with balance. Taking a child by the hand and skipping with him often helps. It may be that this particular child needs a faster tempo until he has the feeling of skipping on both sides. *Or there may be more serious motor perception problems for which the skip was the indicator.*

Following are some ways to improve skips as well as to have fun:

Clapping the rhythm of the skip, clapping the two uneven sounds, responding to the rhythm with shoulders, heads, tongues, noses, and feeling the rhythm through the whole body.

Swinging just with the upper part of the body, particularly the arms, and saying "skiiiiip and skiiiiip."

Skipping in place, pushing off the floor as hard as we can. (The slower we go, the higher) —increasing the tempo and the faster we go, the lower to the floor (we come). Changing tempo.

Skipping, changing directions.

Skipping down as low as we can go and then as high. Playing skipping games.

Skipping around the room, stopping on a signal, and while resting in place continuing the skip by just clapping or carrying the rhythm with the head or hips, then start skipping through space again.

Working on feeling smoothness in the skips.

Skipping in and out of space around each other in the room. making complicated designs while skipping.

Skipping with a partner and to a drum sound, changing partners and continuing skipping.

Skipping, covering as much space as possible with a swing that helps and feels good. Feeling the extension in the swing by new ways.

Finding many new ways of skipping, doing different kinds of things with our arms, legs, shifting body weights and upper parts, staying in one place skipping forward and back pushing on the forward skip and pulling on the backward skip, or skipping side to side shifting the weight from side to side.

Inventing skipping combinations and turning them into dances.

In summary, skipping includes going from a confined space gradually into a larger space, working on pushing harder from the floor to get higher skips, constantly working on getting the rhythmic quality of the skip, and working on the swing so that the body becomes "all one unit." These should help in the development of the movement skill of skipping.

DANCE PATTERNS

In addition to the favorite combinations of movements that produce the skip, gallop, and slide, other dance patterns are developed as we work with movement. These dance patterns involve various combinations, such as the Indian or primitive dance patterns, the polka, schottische, and some social dance patterns.

Primitive or Indian Dance Patterns

Various cultures of the world, including primitive societies, hold special fascination for children. Interest and respect for peoples of the world and cultures represented within our classroom groups need to be fostered, and their uniquenesses appreciated and cherished. Through exposure to chants, music, dance, stories, legends, customs, mannerisms, and special movement qualities of peoples, children can relate in positive ways and begin to appreciate one another. As they move together in learning dance activities, children can be helped to sense feelings in different kinds of cultural movements. As they grow older they recognize that some ways of moving are culturally oriented and that they may not be as comfortable moving with some patterns or styles as others, but it is the fun in *moving* that is and should be important for children. They know they cannot move just like Indians, but they love the "feeling" they get from doing Indian or primitive movement patterns. (Children commonly use these terms interchangeably for locomotor movements of the walk-hop in even duration.)

Movement Combination	walk-hop
Rhythmic Pattern	⎯ ⎯
Underlying Pulse	⎯ ⎯
Direction	any

Our Indian step pattern has the same combination of locomotor movements as the skip, *but it is not the skip.* Instead, it is an even *rhythmic pattern*, while the skip is an *uneven rhythmic* pattern, so they sound entirely different. The Indian or primitive dance step differs from the skip in spatial design, rhythmic pattern, sounds, feeling, quality, and purpose. There is not the feeling of taking off through space in this way of moving as there is in the skip—rather we feel a strong beat pulling us down.

When comparing the primitive dance pattern with the skip, children have said, "It makes us go down into the ground. We stay down, close to the floor. It sounds

heavier and feels much faster and makes us bend all up as our feet are going. It seems easier than the skip." Many children have responded more readily to this movement pattern than to the skip—probably because of the less complicated rhythmic structure and because they do not need to balance themselves as much to stay up in the air on the hop part of the pattern. The accent on the walk part of the pattern helps boys and girls to readily establish the rhythm and "feel" of the step. Children say the primitive step sounds like "walk hop walk hop walk hop" or "dum daa dum daa dum daa."

In working with walk or hop movements or combining the two, many boys and girls just seem to "stumble" upon this pattern we call the "primitive." Others have picked up the movement combination from a film, listening to a record, or observing real Indians dancing. Learning the step starts with even walk-hop, walk-hop, and children respond to the suggestion that the walk and the hop take the same amount of time as they pull their *knees up* as they hop. As soon as an *even walk-hop* has been *established*, the tempo can be gradually increased. When this happens the movements become much shorter, there is hardly time to leave the floor on the hop, and there is a tendency for the body to go lower. Bending the knees and elbows and lowering the head to accent the walk make the children feel the association with Indians or primitive peoples. When more stress (accent) is put on the walk part, we have an interesting combination. *The faster the tempo, the shorter the movement, the lower we can go to the floor, and the more pronounced the accent seems to be.*

Children find ways of continually shifting their weight, adding a variety of other movements, and devising interesting space and movement designs. When chants, tom-toms, or music are added, new changes occur. Sometimes it is helpful to develop this "primitive dance" even before developing the skip; for often the children can immediately discover the skip if the teacher changes the *even*-sounding rhythmic pattern to one of *uneven* relationship. This may be particularly helpful if there are one-footed skippers in the class. This movement skill (Indian or primitive) and its many varia-

INDIAN CHANT

Arr. *Joyce Eldridge*

PRIMITIVE

Arr. *Alonah Stith*

tions have become widely used in many children's dances.

Polka Dance Patterns

Providing opportunities for boys and girls to have increasing experience with skips, gallops, and slides leads to learning the polka. This dance step can be developed from a combination of the slide and skip, or gallop and skip. There are four parts to the polka the way children like to do it, and therefore there are four sounds made by the feet. These sounds are of an uneven rhythmic pattern. Children refer to their movements as long and short, sounding like "sliiiiide skiiiiip." The polka can begin in a sideward direction with the slide or in a forward direction with the gallop. It is a lively step, space is necessary, and children need to have enough coordination and strength to hold themselves up in space.

POLKA (With Downbeat)

Arr. *Joyce Eldridge*

POLKA (With Upbeat)

Arr. *Alonah Stith*

It is not unusual for a class to need vigorous physical activity at times. In one such class, the following question (leading to the polka) was posed: "You all know the skip, slide, and gallop ways of moving—yes? Suppose you take two of these movement skills, *not three*, just two—the slide and skip, or the slide and gallop, or the gallop and the skip—and see if you can find a new pattern that appeals to you." (The polka clue was evident.) "I saw several interesting patterns. While you rest let's watch Jack, Rita, Susan, and Michael and notice what they are doing." Though it was hard to just sit and watch, eventually the class determined that they were doing slides and skips and Rita was doing a hard gallop and skip. "Do you know, there is a name for what they are doing—it's called the polka." This is a funny-sounding word, and the group rocked with laughter—the word "polka" was repeated and they were asked about the spelling. This was the start of the polka for this fourth grade. (Their Polka Dance resulting from spelling "polka" is in Chapter 14.) Identification of the polka added another word with meaning to their vocabulary; it led the children to the dictionary, to searching out where and when the term might have been used, and to learning about some of the folk dances involving the polka.

Another approach to the polka led to the formation of another group from a presentation of combinations of movements and working on directions in space. The group was asked to face the center of the room. We started sliding in a circle, all facing center, all going around the circle the same way. We continued in the same direction but now all facing out or away from the center. This pattern of slide and change, facing first in and then out, was this group's first meeting with the polka. The children easily recognized it as a combination of locomotor movements—of the slide and (walk-hop) *skip*. By doing it in slow motion we determined that the change is really on the hop, or the hop is what first turns us away and then toward the circle. This step pattern was identified, clapped, discussed, and analyzed as it was being done. Breaking away from the circle, we tried the pattern with partners. Partners start facing each other and then turn away from each other. As they start to polka, the children often say, "in and out," or "face to face and back to back." Sometimes it seems easier if two hands are joined while facing, and one hand is dropped on the turning out or away. The polka can be tried in other ways with partners, such as with hands both joined or one child putting hands on hips and the other on shoulders. This time it isn't a matter of turning in and out but rather of turning completely around. Watching, demonstrating, clapping the rhythm, changing direc-

tions, listening to the polka music, and changing partners frequently help to establish the dance step.

Polka with Downbeat

As the polka becomes familiar, it is executed in various ways, with many qualities and variations, depending upon the music and where the step is *started*. As it is developed above in the circle, starting with the *slide*, the polka starts on the strong downbeat (the step pattern becomes a combination of the slide and skip).

Polka starting on the downbeat with a slide:

Movement Skill	slide	skip
Movement Combination	walk-leap	walk-hop
Rhythmic Pattern	—— —	—— —
Underlying Pulse	——	——

Polka starting on a downbeat with a gallop:

Movement Skill	gallop	skip
Movement Combination	walk-leap	walk-hop
Rhythmic Pattern	—— —	—— —
Underlying Pulse	——	——

The downbeat occurs when we start with the accent on the walk, part of the slide, or gallop. We have a feeling of starting down on the floor with the walk or the long sound. There are different ways of doing the polka—most frequently it is done to $\frac{2}{4}$ or $\frac{6}{8}$ meter.

We have found that most boys and girls readily respond to the polka when they can start with a strong downbeat on the walk part of the gallop or slide.

Polka with Upbeat

With the polka established, based on their background in rhythmic elements, children find that they can recognize the upbeat and can analyze the polka pattern accordingly. Of the upbeat they say, "It is the short sound that helps to get us up in the air—the lift as we draw in our breath and pull up." The difference then is in the start of the polka.

Polka starting on the upbeat with a slide:

Movement Skill	slide		skip	
Movement Combination	hop	walk-leap	walk-hop	
Rhythmic Pattern	—	——	—	——	—
Underlying Pulse		——		——

Polka starting on an upbeat with a gallop:

Movement Skill	gallop		skip	
Movement Combination	hop	walk-leap	walk-hop	
Rhythmic Pattern	—	——	—	——	—
Underlying Pulse		——		——

On the upbeat the polka is started with the hop—this seems as though we start ahead of time on the *and*, rather than on the accent. Teachers need to be aware of the upbeat or downbeat—or they may lose the polka pattern. The upbeat or downbeat is only on the start of the polka—after the start, the pattern is the same. In the accompaniment of the polka if the group starts with the hop (up in the air), the first sound on the drum or the piano needs to be short (as children say, a "get-ready feeling sound —"a da *dumm*"); if the group starts down on the floor with the walk or the slide or gallop, the first accompaniment sound needs to be long and strong or accented—*dumm da.* The polka is vigorous and therefore the tempo is important; as Michael so aptly said after having experienced too slow a tempo without accent or feeling of intensity, "There is nothing worse than a slow funerally down to the floor polka." We all had to agree.

The following was recorded on tape one day as a group of fifth-graders created a polka study:

We love to polka,
To polka this way.
We have such fun,
We feel so gay.

It makes us laugh,
It makes us gay.
Polka Polka,
Polka our way.

The Schottische

The schottische and polka dance patterns have been used in a variety of ways by children. These dance patterns are particularly suited to older boys and girls when they have developed coordination, movement knowledge, and awareness of rhythm and space. When boys and girls have had a background in movement, these folk dance steps are developed easily, and they are recognized as a progression in the movement skills.

The schottische is what children recognize and analyze as a combination of basic movements—three walks and one hop (*walk, walk, walk, hop*). This step is different from the polka in that the melodic rhythm or rhythmic pattern is composed of four sounds, all of which take up the same amount of time and give a feeling of smoothness. Children refer to the schottische as having even rhythm.

Movement Combination	walk	walk	walk	*hop*
Rhythmic Pattern	—	—	—	—
Underlying Pulse	—	—	—	—

The interesting feature of the schottische is the *movement accent.* This movement pattern is distinctive because the *hop,* the fourth movement in the series, is given the accent. This differs from many of the other movement patterns. The schottische music

SCHOTTISCHE

Alonah Stith

Fine

D.C. al Fine

has the accent on the first beat of the measure of music but the accent "felt" in moving is on the last sound. Saying the pattern as we do it becomes walk walk walk *hop*! Just as children found that the slide seemed a little dull or restrained in contrast to the gallop, so they seem to feel that the schottische is not nearly as much fun or as lively as the polka, "but useful."

Boys and girls vary the schottische by changing tempo, force, direction, range of movement, and by using various combinations of body movements such as swings, bends, and stretches to the elevated leg on the hop part of the dance pattern. To a fast tempo the *walk* part of the schottische becomes a *run,* (run, run, run, *hop*). Often the length of the runs differs and they become a long-short-long (run), with the second run not "catching up to the first." In other words, as children vary the length of their locomotor movements they find com-

binations they have not experienced before. This is apparent as they find different ways of using the elevated leg on the hop part of the pattern, and combining that with changes in direction—for example, walk, walk, walk, *hop*—finding different ways to bend, stretch, or swing the knee or heel of the elevated leg (across in back, in front, out to the side, etc.); and forward, forward, forward, *hop* (bringing second walk or run up to the first as in two step), swinging the elevated leg in the hop. This can be done in different directions. The position of the elevated leg has given a different feel and quality to the schottische.

A variety of other patterns have been added to the schottische such as walks, hops, leaps, walk-jump, and heel-toe. Variations in groupings also add interest to the schottische. Larger groups have used space in various ways for this step; such improvisations are often unique and have led to many dance studies. The procedure of devising variations in the schottische makes use of arithmetical relationships—because this step has four parts or four sounds, additional movements must have multiples of four. Children have danced the schottische in regular folk dances, such as the Swedish schottische, which was appropriate when children had been studying the Scandinavian countries. They have also combined it with calypso music, "soul" music, rock and roll, and jazz. In addition, some of our schottische improvisations can be recognized in the folk dances of various cultures.

The Jig

Older boys and girls get the "feeling" of the *jig* when they are involved in finding combinations of the *jump* and the *hop*. They soon get a jig-like pattern going if they put a decided accent on their jump and alternate feet on the hop. When this pattern emerges in a group we talk about it and relate our new-found dance pattern to the *jig* as found in *folk dances*. We once had quite a controversy over its relationship to

gigue, found in classic forms of music. The music teacher joined us and some of the group set out to find more information. Thus the children increased their knowledge in other areas as a direct result of their study of this dance pattern.

Movement Combination	jump	hop
Rhythmic Pattern	————	————
Underlying Pulse	— — —	— — —

The jig has a $\frac{6}{8}$ meter that gives a quick, lilting feeling. When this combination is picked up the group often says "jump and hop and jump and hop" as it moves, putting stress on the jumps and in their voices. The two sounds are even, with the same amount of duration given to each movement. Because of the *accent* some children think the jump sounds longer, but as they watch, listen harder, and start to analyze and again "do," they realize that the jump and hop have the same time sequence.

Once children have responded to the accent and the increase in tempo, the lively spirit of the jig pattern is obvious. Adding such variations of heel and toe touches or

JIG

Alonah Stith

D.C. al Fine

taps while hopping, changing weight from one foot to the other by leaps, and adding directions to the movements extends the already established jig pattern. The quality and the spirit of the jig are enhanced when appropriate music is provided for accompaniment. Depending on the group of children, and if the purpose for the time being seems to be on wanting to perfect and improvise on the jig, attention can be given to use of the arms, head, back, toes and heels, etc. It is impossible to become involved with a jig form without expending physical energy—the jig is lively and takes stamina.

Around St. Patrick's Day seems to be a fine time to work with boys and girls with the jig. At this time, what is seen and heard on TV and radio (and sometimes what they are fortunate enough to witness as an audience in a live program) helps children listen more acutely to the rhythm, become more discerning of movements, and tends to get them into the spirit of the jig. On occasions this has necessitated trying to duplicate intricate patterns that must be analyzed. This involves critically looking at jig steps and being able to better appreciate the dance form. Later on, when boys and girls have participated in folk dances, they find that many dances use a jig pattern or movements employing combinations of the jump-hop. When this happens, children

readily apply themselves to the fun, spirit, style, and meaning of the dance rather than having to concentrate on the specifics of the movement pattern.

We have had pleasurable experiences improvising on the jig-like movements and developing dances on many themes. The "Hello Dance," reels, adaptations of the Scotch Highland Fling, and sailor dances have developed from the jig. As children are allowed to move freely, with control and understanding, they continually find new means of expressing themselves. Although they may work with the same rhythm and from the same movement pattern, they continue to add new patterns and new variations to develop their own dance forms— their own jigs.

The Mazurka

Challenges motivate older boys and girls. The *mazurka* has served in this capacity with an introduction such as, "Today I have a hard, unusual movement combination in mind. I wonder how long it would take us to learn a mazurka pattern?"

The mazurka pattern is a combination of two walks and one hop, or two runs and a hop. Our weight is on each movement. There are three sounds made by the feet and and each has the same amount of time

MAZURKA

Alonah Stith

or feeling of even duration. The accent is on the two walks or runs. The mazurka is danced to a $\frac{3}{4}$ meter having a strong forceful quality.

Movement Combination	walk	walk	leap
Rhythmic Pattern	—	—	—
Underlying Pulse	—	—	—

This dance pattern is performed by taking one walk step to the left, pulling the right foot over to the left, and hopping on the right foot. Walk side left, walk with right foot over to left, hop with right foot, bending left knee. Continue moving to the same side. Sometimes we say walk, cut, or hop, because it seems as though the second walk and hop cuts or pushes the first walk out of place. In order to change and go to the other side, we use a stamp, three walks, or a similar break or change. Although it seems easier to start the mazurka in a sideward direction, it can be done in any direction. It is usually a very forceful pattern and is found in many folk dances.

Children can make sequences of the mazurka pattern—such as three mazurkas and three stamping walks. When this is done, they find that they are now free to do the mazurka pattern to the other side. Having accomplished that, they can improvise to find various combinations that seem to fit with the mazurka. Most of all children seem to like arrangements of forceful leaps.

The Waltz

When improvising on the walk, a few boys and girls sometimes discover the *waltz* pattern, and then the rest of the class can learn it. The waltz is made up of a combination of three walks, with the accent on the first.

WALTZ

Alonah Stith

Movement Combination	walk	walk	walk
Rhythmic Pattern	—	—	—
Underlying Pulse	—	—	—

There are three even sounds to the waltz. Each walk step takes the same amount of time, with a transfer of weight on each one, even though the third walk (the one drawing to the side) seems shorter. The waltz is danced to $\frac{3}{4}$ meter.

Starting, we suggest that everyone take one walk in a forward direction starting with the left foot—slow, walk sidewalk with the right foot—slow, walk (pull or draw) left foot to side of right foot—slow.

The space pattern for the forward waltz is forward, sideward, and sideward. Boys and girls often say (left) "forward-side-together and (right) forward-side-together."

Often, the biggest problem in learning to waltz is putting the weight on each walk and starting each waltz pattern with an alternate foot. As boys and girls become familiar with the transfer of weight, they find they can waltz in a forward direction, in a backward direction, or in a combination of the forward and backward directions. Combination of the forward and backward direction seems like waltzing in place and becomes:

Walk left forward.

Walk right to the side.

Walk (or pull) left to the right side (feet are together).

Walk right backward.

Walk left to the side.

Walk (or pull) right to the left side (feet together).

In describing the waltz, children say "forward-side-together; backward-side-together."

As the waltz is accomplished in a confined space with a forward and backward combination, boys and girls find that they can easily add a turn as they move forward and backward. This comes naturally because of their previous experience with movement.

The faster the waltz music, the shorter the steps; the slower the music, the longer the steps. The Viennese style of waltzing includes a fast tempo, short steps, and much turning.

Probably the waltz is one of the most difficult of all folk or social dance patterns for boys and girls generally because of the smooth, gliding quality of the step.

The Two-Step

The majority of the simple folk-dance patterns and most of the social dance patterns come from the walk. In the previous chapter, we found that different combinations of the walk affected by time and spatial elements changed the very character of the walk. The *two-step* danced in both folk and social forms is a combination of three walks, holding the third walk.

Movement Combination	walk	walk	walk(hold)
Rhythmic Pattern	—	—	——
Underlying Pulse	————		——
Direction	any		

Boys and girls often say "walk, walk, walllk," or "walk, walk, walk-hold" as they are two-stepping. The two-step is usually danced to $\frac{2}{4}$ meter. This step is found as children are working on various combinations of walks. If the group has not discovered the two-step, or if students or teachers ask for the pattern, it may be introduced in the following way. With each foot taking the weight, walk in a sideward direction—walk side, walk other foot over to first walk, and walk side again with first foot and hold; or walk side right, draw left to right, walk side right and hold. Repeat to other side, starting left foot. Boys and girls often say "walk, together, walk, hold." As this pattern becomes familiar, it can be tried forward and backward (walk forward left, draw right foot up to left, walk forward left and hold). Repeat walk backward

TWO-STEP

Arr. *Joyce Eldridge*

right, walk back to right with left, back right and hold. When boys and girls can perform the two-step going forward and back or from side to side, they can progress forward alternating leading feet. (The slower the music, the longer the steps; the faster the music, the shorter the steps.)

A variation of the two-step often used in social dancing is a combination of one two-step and one slow walk, with the walk getting the same amount of time as the two-step, or the walk getting the same number of underlying pulses as the two-step

Movement Combination	two step	walllk
Rhythmic Pattern	– – –	——
Underlying Pulse	— —	——

In this pattern, the two-step is always leading with the same foot, and the single walk part of the pattern falls on the same foot.

Social Dance

As we consider the sample of dance patterns and movement skills that have been presented, we can see that they involve combinations of basic movements affected by spatial and rhythmic elements. The particular patterns have been analyzed and included because they are the selections most frequently used by boys, girls, and teachers with whom we have worked. Although this is not a complete list, those included appear to be favorites of children and useful for teachers in rhythmic activities.

We have found that is is fun to combine movements in all possible ways and then select those that appeal to us to use in achieving whatever purpose we desire. The purpose may be to communicate with another person, to interrelate with others, to enhance our skills, to be a more informed member of an audience, or to create a new form. Whatever the purpose, creative dance activities bring about discovery of self and new knowledge of others.

Just as the polka has been a folk dance pattern of people handed down, so have the waltz, two-step, and other popular or social dance patterns. At one time, someone discovered each of the forms we know as the waltz, two-step, fox trot, Charleston, lindy, tango, samba, cha cha cha, frug, twist, monkey, swim, robot, (just to mention a few). These involved combinations of movements affected by elements of time and space, used for specific purposes and *named*. They were current dance forms, or popular social dances of their day. Some of these forms have persisted and are now used for different purposes. Today we have a new form of social dance or popular dance . . . the young people call it "fad dance," and "fad" it may well be because already some of the current forms have passed. There is no telling what other social dance forms will emerge but for the moment the popular dances involve the whole area of body movements in varieties of combinations and qualities.

Across our country we are seeing and feeling the influence of various ethnic groups with their unique movement and rhythmic characteristics reflected in some of our "fad" dances in the popular music of the day. Most of the fad dances of the moment are done by isolating a nonlocomotor movement and using it in unique ways. Culturally, we might say that we are loosening up, and this is evident in the dance forms our young people are enjoying. Whether or not any of these will survive and be handed down is unimportant. What is important is the many ways people are using movement and creatively responding. They are finding joy in making up combinations of movement that they can name, that they call their dance form or that serves their purpose at the time. Boys and girls who have experiences in creative rhythmic movement will be active contributors to possibly new and entirely different forms of dance for tomorrow. It is anticipated that out of such experiences may come quality art forms—and a new and different kind of dancer—who knows?

DANCE FOR ALL

When children understand basic movements, combinations, and qualities of movement, and have opportunities to find new movement possibilities that are satisfying to them, they become increasingly comfortable with themselves. As they are helped to identify body parts and readily use these parts in various ways they begin to realize that they have an important potential for expression which can accomplish wonders for them. As they grow in their ability to listen, to discriminate, to respond kinesthetically to any pulse or rhythm, they find that they possess another dynamic power, that of moving rhythmically. As they begin to effectively use space they have added another dimension to their moving world. As their movement vocabulary and competencies increase they find that they are able to create, analyze, use, and appreciate dance patterns. All of this contributes to a knowledgeable background in movement to be used by boys and girls for fun, for relating to others, for communicating, for composing dances, and for appreciating cultural movement and dance forms.

III

Initiating Movement and Dance

7

Getting Started

There are many ways to start on this venture of providing rhythmical movement experiences for children, but there is no one best way. Experiences can be initiated with groups of children—preschool through the elementary grades—in any indoor or outdoor space. It may be that we begin at desks in the classroom, in an all-purpose room, in the auditorium, in an outside area, or in the gymnasium. Every day all these areas and the children themselves provide situations for *getting started*. One may start at any time and for varying periods of time. One can also start with a teacher of physical education, a dance teacher, a classroom teacher, a librarian, or an art or music teacher.

Regardless of the teacher's own competency in the areas of dance, movement, or creativity, some rhythmical movement experiences can be initiated as long as there is involvement on the part of the students and their teachers. The earlier these experiences are started, the better. It is to be hoped that there will be no stopping point, but that children throughout their school life will have rich and varied opportunities for expression through movement.

To teachers who say, "I'm no good at that," "I never liked physical education," "I can't dance," "I'm not creative," "I don't

have time," "Children want to play games," we say *just try ... start ... offer children the experience that perhaps you never had.*

We must realize at the outset that the *way* of starting is unimportant; the essential element is to *get started*. How one approaches a group and what one starts with depends on what one knows about children: their needs, varying stages of development, interests, and former experiences. Teachers begin with first-hand meaningful experiences with children which initiate exploration, investigation, and discovery of movement and rhythmic possibilities. Often questions children themselves ask or questions from the teacher initiate exploration. Our purpose is to explore with children and then to provide additional opportunities so that they can extend and use their own explorations in diversified and meaningful ways.

Extensive opportunities exist for *getting movement started*. This chapter is intended to provide a series of suggestions. These suggestions are built around a variety of ideas including trips, surprises, stories, games, music, and various other situations that can be developed with boys and girls. Such illustrations demonstrate the dynamics of beginning with a specific movement, situation, or thing and allowing investigation to occur and creative expression to emerge. The teacher plays a key role in encouraging and assisting children in creative rhythmic movement.

The surest way to start is with a question or an area in which the teacher feels most secure. This may come from movement, words, games, stories, song, field trips, classroom experience in mathematics, vocabulary building, reading, social studies, or any other content area. It might be as direct as the simple posing of questions and problems—"What can you do with your arm? Try again, what else? How does it feel? What can you do with this part of you? Work with your friend, what can you two do together? How can you get from here to over there?" There are numerous alternatives for *getting started* in the exploration of movement. One of the most obvious ways is that of guiding boys and girls in finding out how they move.

We create situations in which individuals move, in which they recognize that movement is fun, in which they observe that movement provides delicate and subtle ways of expressing feelings, ideas, and thoughts. It is another way for one to learn controls as well as to express himself.

This process of exploration is exciting because it involves trying out, seeking, imagining, sensing, experimenting, feeling, discussing, expressing, guessing, probing, looking, listening, and becoming aware. Children become aware of themselves, of the group, of things. This quality, when represented through movement, gives a particular kind of immediate satisfaction, enthusiasm, and sense of accomplishment. It deals with the world of childhood. In a way, the process serves as a reflection of the individual's perceptions of the moment as well as his ability to relate motor and sensory perceptual responses.

In working with older girls and boys, some modifications are often desirable. Although the intent is the same as for younger children, it has been found that the technique at the start must focus on the individual and what he can do rather than on things, ideas, and emotional expressions. The adolescent, if he has not had previous sequential movement experiences, may be self-conscious and need vigorous and challenging opportunities in movement and dance. Boys and girls at this stage respond well to situations that call for power, control, and skilled coordination. They like to defy gravity and to explore how high they can go, how long they can extend themselves while in space.

The older group responds to abstract and complex situations and ideas, space, inventions, gravity, historical events, and challenges. Profound human qualities such as aspirations, brotherhood, and dignity of work have often been used. These responses come *after* they have been exposed to movement.

USING KEY QUESTIONS

Having a few key questions pinpointed to a particular group is a good starting place in teaching about the use of the body as an instrument of movement expression. The following questions are only a few of the hundreds that have been used with various groups of children and adults to set them in motion. These questions suggest many more. Each of them involves concepts, thinking for oneself, finding out, exploring, and communicating through movement. Every teacher finds questions that can be used to advantage. Because groups of children, situations, and teachers vary greatly, there is no one question or first question that is preferred.

Let's see if we can move our very smallest part. Now, can you move two small parts?

Can you move the biggest part of your body? What different ways can you move this big part of you? Can you move three parts? Can you double these three parts and move six all at once?

Do you suppose that you can move a part from your neck up and at the same time a part from your hips down?

Can you move a part of you that begins with *e* (ears, elbow)? What can you move that begins with *h* (head)?

Who can make a sound using hands? Can we move to that sound?

While sitting at your desks, can you move your head. arms, knees?

Can we walk through empty spaces without touching anyone?

Can we walk fast—faster—even faster? Can we stop (freeze)?

How slowly can we walk?

Can you swing your shoulders? How can you swing your shoulders while you are walking?

What is another way we can move around the room besides walking?

How high can you jump?

What do you suppose is the difference between a jump and a hop?

How long do you think you could stay up in the air? What would help?

You have been studying about levers and pulleys—let's find out about some of our levers in our bodies.

Suppose we had puddles all over the floor. How could you get over them?

I watched you as you came into the room today. Some of you walked fast, a few slowly. Justine, could you show us how you walked in here?

THE IMPORTANCE OF EXPLORATION

The entire first experience in movement need not be confined to one activity. Rarely is one period confined to one particular movement. Such a procedure not only causes boredom and loss of attention for some children, but does not constitute good teaching, any more than does spending an entire reading period on the comprehension of one word.

An approach to movement exploration may be started by such questions as "How can we get from here to there, from this spot to that spot, from this door and around the room and back to the door again?" When movement is started in this manner, children have opportunities to devise new and different ways of moving from one place to another. Exploring movement becomes a game.

Some exploration of body movement can be started while groups are sitting on the floor, or even if they are on chairs or at desks. "Here's an arm ... what can we do with it? Can we move it? How? Let's see if we can move it another way?" "Sure," says Ginny, "I can move mine around and around like this." "Can you move any other part of your body besides your arms? Let's see if you can move five different parts, one right after the other." Again, movement exploration has begun! Encouraging children to think further and to make associations we might use such questions as "What does it make you think of when you shake your middle?" A universal response is "Santa Claus' tummy" or a "bowl of jelly."

Further questions and discussion may elicit the many different ways people can walk: high, low, bumpy, smooth, cross-legged, loose-legged, with a sore toe, with a walking cast, and many others. Exploration of animal walks may result if we are alert to cues from children. Susie says, "Look at me, I'm a turtle." Sure enough, Susie is a turtle. Then, immediately, there may be forty-two turtles, because Susie suggested it, and because it is fun to be a turtle. However, this might be a cue to talk about different animals, with each child suggesting the animal he wants to be. Perhaps the group needs more time before its members can suggest a variety of animal ideas and walks. *No two groups of children or all children within a group will react in the same way to these questions or to this approach.* In any case, the children are moving, and exploration has started.

FOLLOW, FOLLOW ME

Exploring with a Song

A simple melody often leads children into movement exploration. The following is a favorite of many groups. As the group sings the song, the movements of first one and then another child are followed. The teacher or a child starts with such a movement as swinging the arms, and the group does likewise. During the last line another person is designated to continue by pointing, calling out a name, taking turns by seats, and so on. The song is continued until all have had a chance to suggest a different movement. Lack of space is not prohibitive as far as opportunities for discovering movement are concerned.

Moving heads, arms, legs, or eyes while singing this peppy song may be, for boys and girls, an initial way of exploring movement. Dance songs designating specific movements are good motivating devices.

Exploring with Talking Sticks

Another approach to movement exploration is using *rhythm sticks;* this has a game element that readily attracts a group. As two sticks are hit together the children are asked to respond to the sound; as the sound gets louder they move at a higher level; as the sound gets softer they move at a lower level. The same idea has been used in the discovery of range and direction and other variations of movement.

The use of percussion instruments by the children (see Chapter 13) affords another way of initiating movement exploration. Each child has some piece of percussion to play so that all may participate at once. Percussion devices may be drums of cardboard cartons, rattles, pencils, sticks, keys —anything that will make a sound. Even though a tumultuous din may result in the beginning, controls that are set up by the teacher and the children can make order out of chaos. Just as an orchestra has a leader, we may have ours, helping to keep us together—starting and stopping with a signal that has been agreed upon. The discussion of an orchestra recently seen on television has been an introductory cue. As children become more familiar with their instruments, one of them is bound to move some part of his or her body, thus giving the teacher a cue to say, "Look, Margie is play-

ing her instrument and moving her head at the same time. Could we move a different part of us while playing our instrument?" Once more movement exploration is underway. This exploratory method has been used effectively with beginning adult groups who are reticent about moving out on the floor. Sitting together and having the percussion instruments in their hands often gives them the security needed to start relaxing, releasing, and responding. After discovering the many ways their instruments can be played they often forget about the instrument and are moving body parts before they know it.

Exploring Space: A Second-Grade Class

The following is an example of a lesson in movement used with a second-grade class, emphasizing space.

Teacher: Can everyone find a launching pad that is all yours? A space bubble or spot that for the time being belongs to just you? What else might we call "your space"?

Eddie: This is my space station and I'm in my space station and nobody can be here but me.

Teacher: Anyone else have a name for his space?

Children: Bubble. My house. It's my dock and I'm at my dock.

Teacher: Be sure that your space station or bubble is not next to another one. Vernon, you move so much maybe you had better go 'way over there so you have more space. Now let's see what we can do in our spaces. Can you sit in the middle of your space? How wide do you suppose your space is? Show me by the way you stretch and move. Can you stretch just your arms to show how wide your space is, or how far your space is, or how much room you have on both sides of you? I see Penny using her arms and feet and legs. What else can you do to show us how wide your space station is besides sitting? (Some move around, others are lying down, and some stand up.) I didn't see anyone on their sides. Now start from lying on one side. Now how wide is your space? Again, can you put yourself in the middle or center of your space? How do you know where the middle is?

Nell: Because there's empty space around me?

Teacher: And where are you, Nell?

Children: She's in the empty space. Like this— (Jack goes over to Nell's space, pointing out that she is in the space and all around her is empty.)

Teacher: Yes, Jack, but what happened to some of Nell's empty space when you came in?

Children: They're both in Nell's space. Two in one space. A bigger "blob" in Nell's space.

Teacher: Why don't we all find out all of the ways we can move around in the middle of our space? Be careful to leave empty space. I see hops, stretchy walks, some gallops, twisting, and turning.

Children: I was twisting so fast I got dizzy. I'm a horse that's tied to a stake, that's why I was galloping so fast, I wanted to get away.

Teacher: This time find three different ways you can move *around in* or on all of your space station. Be sure they are different ways. What does *different* mean?

Children: Not the same. Not like the one we just did.

Teacher: What else can you find out about your space? Can you show us how big you think it is? Find all the ways to show how big your space station is—careful not to get into anyone else's space. I see all kinds of biiiiig stations. Now let's see how big you can make yourself in your big station. How much space can you take up in your station? Does big just mean how high it is?

Children: Look at me. Did you see how big I was? Look, I'm big all over! So am I. Look!

Teacher: Now let's see what is the smallest amount of space you can take up in your space bubble. Even smaller—make yourselves little—smaller, smaller, smaller.

Children: I hurt! Wow! Look!

Teacher: How high can you go in your space without going out of it? How low can you go? What are some ways that you can go from low to high and back down to low again? Show us. (Most start to stretch, a few jump, others push their knees up, some just stand to go up. Some go from lying on the floor to almost a stretchy jump, others from bending knees to standing.)

This time let's see how fast you can go from 'way down low in your space to 'way up high. (Much activity with the idea of fastness detracting from discovering movements.) This time let's see how slowly you can go from 'way down low to 'way up high, and when you get up high, just stay there—slower, slower, careful—*very* slowly. (Some fall over. This is to be expected because they cannot hold their stretches.) Oh, I saw some great big stretches, some real pushes. Donny was doing something different trying to get up high—suppose we watch Donny.

(Donny is swinging from side to side from low to high, with his arms together, but the rest of his body swinging.)

Donny: Do you know what I was? Well, my space was a dock and I wasn't exactly in the middle of my space because I was the sail on my boat and I was pulling up.

Teacher: Do it again for us, Donny. Do you suppose that Donny was a little sailboat or a big one? Donny—show us the edge or side of your dock space.

Donny: Right here and it's this big (meaning long)!

Teacher: Suppose we all show the side or edge of our space. Now show us how far around your space is.

(Some sit and use their feet to show the distance, others walk-run, and some stand up and stretch in various ways. Discovery is underway with the teacher acknowledging different ways, encouraging, thinking of another way.)

Teacher: Careful not to go out of your space station. Remember, your space station is pretty big—it's high as well as wide and low. Remember where the edge is.

(Most of the children stay on one plane or level. If they start exploring at a low level they are apt to continue at that level. Only two in the group go from high to low or change their levels. Some are becoming aware of levels.)

Teacher: Curtis gave us an interesting idea a while ago when he said he was tied to a stake in the middle of his space. What was he? How did we know?

Children: Curtis looked like a horse. He really was mad!

Curtis: Of course I was. See (holding himself up like a horse on hind legs)?

Teacher: Yes, he looked different! Look at Curtis now—he is making a Curtis shape. Looks like Curtis as he stands there. Curtis—now make the shape of your horse. "Feel" like your horse and show us.

Children: Hey, he does look like a horse on his hind legs. He's mad!

Teacher: Could we all think of something that would tie, or keep us attached to, the middle of our space—something that could move around, or up and down, but be attached, like Curtis was? (Taking cues from children.) (Some conversation follows about being stuck or hitched. Then ideas start. The children are lollypops stuck to the floor, snowmen melting, light bulbs in a lamp going on and off, trees with different-sized branches, a bubble getting bigger and bigger from a bubble pipe. Patti keeps moving back and forth not moving her feet, making the rest of the children move back and forth with her as they watch.)

Teacher: Wonder what Patti is doing? She's Patti-shaped all right, but something has happened to her. (After much discussion Patti tells us that she is stuck in the glue that she and Salina spilled this morning.)

Here I am all alone on my great big launching pad. Look, I'll show you how big it is. Suppose each of you think of a special way you could leave your spaces and come to my space. (Children are called individually by name, and by some of the ideas or shapes they have assumed, such as horse, sailboat, lollypop, haystack, kite.)

Using Lines and Space: A Sixth-Grade Math Class

Teacher: Right where you happen to be, can you make a straight line with your arm? How can you make it straighter? Make *another* straight line with some part of you. Make a *long* straight line. Feel "longness" and "straightness." (The group starts to move, realizing they need more space.)

Now make yourselves into long straight lines another way. (Exploration has started, and emphasis is on lines rather than on how this group of boys and girls looks.)

Find all the ways you can of making a single straight line. Who has a very different way? Look over here—this line goes on the diagonal. Can you make a vertical line with your body? Turn to another person—can the two of you find ways of making vertical lines? (Finally verbal responses come forth, with much trying out and remarks about the different ways of making vertical lines.)

Still working with another person, can you show us a horizontal line? Find different ways of moving so that you can make horizontal lines. How can the two of you make one long straight line? (Here is variety on the floor, on sides, in all kinds of positions.)

Now let's see all the ways you two can make straight lines and balance each other. Find where your *point of balance* is and don't let your line break.

Let's see sets of parallel lines. Keep on finding ways that two of you can make parallel lines. The first group that has found six pairs of parallel lines, please sit down.

Toby and Jim: Do you mean six sets all at once?

Teacher: It might be a set of six, or you could do first one and then another until you have six. (Various kinds of movements, particularly forms of bending and stretching, are taking place. Relating to one another is evident.)

Soupy: We found ten sets of parallels.

Tom: Oh yeah, show us!

(Some argument about whether two sets were really parallel and whether parallels had to be the same distance in length.)

Teacher: Back to your straight line—make yourself into one straight line. Now break your line. Break it again, and again. Let's see and feel a series of broken lines. Break, break, break. Where in this room do you see broken lines? Where do you see a long straight line?

Children: Over there. On the floor. Chairs. All around.

Teacher: Can you curve your lines? Curve your lines another way. See how many curves you can make with your body. Turn to your partner again and find out all the ways that you two can make curved lines. What's the difference?

Children: Feels looser. Not as rigid. Seems more continuous.

Teacher: Can one of you make a curved line and the other a straight line and find a way to attach them? Find another way. Let's look at some of these ideas of straights and curves.

Children: Wow, that's hard! Let us show you.

Teacher: Suppose you and your partner connect your line to two others so that you are working in a group of four—try to discover different ways that the four of you can move across the room making only straight lines. You can make many of them, but keep them straight. (Much communication, much involvement. The ideas start to come.)

Suppose we take a look at some of these line patterns. Do any of them make you think of anything? Your world is made up of lines. (The class realizes that many shapes came from their line exploration with fours.)

Just before we finish, suppose four of you see what you can do with lines and balance. Can you find a way to have four of you in balance and still have a line?

The essential ingredients in exploration are to set problems, provide meaningful experiences, and use time and space for children to make movement discoveries.

When the concentration of finding out results in a series of movements that feel good, often one hears enthusiastic outbursts of "See what I can do," or, "Whee, look what Mapes can do with her middle."

As children become accustomed to movement, they enjoy it for its own sake, for the exhilaration they receive and the fun of just finding out and exploring. Learning is accomplished by "doing." Through the use and development of skills and tools in creative rhythmic movement, children have a chance to explore and to grow. They give vent to their imaginations and interpret meaningful and timely happenings. *In this process of creative expression in movement what happens to the boys and girls is of vital importance.*

GETTING STARTED USING MOVEMENT

Empty Spaces

The purpose of this game is to establish controls that will help children handle their spaces and be able to move freely without bumping into each other.

Teacher: Let's see how close we can get together without touching, and keeping some empty space around us. Just pull yourself in so that you are all alone in your space. We can come even closer and yet keep some space empty around us. Careful, keep some space empty. Joy, what does empty space say to you?

Joy: It is where no one is. Nothing there; it's all open (with gestures).

Dave: I'm here and Sal is there and—well—there is nobody between, just space.

Lenny: Yeah, like here (poking his tongue through his two front teeth).

Teacher: Yes, there is space there but look what happens when Lenny takes his tongue back. Try Lenny—take your tongue away from your front teeth—now what can we see? What do we call that space between Lenny's two front teeth?

(We are beginning to explore empty spaces within our own bodies, among us, in different parts of the room.)

Teacher: O.K., let's see if we can play a game of moving through empty spaces. We will have to think about this and more so that we keep the spaces empty. Peddie, *you start to move* through all the empty spaces you can find. Memmie, *you start to move too*—keep on going, find more and more empty spaces. Stuart and Jake and Rosemary—start to go through spaces—keep on going. Everyone with blue on you start going through the empty spaces—be careful we do not touch another, because then there will not be any more empty spaces. *Everyone with a birthday this month* join them. *Everyone with shoelaces. Now, everyone move through the empty spaces.*

This dialogue represents only the start of this game. Of course there is some touching in the beginning, but constant reminders help. Also we may start with one or two youngsters who have fairly good control of themselves to emphasize the point, gradually adding to the number moving to assist the class in control. In time boys and girls find it fun to move through the empty space, including between another's legs, under arms, and finding all kinds of empty spaces in the classroom, under chairs, and under desks. They enjoy moving to accompaniment and they can go from "inner" space (where we all are) to "outer" space (away from the group) and gradually back again.

This, in time, leads to use of a variety of locomotor movements. With an increase in tempo comes an increase in control.

The Hopping Game

This game helps children realize that they are inventing various forms of the same basic movement. One child starts across the circle with a hop, stops in front of (or circles around) another person who immediately starts across the circle or to another child with a variation of the hop. *Each child finds a different way to hop.* The game continues until all have had a turn adding variations. As children become familiar with this game we try to pass the movement on without having a break—even though the movements are varied, they seem continuous.

This same idea has been used with a jump, or any of the basic movements or combinations of movement—*movements that start with the letter "S," etc., movements that end in "ing," and with consonant blends* (s*t*amp, s*t*op, s*t*oop) .

Using Body Parts

For a group of very young children the teacher might say "We are made of all kinds of parts. I have a nose and it is here (I start moving my nose). Where is your nose? What can you make it do? Where are your eyes, shoulders, arms?" At first very young children may just point, but in time they will respond by moving the particular parts of their body mentioned. The same idea may be used by saying, "I have a head and it goes like this ... what do you have that goes like this?" (The teacher starts by moving her head up and down and the children find a part that they can move up and down.) This is followed by having a child becoming the leader. Soon all are involved and movement responses have been started. The older the group, the more complicated the task and the question.

"Connected" Chant

A similar game is the "connected" chant, which identifies body parts and indicates how they move.

Our toes are connected to our foot bones.
Our foot bones are connected to the ankle bones.
Our ankle bones are connected to the leg bones.
Our leg bones are connected to the knee bones.
Our knee bones are connected to the thigh bones.
Our thigh bones are connected to the hip bones.
Our hip bones are connected to the back bones.
Our back bones are connected to the shoulder bones.
Our shoulder bones are connected to the neck.
Our neck is connected to the head.
Our head is connected to the neck.
Our neck is connected to the arm bones.
Our arm bones are connected to the elbows.
Our elbows are connected to the forearm bones.
Our forearm bones are connected to the wrist bones.
Our wrist bones are connected to the fingers.
Our fingers are a part of me—.
I am connected to you and you.
We are all connected to each other.

The following is another way of using the same identification idea in order to make a Spanish-speaking child comfortable in class. José was asked to tell us or put on the board the Spanish word for "toes." For instance, the following came from José and the fourth-grade group.

(Toe) El dedo is connected to the foot—el pie. (Foot) El pie is connected to the ankle—el tobillo, etc.

el dedo	toe
el pie	foot
el tobillo	ankle
la pierna	leg
la rodilla	knee
el fémur	thigh
el cadera	hip
el torso	torso
el hombro	shoulder
el cuello	neck
la cabeza	head

GETTING STARTED USING IDEAS

What's in the Box?

One day we sealed up a small shoe box with an object (a ceramic duck) inside. We left it on the piano and sure enough, because it was something different and this "something" was not usually on the piano, Nick stopped what he was doing and started to handle the inviting-looking box. The class soon gathered around and the box was passed to each—they handled it, shook it—each examined the box in his own way, and the question was asked of each child, "What's in the box?" All attention was on the box—eyes were glued to it, ears were cocked to hear sounds made as it was shifted into different positions, and each child felt the box. The children made such observations as "Gee, it's heavy," "It's little," "It sounds funny," "It's as hard as a golf ball," "It goes back and forth," "I think something is rolling in there," "How did it get in here?" All kinds of surmises came forth and in the course of the "supposing" the children developed this chant.

> What's in the box?
> What's in the box?
> Tell us!
> Tell us!
> What's in the box?

Then each of the children was asked to show the class by movement what he thought was in the box.

Surprises

Children love surprises, and they love to be "in" on them perhaps even more than being the recipient. We knew that it was Macguire's birthday because his classroom teacher told us.

Teacher: Because today is a very special day, suppose we try to make it more special for Macguire by making a birthday cake for him. No, we can't bake it, but can you think of another way of making it for him?
Children: Yes, we could all make a picture of one. Or maybe we could do a "make-believe" one out of cardboard.
Teacher: Can you figure out a way that we all might be able to make *ourselves* into a great big birthday cake for Macguire?

The class made the birthday cake through movement—two layers, with frosting dripping all over and seven birthday candles that were "lit" with a blow and "went out" as they slowly went into the cake!

Part of the class became the bottom layer by lying flat and filling up all of the spaces; for the top layer the children stood up, spreading their feet and hanging their heads. (They had to do this because the candles had to be taller.) The frosting was the most fun of all because for this the children could move in and out among the legs, swirling around the bent heads and shoulders and then settling down so that the seven candles would show. Words cannot adequately describe this spontaneous half-hour of labor. That birthday cake will never be forgotten by the class, Macguire, or the classroom teacher. Suggestions came from all the children. Not only was an approach to creative rhythmic movement realized, but Mac grew two inches taller that day!

GETTING STARTED WITH NAMES

"Who has a name that has just one sound?" Ann, Tom, Jeff, Sue. "Who in this class has a name with two sounds?" Jeff answered, "I do—Jeffry." The class was now looking around the room in anticipation of what might be be coming next. "How many with three sounds?" Roberta, Evelyn. "Any with four?" Antonio and Penelope. This continued until all in the class had been identified. "How do you suppose our names would sound if we put them with another?" "How does this sound? Roselle, Ann, Timothy." "How many names did we put together and how many sounds in all?" "Is there another way you could put these names together with the same six sounds by rearranging them? Roselle could change places with Timothy. How would that sound?" The class answered in chorus, "Timothy, Ann, Roselle." "Is there another way we could arrange these names?"

With sufficient space and with an older group an initial experience on the first day of school has been moving out the letters of names on the floor (see the section on "space" in Chapter 11), and making a floor pattern or picture of the name or letter on the floor. "Let's see if I can determine the first letter of your first name by the way you walk it out on the floor. Just make the first initial of your first name and then stop. Now can you find a way to make a period so that we can tell it is a period?" (Some squatted down, others jumped, one hopped.) "Redo the first initial of your first name, add your period, and then make the first initial of your last name and show us another period."

GETTING STARTED USING ADVENTURES

What Did You Do This Summer?

The question "What did you do this summer?" provides an opportunity to initiate many movement responses. If a child answers "This summer I went to the zoo," for instance, the class is stimulated to create movement by discussing the many zoo animals. Children can portray and describe the animals, form a zoo of their own, and even make up a zoo dance.

Other adventures we have used to help children get started are built around such things as special trips (to a farm, fire station, etc.). One example follows:

Visit to a Construction Site

Several weeks ago we watched the workmen dig a big, big hole at the corner. It took up most of the block. We watched them put the wooden fence around it. We were fascinated with the bulldozer and we became human bulldozers and started to move the way the bulldozer moves. We looked through all kinds of peek holes to watch the "digger" dig. Last week we spent most of the morning at the construction spot. The hole was filling up with steel, frames, bricks, girders, wires, wooden walk ways and platforms. The bulldozer was digging away at another spot, the crane pushing up the steel girders while an elevator shaft went down and then back up. The children made such observations.

"Remember what you saw this morning when we were at the construction site and the sounds you heard at the construction site. Now, talk to the person next to you about what you liked most, or what really made you *look*." "Let's move our chairs back so that we have a little space that is all ours. You find your space for your construction. Who can think of something we saw this morning that went up, up, up? The elevators, the girders, the workmen. What was something that went round and round?" (Creative rhythmic movement exploration was started.)

The same experience provides a way of starting through listing and trying to recall all of the sounds connected with construction and then moving accordingly. Later, we taped the sounds we heard as we looked at a building going up, and this venture in listening and then translating into movement later terminated in a dance composition, "The Hole: What We Saw and *Heard.*"

GETTING STARTED USING MUSIC, ART, AND BOOKS

Music

Records

Music provides unlimited opportunities for getting children started in creative rhythmic movement. Over the years Prokofiev's *Peter and the Wolf* has remained a favorite piece. It is particularly appropriate for older children as they are having some music listening opportunities. When they begin to develop their understanding of this music they often want to refine their interpretations and movement into a dance that they can share with younger children. While the class is listening to this music, it is helpful for the teacher to ask such questions as the following: "What does that bassoon sound like? Is it heavy? Does the melody go up and down? What is the difference between the sound of the bassoons and the sound of the flutes? Listen again to the bassoon and start to move your body the way the bassoon seems to suggest that you move. You can stay right there while you move if you like, or you can *go* somewhere. Why do you suppose this bassoon music was selected for the Grandfather in the story of Peter and the Wolf? What kind of a grandfather do you think Peter had— was he young? Was he older? Had he worked hard? Was he irritable and grumpy? Listen again and show us your interpretation of the Grandfather. Why does the bassoon part of the orchestra seem to suggest Grandfather? Let's go back and listen to the flutes. Do you hear any other

sound? What kind of sound? What kind of movements do you think we might do to this flute and piccolo part of the music? Can you visualize what kind of bird you think this might represent? Is it a great big bird? A smaller one? This time as we listen, who would like to show us the kind of movements suggested by the bird you have in mind or just move with the music and let the music 'take you through space'." This invariably invites discussion, after which more movement activity can be tried.

A record that is particularly helpful in initiating children's dance activities is *Come and See the Peppermint Tree,* by Evelyn Lohoeffer. The music on this record is whimsical and charming, and children almost always react to it with enthusiasm. For example, the song "My Shoes Went Walking" started an older group in the exploration of movement, and their findings were developed into a dance composition. One "tight," overstimulated group of eight- and nine-year-olds who were particularly interested in space were introduced to "Riding on a Star." They listened to this song again and again and talked about what it might be like to ride on a star rather than on a bicycle, automobile, etc. The teacher asked, "Suppose each of us were up there on our own star? What do you suppose it would feel like? What would we see? Alone or in groups of no more than four, move out, or act out what you saw from your star. We will try to guess what you saw." Movement that communicated was underway as well as an introduction to a play they subsequently wrote about space.

Children's Own Creations

Noisy Song by Barbara

The water faucet is singing a song,
 bleep, bloop, bleep, bloop,
 bleep, bloop, bleep, bloop.

Its merry music goes singing along,
> bleep, bloop, bleep, bloop,
> bleep, bloop, bleep, bloop.

Some of the most delightful songs and melodies "pop" out of children; these also can be used as cues for getting movement started. The beginning experience of such a verse as "Noisy Song" can progress to a discussion of various kinds of sounds coming from faucets, showers, and water sprinklers and from there the children are easily stimulated to make up their own rhythmic movements.

Folk Music

Folk songs are marvelous sources for helping groups start to move. "Go tell Aunt Rhody," "Blue Tail Fly," and "Puff the Magic Dragon" are just a few of the well-known songs that easily lead children into creative movements.

Art

Drawing

Many kinds of art can help encourage movement in children. In "Dots, Lines, and Curves," for example, each child is given a large piece of paper and a selection of crayons or chalk. The class is then asked to make three dots or points any place on the paper; then three straight lines. "Now will you add three curved lines? Put them anywhere but take a good look at your paper before you draw them in. Now what does your paper look like? Suppose you walk around and look at all the pictures. Are they alike? What do you see? Now go back to your own pictures. Take a good look at it and instead of making a dot with the crayon or chalk, make a dot with your whole self—let your body make the dot. Now see if your body can make a straight line. How about a curve?" This is only a sample of using the children's own art to

help get movement started. The same idea has been used with older groups—having them combine forces and work from one drawing which the group selects and then through movement translate the picture. This is valuable because it takes attention away from individuals and places it on relationships of visual symbols and then representations through movement.

Clay

Another tactile medium for evoking unself-conscious movement activities is clay. A teacher begins by saying, "Can we find a spot that is all ours? Sitting or standing makes no difference as long as you have your own space alone. Make yourself heavy, heavy, heavy. Think about that clay over in the bin. Think about the glob of it you had in your hands. Try to make yourself into that lump of clay. Make yourself feel like that lump of clay—no shape, no form —just a heavy, heavy, lump of clay. Now think of some part of you inside. See if you can establish a point inside you and gradually, slowly start moving 'you' from inside. Keep moving from that point inside out; let one part involve another part until you form a shape—freeze! Now smash, pound, wad your clay-self until you are just a lump of heavy clay again. Try once more to feel 'clayness' and this time even more gradually than before try to move from the inside outward, consciously holding onto that inside point you established. Keep on moving, moving gradually, letting other body parts become involved. Do not break any part—freeze!" This experience will encourage the children to "sculpture" their own ideas and movements—*form* will emerge from their imaginings around the medium of clay.

Mobiles

Constructing mobiles acquaints older boys and girls with mobility and motion. The esthetic experience is heightened if the children are then given opportunities to demonstrate making themselves into a human mobile from those they have constructed.

Dimensional Forms and Shapes

A group of older children was discussing and trying to understand two- and three-dimensional forms. They considered translating specific forms into movement, and this increased their understanding of geometrical shapes and principles as they created such things as squares and triangles with their own movements. This is a good example of relating creative movement to other activities.

Books

Books and stories provide many opportunities to encourage creative movement. One useful book is *The World of Push and Pull*, by Earl Ubell (New York: Atheneum, 1964). The author discusses force and energy in a way that makes clear to youngsters the principles involved in movement: "Everything that starts to move, moves because of pushing and pulling forces" (p. 3). What better way is there to bring about enthusiastic experimentation with ideas and expression than such a lucid explanation of scientific bases to everyday activities?

Poetry can also provide the beginning for exploration of movement response. Sometimes it can be used to initiate movement, other times to elaborate and suggest additional ideas to be extended and translated through movement. Carl Sandburg's work, in particular, makes children think about and identify with ideas that can easily be developed along the lines of moving in expressive ways.

Still another beginning has been from the idea of "taking a line, or lines, for a walk." After establishing that our bodies can make all kinds of lines, we think of ourselves in terms of one straight line. We take our line for a walk and let it go anywhere all over the room. Here is movement starting again without the emphasis on self-consciousness but on conceptualizing and perceiving with the body.

Much of the material boys and girls are reading today is about lines, shapes, and space. These provide excellent opportunities for getting started with children in movement experiences. For instance, a favorite is *What's in a Line* by Leonard Kessler. The story ends with Kessler saying "the lines in this book were my ideas, what's yours?"

Those interested in dance experiences for children immediately want to answer Kessler by using his challenge in dancing ways. The children are most ingenious in the book of lines which they make through the medium of movement, sometimes individually, sometimes in groups. A good starter!

Mary McBurney Green's *Is it Hard? Is it Easy?* is a story about children trying to do different activities involving movement, such as hopping, skipping, and bouncing a ball. The stories can be translated into action, and have provided many opportunities for children to start putting various movements together in a small sequence.

We have used every page in *A Dog's Book of Bugs* by Elizabeth Griffin (drawings by Peter Parnell; New York: Atheneum, 1967) at some time or another to initiate a movement experience. The range goes from the way small bugs move, to the sound that bugs make, to the way different bugs in different situations in the book feel and respond to the space walk they take. This is a delight for all ages. It offers innumerable opportunities to sense and respond through movement.

GETTING STARTED
USING CONTENT AREAS

Experiences in movement are initiated by using the learning that results from all content areas the children come into contact with in the school. For example, when a class has been studying the desert for their science class, such a question as, "How would you move if you were a creature in the desert?" brings about new knowledge of both the subject matter and the area of movement. The study of magnets provides a rich field for "attracting" and "repelling" movements. "My hand is the magnet and I am going to magnetize all of you. Concentrate on my hand, keep looking at it. Be careful not to look away—let your bodies follow wherever my hand goes. Feel me pulling you toward me. There are lines all over this floor—let's imagine that they cause *you* to be magnetic. You can only move along the line as a magnetic field. How can you go? Try various ways, but remember that the line is magnetic." (Not only has movement started, but scientific learning is also enhanced.)

GETTING STARTED USING SENSORY AWARENESS

Another way of starting movement is through sensory awareness. Many situations can be proposed for sensing and responding. We ask that boys and girls show by their movements how they feel in each of the following situations:

You knock over a big jar of glue and while trying to pick it up, you get your hands in the glue. Try to get the glue off your hands. It becomes stickier and stickier.

Your dog is lying in the sun; his back looks so smooth and velvety and shiny. Start to stroke him, running your hands down his back so that he won't wake up or won't move. How does it feel? Show us.

You are stuck in a cobweb. You cannot see it but it feels as though it is all over you. Try to get away from the web.

You are at your friend's house. It is time for you to go home and as you open the door there is nothing but fog. What does it do to you? How do you feel? How can you see? How can you get yourself through it?

We are all starting across the street and all of a sudden the traffic starts coming at us from every direction—from everywhere. What happens to us?

It's such a beautiful day and you and your friend are lying in a sunny, quiet spot, just watching those friendly clouds float over you. You start to float with them. Feel as though you are just moving along with the cloud—going, going.

Imagine that this whole floor is one big, clear, shiny piece of glass. How can we move on it or over it without breaking or cracking any of it? Let's try moving over the glass some other way than on our feet. Be careful not to break through.

Other ideas and sensory suggestions which we have used include going through leaves, over and through tar, ice, getting across a street that is covered with big puddles, getting stuck in a hole while trying to watch a construction crew. *Possibilities are endless.*

Much attention has been given to *getting started* in movement activities. It must be stressed that this is beginning *dance,* and dance can only emerge as movement skills are developed and refined. Quality expression of self and of ideas comes about with extensive movement, perfection, and careful attention to subtle ideas, details, and modes of expression.

Future chapters will extend the development of creative movement and dance emphasizing dance songs, relaxation, space, time, force, sound, and folk and children's dance compositions.

8

Chants

Chants are found all over the world. Universally, they appeal to boys and girls. They are a part of the child's world in which wonderful discoveries of sound and movement merge.

If we listen carefully we hear the beauty and the simplicity of expression in the things children say. In the repetition of sounds and words we hear *chants*. We hear children repeating sounds over and over again with a simple rhythmic sequence or pattern. A chant is like a simple song with few tones. It is a sound or a series of sounds repeated and recited. A chant is a short, simple melody with limited sound gradation. It can consist of variations of one sound or a series of short simple sounds repeated over and over. Chanting is a basic form of musical expression; it lies between speaking and singing.

CHANTS—TALK SONGS

Chanting sounds come naturally to children. They chant before they speak. Even after they begin to communicate with adults, they are often heard chanting to themselves. But chanting is more like talking or speaking than it is like singing. As children say, "it is a talk song."

Often children discover sounds and tones as they discover movement. Chanting, responding in a rhythmical way, repeating, and inventing new movements are a child's ways of expressing himself. Later the process may be extended so that chants include more of what he consciously feels, hears, sees, thinks, and imagines. *Chants are characterized by simplicity, repetition, rhythmical elements, and dramatic qualities.* They are often spontaneous and emerge out of work or play, fact or fantasy, enthusiasm or concern. To a child, chants are about life itself: they are about the world of children, the enchantment of childhood.

Chants are sometimes handed down from generation to generation and acquired during childhood and adolescence; the ideas in them are often completely meaningless to grownups. But even though some chants seem nonsensical, they have a quality, a fascinating charm. They seem to be a natural, extraordinary component of childhood that lives on in adults often tucked away in a storehouse of pleasant memories and sensations.

Where Do Chants Come From?

Chants come from children and from people, places, and events of both the long

distant past and today. They come from fleeting ideas of what was, what is, and what is to be. Chants are found in all countries and cultures. They are orally recorded in the reflections of primitive people. Many have been handed down from parent to child—such a chant is "Patty-cake, Patty-cake," which includes movement, rhythm, and sound. Some of the best-loved chants are those the children make or discover themselves, often referred to as *street songs*. As children become older they have favorites, many of which come from other cultures.

Fascinating origins, sources, and illustrations have been found in chants. This not only helps children realize the smallness of the world, but it also points out similarities between peoples and societies. The wonders of rituals of people and places, traditions and customs, are of interest to boys and girls, as are the ritual quality of the chants that have to do with coming of age, getting married, bearing children, fear of punishment, articles for sale, bits of gossip. As we participate in some of these chants our own feelings, longings, and aspirations are sometimes drawn out.

We often wonder where and how children acquire a particular chant. In a secluded area of northern Japan, we once heard children chanting far in the distance. Upon following the sound, we discovered that the chant was familiar but the words different—it was similar to our "Scissors, Paper, Rock." How quickly we were drawn into a bond with these children because we could, in our own way, participate in and appreciate something that was meaningful to them.

The following illustration may well demonstrate some of the characteristics and qualities of chants. This episode had to do with a play by a second-grade group.

An Episode of a Chant

Children: We need to find a way to start our play; will you help?
Teacher: I'll try. I know that it is called "A Case against the Weatherman," but tell me more about it.
Ambrose: Well, we got a court case and we are going to "try" the weatherman and we have lawyers and Sammie's the judge.
Children: We're the jury and Bert and Salvadore are lawyers.
Teacher: Why are you putting the weatherman on trial?
Children: Because he made it rain and storm.
Teacher: What kind of rain?
Mattie: An awful lot—like pitchforks.
Teacher: Like pitchforks?
Mattie: Yes, my father says, "It's raining hard … it's raining pitchforks."
Teacher: Often when I look out the window in the morning and it's raining hard I say:

It's raining
It's pouring
The old man's snoring.

Children (repeating):

It's raining
It's pouring
The old man's snoring.

Teacher: That's a chant. Repeat it again, Ronnie. Watch how he is bouncing as he is saying

the chant. Let's all chant "It's raining"—make yourself move as you are saying it. Does anyone say anything else when you don't want it to rain, or when you want it to stop?

Pauline:

Rain rain go away,
Come again some other day,
Come again on fish day.

(The children start to move spontaneously as they chant; with a jazz quality, some snapping their fingers, bouncing, and swinging their torsos back and forth and up and down.)
Renie: My Mom sometimes says to me, "It's raining *cats and dogs!*"
Children: Cats and dogs?
Teacher: When I was a little girl we used to say

It's raining
It's raining
It's raining
Puppy dogs' tails.

(Children respond with much hilarity, and they start moving like dogs wagging their tails, shaking, trying to get the rain off.)
Sidney: I've got one …

It's raining,
It's raining,
It's raining
Pussycats' tongues.

(This immediately brings forth other related ideas—pussycat whiskers, paws, etc.)
Teacher: Do you know what we are doing? We are *making up chants about* the rain. Why don't we make up some chants about the rain and the weatherman and put them into your play?
Bert: I guess we could.
Teacher: A chant is something we say over and over. Just like we have been doing about the rain or as you do when you jump rope. When

we have some of our chants made up we will try them out and *move* to them as we chant.

From this experience came a group dance-chant about the rain and the weatherman that was used to introduce the play, as well as a variety of chants to be used with movement throughout the play. Some of these follow:

Weatherman, weatherman,
You're on trial.
Today today,
You're on trial.

What's your defense?
What's your defense?
Weatherman, weatherman,
Defense defense defense?

We have a case
We have a case
We have a case
Against the weatherman.
Rain
    Storm
        Rain
            Thunder
                Rain
                    Lightning

Rain, rain, rain
That's the case
That's the case.

No picnic
No hotdogs
No fishing
No fun
NO NO NO!
That's the case
That's the case.

Sore throats
Wet feet
Earaches
Runny noses
Medicine medicine UGH!

We rest our case
We rest our case

Against the weatherman
Against the weatherman
        on
RAIN RAIN
NO NO NO
MEDICINE—UGHHHHHHHHHHHH!

THE DYNAMICS OF CHANTS

Chants help children feel as though they are "in" on what's going on in their world, and they want to share this with others. When they were babies we shared with them ("Patty-cake"). As they learn or create chants, they share them with their peers and with us, which contributes to the on-going stream of communication from generation to generation.

Chants establish a bond between children and adults. "I used to say that same one when I was a child." "Why don't you say, One-Two, buckle my shoe?" "One potato, two potato, three potato four...." "Thirty days has September, April, June, and November...."

The chants of older children or adults are more sophisticated and the rhythm and beauty of words may be expressed as a kind of art form. As associations and relationships are recognized, this makes for a learning experience as well as an artistic representation. *Chants are important to this study of creative movement because they can contribute to, accompany, and sometimes serve as the central idea of dance studies and compositions.*

Chants help us rhythmically—because we are *saying*, yet moving at the same time. They help us to move readily and to spontaneously invent and extend movement. Chants provide opportunity for us to feel rhythm and move in rhythmical ways. Through chants we can spontaneously improvise and add to, rather than just follow, a particular pattern. Because of their rhythmical structure, chants help some children perform skills.

Chants lend themselves well to both individual and group work. They are excellent for short-term group planning and presentation. Chants can call a group together and even unify it.

Chants have been used in limited space —even in the small classroom. They enhance and bring another dimension of learning to the classroom, particularly when the focus is on trying to understand the cultures of the world. They are particularly applicable to social studies, music, literature, geography, and the humanities.

All aspects of dance are served by the uniqueness of chants; throughout the dance continuum there are countless opportunities for them. They serve important functions for both young and older students in their growth in rhythmic and dance competence.

The classification of chants includes work chants, sea chants, religious chants (taking the form of prayer and worship), street chants, and nonsense chants.

Boys and girls have found that in addition to chanting and moving or dancing, chants have also been accompanied by body sounds, clapping, and stamping of the feet. All over the world some chants involve sticks of various kinds and dimensions. Sometimes the sticks accompany the chant, other times they are an integral part of the chant. Sticks sometimes signify a symbol of power and become the challenge or the purpose of the chant. Various kinds of percussion and stringed instruments have been used to intensify the movement or add to its enjoyment.

Illustrative material in this chapter will include chants related to sounds, words, questions, situations from the child's world, special days, ideas of older boys and girls, work chants, chants from other cultures, and hand and stick chants. These illustrations are by no means inclusive, nor are they presented in any progressive or sequential manner. They are not to be used as units of work, but rather to initiate, encourage, enhance, set, and solve problems.

Chants do not take the place of music. They do, however, provide a rich source of accompaniment for work with basic movement and dance; they have been used at all age levels to stimulate and accompany movement. Through chanting children can get the feel of accent, rhythmic pattern, and tempo. Chants can help a person initiate and intensify movement, portray ideas and understandings, and to sense and respond.

Chants Related to Sounds

Sounds we hear, or sounds we associate with experiences, make fine material for chants—bird calls, airplanes, buses, traffic, the waterfront, machinery, commercials, and countless other examples.

Just after one group had returned from a trip on the ferry boat, the children and teacher started to work with some of the sounds they had heard. This chant developed:

Ferry Boat Ride

Hoo   oo   oo
Sh   sh   sh   sh
Spppplish   spppplish
Bong   Bonggggg   Bongggggggggggggg

Another group, constructing rockets in art class, developed the following chant:

> Rockets   Rockets
> Sirrrrrrrrrrr
> Up   Up   Up
> Gone

This group liked the sound of the word "supersonic." The members started another dance-chant with that word and added appropriate movement.

Supersonic   Supersonic   Supersonic
  Supersonic
Count-down
  1 — 2 — 3 — 4 — 5
Blast   Offfff   Orbit!

Sounds of Words

A group of boys became interested in the music and percussion used in different cultures. As they repeated some of the classifications, they made the following chant.

> Chordophones
> Aerophones
> Idiophones
> Xylophones

(repeat)

This idea was transmitted to the rest of the class, which picked up the chant and started snapping their fingers and doing a bit of "jive" using their feet. Soon all of their bodies were involved in changing designs of movement applied to particularly interesting and difficult words.

There are a number of words that children consistently mispronounce. Often these are not corrected, and adults use the same word patterns. Such words are:

> jist for *just*
> kint for *can't*
> git for *get*
> gonna for *going to*

The following is a chant based on boys and girls trying to remember differences in the pronunciation of these particular words.

> I jist kint git it, an' I ain'a gonna try!
> I jist kint git it, an' I ain'a gonna try!
>
> You *can get* it, and *we are going* to try!
> You *can get* it, and *we are going* to try!
>
> We got it, gang, just because we tried!
> We got it, gang, just because we tried!

Mechanical Sounds

Boys in particular enjoy improvisations that originate from the sounds of mechanical devices and emphasize related sounds as well as various qualities of movement. One group visited a bottling works and developed a dance from their observations of soda pop production. They worked, out the movements of such devices as the conveyor belt, the filling of the bottles, and the capping of the bottles. The following chant is their version of the sounds that went with various parts of the process. This served as part of the accompaniment for the dance they later composed. As the boys said, "It took some doing to put the sounds into the right kind of syllables—we had a hard time agreeing." They taped their sounds as they were working on their chant so that they could listen more carefully to what they were trying to write. Needless to say, they could not really write the chant without saying the sounds and doing the movements at the same time. It proved to be a marvelous improvised lesson in phonics.

Chant in Sound

Uh   ah   uh   ah   kling   kling   plunk
Uh   ah   uh   ah   kling   kling   plunk

Zing   zing   zing   zing   putt   putt   putt
Zing   zing   bong   bong   tap   tap
ssssSSSSSSSSSSSSSSS!

The chant became a musical composition and accompanied their dance study.

Word Sound Chants

Chants can begin with word sounds children love. "Tim Tam Toes Tap" is the kind of tongue twister that children enjoy making up to fast tempos.

Tim Tam toes tap,
Stretch your arms and then clap.
Tim tam toes tap,
Bend your knees and clap, clap, clap.

Tim Tam toes tap,
Click your heels and then clap.
Tim tam toes tap,
Shake your feet and tap, tap, tap.

Who Put the Cookies in the Cookie Jar?

(Anyone's name)
Who put the cookies in the cookie jar?
Did Kathy put the cookies in the cookie jar?
Not I put the cookies in the cookie jar!
Not Kathy put the cookies in the cookie jar!
Then who put the cookies in the cookie jar?

By chanting this, a rhythmic pattern is established. Groups enjoy doing it in a circle with all moving according to the rhythm. This chant is continuous with no break in the rhythm. One person starts and asks the question of the whole group, and after that a person named or pointed to comes in on the response. This continues until all have had a turn, or until someone says, "Yes, I put the cookies in the cookie jar." We have turned this into "Who Popped the Corn for Halloween?" "Who Made the Home Run at the Ball Game?" "Who Put the Sneakers in the Fish Pond?"

After young children have been involved in chants—using them as accompaniment for movement, to find movement, or to enhance ideas they are trying to communicate—they often develop chants for riddles, or asking questions of why and what. Sometimes these are passing experiences shared only with the teacher; other times they are shared with a class.

Using The Child's World

One day it was necessary to locate the garbage truck to have the attendant collect tree branches and cuttings from shrubs. Newell, a four-year-old neighbor, and Staff, the boxer dog, joined in the trip. An immediate discussion started with "Where are we going?" "Why?" "Where is the garbage man?" This was put into a simple chant which was repeated over and over throughout the journey, eliciting both movement and rhythmic response.

The Garbage Man

Looking for the garbage man,
Looking for the garbage man,
Looking for the garbage man,
Where can he be?

Who will find the garbage man?
Who will find the garbage man?
Who will find the garbage man?
Newell will find the garbage man.

Staff will find the garbage man.
Bob will find the garbage man.
No, Newell will find the garbage man.

After finding the garbage man, the following chant spontaneously arose from Newell:

Newell found the garbage man,
Newell found the garbage man,
Newell found the garbage man,
Riding in his truck.

Staff didn't find him,
Staff didn't find him,
Bob didn't find him,
Over in Shady Brook.

Ice Cream

Strawberry, chocolate, butter pecan.
I like ice cream, man oh man!
Lick it from a cone,
Lick it from a stick,
I eat ice cream
Quick, quick, quick!

This chant involves a continuous movement response to the rhythmic pattern. It is sometimes done with feet, other times with hands added, and each time adding different flavors of ice cream. This has been adapted to cars, horses, and other special likes of children, depending on such things as their interests and the time of year.

I Went to the Store

I went to the store
And what did I see?
And what did I see?
Bags of oranges as *orange* as can be
    Looking at me.
    Looking at me.

I went to frozen foods
And what did I see?
And what did I see?
Packages of spinach as *green* as can be
    Looking at me.
    Looking at me.

I went down the aisle
And what did I see?
And what did I see?
A bottle of tomato juice as *red* as can be
    Looking at me.
    Looking at me.

I bought all the groceries
    Looking at me.
    Looking at me.
I bought all the groceries
    Looking at me,
And walked right out of the store.

As soon as the rhythmic pattern is established movement improvisation is started. The words reflect the movement. This chant has taken us to the department store, the planetarium, the art museum, the Christmas store, and the zoo.

Trains

All aboard! All aboard!
Climb on the train.
(repeat)

The train starts to go
The train starts to go
GO   GO   GO!

It pulls up the hill
It pulls up the hill
The train pulls up the hill.

It picks up speed
It picks up speed
The train picks up speed.

It goes around the curve
It goes around the curve
It goes around the curve to the city.

It goes in the tunnel
It goes in the tunnel
Dark in the tunnel, dark in the tunnel.

Pulls to the station
Pulls to the station
And now the train stops.

In addition to putting movement to this chant, kindergarteners and first-graders have extended the idea to buses, boats, and bicycles.

Signs and Words

The chants that can be found or adapted from signs around the city or suburb and familiar "sayings" are most meaningful to boys and girls. Here are only a few from which we have worked in finding appropriate movement to go with our chanting.

Curb your dog,
Curb your dog,
Walk him on a leash,
Curb your *dog!*

Off the grass,
Off the grass,
Offfffffff.

Keep Out!
Keep Out!
Keep
Out.

Post no bills!
Post no bills!
Against the law!

NO PARKING
NO PARKING
NO PARKING
TUESDAY.

Don't, Don't, DON'T
Don't, Don't, DON'T
    Don't climb that tree
    Don't tear your pants
    Don't chew that gum.
DON'T, DON'T, DON'T

WHERE EVER I GO,
WHATEVER I DO
    Don't, Don't, Don't is said
I wish, I wish, I wish
OLD DON'T WAS DEAD!

Don't be a litterbug

A litterbug

Don't . . . . . . Be

A

Litterbug!

Pitch In

Pitch In

Pick it up

Pick it up

Litter litter litter.

Following Directions

Chants for young children tend to involve their daily activities. These chants are especially useful for following directions.

Pulling on the sneakers
Pulling on the sneakers
Pulling on the sneakers

Don't forget the laces!
Don't forget the laces!
Don't forget the laces!

Pull, pull, pull!
Pull, pull, pull!
Pull, pull, pull!

Tie them tight!
Tie them tight!
Tie them tight!

Putting on the snow suit
Putting on the snow suit
Putting on the snow suit
Zip Zip Zip Zip!

Zipping up my snowsuit
Zipping up my snowsuit
Zipping up my snowsuit
Up to the very top!

Going through empty spaces
Going through empty spaces
Going through empty spaces
Careful not to bump
Careful careful careful!

Going through empty spaces
Going through empty spaces
Going through empty spaces
Looking looking looking
For an empty space.

Going down the hall
(whispered)
Going down the hall
Trying to be quiet
Trying to be quiet
  Others working
  Others working
Quiet! quiet!
Going down the hall.

Picking up the room
Picking up the room
Picking up the scissors
Putting them away.

Picking up the room
Picking up the room

Picking up the chalk
Putting it away.

Picking up the room
Picking up the room
Picking up our toys
Putting them away.

All pick up,
All put away.

Using Special Days

Chants come naturally from children on special days of the year. Birthdays, for example, provide opportunities to develop and use chants. As one group assembled, the teacher asked, "Did anything special happen today?" Frances replied, "Betty has a birthday." I repeated, "A birthday!" and Frances returned, "Yes, Betty has a birthday." Frances had started a chant. We talked about chants and suggested that we might finish the one Frances had started. After a few tries (with too many words) we decided on the following:

Betty has a birthday
A birthday
A birthday
Betty has a birthday
And now it is here!

"What could we do with this chant other than just say it to Betty?" Movement exploration was started, with Betty in the center of a circle and the group chanting as they went around with slides and skips.

A different birthday chant developed as another child's birthday was recognized. The boys and girls were asked if they could think of something different to do rather than sing "Happy Birthday" to Olaf. They were asked to form small groups and think of ways that they could congratulate Olaf on his birthday. The result was this chant:

You're one year older today, Olie
You're one year older today.
How many birthdays, Olie
Before this one today?
One
Two
Three
Four
Five
It's birthday six for Olie,
Olie is six years old today!

The class started chanting and said it was too short, so they repeated the whole thing. This chant became the source of movement adaptations; everyone in the room was moving to Olie's birthday chant.

Valentines

Valentine, valentine,
Who will be our valentine?
Valentine, valentine,
We will all follow you.

Debbie is our Valentine,
Debbie is our Valentine,
Debbie is our Valentine,
And we will follow you.

Debbie started her movements and the group followed, repeating the chant until Debbie called another. As each child was called, the groups followed his movements. Often there was no wait between movements and the chant was continuous.

What shapes can you be
On Valentine's Day?
What shapes can you make
On Valentine's Day?
What Valentine shapes
Can you be?

Children turn themselves into different shapes each time the chant is repeated. This has also been adapted to Thanksgiving and Easter time.

Snow Time

Push the snow,
Pile it high,
Push the snow,
Pile it high,
Clear the way
For passersby.
Snow keep falling,
Snow keep falling,
Work all night
And pile it high.

Experiences of Older Boys and Girls

Chants have been used to add vitality and enthusiasm to many group studies. One group of sixth-grade students had been studying their state (New Jersey). Although they had learned a great deal about basic factors such as size, population, resources, topography, climate, and history, chants were introduced to develop some esthetic pride in local places. They began with towns; local maps made it possible to find picturesque names in which rhythm and beauty existed.

Weehawken	Egg Harbor
Matawan	Bay Head
Shrewsbury	Red Bank
Hackettstown	Batsto
Wyckoff	Pennsauken
Sea Girt	Paramus
Absecon	Mahwah

We had fun chanting these names over and over with different emphasis, and we found many ways of saying them using different qualities of voice, different body movements, and varying accents and rhythmic patterns.

Some of the most unusual chants come from boys' major interests. Art and a group of his friends were showing each other some of the boxing movements Art's older brother had demonstrated to them. The following chant, accompanied by vigorous movements, resulted.

> Rock and sock,
> Knock and block,
> Slash with your right,
> Pull with your left!
> That's the way to fight!
> That's the way to fight!
> Shift your body,
> Don't retreat,
> Better not flinch
> Or go in a clinch.
> That's the way to fight!
> That's the way to fight!
> Or get a clout
> And be knocked out
> For that will be
> The end of the bout—sooooooo
> Rock and sock,
> Knock and block,
> That's the way to fight!
> That's the way to fight!

Work Chants

When older boys and girls have opportunities to add movement to a work chant, the sound of the chant and the ideas they are trying to communicate become more meaningful. Work chants are often found in connection with social studies, literature, and music. The best sources are the people themselves. From work chants we learn more about the kinds of work patterns and the life and customs of the people in various far-off places.

Balancé, Oh!

"Balancé Oh!" is a call made by West Indian women when they are ready to have their baskets put on their heads in preparation for going to market. The huge baskets are filled with fresh fruit and vegetables, and are large and heavy—a woman cannot put it on her head by herself. These beautiful women have excellent posture as a result of their labors, and they walk very fast for miles, singing and chanting to each other on their way to the market. This chant is in calypso rhythm.

(chorus)
> Balancé Oh! Rise up from dat bed
> Balancé Oh! Basket on your head.
> Oh, day done break—O, see her basket balancing
> Oh, day done break—O, listen how she shout and sing.
> Balancé Oh! ugh!
> Balancé Oh! wah!

(verse 1)
> Early in the mornings just before dat heat o' day
> You see dem women coming down to market how dey sway.
> Dem basket full of plum, plantain, mango, tangerine
> Der faces shine as dey join de line
> With de aprons bright and green.

(chorus) Balancé Oh! Rise up from dat bed.

(verse 2)
> When de people hear der shout dem basket women make
> Dey pile into de market place to buy and celebrate
> Dey trade an ear for a peck o' meal, you hear dem to and fro
> Got something nice at a bargain price
> And a shanga on the go.

(chorus) Balancé Oh! Rise up from dat bed.

(verse 3)
> And now it's early evening and you see de sweepers come.
> Dey clean de street as de music sweet
> Start sounding from de drum
> And everybody start to sing and move dem-selves about
> And all de night till the morning light
> You hear dem basket women shout

(chorus)
> Balancé Oh! Rise up from dat bed
> Balancé Oh! Basket on your head.
> Oh day done break—O, see her basket balancing
> Oh day done break—O, listen how she shout and sing
> Balance Oh! ugh!
> Balance Oh! wah!

Work on this chant initiated a story in dance, accompanied by chanting. So what started out to be just a chant developed into finding out about another culture, and included making steel drums and learning how to play them. In finding out what a market in Martinique looks like and trying to capture the impression, the children created appropriate movements to the native work chant and connected this rhythmic activity with social studies and art.

From early times there have been many work chants involving the necessities of life, one of which is water. The following chant calls for a leader and then a group answering; it has been used to develop quality creative dance movement.

Water

Leader: Water—we need water today.
Group: Let us pray. Let us pray for de rain.

Leader: Water. We got to have water today.
Group: Let us pray. Let us pray for de rain.
Water will make de banana tree grow
And de rain is good for de grain.
Leader: Bamboo. I never see bamboo so dry.
Group: Let us pray. Let's pray for de rain
Water, we got to have water today.
And de rain is good for de grain.
Leader: Water, we got to have water today.
Group: Let us pray, pray hard as we can.
Water for cooking de rice and de peas
Water please, to put in de pan.
Leader: Water, we got to have water, today.
Group: Let us pray. Let's pray for de rain
Water will make us so happy again
Let us pray. Let us pray for de rain.

The main topic of study for one group of children was their own state of Alabama. Included in their study were occupations and industries. The children were asked to divide into groups to develop a short dance study communicating through movement

WATER

From *Victoria Winters*
Arr. *Alonah Stith*

some phase of work in Alabama. Seven boys accompanied their presentation with the following original chant, done with appropriate expressive movement.

Digging in the mine
Digging in the mine
Turning out the coal
Turning out the coal
To heat and melt iron
To heat and melt iron

Digging in the mine
Turning out the coal
To heat and melt iron
To turn into steel
To turn into steel

Digging in the mine
Turning out coal
To heat and melt iron
To turn into steel
To make an automobile

To make an automobile
To make an automobile
That started in
   Alabama—in Alabama.

Films, sound tracks, tapes, and such media can be useful sources for developing chants and accompanying dances. When one group was studying construction, the film *The Skyscraper* was shown. Some exciting chant-dances were created by the class as a direct result of seeing this film.

Skyscraper

It takes a lot of men,
A lot of time,
To put a skyscraper in the sky.
A lot of men
A lot of men
Time time time
To put a a skyscraper in the sky.

We are building a building
And building it high

Building and building
So it will reach the sky.

We take a city block
   tear it down
To put a skyscraper up
   from the ground.

Dig Dig Dig
Dig Dig Dig
Wssht Wsshttt Boooommmmmm.

A Building Grows

See the building go up!

The owners depend upon the architects,
The architects depend upon the contractors,
The contractors depend upon the excavators.

See the building go up!

The excavators depend upon the drillers,
The drillers depend upon the diggers,
The diggers depend upon the blasters.

See the building go up!

The blasters depend upon the ironmen,
The ironmen depend upon the plasterers,
The plasterers depend upon the masons.

See the building go up!

The masons depend upon the electricians,
The electricians depend upon the carpenters,
The carpenters depend upon the plumbers.

See the building go up!

The plumbers depend upon the decorators,
The decorators depend upon the tenants,
The tenants depend upon the customers.

See the building high in the sky!

Work chants also come from sea chanteys, which reveal human feelings about work, love of the sea, humor, and fun. Stan Hugill's book *Chanteys and Sailors' Songs* (New York: Praeger, 1969) is a good source of this type of work chant.

A YO HO HO

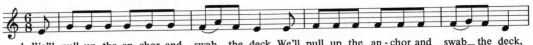

1. We'll pull up the an-chor and swab— the deck, We'll pull up the an-chor and swab— the deck,

We'll pull up the an-chor and swab— the deck with a yo ho ho.——

2. We'll hoist the sails and sail away.
3. We'll scrub the clothes clean, ugh!

A movement-chant experience can help children create such compositions as the following:

Top Sails

Only one more day—only one more day
Away hey oh—
Raise him a hoy
Raise him a hoy
Away hey oh—
Haul him ahoy
Oh Oh Oh
Raise him ahoy.

Calling the Watch

Hoy-a-a-you sleepin
Eight bells are gone.
Hoy-a-a-you sleepin
Eight bells are gone.
(repeat)

Haul on the Lines

Haul on the lines, boys
Haul on the lines

Our bully ship's a' roll in'—
Haul on the lines.

Our captain he's a groan 'in—
Haul on the lines.

Haul on the lines, boys
Haul on the lines.

Chants from Other Cultures

The chants of other cultures, as has already been noted several times, can increase and encourage children's knowledge of history, people, music, and creative dance movements.

There are many original Indian chants as well as creative versions or "home-made" chants. This made-up chant used Indian tribal names with an accompanying drum beat and primitive step patterns.

Mohawk, Cherokee, Paiute, Apache
  Hayya, hayya, hayya, hayya

Mohawk, Mohawk, Mohawk, Mohawk
  Hayya, hayya, hayya, hayya

Cherokee, Cherokee, Cherokee, Cherokee
  Hayya, hayya, hayya, hayya

Paiute, Paiute, Paiute, Paiute
  Hayya, hayya, hayya, hayya

Apache, Apache, Apache, Apache
  Hayya, hayya, hayya, hayya

Hay!

STOMP DANCE CHANT

Elizabeth Bess

O - na we,_____ O - na we,_____ he, he, he. O - na we,_____

O - na we,_____ he, he, he. Ki wa No he no,

Ki wa No he no, Ki wa No he no, Ki wa No he no.

Stomp Dance Chant

The stomp chant is a gay and friendly Indian chant introduced to us by an American Indian, Elizabeth Bess. We always felt special because Miss Bess shared so much of her culture with us. Her father served as chief of the Shinnecock Indians in the Algonquian Nation on Long Island, N.Y.

This authentic chant is done with a group in a large circle moving with short walking steps (walking with a push or shuffling the feet and accenting the heel part of the walk), one walk to a measure with the heel accented on the *we* part of the first measure.

A group of young children in Bronxville, N.Y., made a special study of Indians. They knew that Indians had lived in their area and this heightened their interest. Extensive materials were brought in from homes and from local libraries. Authentic stories, dances, songs, and music were used. The children dug clay and made pottery; prepared dye and dyed yarn to be used in weaving; they built a teepee, wrote stories, and revised and made up songs and chants. They also experimented with percussion and recorded the many chants they originated. Most of their chants were expressed through movement and one, the "Gramatan Chant," is illustrated below.

GRAMATAN CHIEF

Jean Scott

Do o Gra - ma - tan chief, Chief go buf - fa - lo hunt.

Repeat 4 times

Chief find buf - fa - lo, Do o Gra - ma - tan chief.

One group was reading about Pueblo Benito,[1] an old Indian town in New Mexico that had disappeared; archeologists had pieced together some of the incidents that led to its disappearance. As the children discussed what might have happened to the town, they evolved this chant that became a departure for several other dance studies.

Pueblo Benito

Pueblo Benito
Pueblo Benito
Where did you go?
Where did you go?
Pueblo Benitooooooooooooooooooo
Pueblo Benito
Pueblo Benito
Where did you come from?

Where did you come from?
And where did you go,
Pueblo Benitooooooooooooooooooo?

Chants from Parents

Some of the best sources of chants are children's parents. Frequently children become so fascinated with the variety of movement and rhythmic and dance possibilities involved that they ask for more opportunities to use chants. When this kind of interest is manifested, we suggest that they go on a *chant hunt.* Some of them even bring their parents to school! Maxine brought these chants, saying excitedly, "Here are just a few of the German chants my mother has taught me." We had a great time with these after Maxine's mother translated them for us.

German Chant

Ele mele mu
Miller's kuh
Miller's esel
Das bist du.

Ele mele mu (nonsense words)
Miller's cow
Miller's donkey
That's you.

Ringle rangle rose
Schone aprikose
Veilchen und fergestmeinicht
Alle kinder setzen sich.

Ringle rangle rose
Pretty apricot
Violets and forget-me-nots
All children sit down.

Hoppe hoppe reiter
Wenn er falt
Dann schreit er
Falt er in den graben.

Hop, hop rider
If he falls
Then he screams
He falls into the ditch.

Fressen ihn die raben
Felt ehr in den sumpf
Macht der reiter plums.

Then the ravens will eat him.
He falls into the swamp
Makes the rider go FLOP!

[1] Mary Elting and Michael Folsom, *The Secret Story of Pueblo Benito* (New York: Harvey House, 1963).

SAMBALELE from Brazil

Arr. *Alonah Stith*

Sam - ba, Sam - ba, Sam - ba   O - lé.   Pi - sa, Pi -

- sa, Pi - sa mu - la - ta.   Get here be - hind me and

do as I say.   Pi - sa na_____ ba - rra da sai - a mu - la - ta.

Sam - ba, Sam - ba, Sam - ba,   O - lé.   Pi - sa, Pi -

- sa, Pi - sa mu - la - ta.   Soon you'll be want - ing to

dance it all day.   Pi - sa na_____ ba - rra da sai - a mu - la - ta.

Chico's parents told us that this samba chant was like "Follow the Leader." Chico started as the leader and asked other boys and girls to join him; soon the whole class became involved in chanting and dance.

"Kili Mabah Balu" was shared with us by Alonah Stith, who composed it from symbolic sounds of African culture and

KILI MABAH BALU

Alonah Stith

Ki - li ma - bah ba - lu, Ki - li ma - bah ba - lu, Ki - li ma - bah ba - lu deh kaht doo soo.

Se_ gore_ dey ya_ munde,_ Se_ gore_ dey ya_ munde._ Ki - li

ma - bah ba - lu, Ki - li ma - bah ba - lu, Ki - li ma - bah ba - lu deh kaht doo soo.

from syllables of names of some of her African students. It is a playful chant that we used for movement and percussion improvisation.

Another chant that we use over and over is "Ev'rybody Loves Saturday Night." It is found in many parts of the world in a variety of languages. Boys and girls have adapted this chant-song to numerous situations and occasions; it has become "Ev'rybody Loves Christmas Time," "Holiday Time," "Jellybeans," "Easter Time," "Vacation Time," and so on. Movement improvisations, jiving, finger-snapping and hip-bumping, the soft shoe and tap dance have also accompanied this selection.

Hand and Stick Chants

Many cultures use sticks and chants to accompany their dances. The stick in many instances signifies power, and is often used in primitive dances to express feelings, to tell stories, or to challenge another. It is of particular interest to boys that sticks are used in many cultures only by men.

Sticks have been used in our work in movement and dance in several ways, stimulating movement, accompanying movement that has been specified or made up, creating movement and stick patterns, and sharpening rhythmic perception such as understanding pulse, rhythmic patterns, tempo, and feeling accent and phrasing. Sticks are also used to provide opportunities for boys and girls to work together in pairs or as a total group. The chant keeps the group together and also helps with eye-hand coordination.

We have found that a stick of from ten to twelve inches is desirable in starting work with stick chants. Boys and girls easily become skillful in handling sticks, which represent a challenge to them. Patterns may seem structured in the beginning, but chil-

CHANT: EVERYBODY LOVES SATURDAY NIGHT

158

dren soon become adept and begin creating many patterns of their own. A great variety of stick chants have been developed with children starting from the second grade on up through to adulthood. *However, they are most appropriate for older boys and girls because of the coordination and involved patterns.*

An approach to stick chants we have found most successful has been to start with hand clapping.

Hand-Clapping Chants

Some hand-clapping patterns have been discovered while the group was sitting in a large circle, by having one boy start clapping his hands and all following, changing from using the hands to using other parts of the body or the floor. Illustrations of patterns have been:

Clapping hands, hitting one knee, clapping hands, hitting the other knee, clapping hands, hitting both knees.

Clapping hands, hitting knees, hitting the floor, clapping hands, and shaking hands stretched above the head.

The chant to this rhythm is:

clap clap hold hold snap snap hold hold
clap hold snap hold slap slap slap hold

Soon the boys and girls could do this using only the words and feeling the silence, or the syncopations.

The chants "Ja Su Ce" and "Ra Kooma Rango" are samples of children's own creations accompanied by movement. The first chant was made up of the first two letters of Janet, Suzanne, and Celia's names, and is performed with children sitting in a circle back to back with legs pulled up against chests.

Ja Su Ce (extend one leg to the floor—slow slow slow)
Ja Su Ce (extend other leg to the floor—slow slow slow)
Su Ce Ja (cross one leg over partner's leg—quick quick quick)
Su Ce Ja (cross other leg over partner's—quick quick quick)
Ja Su Ce (pull legs back to extended position in front—slow slow slow)
Ja Su Ce (pull legs up to chest—slow slow slow)

Ra	Koo	Ma	Koo	
left elbow to left knee	right elbow to right knee	clap hands together	clap both knees with hands	hit floor with both hands

Repeat first line.

Ringo	Rango
swing body and both arms to left again, clapping floor	swing body to right—clapping against floor

Ra	Kooma	Rango
right hand to left shoulder	left hand to right shoulder	clap both knees

Stick Chants

When boys and girls become familiar with chanting and moving, they find that it is comparatively easy to switch to sticks, which really become extensions of the hands. An introductory experience to working with sticks went like this:

Teacher: We are going to do something new and different with our chants today. Get yourselves sitting comfortably and let's all start to clap. Let's chant as we are clapping. Can you make your claps more interesting by stressing your clap every once in while? Yes, by giving your claps accent. Let us try to keep the claps steady so we sound like one person instead of thirty-seven. Good! What else could we do with our claps to vary them?

Children: We could clap another part of us. We could clap our hands and then the floor. We could make one part an accent.

Teacher: This time try Leon's way. Clap your hands and then your thighs or legs twice. How does it sound?

Children: Hands, thighs, thighs.

Teacher: Suppose you face another person, a partner, and see what patterns you can discover together. This is like patty-cake. (With time there is a great assortment of hand clapping and hand slapping.)

(Taking the clues from patterns discovered.) Let's all stop for a few minutes and watch the patterns that Roger, Clem, and Stokes are doing.

(Roger, Clem, and Stokes are facing each other sitting cross-legged. This is their pattern: clap both knees, clap hands, clap one knee and then other knee, clap hands, and then partners on each side. Clap own hands and then clap knee. Their chant is "Knees, hands, knee, hands, partner's hands, knees." They repeat this several times.)

What makes that pattern interesting?

Children: It's different. Roger is clapping himself, then clapping with Clem and Stokes' hands.

Teacher: Do you notice anything about the last time they hit their knees before they start their pattern again? Yes, they are holding the last sound on their knee.

Maggie: That's sort of like getting ready to start over again.

Teacher: Many of your patterns remind me of those that the African people use in many of their dances. They dance with their whole bodies and often use their hands and feet to make percussion sounds or patterns, just as you have been doing.

Now I have a surprise for you. In many parts of the world games and dances are done with many kinds of sticks. I have sticks here. You will each need a pair and then we will discover what the sticks can do. Select one of the patterns you have made that you particularly like and we will try it out with the sticks rather than your hands.

(In order to set some limits and controls so that the group can work efficiently together, we establish a starting signal.)

Before you start working with your sticks and trying out some stick patterns, let's find out one thing you can do with the sticks. Good, you can clap them together as you did your hands. What else could we call this other than clap?

Children: Strike, slap, hit, push them together.

Teacher: Yes, we can use any of those terms. Now try hitting your sticks on the floor—try various ways.

(They find that they can hit the ends, or hit first one end and then the other. They can also hit them flat on the floor. As children use the sticks they discover that they can also throw them in the air and catch them, toss them to each other, or pass them around a circle. They use these discoveries in their chant patterns.)

Teacher: What kind of signal could we all agree on so that I can get your attention—so that we will all stop hitting the sticks?

(After much discussion and suggesting, we usually determine that an effective way is to hold the sticks over the head, stretching arms up, or crossing sticks over the head. This way all can see the signal and it also gets the sticks off the floor.)

Remember the hand-clap pattern you worked out with your partner? Well, let's see if we can do the same pattern with your sticks. Be sure you say your chant while you are using the sticks, or say what you are doing so that you will establish a rhythm, and this will help the two or three of you to stay together.

A variety of ways of using sticks have been discovered by different groups. For example:

Hitting floor
Hitting own sticks together
Hitting partner's sticks

Hitting sticks to floor on each side
Hitting own sticks together
Hitting partner's sticks

Hitting own sticks
Hitting partner's
Hitting own

Hitting own sticks
Hitting right stick of partner
Hitting left stick of partner

Hitting own
Hitting right stick of partner with right stick
Hitting left stick of partner with left stick

With practice, boys and girls find that they develop dexterity in handling the sticks and perform many complicated patterns, such as throwing, flipping, and twirling.

After working simple patterns with the sticks in pairs, we work in larger groupings. One group developed this chant, which was carried out in a circle formation:

1. *Here we go, here we go*
   (Click sticks in front two times)
2. *Up and down, up and down*
   (Click sticks above head, then at feet)
3. *Up and down and out, up and down and out*
   (Repeat as in second part [up. down], then by clicking sticks with neighbors.)

Flight in Space

Phillip and Ted needed two others to develop their chant when they decided to work from a square. They used this sequence:

1. Hit sticks on floor, tap both to corners, and stretch arms and sticks up.
2. Hit sticks on floor; two people tap each other's sticks.
3. Hit sticks on floor; other two people tap each other's sticks.
4. All flip sticks in air and catch them.
5. Stretch sticks upward touching corners, come down and hit sticks on floor.

BLAST	OFF	HERE	WE	GO

(Hit sticks on floor)   (Hit sticks to both corners and then hit sticks above head—stretching arms up)

TO	MARS	TO	VENUS

(Hit sticks on floor) (Two boys hit each other's sticks) (Hit sticks on floor) (Other two boys hit each other's sticks)

FLYING OUT IN SPACE
(All four boys twirl [flip] sticks in the air and catch them)

AWAY AWAY FROM EARTH
(All stretch sticks upward, hitting sticks at corners, and then come down and hit sticks on the floor)

LE LO LAI

Merreditan Carazo

Le lo-le lo-lai, lo   le lo-le lo-lai lo   Le lo-le lo-lai, lo - le lo-le lo-lai!

Merreditan Carazo of Puerto Rico shared "Le Lo Lai" with us, and we improvised hand and feet movements to this chant. We also adapted it to patterns with sticks of various lengths, shakers, and shells; in Puerto Rico long seed pods of the flamboyant tree were used.

Chants, as we can see, take many forms. Those presented in this chapter have pro-vided for extensive creative expression. Because boys and girls say rhythmically what they are doing when they use chants, this presents a great opportunity to reinforce and enhance many areas of learning and to give zest to daily work, as well as to teach and evoke the many components of creative rhythmic movement.

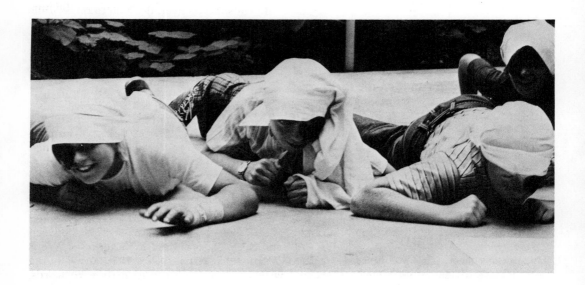

9

Dance Songs

Dance songs (movement or action) are songs that facilitate movement, foster creativity, and provide varied rhythmic experience. In this form of rhythmic activity, singing and moving go together to support and enhance each other.

Young children say, "We dance what we sing," or "We sing what we dance." Older boys and girls think of this way of using movement as a group activity and often refer to "movement songs" that provide for group experiences in creating movement as well as for socializing. These boys and girls have said, "Sometimes it is easier to find more movements that feel right when we hear ourselves singing as we move." "The singing and the moving helps us to be free inside and outside." "Songs help to keep us moving together, give us good feelings, and pep us up."

No matter how they are termed, *dance songs* involve singing about *what, how,* and *why* we are moving. Or they involve moving about *what* we are singing. At times a melody is made to go with certain movement experiences; at other times the movement experiences initiate the melody; or moving and singing might emerge together.

The songs included in this chapter have come from individual children, from groups of students, and from teachers and other adults working with boys and girls. Some of the songs have originated for specific purposes and occasions but have been used in multiple ways afterwards. One can never predict when a dance song will "pop" from the group and become a favorite. Most of the songs presented here are open-ended and can be adapted to many situations.

The songs have to do with "me," "us," and "our" movements. They require exploring, identifying, inventing, and improving movement qualities. They are concerned with our environment, our world, special times, and what seems important to us. We sing and move or dance out our ideas, and thus reinforce our understandings.

Dance songs are a way of helping children identify and show relationships between movement, sound, and experiences; there is far more to dance songs than just singing with motion. Children identify with words, actions, feelings, relevancy, and concepts as they move and sing. Those participating must follow directions, recall past movements, make applications, formulate sequences, identify relevant responses, and clarify relationships. These activities require children to listen, to observe, to respond quickly, and to create new or different movements. *They enable all children to have feelings of achievement and accomplishment, for all dance songs are full of meaning and serve as reinforcement for learning.*

CHARACTERISTICS OF DANCE SONGS

Dance songs are short and repetitive with simple melodies to which one can readily respond. Their words should be at a minimum and should initiate, suggest, or give direction to the movement. Emphasis is usually on one idea or one movement rather than on a series, because it is important to be able to coordinate the movement to the song. The range of the melody is limited so that it may be sung, recognized, and repeated easily. Pitch should be at a level making it easy for children to sing. Music educators suggest that songs for young children seldom go below middle C. The phrases are usually short. The tempo is usually lively rather than slow and dragged. In other words, the tempo provides for spontaneous, vigorous activity.

Dance songs may be used in small spaces, in classrooms, in open space, in special centers, or in large auditoriums. They may be used with people sitting or standing in crowded areas. Dance songs may be used while moving about in circles, lines, or rows, in formal or informal groupings. When they are used in a first movement experience with a group, regardless of age, people seem more comfortable when sitting close together in a confined area. As they become more secure in moving, they tend to call for more space.

DANCE SONGS ARE PURPOSEFUL

There is no one way or single purpose for using dance and movement songs. They can be used for such varied purposes as:

Getting movement started

Kinesthetic awareness

Having fun together

Helping children learn to carry a tune

Helping children to listen and to take turns

Participation for all, regardless of size or age

Accomplishment for all

Sensing and responding

Thinking and problem solving

Expressing thoughts and feelings

Achieving in a comparatively short length of time

Cutting through barriers involving a new group of children or teachers

Changing the pace, to give variety and balance to a child's day

Initiating an experience planned for the day or summarizing an experience carried on during the day

Getting a group back together after individual work

Enhancing an experience

Providing opportunities to compose songs

Intensifying a field trip or give added meaning to a trip by recalling it through words, song, and movement

Starting or ending a day—"hello or goodbye"

Quieting a group down after overstimulation or exhilaration

Reinforcing concepts and learnings

Learning more about movement

Sending a group off on a vacation

Uniting a group of children again after a vacation

Coordinating words, sound, and movements

Highlighting an important special day or event in the life of a child or a group

Helping the shy child become a part of the group

Having a creative experience quickly

Initiating a creative experience

These songs are used effectively with or without musical accompaniment. Rarely

I'M HAPPY TO SEE YOU

I'm hap-py to see you, hap-py to see you, Hap-py, hap-py, hap-py, hap-py, hap-py to see you,

Hap-py to see you, hap-py to see you, hap-py, hap-py, hap-py, hap-py, hap-py to see you.

does a teacher have an accompanist each day, but as we sing and move together we become our own accompanists—thus we can use these songs at any time.

Dance songs are resources to be drawn on spontaneously to fit a situation. One fourth grade used a familiar action song spontaneously when a very important person to them suddenly appeared in the room. The group seemed tongue-tied until Vernon started singing (with the group immediately joining in) "I'm Happy To See You." The teacher and the class really felt this movement song expressed what they could not express in words.

The dance songs in this book serve quite a different purpose from the traditional singing games handed down to us from generations past. Singing games, however, are an important aspect of our culture, and they need to be preserved for their rhythmical qualities as well as their link to the past. They provide another vehicle for communicating, having fun, comparing, appreciating and inquiring, and learning about folk material; much of value can ensue from the use of traditional singing games. (A discussion of singing games is presented in the chapter on folk dancing.) The dance songs that are described in this book are aimed specifically at encouraging learning about creative rhythmic movement, and share some qualities of singing games.

YOUNGER CHILDREN AND DANCE SONGS

During early childhood (the "I" period), children's thoughts and actions are largely centered on themselves as people. Dance songs can be used to give them opportunities to say "*I* wish," "*I* can," "When *I* grow up *I* want to be. . ." *The simple dance form lets youngsters think and express thoughts and feelings about themselves.*

After having developed a highly successful dance song, a second-grade group was asked, "Why do you suppose we have dance songs? What are they all about and what do they mean to you?" Responses included: "They tell about what I can do, what I like, what I think about, what I dream about, what I want, what I have to learn, wishes, people I like, my pet, my friends, my fun, my silly stuff." These responses actually explain the substance of dance songs for children. They also provide opportunities for the audience to join in.

In any age group what really makes a difference to boys and girls is that which they conceive and express *in their own way*. Dance songs and movement songs provide opportunities for them to reveal their inner selves at a particular time in an outward form of sound and movement. Yet we cherish these spontaneous expressions. As suggested earlier they have to do with people, movement, concepts, seasons and holidays, special times—songs that come

LOOK! SEE!

Arr. *Betty Lu Fitch*

from the child's world and moments of just having fun together. As these songs are used, some may lead to dance, while others may serve only to express an idea at the moment; to initiate, review, or extend movement; or to give vitality to learning. *There is no particular sequence to the dance songs or the way in which they are used. Their use is determined by the purpose they serve.*

This song is about three words—look, see, watch—and it provides a chance to move expressively, learn about others, achieve, and to develop other curriculum areas, such as vocabulary development. These three words of varying shades of meaning, when put into an action setting, seem much less complicated.

Immediately this song gives emphasis to the "I" of early childhood. It utilizes constructively the "look at me" stage. With its use, "Look! See!" invites children to observe, follow directions, respond, cooperate, and even be leaders in the creation of new movements.

For some young children it is difficult to think and express a movement while singing, or to be singled out as the leader. But with the encouragement of the alert teacher even the shy child can assume a leadership role. *Any* movement is acceptable!

Another learning involved in this song is adjusting a movement to a particular rhythmical structure. For some children this is also a means of helping them with pitch and verbalization of words, all of which is important in their development.

As younger boys and girls become adept to the form of rhythmic activity introduced with a dance song, they enjoy the change of pace supplied by this song. The leader supplies a movement and during the last line designates another person to continue. The words are repeated, with new movements, without losing the rhythm or changing the tempo. The song is continued until all have had an opportunity to initiate a different movement. If a group of children seem to have difficulty relying on themselves to start a new movement, or cannot seem to think of another movement the teacher has only to suggest what might be done with a head, an eye, a "sitter." These songs do not require large open spaces, although they can be used with expansive movement. They can be used to initiate movement experiences in the security of the children's classroom or even at their desks.

This dance song puts emphasis on "I can do this." When working with small children at least in the beginning, we start and stop the song with each child. In this case, a child is designated to initiate the activity and time is provided for the child to think of a movement and then execute it. The same action song may be used to encourage cooperation, with groups of two or more children suggesting movements or ideas. When used this way, the response is faster, the group movements more ingenious, and the tempo increased. This dance song has also been used as a round and as a simpler folk-type circle dance.

THIS IS WHAT I CAN DO

Arr. *Joyce Eldridge*

This is what I can do. Ev - 'ry - bo - dy do it too.

This is what I can do. Now I'll pass it on to you!

I CAN MOVE

I can move my el - bows. So can you. I can move my el - bows. So can you.

I can move my el - bows. So can you. Show us an - oth - er part we can move.

"ME"

Willa Cwik

I've got a head and I've got feet, And they both be - long to me.
(arms)
(legs)

I've got a head and I've got feet, And they both be - long to me.
(arms)
(legs)

KEEP IT MOVING

Keep it mov - ing, keep it mov - ing, I've got a hand so keep it mov - ing.
(foot)
(knees)

Keep it mov - ing, keep it mov - ing, I've got a hand so keep it mov - ing.
(foot)
(knees) (them)

The three songs on page 167 provide opportunities for boys and girls to clarify the first- and third-person—I and we. When asked what "Keep it Moving" means, children make such responses as "Keep going. Don't stop! Continue. Go on. Increasingly. No end." This is a good way to develop vocabulary. Here also can be identification of body parts. Sometimes children enjoy another version of "Keep It Moving," adding one movement to another until various parts of their bodies are moving at the same time.

A song like "Discovering" provides young children with opportunities to explore various positions they can take. The surprise element of what there is to discover is very appealing. Note that the children are responding to directions and at the same time expressing movements in their own way.

"What Do You Want To Be?" is a good example of a dance song written by children to describe, in words, music, and movement, their wishes and dreams. There is also a game element involved in this type of movement song which appeals to youngsters.

DANCE SONGS ABOUT CONCEPTS

Is there a better way to reinforce concepts than to actually experience them? *How can a youngster know about fast, slow, down, and up unless he is made physically aware of these concepts?* The world in itself may mean little, but the experiencing of "fastness" or "upness" *results in learning that lasts.* Many of the dance and movement songs emphasize concepts and associations with ideas and are useful to all age groups.

"Up, Down, Around Song" emerged out of exploration of movement with a kindergarten group. We were working with our hands, finding out the many ways they could move.

Teacher: What can your hands do besides stay right here? Where could they go?
Children: Uppppp (stretching)—'way up here!
Teacher: Show me how high your hands can go up up up upppppp. Say up up up up as you make your hands go still higher up.
Can we make our hands go low? How would you do that?
Children: Down here on the floor.
Teacher:

Our hands can go up—high—
Our hands can go down—low.

Let's say it as we move. (Our chanting started to have tones, so a melody resulted).

Exploration began with different ways of moving the hands; the concepts emphasized were out–in, back–front, together–apart,

DISCOVERING

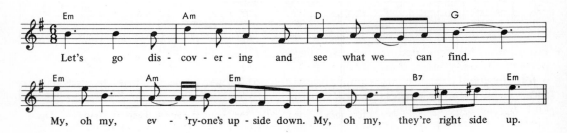

Let's go dis-cov-er-ing and see what we___ can find.___

My, oh my, ev-'ry-one's up-side down. My, oh my, they're right side up.

WHAT DO YOU WANT TO BE?

Arr. *Joyce Eldridge*

All: O what do you want to be——— when——— you grow up?

O what do you want to be when you grow up?

Ind.:   I want to be a scuba diver and go down low.
          So I can see what's in the sea.
All: What do you want to be when you grow up?
All: (Repeat)
Ind.:   I Want to be cowboy in the West.
          So I can rope a steer the very best.
All: (Repeat)
All: What do you want to be when you grow up?
All: (Repeat)
Ind.:   I want to be a pilot in a plane,
          So I can beat the railroad train.
All: (Repeat)
All: What do you want to be when you grow up?
All: (Repeat)
Ind.:   I want to be a fighter in the ring.
          So I can hear the gong go bing, bing, bing!
All: (Repeat)

UP, DOWN, AROUND SONG

Arr. *Clark W. Graves*

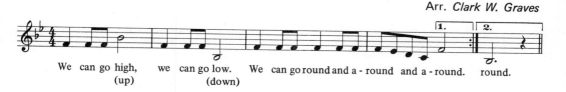

We can go high, we can go low. We can go round and a-round and a-round. round.
    (up)   (down)

fast–slow. This extended to use of other parts of the body—feet, shoulders, all of us.

On the next page are two similar dance songs using the same concepts of up, down, and around but extending them through ideas. It is amazing how quickly the ideas

and song develop when boys and girls get into the spirit of making associations.

When one class was asked: "What can you think of that involves the concepts of *up, down,* and *around,* and what ideas do you have that involve in some way all three

LET'S ALL GO TO THE FAIR

Judy Hogan

Let's all go to the fair. Let's all go to the fair.

Things go up, things go down, Things go round and round and round. Let's

all go to the fair. Let's all go to the fair.

WE'LL GO UP, UP, UP

We'll go up, up, up, We'll go down, down, down, We'll go round and round Like a spin-ning top.

of these concepts?" the children responded after discussion and work with the following verses and accompanying appropriate movements.

We'll go up up up,
We'll go down and up.
Our space ship
Goes around the world.

We're up up up,
We'll open up wide,
We'll go down down down
With our parachute.

I zing up high,
I zing way down,
I zing round and round
Until I *sting*—you!

We fly up North,
Turn right around.
Our birds say it's time
To fly down South.

Our smashing machine
Turns cans round and round,
Pushes them up
And smashes them down.

Let us spread our wings
And shake our tails.
Let us point our noses—
Round and round we will sail.

We'll turn round and round,
We'll turn down, up, down,
Our hoola hoop
Falls on the ground!

Squirt 'way up high,
Squirt 'way down low,
Squirt round and round
As our sprinkler goes.

We go round low,
We go round high,
We go round and round
Like clothes in a dryer.

Adaptations and new tunes emerge as children have opportunities to work on concepts and associated ideas and then dance them. A dance song never elicits the same responses; it produces a variety of types of movement ideas from various age groups. Adults also often respond to dance songs in a highly positive way. The simplicity of the song and movement possibilities often facilitates the development of concepts that are difficult to define verbally.

"How I Feel Is How I Move" was composed by a small group of students involved in discussing "feelings" in a Social Studies class. Several sessions in improvisation were instigated by the use of this song. One class turned its improvisations into a dance which they called "Happiness Is," using such words as proud, giggly, mean, mad, sad, embarrassed, cocky, scary, apprehensive, curious, bossy, silly, and sassy.

The portion of the movement song below was developed with older boys and girls but was adapted to young children to identify body parts and work with various concepts such as fast–slow, out–in, and left–right.

HOW I FEEL

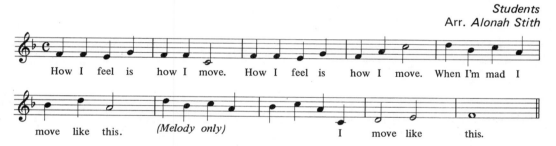

Students
Arr. *Alonah Stith*

SOMETIMES FAST, SOMETIMES SLOW

Sometimes we make up a melody such as "Listen to My Song" to go with a selected experience or with a certain movement that is to be emphasized for a specific purpose. This encourages the group to listen and helps establish controls, thereby increasing a child's feeling of self-confidence.

At other times the movement experience seems to dictate the melody. For instance, when one class was swinging, a natural

These songs illustrate how the teacher can take advantage of experiences as they present themselves, because she is with the children when these events happen. This group was excited about Hallowe'en, and they had quite a discussion about the day for "dressed-up faces." Their discussion finally centered on sounds. Together, they listed the sounds they could think of that suggested Hallowe'en, while the music

LISTEN TO MY SONG

SWINGING

rhythm established itself, and a tune seemed to develop on the spot. The song that evolved from that experience has been used for reviewing movement and for rhythmically responding to others. It has also provided many opportunities for taking turns and being a leader.

SONGS ABOUT OUR WORLD

Special seasons lend themselves well to movement and dance songs that have special meaning to children. In the fall children sing about leaves and Hallowe'en.

teacher recorded them on the board. Using as many of the sounds as possible, the class created the song. As they said the words and made the sounds, they caught a tune, which was also recorded. In their enthusiasm the experience was taken one step further; they decided that they would like to dance to their song (right there and then). This experience was enhanced by the movement interpretations that they worked out together.

"Pumpkin Time" is a dance song that is open-ended, providing countless opportunities for individual or group creative expression.

LEAVES

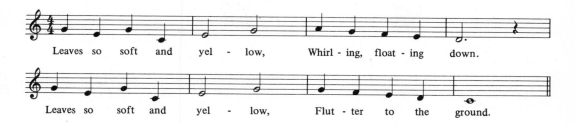

Leaves so soft and yel - low, Whirl - ing, float - ing down.

Leaves so soft and yel - low, Flut - ter to the ground.

THE WITCHES SAY "OO-OO"

Arr. *Mary Robinson*

The wit - ches say "Oo - oo." _____ The black cats

say "Me - ow." _____ The gob - lins laugh _____

"Ha - ha - ha," To - night is Hal - low - een. _____

PUMPKIN TIME

Abitanta and Jané

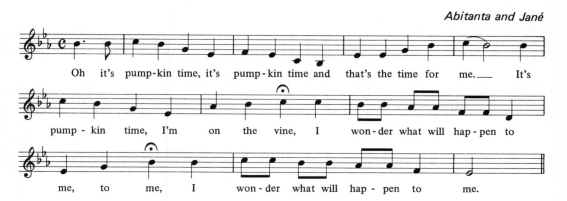

Oh it's pump-kin time, it's pump-kin time and that's the time for me.__ It's

pump - kin time, I'm on the vine, I won - der what will hap - pen to

me, to me, I won - der what will hap - pen to me.

Children respond to a line like "I wonder what will happen to me" with appropriate movement and lyrics such as these:

They threw us in a truck
And bumped us to town,
And now we're for sale for sale
And now we're for *Sale*.

They rolled me over
Next to my scarecrow friend,
And that's what happened to me to me,
And that's what happened to me.

They cut two eyes,

A nose and mouth,
And made a jack-o'-lantern out of me, of me,
A jack-o'-lantern out of me.

They cut us open
And made pies out of us,
And that's what happened to us.

They cut us open
And made pies out of us,
And that's what happened to us to us,
And that's what happened to us.

Winter brings snow and Christmas and holiday time.

I AM A SNOWMAN

I am a snow-man so round and so fat.
I'm wear-ing a fun-ny, flop-py old hat.
I love the cold, the wind, the ice.
But when it gets warm, it is-n't so nice.
When the sun shines, I can-not stay.
Slow-ly, so slow-ly, I soon melt a-way.

THE SNOW

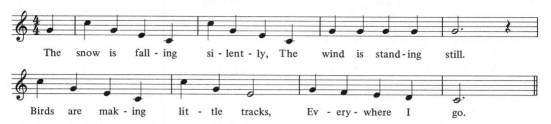

The snow is fall-ing si-lent-ly, The wind is stand-ing still.

Birds are mak-ing lit-tle tracks, Ev-ery-where I go.

Squirrels making larger tracks everywhere in the snow.
But I make great big tracks everywhere I go!

HAPPY HOLIDAY

Linda Smalline

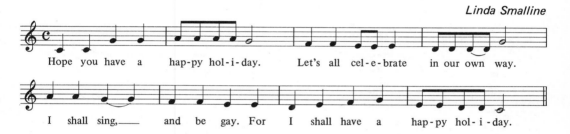

Hope you have a hap-py hol-i-day. Let's all cel-e-brate in our own way.

I shall sing,— and be gay. For I shall have a hap-py hol-i-day.

And then there is spring:

NOW THAT IT IS SPRINGTIME

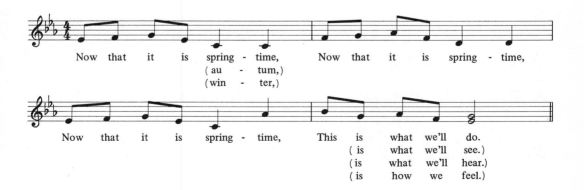

Now that it is spring-time,   Now that it is spring-time,
   (au - tum,)
   (win - ter,)

Now that it is spring-time,   This is what we'll do.
      (is what we'll see.)
      (is what we'll hear.)
      (is how we feel.)

We have many dance songs about animals. "Keeper of the Zoo" was made up after a field trip to a zoo. Boys and girls move around the room doing any movement of locomotion (skip, polka) singing the song until one child goes into the center of the group on the words "see see see." He then performs the movement of an animal and calls out the animal's name. All others follow the movement. The song is repeated with a new zoo-keeper each time. Adaptations of this song include "Man in the Pet Store," "Ranger in the Park," "Curator of the Museum," and "Commander of the Space Ship."

"I Have a Little Donkey" provides an opportunity for the teacher to solicit new ideas and concepts describing an animal. We have also substituted other animals' names.

"The Puppet Song" not only provides for identification of moving parts but reviews movements that have been learned. In addition, parts of this song emphasize the control factor ("still as can be").

We find it fun to be a part of a band. Sometimes we make the sounds of the instruments as we parade.

KEEPER OF THE ZOO

Arr. *Alonah Stith*

I HAVE A LITTLE DONKEY

Karen's Song
Arr. *Alonah Stith*

THE PUPPET SONG

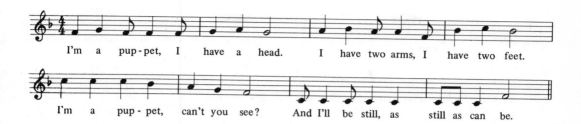

I'm a puppet, I shake my head.
I shake my arms, I shake my feet.
No more shakes left in me —
I will be still, as still as can be.

I'm a puppet, I bend my knees.
I bend elbows, I bend my back
No more bends left in me —
I will be still, as still as can be.

LET'S MARCH

Arr. *Elizabeth Sutherland*

2. Let's strut like the leader in the band.
3. Let's beat like the drums in the band.
4. Let's toot like the horns in the band.
5. Let's crash like the cymbals in the band.

The movement song "You Can" is useful for groups of older boys and girls. The tempo is fast and the song is readily adapted to group work and may be used in a variety of ways. When *using movement,* it calls for following different leaders or different groups performing a particular movement.

YOU CAN

To the beat of   the mu - sic   you can   *(movement)*

To the beat of   the mu - sic you can   *(movement)*   To the beat of   the mu - sic you can

(movement) -

This song has also been used to illustrate instruments in a symphony orchestra through sound and movement. Children decide on the instrument they will play, and then move and make the sound of the instrument when cued in by a conductor. The possibilities of varying the content and thus the movements are limitless—we can use such lines as

When we visit the waterfront we see (hear) ...
When we visit the farm we see (hear) ...
When we go to the fair we see (hear) ...
When we're caught in a snow storm we feel ...
When we take our test we feel ...
When our team wins we ...

Not only do children enjoy the minor key of "We're a Pond of Water," but they wait almost breathlessly for the rock to disturb their stillness. The element of anticipation adds to interest in such a song, and shaking and vibrating characterize the children's movement. Other ideas can also be tried that focus on contrasts in feeling.

"Catch a Star" serves as a quieting-down or relaxing song—providing a time when the children can catch their breath, move easily, and just dream about riding a star.

No matter where we live, there is hardly a place without construction underway. The sounds, the work, the equipment, and materials, as well as wondering what is being made hold fascination for children. Songs about construction can help children imagine the movements of caterpillars, piledrivers, drills, air hammers, and tractors. It is also fun to create the sounds they make.

The open-ended dance song on page 180

THE CIRCUS

The   cir - cus,   the   cir - cus,   I'm   go - ing   to the   cir - cus.   The

cir - cus, the cir - cus, Oh, what do you think I'll be? (see.) I'll

be a jug - gler, jug - gler, jug - gler, Oh that's what I will be, I'll

see the hors - es pranc-ing, pranc - ing, pranc - ing, Oh that's what I will see.

WE'RE A POND OF WATER

ACEI Workshop—Ohio

We're a pond of wa - ter stand - ing ver - y still.

Some - one threw a rock in and now we're not so sti - - - - ll.

CATCH A STAR

I want to go up, up in the sky, and catch a star as it floats by.

I'd ride my star all o - ver the sky and look down at you as I ride by.

has provided opportunities for creative expression in relation to what we see and hear. Children respond vividly to the idea of something falling and smashing.

In an experience involving a train, one person (or several) as "engines" start chug-

ging around the room, stopping in front of the child whose name is sung in the song. Singing "choo-choo" or making any appropriate sound or signal, the engine performs any movement he can think of for the other boys and girls to follow. At "All aboard,"

FOURTH AND MAIN

Willa Cwik

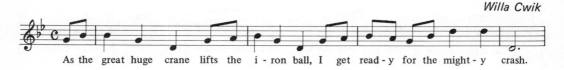

As the great huge crane lifts the i-ron ball, I get read-y for the might-y crash.

Then they let it drop on the old brick wall, And the tum-bling piec-es fall and smash!

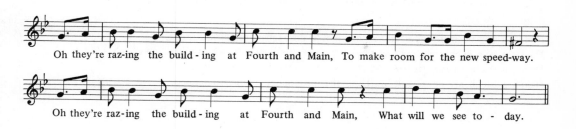

Oh they're raz-ing the build-ing at Fourth and Main, To make room for the new speed-way.

Oh they're raz-ing the build-ing at Fourth and Main, What will we see to-day.

the engine turns around and the individual named hooks on and becomes a caboose. The train moves on to another boy or girl. The song is repeated, and another caboose joins the train. This action is repeated until all are included in the train, each having had an opportunity to be the engine.

Other possible variations for the train song are the following:

Here comes the school bus
Bumping down the street,
Stopping at the corner
To take us all to school.
Hurry up hurry up hurry up

Here comes the jet
Zooming through the air,
Stopping at the airport
To take (child's name) aboard
Z-z-z-z-ooooo-m-m-m-m-m-m-m-m

Here comes the fire engine
Racing down the street,
Watch out, kids
Out of the street!
EURRRRRRRRRRRRRRRR!

This is the space lab
Whizzing through space,
Recording scientific facts
For all to use.
Blip Blip Blippp

HERE COMES THE TRAIN

Here comes the train Chug-ging down the track,

Stop-ping at the sta-tion to take *(Child's name)* back. *Fine* Choo-choo, choo-choo, choo-

choo, choo, choo, choo, choo, choo-choo, choo-choo, "All a-board!" *D.C. al Fine*

Additional dance songs for boys and girls follow.

INNER CITY BLUES

Phyllis Borucki
James Raines

There's a drip in my fau-cet and it hits like this___ Splash, splash, splash, splash, splash.

There's a squeak in my door and it sounds like this—squeak, squeak, sq-sq-sq.
There's a hole in my window and the wind comes through—whoosh, whoosh, wh-wh-wh.
There's a shade on my window and it moves like this—flap, flap, fl-fl-fl.
There's a cat in my house and he chases the rat—pounce, pounce, po-po-po.

THE TEXAS COWBOY

Jane Murphy

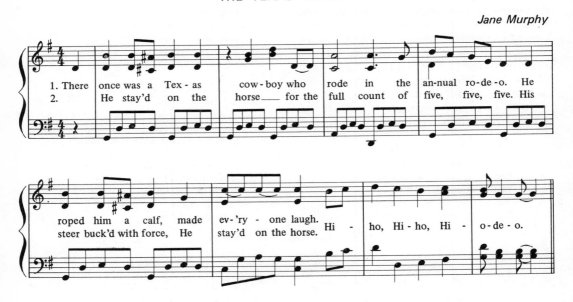

1. There once was a Tex-as cow-boy who rode in the an-nual ro-de-o. He
2. He stay'd on the horse___ for the full count of five, five, five. His

roped him a calf, made ev-'ry-one laugh. Hi - ho, Hi - ho, Hi - o-de-o.
steer buck'd with force, He stay'd on the horse.

THE KENTUCKY RACE

Arr. Judy Hogan

Here they come, here they come, here they come to the gate.

Hors-es and rid-ers in green and in red.

182

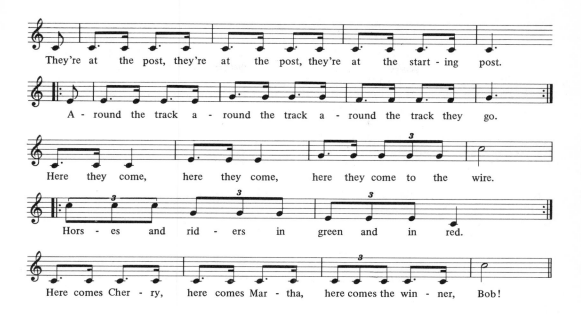

They're at the post, they're at the post, they're at the start-ing post.

A - round the track a - round the track a - round the track they go.

Here they come, here they come, here they come to the wire.

Hors - es and rid - ers in green and in red.

Here comes Cher - ry, here comes Mar - tha, here comes the win - ner, Bob!

BLAST OFF

Willa Cwik

We're strapped in at the launch - ing pad, The count - down has be - gun. The

go sig - nal flash - es, Five, four, three, two, one, zero, Blast off___ Blast out___ Blast a -

way gone! Blip, Blip, *(Repeat:* Blip . . . .

Weightlessness serenity quietness faster than fast. In or - bit,

(Spoken) (Sing)

All A. O. K. In or - bit.

SONGS TO SAY HELLO AND GOODBYE

Ways of greeting are important to groups. Frequently it is important to greet a group in a new and different way. Now and then a dance song is just what is needed for this.

Sometimes we use this in a double circle for motion—one group moving clockwise, the other counterclockwise. When we sing "There are many ways to greet" we all stop and greet the person next to us.

The "Goodbye Song" is a dance song that was originated for the purpose of terminating work with a particular group of children. It was used so that they could say goodbye to one another, to the teachers, and to the audience. It also served as a way to engage the total audience of adults in joining the dance activity of the boys and girls.

Goodbye in other languages:

Adieu—French

Addio—Italian

Adios—Spanish

Vaarvel—Dutch

Ohio—Okinawan

Shalom—Hebrew

Cheerio—British

Aloha—Hawaiian

auf Wiedersehen—German

Do Svedanya—Russian

PETER'S SONG

Peter

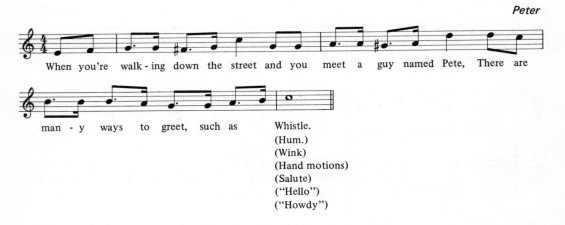

When you're walk-ing down the street and you meet a guy named Pete, There are man-y ways to greet, such as

Whistle.
(Hum.)
(Wink)
(Hand motions)
(Salute)
("Hello")
("Howdy")

GOODBYE SONG

Arr. *Ruth Korman*

There are man-y, man-y, man-y ways to say good-bye. There are

man-y, man-y, man - y ways to say good - bye. There are

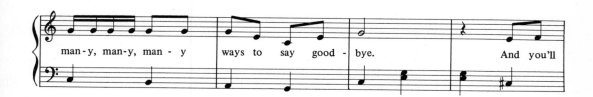

man-y, man-y, man - y ways to say good - bye. And you'll

hear it where - ev - er you go. Good -

bye, good - bye, good - bye, good - bye, good - bye. You will

hear it where - ev - er you go. Good - go.

As can be seen from the contents of this chapter, there are many lively dance songs that can be used and even created by children in their guided attempts at discovering dance movement. *Obviously, the best ones are not to be secured merely from a presentation such as given here; rather, they emerge as teachers capture spontaneous experiences of children in creative rhythmic movement activities.* As the children chant, tunes often evolve spontaneously.

10

Helping Children to Relax

Moments of relaxation are essential for children. Everyone needs to "let loose," but we also need to level off and quiet down following periods of intensive learning experience. The strain of mental concentration, physical exertion, and everyday school organization makes this especially necessary for children. Periods of relaxation, in addition, provide desirable breaks in a session or in a day; they give teachers an opportunity to "talk things over" with the group, and can act as starting points for new activities.

SENSING AND RESPONDING USING IDEAS, ASSOCIATIONS, AND FEELINGS

With younger children the approach to relaxation may be almost entirely *ideational*. This type of approach is used primarily to help children gain relaxation of the entire body, as well as to get the group as a whole calmed down. It can also be used to help bring a group together as a unit again after members have been exploring movement in individual ways. In using the ideational approach, the teacher sets the mood both by voice and manner, suggesting ideas, associations, and feelings that evoke a

relaxed mood. In response to suggestive or descriptive words, each child reacts in his own way—*the tone of voice and tempo of speaking are as suggestive as the words themselves.*

The short period of relaxing involves body control and provides release of tension. Some of the ideas for relaxation that have been used effectively with younger children include becoming balloons slowly deflating, or balloons blowing up and floating away; elastic bands shriveling up; faucets dripping; salt pouring from a shaker; smoke rising, whirling, and disappearing; icicles melting; bubbles getting smaller; ice cream cones melting; and feathers rising, floating, and falling on the ground. Some of these approaches are described below.

Clothes on the Line

The children sometimes choose the article of clothing they wish to be and respond with movement to the following verbalization:

I am a shirt hanging on the line. There are clothespins holding me up. The wind is blowing and it blows and blows and blows, and it tugs at the clothespins. All of

187

a sudden one of my clothespins falls out (and one of my arms falls down) and there I am, left with just one clothespin. The wind blows and blows and blows some more until all of a sudden it pulls the other clothespin out, and then the wind blows me right down to the ground.

Ice Cream Cones

I am a big, big, big ice cream cone, and it is a very, very hot day. I begin to melt. And I melt and melt and melt, and that makes me grow smaller and smaller and smaller until finally I just melt away into a little spot on the floor.

Kittens

My, my—what do we have here? Tiny kittens all curled up. As I come to look, they open their eyes and stretch one paw, then another, and then their backs stretch. Those cuddly kittens tuck in their paws and just quietly curl up again and go off to sleep.

Quiet Music

I listen to a music box or quiet music; sometimes I close my eyes, and just think my own private thoughts. I respond in my own ways—sometimes I move and sometimes I just listen and dream.

QUIET SONG (Relaxation)

Alonah Stith

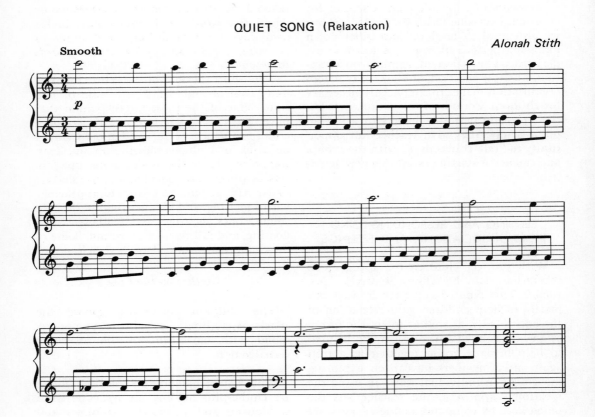

Snowman

Ho, ho, hum, hum, hum. I am a snow-man, disappearing by the minute in the hot sun. One arm gone, now two arms gone. And plop, there goes my head. My middle melts; my knees melt, too. I'm all gone. All but my funny hat.

Dandelion Puffs

Just look at this field—it's all covered with dandelion puffs. Look at their soft, puffy heads moving just a little. I'm going to walk through this field and blow off these beautiful puffs and watch them float away, away from here.

Seagulls

I am a seagull, and I'm flying over the sea. I gently glide and softly swoop and sail and swoop right down to the sea.

Pancake Syrup

I am syrup in a big, big pitcher. But the pitcher starts to tip and I begin to run slowly because I am so thick. It takes me a long time to reach my pancake, but when I do I spread all over it and then I stick.

I Am Heavy, I Am Light

I am making my whole *self heavy*—I can feel heaviness in my feet, arms, back, and even in my tummy. No one could even pick me up. Now I am feeling *light, airy,* and soft as a breeze. I am letting go. My head feels as though it might just come off and blow away. I feel as though I don't even have a backbone. I am *so* limp and relaxed and light.

TAKING CUES FROM CHILDREN

Occasionally children suggest ideas for relaxing. When this happens, we try to follow the suggestions. Boys and girls are encouraged to use ways of their own choosing.

Sheila suggested that we turn ourselves into faucets and drip away.

> The faucet drips and blips all day.
> If it doesn't stop it will blop away.

Now and then we all discover something that can serve this purpose. For example, after watching a beautiful snowfall and talking about different kinds of flakes and trying them out in movement, the "Snow-flakes" poem just happened. Throughout that winter this particular group of children were eager to relax using *their* idea of the snowflakes.

Snowflakes

From behind a cloud one wintry day
Some little snowflakes came to play
They floated high, high up in the air
So high folks couldn't see them there.
They drifted contentedly round and round
'Til Richard said, "Let's float on down."
So first came Elspeth and then came Robin
And Mia and Martha, gently bobbing.
Then Norton and Helen and all the rest—
The snowflakes floated their very best
'Til gently and quietly on the ground
They finally settled without a sound.
And when folks pass them by they say,
"What a lovely snow we've had today."

A variety of approaches to relaxation have been given. For elementary school children it seems highly desirable to seek balance, to change the pace, to avoid pressure, to be able to accept and approve each child, and above all to have a good time. A teacher's sensitivity to the group (and to individuals) is essential. *Helping children to be happy, to relate to each other and to the group, is basic to positive mental health factors.* And relaxation "activities" can be just as important to learning creative rhythmic movement as is participating in a vigorous dance.

IV

Elements of Dance

This section is concerned specifically with the *space, time, force,* and *sound aspects of movement.* Knowledge of these interdependent elements helps us to respond in unique ways to movement because within them there is organization and opportunity to use movement specifically in various forms of expression and communication.

As we examine the language children use to describe themselves moving, we find that they tend to establish different categories. Words such as tall–small, low–high, in–out, much–little, forward–backward, and straight–curvy all seem to characterize *space.* Words such as fast–slow, even–uneven, and long–short are used to describe some of the ways movement occurs in *time.* Still other words such as strong–weak, stiff–relaxed, heavy–light, smooth–jerky, tension–release, and continuous–sudden tend to characterize *force* or *energy.* In addition to those already mentioned, other words like loud–soft, beat, meter, accompaniment, and percussion are associated with *sound.*

We recognize the interdependency of these terms when we think about movement and rhythm. For example, the gallop is a movement in some direction (space); we gallop at a certain speed or tempo (time) ; we add a burst of energy to the first part of the gallop and give a special heavy quality (force); and we hear our feet gallop (sound). This section will describe each of these elements separately so that we can extend our understanding of each of them in dance.

11

Conquering Space

Space is infinite, crowded, endless, and empty. In this chapter attention will be given to space as it enhances, relates, and gives purpose to our ways of using movement in dance. We are concerned with how we feel in space, how we use various concepts and amounts of space, as well as how we design with or in space.

SPACE IS TO BE USED

What an extraordinary experience it is when boys and girls master the igniting, controlling, and propelling power to command their bodies to take flight, to soar, to go down under, to squeeze around, and to weave in and out of space! Space is their world to conquer. Children's perceptions of space are fascinating; those of each child depend on individual experiences. Many city children tend to think of space as *up;* those living in crowded developments often think of space as *in* and *through;* those living near mountains refer to it as *up* and *down;* rural children often refer to space as *around, over,* and *through.* Regardless of early spatial impressions, children soon become aware of amounts and dimensions of space that are needed for movement. They develop spatial aware-

ness as we provide opportunities for them to explore their *own* spaces. The following is an illustration of one approach.

"Where are you in 'your' space? See what you can do with yourself to take up that space! What is the smallest amount of space you think you can fill. How *much* space can you fill?" (Such questions elicit interesting informative responses. *Smallness,* for example, has different connotations for different children. Suggestions as to how far out, in, down, up, and around one can go emphasize awareness of space rather than the movement involved in apprehending it; children do not have to think about movement as such—that comes automatically as they respond to concepts about space). "Take a good look at where you are now and explore all of the ways you can *go out* from where you are. When the music stops, you stop. See how many ways you can find to "go out' and how many different parts you can make 'go out.' Where is 'out'? Instead of telling us, show us 'out.'

"What is the most space you think you can cover where you are without leaving your spot?" (Children soon become aware of themselves going *through* and *in* space. They try covering space while sitting, on knees, on sides, on back, lying, and standing. Doing this in small groups later leads to considerations of two- and three-dimensional space.) "Without using your arms or legs, how much space can you use? Does it feel any different to you when you seem to be almost on your head rather than on your back?" (When working with others on spatial awareness, balance and distribution of weight is also understood.)

"Can you put one knee in the center of your space? How far away from the knee can you make your other parts go? When you find that something feels good, *freeze*. Notice the empty space around and within you. Now, starting from your two knees, what can you do in the space remaining? This time, instead of the two knees,

put two of something else in the middle of your space—fix your knees or glue them there, then start moving through any area of your space you wish. When you feel you are almost ready to lose your balance, stop and hold your position."

SPATIAL AWARENESS

Empty Space

"Look at the space around you—do you see empty space? What is empty space?" (The responses to this question have often been: "Where I am not," "Where there is no one or nothing," "Air," "Places

without people or buildings or chairs or things," "Out there," "Up there," "Through here," "Down under there.") "Show us where there are some empty spaces *around you,* within you. Can you find any empty space in parts of your body? When you move different parts, can you discover some empty space?" (Children often respond "Under arms, between legs, between fingers, in ears, nostrils, between head and shoulders when head is bent, and missing teeth.") "Is there any difference in the space you have just located? Some is smaller and some is larger. Make yourself so that you see just a very small crack of space somewhere between one part of your body and another. Now start moving slowly until you see more and more space, until the crack is gone. Play a game by changing those bits of space to much more space. Can you look through or go through the space you have created?"

"Try putting your thumbs together and then your fingers, leaving some space to look through. What could we call this space?" ("Holes, circles, glasses, telescopes, cameras.") "Make some holes with different parts of your body. Make little ones and big ones. Now, see if you can put other parts of your body through these holes. Sit on the floor and try the same thing. Does this feel any different than working with cracks of space? Find another person to make holes with and see what you can do with the space in your holes. Instead of talking with your mouths, talk with your feet, hands, backs, sitters, use any parts you can and see what happens to them. Change your *holes* back to *cracks.* What is the smallest crack you can make within you? Try with small parts and big parts of you. How large can two of you make your crack, staying in one of your spaces? Can you make one part of your crack very large and the other part very small—so that we see small and large amounts of space?"

Children make wonderful discoveries as they try to maneuver space. Beautifully controlled movement is observed as they become more and more involved. When one class felt *empty space* between their legs we talked about upside-downness and how different it makes the space, and in fact the whole world, seem.

When a large number of children start moving around a room, or going from *here* to *there,* things are bound to happen. Our game of "Empty Spaces" has been an approach used to avoid the problems that occur as groups move as well as to make children aware of space as not only a concept but a real thing. They tend to identify "inner space" as the area near the middle of a room or where most of us happen to be, and outer space as the space "out there" where most of us are not at the moment.

Empty Space Game

The children are all called into "inner space" and are asked to see that there is some space between each person. One person—a child who can control his movements and can listen—is invited to move through all the empty spaces he can find, without touching another person. (When we touch, we find that the space is not empty and we discuss this.) The purpose of this game is to keep spaces empty and to judge whether or not it is possible to go through the spaces without touching. The child continues through empty spaces and others are invited to join him, finding other empty spaces. This procedure is continued until the whole group is moving through empty spaces. Sometimes the spaces are between legs, under outstretched arms etc. To add variety, sometimes we call for only those having a birthday this month, or those with glasses, or those with hair ribbons, etc., to investigate empty space. This game pays off because children challenge themselves and soon find that they can move through less and less space quickly, using a variety of movements. (The rate at which they can move through specific "amounts" of space, of course, affects the time and force of their movements.) Once this concept is established, children are free to use every available space within a room; no longer do they need to move in the same direction or in the same way. *With control of self, all available space may be used.*

There are times when children may be put in a space that is too large or small for them to handle. This is one reason for starting movement exploration in one spot or in "my space" and helping children relate to and become aware of space; they need help with handling their freedom in space. In addition to the concept of empty space, we also talk about the necessity for rules to avoid collisions of bodies in space. In this regard, such things as traffic accidents can be discussed. Finally the children agree upon their own set of rules.

LINES IN SPACE

Everywhere we look we see things occupying space—in lines and shapes. Often we react to that which is occupying a space by the way it affects us. We respond to closeness, highness, smallness. We ourselves are shapes in space; we occupy space; our bodies consume space; and as our bodies move we can make many (human) lines and shapes. "How can we make a straight line of ourselves?" What can you do so that you look like a line?" Exploring questions like these helps children discover that they can make their own shapes take many forms in space. They get themselves into some almost impossible positions. "Can you make a straight line any other way? Let's see how many straight lines you can make in space with just parts of you." Depending on the age group, this

is where we have experienced and added to understanding of the concepts of vertical, horizontal, and parallel. We move our lines so that we become flowing human lines moving through space. As we do this, we find that all lines are not straight, that many are curved or bent. We discuss how, with our whole bodies or with parts of them, we can feel and look different when we curve our lines rather than concentrating on straightness. Working with others, we try to find many ways of extending and combining straight or curved lines. When we work with linear qualities we try to transform ourselves into such lines as:

thin	meandering	jagged	broken	sharp
cracked	flowing	spiral	heavy	slanted

We make associations with concepts. For instance, broken lines made one group think of the rickrack on Shirley's dress, bolts of lightning, a wooden fence, Indian designs, bleachers, zig-zags, jungle gyms, lookout towers. All these ideas depend on how we perceive things. We become sensitized to lines and look at the outside world to find linear qualities in our environment: There are *man-made lines* in buildings, machinery, furniture, vehicles, and *natural lines* in rocks, stones, leaves, trees, water, rainbows, animals, clouds, and flowers. We develop a better understanding of lines as we discover them, discuss them, and then respond to them by moving ourselves. It is interesting to see that children respond kinesthetically when various types of lines are discussed; they look up, down, move sideways sometimes almost to the point of losing their balance. We find it interesting to bring into class things that have lines to which we can move—corkscrews, pencils, yarn, fabrics, toys, ropes, pictures, lace, magazines, patchwork quilts.

Among other things that can serve as aids to our understanding of lines are books. A favorite book is Solveig Paulson

Russel's *Lines and Shapes: A First Look at Geometry* (New York: Henry J. Walck, 1965), which has stimulated many kinds of movement and dance experiences. Other books that have been found helpful include Irma Hovan's *Look Again* (New York: The Macmillan Company, 1971), Mannis Charosh's *Straight Lines, Parallel Lines and Perpendicular* (New York: Thomas Y. Crowell Company, 1970), Ann Samson's *Lines and Spines and Porcupines* (Garden City, N.Y.: Doubleday & Company, Inc., 1969), and Leonard Kessler's *I Made a Line* (New York: Grosset & Dunlap, Inc., 1962). Some of the dances developed from such sources in our attempts to sense and respond to linear qualities include "The Shortest Distance Between Two Points," "What the Funny Squiggly Lines Said to the Sad Dotted Lines," and "Curvy Curvy is My Name—What's Yours?"

SHAPES IN SPACE

Shapes are discovered during experimentation with lines; *when lines enclose space, shapes occur.* If one extends both arms sideward, shoulder high, they make a straight line. Moving the arms forward until the fingers touch makes a shape of roundness or ovalness. Not only are we lines in space, we are shapes in space and as we move, our shapes change. We become more aware of space as we transform ourselves into circles, cylinders, ovals, spheres, arcs, triangles, squares, pyramids, and irregular forms of two and three dimensions. We realize that we feel different when we make angular shapes than when we make circular or arc shapes.

As the children experiment with various lines and shapes that they design in space, associations that come to mind from shape discoveries can be discussed. For instance, one group was asked to make themselves long and to stretch every part they could to feel longness, then to find at least five ways to make themselves long and to end up in a long shape which they could describe. The following associations were recorded: one-mile road, tightrope, hot dog, snake, stick of licorice, dinosaur, city building, a bridge, elastic band, and Dodie's hair.

When we move in space we take up space. When we move in different directions and within varying amounts of space the body can make different shapes. We can make little shapes in a big space, or we can make big shapes in a little space. We can visualize and feel the space around the shapes we make. We can internalize the experience of moving as shapes in space as we have opportunities to experiment and relate to space. The following is an example of guiding questions:

"Can you visualize a big circle on the floor around you, like a big capsule or a big roundness? Enclose yourself in the capsule and leave plenty of empty space around you. How does it feel to be in your capsule? Can you touch the top of it? Now try touching the side. If you tried with your hands, now try with your feet. What kind of shape do you think you are making within your circle or capsule shape? Do it again and see. How far away from your eyes is the outside of your capsule? How far away from your toes? Can you move around inside of your capsule or shape? Now try moving around different ways, changing your own shape as you move. How long can you make your shape and still be inside your capsule? Now how small can you make the same kind of a shape? Does it look different, and does it feel different? Think about the kind of shape that you would really like to mold inside your capsule. What kind of shape would be interesting and fit into the capsule? When you have created your shape, "freeze" so that we can really take a look at the picture or form you have made."

Concepts take on meaning when children are asked to make themselves into

different shapes. They have been asked to make themselves *round*—to *feel* the roundness of a shape, *feel* that every part is round (wheels, the earth, manhole, ball); or flat (paper, pancakes, a dime, the floor); or to pull themselves *"in"* (pretzels, snails, cocoon).

It helps to have children respond to situations—for example, "You can be little or big—what kind of a shape will you be? You can be heavy or light—what kind of a shape will you be?" A study of the sea stimulated one class to make shell-like shapes with themselves. The shapes seemed to take on added meaning when feelings of roughness, smoothness, delicateness, hardness, and sharpness were added.

When open space within shapes is identified, a discussion has followed about *negative space*. In small groups the children have created shapes with empty spaces

between them—spatial awareness is sharpened when others can move through such empty or negative space made by human shapes. Sometimes children have crawled or traveled in space in various positions. This feels quite different than when they go through space standing up. Shapes can be connected, making the room a massive sculptural shape. This particular idea has instigated such student dance compositions as "Webs" and "Cavern of Stalactites."

Additional Approaches to Moving as Shapes

"Make yourself into a blob of clay—think of the blob of clay you worked with last week. Do to yourself what you did to the clay." (Boys and girls flatten, pound, roll, push and pull themselves.) "Feel like clay—now, start to feel as though you are growing into a definite clay shape. Try to grow into an abstract shape. When you have your sculptural shape, stay motionless." This is an experience showing how children can be helped to understand how form emerges. First-hand experiences in the "doing" clarify concepts of space for them.

It is intriguing to watch children devise shapes and to see where certain experiences lead them. Five girls were working with oval shapes. When they finally developed one that pleased them, it was too good an opportunity to pass up, so we all stopped and watched. Finally, the group worked out a poem describing these shapes.

> We are chicks about to hatch.
> Peck peck peck,
> Scratch scratch scratch,
> Soon our shell starts to crack.
> Peck peck peck,
> Scratch scratch scratch,
> *CRACK!*

Children are always fascinated with kaleidoscopes. One day we turned the whole room into a huge kaleidoscope and the class was asked to change their shape as it was turned. The music provided the signal for turning. When the music stopped the shape would fade away and then a new shape would form when it started again. Improvization resulted in the following: rubber tires rolling, snowflakes whirling, clouds and smoke floating, rainbows, and half-moons slowly disappearing.

When children are engaged in forming shapes, they often discover that *letters of the alphabet and numbers are shapes,* and that they can turn themselves into the first letter of their names or into short words, or make number combinations.

Another way of relating to shapes has been through shadows. "When you go home, find a spot where you can make some shadows—on the sidewalk, or in your house. Make yourself bigger in the shadow. Change yourself into all kinds of shapes and notice what happens to your shadow. See how it feels to be bigger—smaller."

Some children who had been to the Fair told us of their experience with the magic mirrors and the funny things the mirrors did to them as they looked at themselves. Our room was immediately transformed into the Fair with mirrors all around. Our windows became the mirrors, and we decided that one window would make us very very long and skinny, another would make us round and fat, another would make us tiny. The fourth window could make us any shape we wanted to be. This venture was captured in words.

There are splendid books about space and shapes, in addition to those discussed dealing with lines, which have been used as a point of departure for extending our work with moving shapes. Sometimes ideas from the stories can be translated into movement. Some of these books are Jeanne Benedick's *Science Experiences—Shapes* (New York: Franklin Watts, 1968), Jana Toban's *Shapes and Things* (New York: The Macmillan Company, 1970), and Kessler's *Are You Square?* (Garden City, N.Y.: Doubleday & Company, Inc., 1966).

Using a prop such as a jump rope, and letting the rope fall into a shape, or making a specific shape out of the rope, lends itself to many spatial discoveries and increases spatial understanding and awareness. The boys and girls can move inside it, move on the line made by it, see how close they can come to the outline of the shape without touching it, and try to move in and out of the shape in many ways. Two or three ropes can be put together and made into a large shape that several children at a time can work with. Again, the *feeling* of movement through space in defined areas helps children in their understanding.

With props such as ropes, nets, cardboard cartons, hoops, and even themselves, children can make obstacles, shapes, or stabiles and then move in, out, around, and through them. They learn about space in adjusting to differing amounts of it and working out how they can get themselves through some of the obstacles. When they try to "dance" through the obstacles it becomes even more difficult. Here body awareness, kinesthetic perception, and spatial awareness are evident. Human stabiles are particularly fascinating for children. In making static designs in space, they are helped in recognizing the negative space within the shapes they make. Interest increases when one person does the designing and fashions others into a large stationary shape. If a group has worked on stabiles in art, it provides an opportunity to sharpen artistic observations by reconstructing them through the medium of movement. Pyramid shapes can be made the same way. Once an entire class spontaneously designed a gigantic pyramid using various positions in movement—on heads, on hands, under, over, or through each other.

SPATIAL DESIGNS

The early part of this chapter has been concerned with the spatial designs of lines and shapes that were made by children moving in space. These spatial designs are discernible to the onlooker who follows the sequences our bodies make as we move. Also discernible are the paths made on the floor with our feet when we are moving in space. This portion of the chapter is concerned with these spatial designs.

Children call these spatial designs different terms—paths, floor patterns, pictures, tracks, routes, space trips, trails, feet charts. Throughout the following pages they will be referred to as *paths* or *floor patterns*. As children move through space they realize that they can translate to the floor any designs that they are capable of creating and then *making*.

Approaches to Developing Floor Patterns

"Suppose we think of ourselves as *points*. Locate yourself as a point on the floor. See that you are away from every other point (child) in the room. Think of yourself as the point of a pencil—if you moved like a pencil around on the floor, what would it make? Try and see what kind of designs (paths) you can make on the floor as you move in your space. Can you go back to where you started and make the same path again? This time move your point (you) in a circle and be sure you get back to where you started. Can you make a larger circle? Let's see. What other kinds of path or pictures can you make as you move on the floor? Try some. What could we call what we are doing? And where are you making patterns?"

Another approach is the following: "While you were skipping and sliding in the room something happened. Let's watch Ernie and describe what happened." (The children responded with such comments as "He's all together using himself," "His skip is nice and high," "He looks like he likes to slide and skip because of the way *he goes in and out*.") "Ernie, please do your combination again and see if you can go the same way again. You were making a picture of *in and out* on the floor that looked like this." (This is the cue for visualizing the pictures we make on the floor whenever we move.) "Suppose we try to make a picture on the floor as we move—try to remember your own picture."

Another initial approach to paths has been by making associations with snow, sand, chalk, or tar. "If we were out in fresh snow and started to run around, what would we see? Think of this room as covered with fresh snow—not even the squirrels have made a track. Let's have someone make a path in the snow. The rest of you follow with your eyes and then tell us what you see. Let's all make paths or tracks in the snow. What do we see? Suppose we had a chance to walk on sand that had just been washed by a wave—what might we see? Show us. What could we call what we are doing? Yes, sand tracks, footprints, sand patterns. Now let's do the same thing on the floor—what might we call what we are doing? *Floor patterns.* If you had been playing in the tar out there in the middle of the street and then had come in here and skipped around, just as you have been doing now, what would happen?" ("We'd get the floor dirty and make marks on the floor.") "What kind of marks? Yes, tar marks—whole foot marks.

That's what we call making a picture on the floor—a floor pattern. For instance, if Stanley had tar on his feet, he would make a floor pattern of tar foot marks, and the shape or design or pattern he would make would depend on how he moved in the room. Let's watch Stanley to see what kind of a design or pattern he will make on the floor as he is moving. Could anyone draw on the board the picture he is making?"

The egg-shaped picture that Stanley is making on the floor as he moves starts a discussion on different pictures or floor patterns that could be made. Children often trace with their fingers, toes, or arms, patterns they could make or that have just been demonstrated for them.

"Let's find a space on the floor that you call *your spot*. Take notice of where you are, and where you are in relation to the others in the class. Now take yourself for a walk and come back to where you are now —to exactly the same spot. Can you take the same walk again and think about the *path* you are leaving on the floor as you are walking, and come back to where you started? Let us see some of the walks you took. Could we call these walks you took *paths*? Who will show us the kind of a path he took? Try to remember exactly the path you took and we will follow you with our eyes. Now let's all make a path again using another movement. Remember to be careful not to get it too complicated because we want to try to remember exactly where we have been and the path that we have left on the floor. When you have your path well in mind take some of the colored chalk and draw your path on this brown wrapping paper.

"Let's all try some spirals now—see if you can get across the floor doing a spiral path. Think about how you can do that."

When these explorations are with seven- or eight-year-olds the paths should be simple in design and movement. However, with older children, the symbols may become complicated and may be anything from simple spirals to music symbols to elaborate designs of Indian lore, animals, bird flights, and geometrical figures. The latter make good material for floor patterns and often evoke interesting discussion, analysis, and "finding out more" about such symbols as parallelograms, trapezoids, hexagons, pentagons, cylinders, and cones. These explorations give the teacher an opportunity to point out the products of children, all of whom need the feeling of accomplishment or worth. For children who may not have developed as much motor coordination as others, floor patterns frequently present an opportunity for them to gain recognition.

Often boys and girls are asked to spread out over the room so that each has his own area, like an artist with a huge piece of canvas in front of him on the floor. Instead of having a brush and paint or a piece of chalk, their pictures are the paths their movements take on the floor. Time is allowed to refine the floor patterns. If the group is not too large, it can guess what designs each member is making. If a classroom is used, designs are figured out at seats or on the board and then space cleared on the floor for demonstrations.

A floor pattern can be made by a leader, who should make large, simple patterns so that everyone can follow. If there are too many in the group, it can be broken up into smaller groups, each with a leader. *Here we set up controls*: Leaders can go any place in the room as long as they are careful not to bump into another group and spoil their design. This puts responsibility on the leader and calls for judgment and reasoning. After this kind of an experience, sometimes it is helpful to recall the designs that have been made by drawing them out on the floor, or on the board, with chalk.

The creation of floor patterns can tie in with many other classroom studies. For example, in pursuing the topic of transportation one day, a class was divided into groups of from eight to eleven to see if they could work out floor patterns of a specific mode of transportation. One group of boys made the design, a rectangular-shaped boxcar. They started to move slowly around the room making rectangular floor patterns. The other children could not figure out why the smallest boy was making a zig-zag pattern in the middle of the rectangular shape; it turned out to be a boxcar with a lone cow.

Science studies can be tied in with the study of movement also. Stars, clouds, leaves, and animals can be used to stimulate the children's imagination and add to knowledge of movement and space. One group of fifth-graders worked in groups to identify constellations, and the frieze that they had made in art and that decorated the wall of their classroom became the stimulus for floor patterns. This made their study more vivid and meaningful.

Floor patterns have also originated from drawings, pictures, magazine advertisements, figures in linoleum, maps, and charts. When older children have been working strenuously on vigorous locomotor combinations, such as the polka or jig, the study of floor patterns can serve as a device for quieting them down and resting them. "While you are resting and getting your breath, suppose you look around the room and find a design or picture that might serve as a floor pattern." If they are in an open classroom, then the clock, window, or door is often the first pattern drawn; if they are in the playroom or gymnasium, the basketball hoop, basketball court, lines on the floor, or light fixture is usually the first thing interpreted in floor patterns. However, children have worked out such complicated designs as curtains with folds, patterns in the ceiling, a pencil sharpener, piano, ventilator, and bleachers.

Two books seem to have been favorites

and particularly helpful in our work with floor patterns: Elizabeth Griffen's *A Dog's Book of Bugs* (New York: Atheneum, 1967) has suggested countless paths of the cricket, cockroach, dragonfly etc. We have practically retold the story through our floor patterns. E. B. White's *Charlotte's Web* (New York: Harper & Row, Publishers, 1952) has also been a fascinating source for floor patterns. All patterns have not been as intricate as a real spider web, but we have made the floor patterns of "Web—Some Pig" and "Web—Terrific."

Some of the varied paths created by children and then translated into floor patterns have been: the path made by strikers walking in a picket line; paths of the bus ride home, and the paths made by skiers. Carefully watching and trying to capture graphically the path of a water skier provides quite a different pattern from that of a snow skier. Watching the Olympics and other sport events has also helped many children create varied movement experience designs.

Designs have also been found in fireworks, advertisements in newspapers, and magazine covers. Sometimes we just sit on the school steps and watch people or animals go by and then draw the different linear paths they make as they continue down the street. We have also watched aquariums to capture the paths of fish.

Field trips and holidays furnish additional ideas to be used to study path-making problems in space. A visit to an airport can stimulate an interesting discussion of airplane traffic and the paths involved, with the students' perception translated to the floor later in the classroom.

As developing floor patterns become a part of children's activities, designs and patterns in folk and square dancing are more easily followed. One group found no trouble whatsoever with the difficult folk dance pattern of the *grapevine twist when it was associated with a floor pattern of a figure eight.*

When we compose dances, we often chart our paths of movement. This not only helps us to remember movement sequences but often helps us to improve our designs as well. Understanding floor patterns helps children to both create movements in space and move through it.

Mobiles as Moving Paths

Older boys and girls respond well to mobiles, which are made up of lines and shapes in balance and in constant motion. Designing and then dancing mobiles not only adds to children's understanding of them but also adds to their awareness of spatial human relationships. Here are moving designs in space that invite groups to translate paths and shapes to the floor. Constructing mobiles and then working them out in dance provides vivid feelings and understanding; and it is fun to make mobiles come alive. Alexander Calder's mobiles, for example, have been lived and relived by children using movement to recall them. A Calder exhibit at the Guggenheim Museum in New York provided a fifth and sixth grade with an opportunity to study the spatial relationships in mobiles and to "move out" their interpretations. Mobiles and their interrelated moving parts provide understanding of the interdependency of spatial elements—*direction, levels, range and focus*—and they often furnish ideas for dances.

Planetarium Visit

Their previous study of mobiles led one class to relate a planetarium visit to the principles of moving bodies in space in a way that aided in better understanding of both the solar system and spatial elements. After the visit, the teacher's first question to the class was, "Does anyone remember how our earth moves in space?" James answered, "Well, I could show you if I had a sun to show revolution. I need to rotate as I revolve around the sun." Words soon gave way to movement and the entire class became involved in making a huge solar system of orbiting paths. This venture took several periods to work out and more and more space was needed. As the class added more planets and satellites, they ran out of people, so they had to recruit some boys and girls from another grade. The entire group was active in the planning, in making choices concerning who would be the sun, moon, planets, and their satellites, and then in working out their orbiting paths. Concepts had to be clarified as to rotation and revolution and the relationship of one moving body to another regarding time and space. As understandings sharpened, the group worked intensely to perfect their solar system. They were so proud of their efforts that they decided to put into a dance all that they had learned about an ordered universe. They felt good about themselves and eventually shared their dance with other classes and finally with the school PTA.

Many difficult concepts had to be grasped by the children in that class. There was first the *idea of rotation, or revolution;* then the planning of an ordered way of moving, rather than just random movements; there was relationship of one moving body to another regarding time, space, and distance, one from the other. Some arithmetic was involved. The primary purpose was to help the children gain more of an understanding of *an ordered universe.* Additional time was given to the use of movement to keep building larger concepts of this one idea of space. The potential in this type of learning is vast; the class could have gone on to study our galaxy and other galaxies in outer space and with movement, show the earth in relation to other bodies in space.

Other groups of older boys and girls have recharted some of the moon walks and created walks in imagined and yet unfounded bodies in outer space. Increasingly the new findings of space exploration are of great interest and seem to fascinate the young adolescent. This is an excellent area to use in motivating inquiry as well as in representing findings in aesthetic and exciting ways.

Directions in Space

When children have a background and understanding of many of their own ways of moving—when they feel that they can communicate easily with their bodies and use them readily, they have developed a movement language. When their movement responses are automatic—that is, when they can move freely alone and with others—then they can apply themselves readily to spatial elements. Primarily, up to this time emphasis has been given to *how and why children move,* and awareness of oneself in space and the changes that are made in body shapes during movement. *Now attention can be focused on direction as a spatial element.*

True, we have not been moving and dancing without emphasis of spatial elements, but our concern in this section is not on movement *as such* but on specific elements in space and how they give specificity to movement. *Direction* of movement is the line of motion that our body follows, such as forward, backward, sideward, or up and down. (Children often tend to think of up and down as high and low; this will be discussed in the next section—"Levels in Space.") Children label these as they develop awareness of space and its effect on their movements. In the beginning they often call "around" a form of direction, because they cannot seem to understand that it may be a combination of the other three. Youngsters often think of backward as "backing up." This takes more skill for them than going forward. Therefore, controls must be set up within the group to prevent collisions as the children change their directions.

The illusion of more or less space can be created as we find out directions we can move in space. Likewise, the quality of our movements change as we consciously imply particular directions (forward, backward, sideward, diagonal, and around). We realize that parts of our body can move in different directions—behind, side to side, in front all at the same time. As was indicated earlier, different body shapes, feelings, and associations result as part of our bodies can move in different ways, in different directions.

Direction affects movement. To illustrate, walk across the room, turn around, and walk back to where you began. This is a common procedure and one we ordinarily do not think very much about. But, now walk across the floor in a *forward direction,* consciously turn around, and with emphasis *walk back* to the point from which we started. Our movement has assumed a definite emphasis owing to the *direction* we have added. We walk down the street every day unaware of the space about us, but our walk often changes when we purposely walk toward a specific object, or concentrate upon arriving at a designated spot. The entire quality of our walk has changed.

There are many approaches that can be used to get at the effects of direction on movement. In small groups we have used the idea of "Follow the *Directional* Leader." Leaders can be given titles depending on the season of the year or specific situations—for example, drum major, Indian Chief, or Pirate. Sometimes, depending on the maturity and experience of the group, we have three or four leaders all starting with a different prearranged direction. Previous experience with spatial awareness contributes to groups' abilities to manipulate themselves in various ways using spatial directions. They can respond without interfering with other groups' space. Sometimes groups are able to go through their space in such a way that they can continue moving in the direction they were following—under, over, or around another group. From such experiences in which individuals are directional leaders, dance movements emerge and form becomes evident.

Some examples of directions given to groups starting their learning about directions in space follow.

"Start skipping or polkaing (or find another movement that fits this music) all over the room and when you meet another person *face to face,* keep on skipping (or whatever movement you were using), but *change your direction.* Continue doing this until you have skipped forward, backward, sideward (both sides), and around. Select a partner and the two of you do the same, changing directions as you meet other partners. Try also to find different ways of changing partner relationships as you change directions. Improvise upon your directions and movements." (This can sometimes be done in groups of threes and fours. Confine yourself in a small space area. Right where you are, keep moving continually but change the *direction* of your movements abruptly with each accent you hear from the sticks, percussion, recording, piano). "This time, to percussion accompaniment, all start moving in a forward direction any place in the room. When the accompaniment changes, change the direction in which you are moving, finding another movement or combination of movements. Add some kind of movement emphasis as you are changing directions. Use as much space as possible, but let us feel and see that you are really changing directions. Now try to work only on diagonals, going diagonally forward and diagonally backward, and see what interesting combinations you can make of just moving on diagonals."

"This time we will work on developing some kind of *mechanical* movements and continually change directions of the movement in and through space. Think about the precise directions you are using. Can you make your movements seem even more mechanical and the directions more pronounced? You decide if you want to be in groups or alone. If you want to work in groups, maybe some of you might like to do the same idea on the percussion and accompany the directional mechanical problem."

"Using the different directions in any sequence (including diagonal and around), find movements that feel right to you. Redo and make up a pattern based on changing directions and then share your pattern with us. (You don't have to be on your feet; you can move using any part of you just as long as you use direction.)" (Some children respond by using heads, hands, an elbow, a knee, etc. The most difficult seems to be with eyes looking back over the shoulders.) "Try to let your chin move you in a forward direction. Find other smaller parts of you to lead you in a real forward direction." (To calm the group down after this, we have initiated a discussion about the feelings the children had as various parts led them forward—this involves perceptions about quality and style.)"

"Which of the records you have heard would fit what we have been doing, and would help us exaggerate our movement? Improvise a series of any sequence of directions with different special parts of you leading, and *exaggerate*. What does improvise mean?" (This can also lead to the creation of poems, chants, and songs to accompany experiences of this nature.)

"Glue, or stick your feet, seat, or any specific part of you to the floor and now see how many directions you can continue to move in while you are 'stuck.' Donna brought in a good record today that we can use as accompaniment. I think you will like it."

"This time, *no feet on the floor,* move in directional ways on other parts of you. You decide whether or not you want to be stuck to the floor or not. See if you can find others moving in similar ways to you and join together."

"It's *backward time*—can you move continually in a backward direction until the music stops? Good for you—that's hard! Try for not a 'bump' in the bunch. Mike just suggested that everything we do today in dance we do backwards—how about it?"

"In small groups or alone if you prefer, think of all of the things you can that go from *side to side*. After you have thought of some, try the one you like best and make the sound accompaniment, if it has sound; after five minutes we will try to guess what everyone is doing." (Some of the things discovered included water sprinkler, windshield wiper, metronome, hammock, and dog's tail. When the same problem is done in a forward and backward direction, things that have sometimes been interpreted are a telephone dial, motorcycle, canoe, and crayfish. Forward, backward, and sideward has presented such ideas as checkers and chess, bulldozer, tennis ball, and a police woman directing traffic.)

"Show us how it feels to walk against the wind when it is blowing hard; by your movements, let us feel what direction the wind is coming from. Now let the wind blow you forward and show us how you feel."

"Find some magazine pictures that are clearly directional in design. Select one and bring it into class for a group workout." (The art teacher has helped by assisting children in making collages emphasizing directionality.)

"How would you like to have a *visual adventure?* Suppose we can't go in a forward direction—how could you and your friend make a dance study to this record? Remember, no feet, and you can't go in a forward direction. Can you make us want to look at you and feel it is exciting as we look at you?"

"Who would like to try to be our Directional Announcer? Now direct the class to go north, south, east, and west, with particular dance steps or movements." (Some examples are: "Go north—forward—with a schottische"; "Go south—backward—skipping"; "Go east—sideward—leaping." (This can lead to a variety of ways of improvising on the directions and movement announced.

"What's the funniest way you can go *backward* across the room? What's the bumpiest way you can go *forward,* around and around any place in the room? What's the stiffest way you can go sideward, from one side of the room to the other?"

"You are running or leaping as fast as you can go across the room—maybe we had better do this a few at a time. When these *cymbals crash,* you are *hit.* By the way you fall or stop, show us where you are hit and the direction from which the object came. What do you suppose the object might be?"

"Think of something that you *like very much.* Show us by your manner how you feel about it and that you are *backing away from it or it is going away from you.* Do this in groups if you like, or alone."

"In groups of six, make up a dance study based upon *directions.* Have a definite beginning and ending."

Levels in Space

The study of *levels* provides a splendid opportunity for boys and girls to experience what it might be like to be the tallest or the smallest in the class. The spatial element of levels calls for multisensory responses of thinking, feeling, and moving. Working with levels involves challenge, control, and awareness of self in relation to one's own spatial environment as well as in relationship to others in various dimensions of space. There is no particular sequence to developing an understanding of what levels can do to movement. Children often find

this a unique activity within itself; by becoming involved in levels of moving, they often sense the emergence of form and its importance to dance studies and compositions.

It goes without saying that when we move we employ levels in space, but we are now directing our attention to what happens when we use levels. When we move we can do so at certain levels. Children think of levels as *"high, low,* and *in between."* As they grow older they refer to levels as being "above the sky—out in space—to the depths of the ocean" (and maybe below) and to earth as being in between what is beyond —"up there and down there." This reflects children's common sense, which we respect. As was mentioned in the previous section on Directions, *up* and *down* might well be considered directional, but children recognize levels in their own way. Moving themselves up and down is considered by them to be different from taking themselves forward, backward, and sideward. Ideas involving the relationship between self, the floor, and the space above seems different, and at times more challenging, than do those that involve space in front and in back.

A few of the approaches that have been used to help children understand levels as related to moving in space are related here:

"Do you suppose for the next five minutes you could zip up your mouths and close off your fingers and instead of using these parts of you, 'speak' or respond with other parts of you? Answer these questions, each time a different way: Where is the sky? Where are the clouds? Where are the tree tops? Where is the moon when it is out? Now unzip your mouths—what about all of those things you were showing us?" (The movements mentioned at this point included reaching and stretching up, swinging high, high, going up, up, and rising.) "Was it all at a *high level?* Right where we are now let's all try to go as low as we possibly can. Can you go anywhere in the room this time, going as low as you possibly can? With only movement again—no mouths or fingers used —answer these questions: Where are the cracks in the floor? Where is the ocean bottom? Where are your feet? Where is the cafeteria? What's the difference in the way we responded this time and the way you moved?" ("Down—'way, 'way down; low, dropped, sank down, fell down, Yuck—I went flat.") "Did it feel any different? It certainly *looked* different! Show us all of the ways you can move at *low levels*—feel lowness as you are moving."

"Now let's see how fast you can change your levels and go from low to high, or high to low. If you can move at different high and low levels, is there any other level at which you can move? Is that a puzzlement? Well, if my ear is high and my ankle is low in relation to my ear, what might you call my hips in relation to my ear and my ankle? Or if the ceiling is high and the floor is low, what might we call that mural on the stage in relation to the ceiling and the floor? Good, Felicia—you made up a new big word for 'not high–not low.' " (Later the group had a separate session on making up new words to dance patterns and danced out words that had been made up.) "Let's get back to what we might call approximately one-half way—not high and not low. Sometimes we go high, other times we go low, and we can go in between. For our purposes shall we call this level 'In between'? But remember, 'in between' has to be in relationship to high and low. Suppose we get into threes and when we say 'levels' the three of you find something in the room that is high, low, and 'in between.' "

"What can you think of that can travel on all three levels?" ("Us, birds, planes, window shades, bleachers when they fold up.") "Suppose you take off and continually *change your levels* so that we see the three. Can you move and listen to the music at the same time and when the music stops

you stop at whatever level you happen to be? This time when the music goes high you go extremely high, when it goes low, you follow, and when in between see what you do, but stop immediately when the music stops. Good—let's do it again and really feel what you are doing, and feel the stop. Try to do the same, only this time with your eyes closed, try to sense where you are and how it feels. Start, with partners, at the same level, with one moving toward a high level while the other moves toward a low level. When you reach the extremes of high and low, *freeze*. If the two of you have another idea of how you might change level, try it. Remember that you have every part of your body to move, not just your arms or knees." (As the boys and girls work they become involved in creating fascinating spatial forms. The concentration is almost startling. Many new ideas emerge from the choices suggested.)

Vocabulary is emphasized in all aspects of dance activities. With levels a group was given the following. "Respond to the following words: *Arise, decend, ascent, elevate, flatten, upward, extending, vertical, horizontal.* What other kinds of words can you think of that we might move to another day?" The other day came, and this group worked their level-kind of words out in groups. (As has been implied throughout this book there is no end to where a suggestion might lead.) For instance one group worked out the way their idea of low-level kinds of words make them *feel*. Their words were *sneaky, slinky, dribbly, squiggly, crawly, wigglewormy.*

"Without using any hands or arms, put yourself on the floor at a low level. Slowly and gradually change your level until you are up as high as you can go. Let your toes, heels, knees, sitters, hips, shoulders do the 'level talking.' Try it again, thinking and feeling continually about changing levels and using many parts of you. When you reach an in-between or high level that feels right or different, then freeze."

"Start on your sitters and twist, turn, or spin around or propel yourself from low to high levels so that you go off your sitters. Some of us will have to spin harder to get up higher." "Hey, look at Randall and Mike, they are spinning on one knee—look at them go. They look like one of those *Gyra things.*" "Do you mean Gyroscopes? Suppose we try what Randall is doing, and then you could find other parts of you that would spin you in space as you changed levels gyroscopically. Look this word up in the dictionary when you get back to your classroom."

Dance songs are often used or created to review or to intensify the concept of levels. From such an experience—the idea of contrasting highs and lows, using a giraffe and an ant—a third grade worked out its version of what they thought Mr. Giraffe *looked down on.* The dance song that resulted follows.

"Boy, what's happened to you today? You seem all charged up like dynamos jittering all over the place. Let's jitter as fast as you can—faster, faster, harder, harder, and freeze. Do you know what the word *disintegrate* means?" Tony suggested "fall apart," and Debra said, "get undone or pull apart, go to pieces?" "Well, let's do as Debra and Tony have suggested when you hear the

MR. GIRAFFE

Arr. *Marie Hunter*

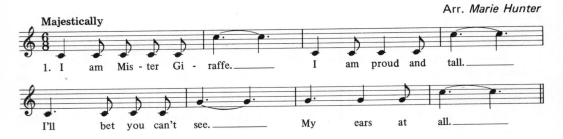

1. I am Mis-ter Gi-raffe.____ I am proud and tall.____

I'll bet you can't see.____ My ears at all.____

2. I am Mr. Giraffe.
   I am proud and tall.
   I can look around.
   And see it all.

3. I am Mister Giraffe.
   I am proud and tall.
   I am looking down.
   On something that crawls.

MR. ANT

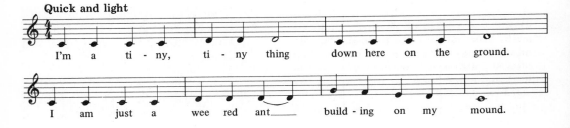

I'm a ti-ny, ti-ny thing down here on the ground.

I am just a wee red ant____ build-ing on my mound.

word *disintegrate*—we'll just fall apart. But when you disintegrate or fall apart stay that way without even moving a muscle. Start at any level you wish and we will play the bongos and steel drum as you keep moving at different levels. When you hear the word *disintegrate* you do just that on whatever level you are and remember to stay that way until we start playing the bongo again." (This was a controlling factor helping them to "hold" their movements and a fun way to work on levels while trying to calm down the group.)

"Suppose that your world was *upside down* and you were you in it. How would you feel and how do you think you would move or what would happen to you in your space in your *upside down world?* Let's be concerned with the actual feeling and moving—not how you look. Show us." We had a hilarious session, in which we experienced feelings of weightlessness as we tried to show which way was down and up, and how to "level off." All of this gave us material to work out for a dance which this fifth grade called *Topsy Turvy World.*

An Episode on Levels

The following is an excerpt from the recording of a demonstration tape, showing the relationship of movement and art. The emphasis of the demonstration was on spatial aspects, of which one part concerned levels.

Teacher: For a short time, could we work on the way levels in space affect our movements and what happens to us as we move at different levels? What do we mean by levels? (Spontaneous discussion.) Class, please show us your ideas of a high level, a medium or in between level, and now a low level.
Chad: I can move like three levels all at once.
Children: Look, I can too. Can we? Sure, let's!

Teacher: Suppose we all get into threes, or not more than fours. Let's watch this group of three for a minute. Jackie, suppose you be the pivot and establish a level you want to start from. Now the other two take another level so that we see three levels. Good. We said that there were three levels, and now we can see those three levels. Do you think that you could change your levels so that we will continue to see three different levels? Let's make a game out of it.
Joel: Can we do it? One can be high. One can be low, and I'll be in between.
Teacher: Shall we all work now at the same time, and see if we can continually change our levels within each group? Use any movements which seem good to you. And be careful to stay close enough together so that you can watch each other and we can tell that you are a group changing your levels. Let's see the pivot person. Now the others in relation to your center of pivot.
For just a second, let's watch Peter's group working out its pattern of levels.
(Three of the boys were completely involved—grunting, and changing qualities of movement and chanting. Finally, when we broke their "spell," we found that they had expressed their changes of levels according to their understandings of a *hydraulic ram.* Time and space is too limited here to include their full discussion of all that was involved, but it contributed to the children's understandings of scientific principles.)

Range—Amounts of Space

Range pertains to the amount of space we fill when we move. Children discover this in terms of how big and how small they can make themselves, and how far out or in they can go. They often say things like "a big movement" or "a little movement" or "Look how wide I can go," "Look how long my leap is and see all the space it covers," If I get much wider I'll split."
Working specifically on range of movements helps us to underscore concepts of self and self in relation to others in space. Trying to find how far out we can go without losing our balance is self-absorbing. The

more easily we move, the greater curiosity we seem to have in seeking range of space to fill or cover. Sometimes we find that boys and girls get themselves into almost impossibly small amounts of space and also get out—by themselves.

Depending upon age and experience, the words children use to denote spatial element of range have included: a lot, a little, skinny, fat, big, little, narrow, wide, much, getting bigger, closed and open, area, amount, small, large, extent, distance covered, size, scope, expanding, and diminishing. We must remind ourselves that the world of children and their environment is different from that of adults. Therefore understandings of small and large often refer to "being" or "feeling" a small movement or a small "something" and then developing into a large movement or a large "something." *The amount of space covered varies according to what a child is trying to interpret*—a tadpole, a frog, a butterfly in flight. The space relationship is in terms of ideas and feelings and concepts, not broad time intervals. Perceptions about range seem to include *feelings*. For instance, experiencing how far out we can go or how wide we can make ourselves "feels" and "looks" different from how we pull ourselves in and how skinny and narrow or little we can be in space.

As was evident earlier, children discover range when they are exploring their own particular spaces. They find that the range of their swings can be tremendous and that combining swinging with other movements such as the walk or leap increases the distance of movement. They must all work to determine their own range of movement. When we work on the leap, this is evident. Some of us try to overextend ourselves in the length or height we try to get. As a result, there is a loss of balance. As Bud said, "My leaping is all out of whack." He was trying to go farther out on his leap than his human frame was capable of going. His expectations of the range of his movement

were beyond what he could actually do at that particular time.

Sometimes we have started with a traditional dance pattern such as the schottische. We commence with the smallest possible amount or range of movement, gradually extending until we have tremendous "rangy" schottisches. At this point we have made many variations on the schottische. We add other movements as we improvise and change the character and quality of the dance step. By changing the range within the movement, we often end up with step patterns of our own creation.

Changing range of movement makes us argue with ourselves, because we find that parts of us can have tremendous proportions of space and at the same time other parts of us consume limited amounts of space. This is particularly apparent when we work in groups. This is "movement magic." Here are some ideas of ways of encouraging boys and girls to explore the concept of range.

"Everyone into inner space. Come on, get as close as you can, but still keep the space around you empty. While you are in inner space, start moving just one isolated part of you and continue to move until you are moving your whole self, but keeping space around you empty. Probably you cannot stay in inner space any longer because your movements have to take off. Now, take off to outer space and use more and more range of movement. Keep going out in space until the percussion instruments call you back to inner space. Find movement that feels good and seems to develop from small to large. How did it feel when you were out there in a lot of space and suddenly were called back to a small amount of inner space?" "This is like *horses* all being in a corral," answered Rita. "You let us out and whoops, do we gallop! Then—yaak!—you call us back into the corral." "Come on, now let's find out about that idea. Where and how will you go if we open up the corral? What do you suppose will happen to you and how do you suppose you will feel when you are 'rounded up' and ridden back to the corral?" (At this point a discussion ensued about slowing *down* our movements and taking less and less space, because we were moving closer to the ground.)

"Be careful that you are in your own space and that it is far enough away from your friend's space. Put yourself on your own space island.

I'm a stretchy, stretchy, streeeetchyyyy baloooon
Growing biigger and biiiigggerrr, growing biiiigggger
Getting fattter and fatttteeeerr, getting fattttterrrr
Someone stickssssssss me with a pin
Pffff-pffff-ffffffffffff—Oh I'm *flat flat flat!*"

"While you are flat, close your eyes and think about what it was like as you were stretching and getting bigger. How much space do you think you covered? Is there any difference in the way you cover space now that you are flat? What happened to your space? Do you feel any different now that you are flat than you did when you were a big stretchy balloon?

"Think of yourself as a fish—you are the kind of fish that swells up and puffs 'way out. Start to feel yourself bloating up or puffing up until you are a bloated Puffer fish. Make yourself into various kinds of fish you know about and think about the different amount of space you fill. Let's try to guess some of the kinds of fish we have here."

"On a fall day our world is full of beautiful colored leaves—just look out the window and see them. Think of yourself as one of them and try to feel like your leaf might feel when the wind starts to blow you off your branch. You are there so long you start to dry up—you get all wrinkled up, shriveled up, and completely crinkled up. What has happened to your range of movement?"

"Can you guess what I am today? I'm a glass blower. Have you seen a person blowing glass into objects? Think of yourself as just molten glass all around me. I'm going to blow air into you through this long tube (use arm as tube). As I turn and point my tube at each of you, you start blowing up or expanding very, very slowly. Feel the space you are filling and when I stop blowing let us see each of you as your own glass object or form. There are so many of you it's going to take a lot of blowing, so maybe Alonah will help me on the piano. Careful, feel the space in you. Whatever you do, don't break!"

"Find different hinges (joints) in you, that make parts of you move. Close up one of your hinges and notice the difference in range of space. Try to open and close several of your hinges and notice what happens to you and the amount of space involved. How does it feel as you try to move with different hinges closed? Can you do the same in small groups when you open and close certain hinges? See if you can combine your opening and closing of hinges and talk about the feelings that you have."

"Today you have been studying about atoms. I wonder how we could be atoms? Would we take up much space? I see atoms all over the place and several atoms are getting together and making molecules. Now how will the molecules move? Where can you move? Wonder what would happen to the molecules if you were in a very small jar? Whoops! off comes the lid and now you are molecules in this very large room. What else could we do as molecules?"

We have felt, seen, and sometimes even heard range as we have worked out associations in groups by developing a little snow into a snow storm, rain, hail, a blizzard. A small coil of garden hose that uncoils to become a sprinkler. We have talked about dropping a pebble into a pool of water and seeing and feeling the circle expanding. Many other ideas can be used to apply the concept of range to our spatial awareness in movement.

Also we were able to clarify these concepts of groupings by moving, emphasizing the range of space involved and the movement qualities:

bee to a swarm of bees
bird to a flock of birds
fish to a school of fish
kitten to a litter of kittens
wolf to a pack of wolves

"In groups, suppose we take no more than ten minutes and make up a dance study showing range of movement using one of these ideas:

bigger—bigger *than*
smaller—smaller *than*
nearer—nearer *than*
wider—wider *than*"

Focus

Focus is different from the other spatial elements. Focus initiates from "within," from an internalized feeling or attitude. We say we focus *on* or focus *away from* a specific point, spot, place, thing, or idea. This point may be direct or deviating; it may be visible or internal. When we apply focus we are giving all of our attention and concentration to a specific point, object, or idea in space. Although focus encases the other

spatial elements, it is that mysterious phenomenon of relating *innerness* and *outerness* which provides for movement projection and atmosphere. Focus may be more difficult to use than other elements in space because of the concentration and esthetic sensitivity involved. It helps us to dramatize, crystallize, clarify movements, and often enhances suspense, surprise, reverence, and other dramatic qualities.

Because of the concentration involved it seems to have little meaning for most young children because of their short attention spans and limited movement discoveries. When they have a background in movement however, older children thoroughly enjoy working with the element of focus and find it valuable when they want to emphasize or change a design or make dance seem more purposeful and cohesive. Certain dance movements cannot be captured without the interaction of focus with time and force. Focus gives an expressive quality to movement. To illustrate, one walks in space and focuses on a specific point in the room, he establishes a direct relationship between his walking movement and that point; it is like a magnetic pull which gives special flavor to his feelings about his walk. This is also projected in the way others perceive him walking. In this case, focus affects the quality of the walk and seems to give definiteness and strength to the movement.

Again, a number of illustrations are presented on activities.

"Put your hands together and look at them. Focus on your hands; start moving your hands but keep looking at them no matter where the movement takes them. Focus on another part of your body and let that part absorb your complete attention as you move it through space. Be careful not to break your focus—if you do, start again."

"Look at the box on the piano—concentrate on it—focus on it and start slowly moving away from the box. Now, even more

slowly, start to move toward the box without losing your focus."

"This time try focusing upon something on the ceiling, other than the lights. In any way move toward your point of focus or be pulled away from it."

"Focus on something over there in the corner of the room. Decide whether you are moving toward or away from your corner point of focus. Concentrate and feel as though a magnet is pulling you toward or away."

"Can you all focus on my hands? Look right at them; give your whole attention to my hands and move wherever they take you, but be careful not to drop your gaze. Now see if you can do the same with a partner. Each of you use one hand, but do not let them touch. Move your own hands anywhere and see what happens, *but be careful to look only at your partner's hand, not yours.* Move slowly until we get used to focusing this way." (At this point it is a good time to talk about what happens when we lose our focus, or when the focus is broken. This is readily apparent in shoulders, head, in fact throughout the body.)

"Sense a point of axis within your body. When you have established it start slowly and gradually moving away, toward, around it."

"Think of something very precious to you and something very light. Focus on it and carry it somewhere and gently put it down. Then, still focusing on it, move away from it. It's a secret and only you know what it is.

"Come close into inner space into a circle shape. I have something in my hands I'm focusing on but I am not telling—instead I will pass it to one of you, and you will pass it on to the person next to you. Keep on passing it until it gets back to me. This time let's pass something that is not so fragile or

special. Someone else start, this time." (One boy who started this—Richard—quickly but carefully lowered himself so that the person next to him also had to lower himself to get it. The whole atmosphere of the room seemed to change, as some tried to pass it quickly and others held on to it. Passing and receiving it on various levels and with increased tempo while focusing is not easy, but the majority in this group were able to maintain the focus. When Richard finally received it back he quickly dropped and stepped on it—what a dramatic moment! This is what focus can do for movement.)

"There is a *spot* over there and you are being drawn toward that spot against your will—you do not want to go, but it 'pulls' you. Have you all found your spots? If so start focusing and moving toward it as though you are bewitched, hypnotized. Most of you seem only halfway—and suddenly, it disappears—How did you feel? What do you feel it was? Now try the same thing, only decide what it is that pulls you and how you will resolve the problem."

"There is a beautiful butterfly—do not let it out of your sight. Chase it; now it stops, lights, and then flies again. Now it lights right on some part of you—and you stay still with surprise. By focusing, let us see if we can guess where the butterfly lighted—right on Jake's toe, on Eddie's nose, on Selma's little finger." (Again, the teacher's voice, timing, and involvement are very important in helping children with experiences of this type.)

"Focus your ear on a sound you hear far away—by your movements feel when the sound gets closer to you. It passes you and then goes away. Let us feel that you are with the sound until it completely disappears."

Focus helps us to dramatize movement, give depth and projection to what we are trying to communicate, and it also helps us create an atmosphere. Focus has been the stimulus for such dance studies and compositions as *Mysteries of the Red Mars, What's Up There?, Worship as We Please, Thanksgiving, The City of the Sea, Something's Going To Happen, Baseball Game, The Scarecrow Who Heard It All,* and *Silent Night.*

Space is an exciting study for boys and girls. It is a basic element in dance. As spatial factors are experienced and understood, an important ingredient of dance is accomplished.

12

Time and Force

It takes *time and energy (force)* to move. This chapter concerns the relationship of time and force inherent in movement qualities. The special arrangements of time and force within a movement (or a series of movements) give it rhythmic structure. Time and force not only organize, regulate, and control movements but also give emphasis, continuity, esthetic quality, and character to our movement.

So far we have been concentrating on helping boys and girls build their own stockpiles of movement to understand and enjoy their own movements and to command their human "modules" to conquer space. Now we turn our attention to the exciting components of *time and force*. Throughout the pages of this book we have referred continually to "feeling" the movement. Our purpose in this chapter is to interpret ways by which time and force factors initiate and characterize movement and make it "felt" in an expressive, spontaneous, and exciting way. When we refer to "feeling" the movement we are sensing, perhaps unconsciously, time and force factors at work. Each of us has our own built-in rhythmic system. It may help to think of our "timing device" as a carburetor; this keeps us moving and serves as our regulator. Our "battery" consists of complex nerve fibers—the energy (force) or accent behind the action; this puts us into action. It relates to the way we exert our energy as well as the varying amounts of energy produced.

ANALYZING TIME AND FORCE

The way our battery acts upon our carburetor can be "felt" in movement. We sense ourselves making *strong* (powerful) or *weak* (delicate) movements; *fast* (exhilarating) or *slow* (tranquil) movements; *long* (sustained) or *short* (sharp) movements. We feel sudden bursts of energy that give our movements character. We sense in an even pulse a steady kind of a movement, in contrast to the excitement found in the kind of movements induced by feeling the irregular pulsations in a rhythmic movement pattern.

We not only "feel" this but we can "hear" loud and soft, fast and slow, long and short sounds. We can hear the beat of an even pulse and the rhythm within a melodic or rhythmic pattern. We usually rely more strongly, however, on the external stimulus (sound) rather than on our own internal time-force stimulators to "feel" rhythm. *We should be able to feel ourselves moving first, and then adjust to or use the sound.*

Teachers need to be able to feel pulsations in order to help children. They need to sense fastness and slowness within themselves and

within their movements in order to sense children's tempos and help them maintain a tempo. Children's tempo in moving is usually much faster then that of adults. Unfortunately, many teachers have had limited experience with rhythmical activities. They often feel that they cannot sing, or that they do not like or understand music. It may be that they were exposed to symbols and terminology rather than being encouraged to experience and enjoy participating.

Teachers and children can learn together to respond kinesthetically and then audi-torily. Together they can experience time and force and sound aspects of movement by accompanying themselves rhythmically when they chant, sing, find sounds within their own bodies, and use percussion and music. This chapter is devoted to sharing experiences in this aspect of children's dance activities and will give accounts of how teachers and children have developed understanding of time and force relationships. The following charts serve to summarize relationships of various rhythmic elements.

WE FEEL RHYTHM IN MOVEMENT—WE HEAR RHYTHM IN SOUND

Time
: Eternal until it is divided by accent.

Accent
: From "strong" to "weak" in force, energy, intensity, weight, and dynamics.

Duration
: From "long" to "short" amounts of time at which movement/stillness and sound/silence occur.

Tempo
: From "fast" to "slow"; the rate of speed at which movement pulses or sound-beats occur.

Pulse or Beat
: Usually even, steady, constant (though it can fluctuate):
  In movement: a steady walk, even jumps, hops, runs;
  In sound: the basic, underlying beat that is heard or felt.

Measure
: A division of the pulse or beat by regularly recurring accents.

Rhythmic Pattern
: *In movement,* e.g., 2 sequences of a slow walk, a pause (a kind of "stillness" or absence of movement), two quick steps, etc.; or a gallop, slide, or skip (which all use the same rhythmic pattern); often emphasized by accents.
  In sound, the duration of the sounds and their relationship to silences; often emphasized by accents.

Phrase
: Natural grouping of movements or sounds that seem to go together.

220

WE FEEL RHYTHM IN MOVEMENT

Time

Use of *Accent*

Force, energy, intensity, weight, dynamics.

If movement occurs regularly and evenly, there is a *pulse*. When an *accent* is regularly added to one of a series of recurring pulses, it creates a unit of movement measurement (e.g., "Three movement pulses to a measure when the first of every three pulses is accented").

Use of *Duration*

Amounts of time movements and stillnesses or pauses last.

If movements (and stillnesses) of differing *durations* are used, a rhythmic movement pattern is created. Movement *accents* are often used to emphasize the movement's rhythmic pattern.

The *Tempo*

Rate of speed, something felt as "fast" or "slow" at which the movement pulse occurs.

WE HEAR RHYTHM IN SOUND

Time

Use of *Accent*

If sound occurs regularly and evenly, we have a *beat*; when one seemingly recurring beat of a number of beats is regularly *accented,* we have a *basic meter,* or a "measure" of music.

Use of *Duration*

If sounds (and silences) of different *durations* occur, we have a *rhythmic pattern*. Accents are often used to emphasize the rhythmic patterns of sound.

The *Tempo*

The rate of speed at which the underlying beat occurs.

Note on the rhythmic analysis used throughout this book: (I) In the rhythmic analysis of standard notation, the top line uses conventional music notation, the lines beneath indicate (a) the rhythmic pattern created by lyric (song) and (b) the basic underlying beat (lower line). In the standard notation, the time signature indicates the meter—the number of beats in each measure (e.g. $\frac{2}{4}$).

I. *Music Standard Notation*

Rhythmic pattern

Look at me,   Look at me,   I'm a Kan-ga - roo.

Underlying beat

In the rhythmic movement analysis, the meter is indicated by a number placed before the first measure (e.g., 2).

II. *Rhythmic Movement Analysis*—One of our dance songs, "Look at Me," is used here to illustrate rhythmic symbols.

and hearing fastness or slowness in sound. When children are conscious of how fast or how slow they are moving, they are conscious of tempo. How does a young child come to understand the concept of speed— fastness or slowness? Words have little meaning unless a child is given opportunities to experience the concept kinesthetically—to feel the speed or tempo as he moves.

As we have worked with movement we have already experienced tempo and often found that we could not seem to make parts of us move as quickly or as slowly as we desired. We have also found that at times we had problems keeping the tempo we set (and not going faster and faster). When dance

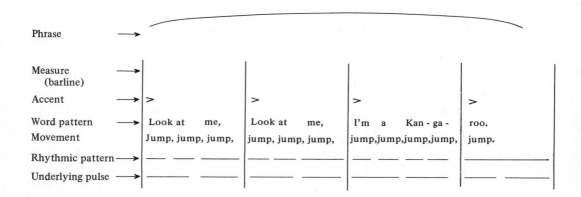

Tempo

Tempo is the rate of speed of the underlying pulse or beat of a movement. Tempo is feeling fastness or slowness in movement

songs are sung too slowly, they are not as much fun as when we find a tempo that seems "just right" for our moving or singing. Moreover, if we sing them too fast, we are unable to accompany them with movement. Children readily sense tempo when they are in group situations and are moving slower or faster than others or when a group doing a dance step increases the tempo— going faster and faster—until they cannot keep up. Variations in tempo can entirely change the character of a dance.

Boys and girls recognize and understand tempo by thinking of it in terms of how fast or how slow they are walking, swinging, folk dancing, or singing. When we accompany our movement with percussion, we sense tempo in still another way. Teachers can also use their voices to change tempo and to verbally assist children as they move.

When working with children, teachers need to be especially conscious of tempo. For the most part, the children should set their own tempo, or the tempo that is right for them, rather than have the teacher or accompanist do it for them. As a group starts to move, a tempo should be established to which most of the children can respond.

When teachers set the tempo for the skip for children, often they set it according to the way adults skip. Because our legs are longer and because most of us have developed a greater awareness of the pulse and beat, we are apt to set a tempo that is too slow for very young children. When a tempo has been established, then it is the teacher's job to keep it steady and prevent it from getting gradually faster and faster, unless working toward that aim. Some children need many opportunities and much encouragement to *listen, to feel, and to respond before they are able to keep up to the tempo of the group.* As children feel comfortable moving and have continual opportunities to express themselves rhythmically, they gain in their ability to hold to a tempo and to adjust their tempo to the rest of the group. Recognition of tempo is particularly important as far as folk dancing is concerned. There is nothing as dead as tempo set too slow, because tempo contributes immeasurably to the spirit of the dance. Tempo, of course, has to be adapted to the group dancing and to the variations within the group. This is just one more reason for children to have a background in fundamental movement before they attempt folk dancing.

We have already discussed tempo in previous chapters; but the following illustrations of conducting a class to make tempo understood by children treats this concept specifically in relation to time and force.

"Can you move your shoulders very fast— even faster? Now gradually move slooooower and slooooower and slooooooooower until you are hardly moving at all, and feel the difference. Find other parts of you in which you can increase and decrease tempo—move fast and then slowly. Can you move one body part at a very fast tempo and another at a slower tempo?" (Illustrations of some of the children's movements included fast feet and slow arms and hands: heads shaking and bouncing fast and slow legs behind or stretching; slow walks and fast push and pulls.)

"How would you like to start class today? It's Rob's birthday. Let's have him select something ... gallop and be horses? O.K., let's all get some space and start to gallop, and Alonah and I will 'pick up' your gallops on the percussion." (This provides a chance to work on tempo and give the gallops another characteristic.) "While you get your breath, can you gallop without your feet— with your heads and hands against your thighs making the gallop sound? Now try to gallop in place, pawing the ground with the forward foot—and now 'take off' increasing speed (tempo) with each successive gallop until the signal 'Whoa' is called. Gallop like the tired work horse that starts out quite rapidly for home and slows down gradually until he almost stops, then sees the barn and gallops fast to his stall. Gallop like the bucking bronco, alternating fast and slow gallops, interspersed with kicks. Gallop like the bandit coming from a distance. Gallop like the sheriff and his men going after the bandits. What can you do as circus horses who come into the ring proud and fast and then slower and slower? Show off your tricks as a circus horse."

Opposites

"One of you start moving some body part very fast, and your partner will try to move a similar part very slowly. Then reverse. See if you can do this moving and respond to each other without talking about it. No mouths this time, but all other parts. Try to find other ways of showing fast and slow tempo. Make it so pronounced that we can readily feel what you two are doing." (This provokes a variety of responses —some go to percussion instruments, some make sounds to accompany their movements, others stay in one spot doing fast and slows, and others use small and great amounts of space.)

There are many times when we consciously work on tempo by feeling amounts and degrees of speed in our movements and in our relationships to each other. One day we were in a confined space and found that we could still move in fast and slow ways without "going anywhere." This seemed to force us to find ways of moving that became different. Bonnie said "It didn't seem like we were people at all—just little bits of things." She had isolated movements using her hands and shoulders adding a feeling of jerkiness or staccato to her fast and slow ways.

"In groups of fours, see if you can develop a sequence of movements that may be done first at a fast tempo and then at a slow tempo. When you find your movement sequence, have two of your group perform the sequence in a *slow tempo* and have the other two perform it in a *fast tempo* and see what happens." (As some of the movements are done faster and faster, movements seem to become shorter and less space and less time are used. Many of the faster sequence movements are done going through space, while slower sequences are in one place.)

"What words can you think of that make you feel as though you move fast?" (Hurry,

scurry, out of the way, Fire! telephone, hold the bus, hurricane, motorcycle, rockets. The inflections and speed in the children's voices denote tempo.) "What can you think of that makes you want to move slowly?" (Hot, lazy, beautiful, church, time to get up, biking up hill, clouds, don't wanna, caution, pokie, my Grandmother. When different movement series are done with some of these words, movements take on different rhythmic qualities.) "Do you suppose we could think of 'tempo' words of people or things which might go together? They might be slow, fast, or fast *and* slow. For instance, Ben might show a fast way of moving as he is motorcycling, Curtis might go slower on his unicycle, and I would go still slower than Curtis or Ben on my roller skates." (Movement episodes usually result that show the children's understanding of what tempo can do to movement. From one group came these portrayals: breeze blowing, leaves mumbling, birds flying, and trees sighing— all going fast and slow.)

Another sample of consciously trying to feel *tempo* in our movements included the idea of slow motion and fast motion. "Sometimes when we watch the TV sports replay what happens? Can you capture this same feeling of slow motion in a dance event? In groups no larger than six, compose a slow-motion study." It is amazing to recognize that even children's speech becomes slower or faster in accordance—in tempo— with what they are trying to do with movement. One class was so turned on or slowed down by the concept of slow motion that they slow-motioned out the gymnasium door back to their classroom. For their next tempo experience we did "fast-motion"— speeded-up—movies.

"We have taken turns to see how fast we can go across the floor, as groups and as individuals, according to movements of our choice. Sometimes we find that the movements we have selected cannot be performed at as fast a tempo as we had set for ourselves. At times the movement doesn't feel right, such as when we are walking on our hands, doing complicated leaps, and flips with jump-turns. Many of you may want to do your movement faster, some of you slower."

A nongraded group enjoyed "Just Suppose's" and "felt" fastness and slowness as they responded with movements to such situations as these:

We are chipmunks and we have been looking all around for "goodies." All of a sudden we spy a piece of bread.

We are a sprinkler hose and all of a sudden holes appear in us.

Your Mother calls you to come home for supper—what do you do?

You are in an elevator in a tall, tall building; show us how you get to the top floor.

You feel "all fast" inside—what happens to the way you move? Or you feel "all slow and pokie" inside—now how will you move?

You are a wind-up toy train that can go quite fast until something is in your way. Now show us what happens to your speed.

You think up a "Just Suppose" ... work it out about something that has a change of speed or tempo.

Accent

Force or energy conditions and characterizes movement. Force initiates movement. Changes in the amount of force used in certain movements gives these movements a rhythmic emphasis. Sudden and successive "bursts" of energy have a clearly felt rhythmic character. The increased energy required in order to execute a basic movement such as a leap or a jump is *felt* as a rhythmic event—the beginning of the leap or jump is accented."

Accent is special emphasis, stress, "felt" in and through movement. When we emphasize a pulse or beat we are exerting energy and we say that we are *accenting*. In speak-

ing we give accent to our words; in playing percussion we give accent to our sounds; in moving we give accent to our movements. Accent is *heard* as louder and softer emphasis in sound and *felt* as stronger or weaker emphasis in movement. Accent gives variety and excitement to movement and gives unity to a series of movement sequences.

A specific approach to acquainting a group of third-graders with the word "accent" included the following. Using both my arms I gestured three times to the group to come toward me; the third gesture was a strong movement. This was repeated twice, the third time I added verbally, "Come, come, *come*," and all the group came. "What did I do?" "You hollered ... you really made us come! As my Dad would say, you looked as though you meant that one!" "Yes, I did mean it. I wanted you to come at once. I was *accenting* both my movements and words. What did I do?" "You surprised me. You said 'Come' louder"; and finally, from Pete, "You used more force." "Yes, I used force in my movement and voice; we call this *accent*. I put an accent in what I did and said. What are other words or ways we might use for accent?" "Speak up, change something, make something different to get attention, make something louder like you did when you called 'Come.' Make something bigger like this ..." from Stuart, swinging and twisting several times and then ending with a huge leap-turn. "That's it, Stuart. Suppose we watch and see if you can feel where Stuart is really accenting his pattern. Everyone take lots of room and see if you can find ways of accenting movement.

"Suppose we just start by shifting our weight from side to side moving various parts of us. Stay wherever you happen to be and start to shift your weight or push yourself from side to side." (Some were standing, some sitting and others half lying down.) "Just see if you can feel yourself moving from side to side ... keep on. Now make it different by adding an accent. Keep on

moving from side to side and find many ways to change the movement by accenting." (For this we used stamping, arm stretching, knees bending, seats and hips bumping, heads flopping, leap and jump turns.) "Now see if you can create a pattern of your side-to-side movements with different kinds of accents. Find a pattern or series of movements that feels good." (As the boys and girls were working some of them decided to combine their efforts and work in groups of two or more. This seemed to give added sharpness to their accents.)

"Let's start walking all over the room at any easy tempo. This is a 'good feeling'

walk. Freeze! This time keep walking, only freeze whenever you can, but make it a decided freeze. *Accent* your stop or freeze. Now, instead of freezing to accent, keep walking and find different ways to change your walks with accent. (This terminated in complicated, unique ways of moving and, in some cases, dramatic qualities were apparent.)

"Take a position on your seat, knees, and elbow, or some such, and start to spin, twist, and push; feel the accent as you start into motion. Push as hard as you can and when you think your spin is beginning to run down, give another accent."

The primitive dance pattern is made up of a *walk and hop* with emphasis, or accent, on the *walk*. It is the sharpness of the accent that gives this pattern a distinct feeling. Accent is not only felt and given to the walk but the accent is also stressed (felt) with the elbows, head, and throughout the body. After classes have acquired this movement pattern, they are able to concentrate on *accenting* the first part of the pattern with ease. They continually find fascinating combinations, which have resulted in many variations of Indian dances. Also, accenting the walk part of the primitive pattern on the drum comes readily (as Vernon said, "My drum is *walk*-hopping"). Vernon and Curtis became intrigued one day accompanying each other—one improvising a primitive dance while the other played the drum. They made a game of changing places on an accent without losing a pulse or beat. This is what being able to accent did for them!

In the schottische, the accent is noticeable on the *fourth* part of the step pattern. This dance is made up of three walks or three runs and a hop (walk, walk, walk, *hop*). As we move, doing the schottische, we seem to accent the *hop*. This movement accent often differs from the metrical (music) accent, which emphasizes the first underlying beat in each measure. The movement and metrical accent may or may not coincide. To illustrate (using the schottische), we notice that in the step or movement pattern the accent is given to the last of the four pulses; in the music or metrical accent, the emphasis is given to the first of four underlying beats —movement accent: *walk walk walk hŏp*; metrical accent: ‾ — — —.

The children know the accent they *hear* as a louder beat or sound; they recognize metrical accent by indicating the first beat in every measure and say, "It helps to keep the music straight." The more they listen to music and the more they play percussion instruments, the more conscious they are of accent. As they experience percussion and

movement, they recognize that there is a certain other kind of accent which is called a *rhythmical* accent. This accent is the natural stress given one or more pulse beats in a rhythmical pattern. Mary Ann Humphrey's name, as beaten out on her drum, shows the accents she gave the pattern of her name: "It has a big accent and then a little accent—I say 'Mary' louder than 'Ann' and 'Humph' louder than 'rey.'" As children become more familiar with movement and as they become more conscious of the rhythmical elements and how they affect movements, their power of perception increases, as did Mary Ann's.

When calling and writing folk dances, boys and girls must be conscious of the metrical accent so that their "calls" will fit naturally with the music or with the underlying beat of the first measure. Older children realize that accent isn't necessarily a loud or hard sound, but that it can be achieved by emphasis, such as omission or differentiation. For instance, a group of children accented the first of a series of running steps by *leaping*; another group accented by omitting the first so-called running step. Differentiation of accent or a displaced accent is recognized in syncopation.

Children of all ages seem to respond well when we work on accenting specific movements and sounds. We have employed accent when we have worked on being or creating such things as

Dynamite igniting and exploding
Mosquito's zisssing and being slapped
Squeaky shoes going down a hall and stopping
Tennis ball between players
Cowboys lassoing
Noise pollution
Oil drills striking oil

Intensity

Intensity is the amount of force exerted or energy expended in movement or sound within a given length of time. The intensity of the movement is characterized by the amount or degree of energy used. Various qualities of movement are created by intensity. Very young children can readily identify with feelings of heaviness, lightness, looseness, stiffness, bumpiness. They can make themselves feel and look heavy and big like a hippopotamus or a tractor, or light and tiny like a butterfly or feather.

Feelings of strength, power, flow, firmness, solidness, sharpness, suddenness, tension and release or relaxation, smoothness and jerkiness can all be experienced by boys and girls as they move. In sound boys and girls hear and create loud and soft, high and low, heavy and light, sudden or continuous. They can apply intensity to their movement or make voice or body sounds or play percussion to project an idea, thought, or feeling in movement and/or sound.

When working with young children to help them sense and respond to different feelings of force and qualities in moving we set the mood by our voice and manner. The tone of voice and the tempo of speaking may be as helpful as the words themselves. Music accompaniments are not necessary and sometimes detract from children's finding their own way to express their inside feelings or to give intensity to their movements.

In response to words, questions, and problems we pose, which may be suggestive or descriptive, children react individually depending upon their own experiences. A child responds one way to lightness while another child may think of and associate lightness in an entirely different way—we must be ready for this. We live in the kind of world, and at a time, when it is important to help children express and project inner feelings. Expressions of intensity can be very personal.

The following are illustrations of ways boys and girls have been helped to express intensity:

"While lying there on the floor, can you make your whole self heavy ... heavvvvvy ... heavierrrrrrrr. Feel heaviness in your feet, arms, back, and even in your tummy. What is the very heaviest thing in the whole world that you can think of? Make yourself that heavy; make yourself so heavy that we would not be able to pick you up if we came to you and tried." (Young children like trying to resist being picked up. It becomes a wonderful game between teacher and child, with the teacher exaggerating and dramatizing heaviness as she tries to pick up a child's heavy arm, head, or whole body. At times children exert so much energy throughout their bodies that they look as though they might burst at any moment.)

"This time just 'let go' and try to make yourself light—make your feet light, let your head go as though it might just come off and blow away ... feel as though you didn't even have a backbone. Think of the very lightest thing in the world." (To add to the intensity of the moment we often tiptoe to different children and ask them in a whisper what they are that is so light. Responses are often as numerous as children in the class, from clouds and stars to dandelion blossoms, Kleenex, dust, and feathers, to mention a few. We also move various body parts of children and sometimes they are so limp and relaxed that we can turn them completely over. At times they can be put into various positions and they tend to hold their lightness, and other times they can get up and start moving all over the room, feeling lightness as they move. Sometimes as we sense *heaviness* or *lightness* we talk about other words that also mean this—soft, hard, stiff, loose, etc. We add to our vocabulary as we talk about how we feel when we move as robots, astronauts, pussywillows popping, rain dripping off umbrellas, and music boxes running down.)

"Now change yourself into clouds in the sky, just floating slowly and quietly, changing shape, size, and density as you pass by.

Now change—you are all sponges washed up on the sand, rolling back and forth with the gentle waves until you are tossed on the sand only to have the sun come out and start to dry you and make you have all different kinds of feelings of intensity."

"We like to think of ourselves as hot dogs waiting for the water to boil and when we are plopped into the water we feel different things happening to our hot dog self."

"An unknown chemical gas has escaped from the laboratory down the street and it has spread all through our school. What happens to us as we breathe it? Do we explode—and then do we feel as though we are floating or flying? Does something different happen to those of us who have on tennis shoes and those in bare feet? Show us the intensity in your movements."

We have related how it feels to be a football being kicked or thrown or carried or bounced or rolled on a field, and what it is like to walk on glass (as though the floor were a sheet of fine glass), walk in mud or glue and then get stuck, be caught in a huge fish net, be afraid of dark shadows following us. *Applying intensity to our movements helps us in our movement expression.*

Other opportunities for boys and girls to express intensity have included touching different objects and then responding verbally as well as kinesthetically. For instance, a long, giant pussywillow was passed around the class and the following responses to its feeling were written down: "Soft, fluffy, like cotton, smooth, like a kitten, slippery, scratchy, furry, hairy, silky, velvety, happy, warm." This was followed by putting the feeling of our own particular word into movement intensities.

Older boys and girls have actually felt the flow and control of energy when they have been trying to swing bigger and longer and continuously improvising with the swing

and combinations of other movements—in and through space and then suddenly stopping. They can feel the build-up of strength and power starting from raindrops, turning into heavy rain, or a river, joining waves to end in a turbulent ocean. Also older boys and girls can experiment with transfer of body weights and feel tension and balance within themselves as they try to reach a point of balance with another person. This can be in conjunction with classroom studies of force, levers, and pulleys. Power, strength, muscle tension, and concentration are experienced in balance.

Duration

Duration has to do with the amount of time it takes to do a movement or a series of movements. Children recognize this as how long or how short a time a movement lasts. It may take a long amount of time to complete a full body stretch, or a short amount of time for an arm stretch. All movement involves duration of time which is "felt" from the beginning to the end of the movement—from the beginning of the stretch to the completion of the stretch.

Duration is also sensed in sound. When we hear rain on a roof we hear short intervals of sound or prolonged intervals of sound. We hear short intervals of sound and short intervals of silence, or we hear long intervals of sound and long intervals of silence, or we hear a combination of these long and short sounds, plus corresponding intervals of silence.

Duration denotes continuity of time. A fourth-grade group, in composing a dance to a song called "I Hear Bells," started by feeling the pulling of the bells and were conscious of how *long and continuous* a movement it took to pull the bell. They had to hold on to the bells for long periods of time in relation to letting the bells go before pulling them again. This group actually felt the duration in their movements.

Children can be helped to understand

duration by making associations with long and short intervals of time: a *long time* is experienced while waiting for Christmas, at night time when there is a fishing trip tomorrow, in the dentist's chair, waiting for the rain to stop; a *short time* is experienced while children are in swimming, eating a banana split, or playing. *Long and short* times are felt while waiting for the merry-go-round and then the ride is over, or when it has rained all day, and finally the sun comes out and then it's dark, or waiting to come up to bat and then striking out; things children like to do seem to take a short time, things they don't like take a long time.

When discussing certain series of movements in a dance, children have become conscious of long and short durations of time by the following type of questions: "When you did your Pollution dance, what was a movement or series of movements that took a long time?" "The garbage can waiting to get full took a long time and when it exploded it was a short time ... Randall *galloping* his horse took different amounts of time."

Even and Uneven Duration

Children come to know duration as long and short time and are conscious of feelings of evenness or unevenness in movement. This is apparent when they analyze their locomotor movements. For instance, they realize that they can do the basic locomotor movements—walk, jump, hop, run, leap—in the same time frame. Each can be done taking a long period of time or a short period of time and each movement makes one sound.

We continually work to feel the pulse and rhythm within our bodies, internally sensing what is happening as we move. We are alert to the sounds we make, using sound to help us clarify, but we do not rely on the external stimuli or use it as a crutch. We avoid counting out using numbers. Rather, we try to feel what we are doing and then say what we are doing, such as saying "jump, jump, jump" rhythmically. What we are doing means to us something quite different from mechanically counting the one, two, three. As we do this and say "jump," we hear even and uneven duration.

The relationship of the various durations of movements and stillness and of sounds and silences creates rhythmic patterns in our movement and sound experiences that are very exciting.

When children perform a series of any movements (such as a walk) using the same amount of time, the evenness of the movement is *felt* and the *evenness* of the sound is heard. We say the movement has a sense of *even duration*. However, when children do a series of any of these movements in *combinations* using different amounts of time, the unevenness of the movement is felt and the unevenness of the sound of the movement combination is heard; that movement combination has a sense of *uneven duration*. If we say "Waaalllk waaalllk waaalllk" we can feel and hear *long* continuous intervals of *evenness*; "Walk walk walk" enables us to feel and hear *short* continuous intervals of *evenness* which we call even duration.

Sometimes children have problems with the concept of even duration. Here they confuse a feeling of *accent* with the amount of *time*. When they are accenting a part of a pattern of even duration, that part seems to take more time. For instance, sometimes when groups are doing a series of jumps,

accenting the first— "*Jump* jump jump jump jump," it seems to them that the first jump is longer in time because of the stress they are putting on the first "jump." This is the opportunity for thoughtful discussions and activities concerning time and force relationships. To help them comprehend *uneven duration*, we experience the following:

"Do a series of walk-hops while you are saying 'Waaalllk-hop, waaalllk-hop, waaalllk-hop.' You can feel and hear long and short intervals—unevenness—in these words; the walk is long in relation to the hop and the sound of the walk in relation to the hop is longer. This time say 'Walk-hooooop, walk-hooooop, walk-hooooop'— feel and hear the short and long intervals of unevenness. The walk is short in relation to the hop and the *sound* of the walk in relation to the hop is shorter—feel the unevenness?"

"Suppose we review the gallop. While you are galloping see if you can really feel the unevenness in your gallop pattern. Close your eyes and gallop in place and sense the relationship of the walk and the leap part of the pattern. How many sounds do you hear yourself making? Gallop again. Does it feel as though you are just walking, or do you feel that the gallop is very different? How do you know? Now try just walking—do you feel the evenness of your walk? Say what you are doing—now try galloping again. What do you feel and hear? Is there evenness as in the walk or unevenness as in the gallop? Clap what you were doing in your gallop. Close your eyes again and listen to Salena gallop. Let's catch her rhythm by snapping our fingers. Again listen to the uneven sounds you are making as you gallop."

After sensing uneven duration in the gallops, the children added accent to exaggerate, and this gave it another quality; the tempo can be increased and decreased to make the gallop feel still different. The boys and girls try different ways of stopping and starting going in various directions, for different intensity—this needs to be bumpy and forceful.

Setting rhythmical problems and recording them graphically comes only after boys and girls are able to sense and understand rhythm within themselves. Symbols of long and short lines can be used to express even (— — —) and uneven (—— — —— — —— —) duration. Some children enjoy a graphic representation of even and uneven duration like that shown in Figure 1. These represent long and short swinging movements after boys and girls have sensed the feeling of duration of longness and shortness. Graphic representation is used throughout this book to specifically help the reader see as well as feel the relationship. Some of us are more visually oriented, and graphic notation may be helpful.

Many older boys and girls enjoy rhythmical analysis of their movements and sounds. There is no one way of graphically representing duration or any other rhythmical element; children create their symbols by doing. Some of the symbols for the leap have been those illustrated in Figure 2. Symbols for uneven duration of the skip have included those shown in Figure 3.

Figure 1

Figure 2

Figure 3

Some boys and girls have been helped to understand fractions in arithmetic by the graphic representation of movement patterns. A few boys and girls who were particularly adept in arithmetic have rhythmically analyzed various movement patterns and movement studies. In order to do this they had to understand duration.

When we have *even duration* we feel the *pulse* or hear the *beat,* which we will discuss in the following section. Also, there are many combinations of long and short intervals giving a sense of uneven duration which can be used to create rhythmic movement or rhythmic sound patterns; these will be illustrated later in the section "Rhythmic Pattern."

Pulse

In movement, *pulse* is *felt* as an *even,* constant, steady, continuing interval of duration. If the accent occurs regularly and evenly we have a *pulse,* or *even pulse.* A constant pulsation—a basic underlying pulse —exists in all motion. In sound (music) this is heard as an even, steady *beat.* If the accent occurs regularly and evenly we hear an *even beat.* We say we are "in time" or "keeping time" when we feel ourselves moving and can coordinate with the beat we hear being played or produced. This is what happens when we say "get the rhythm, feel the rhythm, keep in time." What we really mean is get the underlying pulse—the basic beat. Young children experience pulse in movement when they bounce on their Daddy's knees or on bedsprings: the bounce is the pulsation of even duration. Later they feel their basic pulse when they start to bicycle, bounce balls, skate, ski, or are on the trampoline.

As we help boys and girls become aware of their basic pulse in movement, we are helping them to move with rhythmic accuracy. Throughout this chapter we are specifically concerned with rhythm accuracy.

Children are usually conscious of a pulse even though in the beginning of movement experiences they are not apt to use the technical words. With experiences, they come to feel and understand this basic even pulse in movement and sound. In time, children find that the basic locomotor movements—the walk, jump, hop, run, and leap —resemble the underlying beat in music. They find as they walk that their feet can make the sound of the underlying beat. They also become aware that the underlying steady pulse is the foundation for rhythmic movement patterns. This awareness of feeling and hearing the underlying pulse is necessary to participate in such activities as folk dancing.

We all recognize units of time. We know that sixty minutes make an hour, or that twenty-four hour units make a day. We can think of pulse and beat in this same relationship; and we can measure the length of time of a movement by these units.

As was indicated in the discussion of duration, we hope that teachers and children will feel the underlying pulsations in movement rather than relying on counting. Emphasis should be first on relying on one's own internal feeling of pulse in movement. Counting comes later as individuals and groups want to perfect rhythmic movement and sound patterns. It is important in working with younger children to provide many opportunities for them to move *their* way, to find other ways, and to continually get them to express how it feels. Having the accompaniment follow the children rather than setting the pulse for them will develop their individual awareness of pulse in movement.

Older boys and girls are often helped by trying to locate their own heartbeats in their wrists and moving accordingly. We find out that this pulse is *steady* even though some have a faster or slower beat than others. We close our eyes and try to move some part of us to the pulse, then try to do the same thing moving through space.

Finally we realize that pulse is expressed by our basic movements. It is quite something to be able to change from one locomotor movement to another without losing the established beat. As we consciously work with sensing pulse in movement, we realize that it gives regularity and order to our movements.

In recognizing the basic underlying pulse, boys and girls often observe that it would be boring if they had to just move this way all the time. Once they have the feeling and understanding of underlying pulse and realize its importance, the whole rhythmic structure of movement in children's dance becomes evident; the rhythms occur within the framework of the pulse.

Throughout this book, underlying pulse will be graphically symbolized by lines of long duration (——— ——— ———) or lines of short duration (— — —). Underlying pulses or beats will be grouped by means of a regular accent and shown in groupings such as of two underlying pulses or beats: —— ——; or three —— —— ——; or four —— —— —— ——; etc. Regardless of how they are grouped, underlying beats serve as the constant, even pulsation that exists in all movement.

Rhythmic Pattern

A *rhythmic pattern* is a series of movements or a series of sounds of different durations, often with different amounts of time between them. The stillnesses and silences are an important part of rhythm and accents are also frequently used to emphasize the rhythmic pattern.

In movement, we feel the even or uneven accent and the long or short duration of time; in sound we hear the irregularity. Children refer to the rhythmic pattern in sound as the melody or the word part of the song. To clarify the distinction between pulse and rhythmic pattern, one day Kathy

helped us by saying, "the rhythmic movement pattern is not monotonous, steady, and even like the underlying pulse. The rhythmic pattern can have more 'big and little' movements and I can combine many kinds of movement and make many kinds of rhythmic patterns. With the pulse I can only do one thing at a time. Look, I can show you. This is my pulse." Her entire manner gave us a feeling of slow, deliberate, pushing-down kind of walk taken with her whole body—no variation—each walk exactly the same. "Now look how different my rhythmic movement pattern is." She started out with jump   jump run run run run jump jump   , ending with her long jump. Doing her rhythmic pattern again, she analyzed her pattern in the following way: "I do my first jump long and hard, my next jump is shorter, my four runs are still shorter yet, my next jump is like my second jump and my last jump is hard and long like my first jump."

As indicated earlier, many children have a natural rhythmic sense. Continuing with Kathy's lead and taking a cue from her, the class was asked to take Kathy's first movement pattern of underlying pulse. "Gee," said Eddie, "nothing's going to happen this way." That was another cue. "O.K., suppose you all make something happen. Change from your underlying pulse in some way and make various combinations of movements and make rhythmic patterns."

A great deal of discussion is needed about the relationship of the rhythmic pattern to the underlying pulse and why it is necessary to be able to feel the underlying pulse before we can relate a rhythmic pattern to it. Working with the two, we come to understand that the pulse is ever-present and that it gives organization to the rhythmic pattern.

Groupings of underlying pulse are established and boys and girls make up rhythmic patterns that relate to underlying pulse.

Sometimes we work in couples, one setting the underlying pulse and the other responding with a rhythmic pattern. At other times a part of the group establishes an underlying pulse or beat. We do this by moving with some part of us such as our shoulders; or clapping or playing percussion, singing the underlying pulse while the rest of the group responds individually moving or playing a rhythmic pattern to fit the underlying pulse or beat.

Television commercials are favorite rhythmic patterns to be danced. We listen to TV and look in the newspaper to pick up commercials which we use as rhythmic patterns. Holiday greetings, cheer-leading chants, and nonsense rhymes also furnish opportunities for rhythmic patterns. Our own names and names of visitors to our school have been used frequently and translated into movement. Series of funny words, plays on words, and making up words (*gimme, scrumlicious*) supply rhythmic pattern possibilities.

Many of the chants presented earlier are helpful to us when we work on rhythmic patterns. The following New Jersey town of Pennsauken illustrates various patterns coming from the same word.

which have to be felt and called to an underlying pulse. This is necessary if we are to keep the calls going so that the class can respond rhythmically.

Swing your partner round and round,
Keep on going round the town,
Stamp your foot on the floor,
Swing, swing, and swing some more.

Measure

A *measure* is an equal grouping of beats with one recurring beat regularly accented; this is sometimes called a basic meter. In sound—music, song, words, chants, percussion—we hear groupings of beats. When we listen to a series of underlying beats and start counting the beats from one accent to the next, we can determine the meter or the number of beats in the measure.

In rhythmical analysis, the meter is indicated by a number placed before the first measure—for example, if it is a 2, this means that there are two underlying beats to the measure. In standard notation, the time signature indicates the meter—for example,

PENN	Sau			KEN		
P E N N	Sau KEN			P E N N	Sau KEN	
PENN SAU	K E N			PENN SAU	K E N	

Material in the chapter on dance songs is often reviewed and used for rhythmic pattern responses. Writing our own calls for square dancing is nothing more than making up a series of rhythmic movement patterns

$\frac{2}{4}$—the top number indicates beats to the measure, the bottom number indicates the kind of note that will get one beat. Feeling the pulse in movement and working with groupings of beats in sound, children become conscious of meter—a certain number of beats between bar lines. For example,

2 beats in a measure: 2| >   __

3 beats in a measure: 3| >   __ __

4 beats in a measure: 4| >   __ __ __

5 beats in a measure: 5| >   __ __ > __

6 beats in a measure: 6| >   __ __ > __ __

Children readily understand the concept of measure if it is related to sentences. They often say that a measure is a sentence of beats (or sounds) instead of a sentence of words. The sentence can be long or short, but has a definite start and stop and is a complete thought.

A group of third-graders who had had two years of work in dance as an integral part of their schooling were asked to participate in a convention program of dance with high school and college students. Each group was to present a dance using certain basic movements. It was decided that each group would have a working period to show in sixteen measures the basic movement ingredients of their dance, which included emphasis on the *jump.*

Even though the third-graders had not previously used the term "measure," they worked with the idea readily because a measure of beats was related to sentences they wrote in language arts; and their series of movements could be thought of as a sentence of movements. After working on improvisation with a variety of jumps and other kinds of movements, the children decided to divide into three groups, each group to work out four measures, with the entire group doing the last four measures.

Their dance was to the poem "Jump and Jiggle" and was primarily based on the movement patterns which they developed below and applied to animals.

Percussion and records have been used to help us identify measures. When children have discovered accent, measures have easily been approached by using a recording and by following it with the question, "How can you tell where the accent comes in this music?" "Because I hear it." "Now let's show by moving some part of us when we hear the accent. What do we call where the big accent comes? Can you take turns going around the circle, each playing a measure? Now do the same playing with your percussion instrument." Not all children can respond as quickly as others. With some groups we may never desire to get into these particular rhythm elements. "Now, let's see if we can go around the circle without missing a single measure.

"Listen for two measures, and then we will try to improvise on any movement of your choice to the next two measures—listen—two measures and move—two measures and continue listening and moving.

"Turn to two or three others, and one of you move on the first four measures and then the rest of us will try to repeat the movements on the four measures.

"Now listen to the music and hold up an arm or leg on the first measure. Now, on each of the next seven measures, extend your movement. This time try to keep one movement going continually, really feeling long duration of the movement.

"In groups of six or eight, see what you can do with this problem. You decide how many measures you want to play. Using

1st group	4 measures	jump-shakes, jump-turns in confined space.
2nd group	4 measures	low walks and jumps in various directions, ending with jump-shakes.
3rd group	4 measures	runs, jumps, flips ending with jump-turns.
All	4 measures	walk-jumps, jump-turn, flip and jump-shakes, (walk off floor).

drums, shakers, and one other instrument of your selection, create rhythmic patterns. Keep playing your rhythmic patterns until you are satisfied. When you are ready to share with us please play your measures of rhythmic patterns. Be careful not to use too many measures and keep your patterns simple." (Constant reminders to children to keep patterns simple helps them to get a feeling of accomplishment.)

Phrase

A *phrase* is a natural grouping of measures of beats giving a temporary feeling of completion. We hear phrasing of sounds (or music) and we respond with movement. Children not only hear a grouping of beats, which seems to give a feeling of unity, but they can respond with a series of movements which seems to form a meaningful grouping. In dance we say we respond to phrases of sound with grouping of movements, or we create a grouping of dance movements which a grouping of sounds (phrases) accompanies; sometimes the two are created simultaneously. As we speak, we stop for breath every once in a while. As we write we use punctuation marks. In sound and movement, we naturally group to give that same feeling of completion to a series of sounds or series of movements before starting over again or starting on another. Phrasing usually means to children "a grouping of two or more measures—a paragraph of beats or sounds instead of a paragraph of words." If we listen carefully to children, we find that they naturally phrase as they talk. When speaking of phrasing, children have remarked, "You can tell when to stop or start by the way it sounds or feels."

A phrase may be short or long. Children can be helped to recognize short and long phrases—they come to see that a whole or long phrase represents a *big idea*, and a small (short) subphrase of beats includes a *part* of the big idea. As boys and girls are creating dances they need to be cognizant of phrasing if they desire accompaniment of any kind. If they are creating dance patterns or dancing to folk music, they may need help in adjusting their movement patterns and ideas to the phrases of the music. However, they respond readily to music as they understand phrasing. Most of the chants, dance songs, and dance music in this book provide opportunities to respond to phrasing.

Development of Phrasing

Phrasing can be as much fun for younger children as it can for older children. Even very young children phrase naturally when they speak, and many of their rhymes and repetitive word patterns show phrasing. Children identify phrasing as "the end, and ready to start over." Phrasing has been used in different situations: follow the leader with leaders changing after every so many phrases; identifying phrases by the beat of the tom-tom; stopping the music, using orchestra leaders and working in small groups with the leaders changing after two or four phrases; listening to phrases in folk songs and changing movements to, or with, the phrase. Singing rounds as well as moving to rounds helps in learning to respond to phrasing. Older boys and girls are particularly conscious of phrasing when they folk dance, "call" for folk dancing, and compose their own songs and "call."

One approach to identifying phrasing has been listening to recordings. We listen and then determine that there are sounds in the song that are like paragraphs similar to those you have been writing in your stories. "Listen carefully to the record to see if you can hear several sentences (or measures). When you think you can hear where a paragraph comes, move some part of you. Do you think this half of the group could clap to the first division or part in the music where it seems to stop for just a second? Then let's have the other half of the group clap to the second phrase or division of measures. Let's start with Marjorie this time, and each one of you in turn clap until the music makes you feel as though it is time to stop. Then, the next boy or girl starts. We have to listen very carefully so we won't lose the beat or pulse. Let's try it again to see if we can make it even smoother—just as though one person were doing all the clapping. Now that we are getting better clapping phrases one after the other, let's see if we can do the same thing moving some part of us. What are those divisions of music called? Yes, they are phrases."

Many gamelike activities can be discovered from such devices as the above. "Circle Phrase" and "Silly Phrase" are always popular. The Circle Phrase was composed as boys and girls were working out this game of phrasing. (Many adaptations have been made, depending on the group and their experience.) Boys and girls are in a circle. One is "it" and moves around the circle or across it, tagging off another on the

end of a phrase. The game is continuous, starting and stopping with the phrase, using any kind of movement, or each doing a different movement. "Circle Phrase" has also been played in the classroom while sitting at seats or on the floor. One person starts a body movement on the first phrase and the person sitting in the next seat starts another body movement on the second phrase, and so on around the room, trying not to miss the beginning of the phrase. At times, this is used like "Follow the Leader."

"Silly Phrase," which a group of ten-year-olds originated, came about as a result of one of those days when teacher and children admitted it had been "quite a day." We hoped that maybe something in dance would relax the group and found only that it brought forth more cavorting. After a few futile attempts we asked, "What's the matter with us today, anyway?" This brought forth giggling, until Jake spoke up and said that he guessed we were just silly. (Children are bound to be silly now and then, and sometimes it's their way of telling us about them. It's good when they can evaluate them-

CIRCLE PHRASE

Arr. *Nina Coffing*

SILLY PHRASE

Arr. *Joyce Eldridge*

selves in terms of their own actions. The group's behavior was turned into a learning situation which was as satisfying to the teacher as to the children.) In ten or fifteen minutes these children learned to identify phrasing by use of their silly actions, faces, giggles, and positions. "Silly Phrase" consisted of getting into silly poses or human sculptural forms on each phrase, either individually or in groups, and holding the position for one phrase and then getting into another silly position for the next phrase.

"From the Feet Up" is another game version which a group of older boys and girls originated. One starts moving the feet on the first phrase, the next person moves another part above the feet on the next phrase, and

so it goes on up the body until the head is reached, and then they start from "the head down."

When boys and girls understand phrasing and have had opportunities to create dance movements or studies using phrasing, they are able to sense a feeling for phrasing within themselves. Some older boys and girls have created short dances without sound accompaniment. They have used *silence* as accompaniment—when they do this the relationship of phrasing within the dance is apparent. Dances in silence have gripping dramatic qualities and children are very proud of their efforts.

Children sense a complete phrase which is represented by a long arching line. There can be smaller phrases. If the complete long

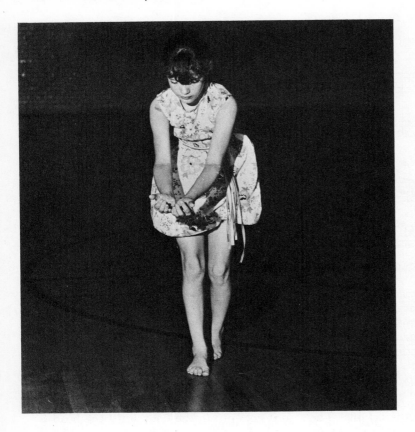

phrase is eight measures, then it might have two subphrases of four measures each. If the phrase has four measures, the smaller idea within the phrase would be two measures. The complete phrase, or the big idea, is represented by the figure below:

Elements in rhythm are interrelated, as they are interrelated with movement. Even though one element may be emphasized at a particular time, children are nevertheless responding to other elements of rhythm. An understanding of the use of the elements in

The dotted line can represent a subphrase idea. When we gain in experience and comprehension with phrasing, we often work to music with uneven phrases or an odd number of phrases.

rhythm gives quality and meaning to their dance movements.

13

Sound

USING SOUND

Finding and using *sound* is exciting and adventurous. In the previous chapter, emphasis was on *feeling rhythm* in movement. This chapter is concerned with hearing rhythm and making rhythm with *sound*. Sounds are made by us—by our hands, feet, mouths, thighs, knees, seats, and other body parts. Sounds are found in our environment and reproduced by us in meaningful and imaginative ways. Sounds are produced by us in the form of musical instruments and used for many purposes.

So much can be done with the sounds coming from oneself, from two sticks, or from percussion of our own making. It goes without saying that a piano accompanist who knows and understands children can enrich the total experience. This chapter will share brief suggestions regarding music, and piano accompaniment when available.

There was sound in the world—in the rhythm of the waves, the rain, wind, thunder, lightning, and utterance of animals—long before man existed to hear them. Because primitive man did not understand such happenings, he believed that acts of good and evil gods or spirits were responsible for all things beautiful and devastat-

ing, in their world. There is a story of long, long ago that has been handed down to us. One day a native gave way to his feelings of joyfulness by pushing his hands together. He made a quick, sharp, sudden sound, different from any sound he had heard or made before. The sound so pleased him that he continued pushing his hands together. He liked his sound so much that he showed his tribesmen, and soon the whole village was making a clapping sound. Movement in the form of dancing developed with the clapping. To please their gods, primitive peoples offered prayers accompanied by dancing and such sounds as hand clapping, foot stamping, and body swinging, swaying, and shaking. As the use of language grew, men repeated the same sound over and over to accompany their movement. This chanting led to singing.

Another story is told about a tribesman in the woods. He suddenly picked up a rock and threw it into the air to see how high it would go. On the descent, the rock hit a hollow tree and produced a long, deep, hollow sound. The native, amazed by the sound, continued to throw rocks into the air, listening for the new sound as the rock hit the hollow tree. The tree trunk was taken back to the village. The sound so pleased the chieftain that it was used in tribal rituals

and probably became the antecedent of the drum. Primitive people discovered new sounds as they began to make utensils for cooking and knives for hunting. Some of the simplest were made by merely striking together two sticks of wood, or clapping stones against each other. Drums were later made of animal skins stretched over hollowed-out stones or tree trunks. Gourds filled with pebbles created an interesting sound.

For primitive peoples, sound served as a means of communication. This is true for us, too. For example, percussion serves as a vital and significant part of our program in dance.

Sounds We Make—Hands, Feet, Mouths

Children use various parts of their bodies to help produce sound. Soon after they begin working with movements, they discover that pushing their hands together make many kinds of clapping sounds. Pushing their thumb and forefinger together (with the thumb pushing away from the nose and the middle finger toward the nose) makes snapping sounds. Hand rubbing, nail clicking, finger tapping, and scratching are only a few of the other sounds we often use.

The following is an example of how we work with hand, foot, and mouth sounds.

Hand Sounds

"Find all the sounds you can possibly make with your hands. Listen carefully to find different sounds. Of all the sounds you made, let us hear the loudest...the softest... soft to loud...and just the opposite, loud to soft...fading away...just one...three...many short ... the one you like best. What do you call some of the kinds of sounds you seem to be making?" ("Whapping, galloping, smacking, bumping, rubbing, rattling, thumping, snapping.")

"What are different ways you can use your hands to create sounds? Discover a sound you have never made before.

"Try making sounds with your hands on various parts of your body...from your neck up...careful—not too hard (your cheeks are not as tough as your knees). Now try your hands with parts of you from your neck to your knees. What other sounds can you make with your hands and thighs (or top legs)?

"Now find what you can do with your hands and other parts of your body. Can

you make fast sounds, then slow sounds...
scary...funny...happy...quiet ones? Suppose
you name some of the sounds you have discovered and play them for us." (Examples
included fantastic, dangerous, horrible, animal, machine, swishing.)

Boys and girls soon find out that they can
create innumerable sounds with hands and
feet together. Also, they find that they get
different results by slapping hands against
thighs, knees, chests, and from beating
against the floor. All of this helps them to
listen, to discriminate, and to add to their
own collections of sounds.

Foot Sounds

Foot sounds are different from hand
sounds. We find that our feet make different
sounds with sneakers than with regular
shoes or bare feet. Some of the sounds we
have identified and used are stamping, tapping, clumping, slapping, shuffling, pushing, digging, brushing, beating heels against
the floor, clicking heels, jumping in the air,
and clicking sides of feet. Some of these
sounds have been recorded on the tape recorder and stored away for future use.

Making interesting and complicated patterns of sounds coming from one's own self
helps boys and girls to realize how special
they are. There was a special light in the
eyes of four young children when they informed us that we did not need music any
more because they were a whole *combo* and
we all should listen to their band! Fortu-
nately, the tape recorder was available for
recording their "band," which was composed of sounds from hands, feet, thighs,
and seats. The playback delighted them as
well as the whole class. When the sound
composers asked the group to dance while
they played for us, we did!

"What sounds can you make with your
knees and your hands? Find sounds that you
can make with other parts of you from your
hips or waist down. Make one sound from
your hips up and one from your hips down.

What sounds can just our knees make? Do
you suppose our elbows or arms make any
sounds?

"I'll bet that we could go around this
circle with each person adding a pattern of
sound that would fit. Take a few seconds
to plan your sound pattern, using any part
of you. Harry, suppose you start and let us
hear each one add his sounds." (When it
was Harry's turn again, he reminded us that
we had a circle of sounds. This same idea
has been captured in various ways with
movement accompaniment.)

Mouth Sounds

Children are ingenious when it comes to
producing numerous sounds with their
mouths. Tongue clicking, clacking, clucking, swerping, swishing, whistling, sissing,
oohing, ahing, a-ing, e-ing, i-ing, o-ing, u-ing,
beeping, slurping, sucking sounds fill the
room when children have opportunities to
find sounds. They work with their tongues,
lips, teeth, and cheeks arduously to produce
different kinds of sounds.

Respect is heightened for vocal chords as
mysterious and magical sounds emanate
from children's mouths. They are able to
vocally and phonetically reproduce sounds
in their environment as they hear them.
This is unlike the stereotyped sounds which
some people associate with rain, wind,
trains, and the like. The rain does not really
say "pitter patter," nor does the wind only
say "wooo." Boys and girls find that there is
no one sound for either of them; they recognize that there are many kinds of rain and
wind and that they are heard in a variety
of circumstances. These they have reproduced as mouth sounds.

One teacher shared the following with us
concerning one of her kindergarten classes.
She asked: "Can you see and hear the wind?
What is he doing?" Mr. Wind (a small boy)
was pushing forward, blowing with all the
lung capacity of a "superman" five years
old, making realistic wind sounds with his

mouth while the trees (other children) were ferociously swinging and swaying, bending and twisting and turning. Finally, our wind turned and said, "You'll just have to get a new Mr. Wind; I'm all out of Stuff."

Boys and girls are full of all kinds of sound interpretations which will come out if opportunities are provided. This is a rich source for movement accompaniment. After children understand movement, sounds are important in helping them to express better a train starting up, an airplane taking off, and the noises of animals, mechanical devices, and so on. They discover a variety of ways they can accompany their movement patterns and give their movement more meaning. One boy and girl move while the class concentrates on the movement, and with mouth or body sounds follow and furnish the accompaniment. This becomes a game of concentration for those following —going fast when the movement is fast, slowing down, picking up uneven sounds, changing and responding to even sounds and dynamics, and even catching the mood of the dancer. This provides an opportunity for improvisation of movement for the one performing and a splendid way to review and enhance the use of rhythmic elements. For those furnishing accompaniment it provides for concentration, perception, and discovering a variety of ways of using one's body and the floor for sound.

Some fascinating spontaneous rhythms of the accompaniment have been taken down on a tape recorder and filed away only to appear again when we have need for certain combinations of sound patterns and effects.

LISTENING AND FINDING SOUNDS

Two of the features we seem to continually work on with children are *following directions* and *listening*. Working with sound sharpens listening. It can be fun to help boys and girls use their ears to listen and hear. All of this helps us in sound discovery, which aids movement and adds to the interest of many of our dances.

Some of our ways of encouraging listening include:

Going on listening walks, finding sounds, stopping, listening and trying to reproduce, identify, and sometimes record them.

Putting on our sound antennas and opening up the windows and just listening and trying to describe the sounds.

Becoming "sound sleuths" and "casing" the cafeteria for all kinds of sounds.

Being "sound catchers" at the corner—listening to traffic going by, people rushing, birds, trees.

Finding a construction site and becoming "sound excavators" writing down all the sounds we hear.

Sometimes we get so caught up watching that we forget to listen. We have listened for God-made (natural) and man-made (mechanical) sounds and used them in various ways. Sometimes we see who can try to find brand new sounds. (Our walkie-talkies, casettes, and tape recorders help us.) Sounds we have heard include: birds chattering, pets whimpering, trains roaring and grinding, chewwwwwwing, clocks ticking, carpenters sawing, radiators pzzzzing and banging, pots and pans rattling, helicopters chop-chop-chopping, as well as diverse sounds of the circus, Christmas, a birthday party, parking lot, church, camp, or street corner.

Our world is replete with sounds for boys and girls to capture and use. It is helpful to have children list the numerous sounds they encounter. From exhaustive listings of sounds often we have tried to sharpen our ears by trying to reproduce vocally or phonetically sounds we hear. Here are a few illustrations:

Acorns—Blopping bloppppBop ... dahhhd dahhhd

Crickets—eric eric

Dogs—aarruh aarruh ... gerrr urr urr ... murmm

Seagulls—eek eek eeeeeeeeeerruk

Birds—tee tee teee kaw kaw kaw ... ch rup chrup ... cheater cheater cheater ... thankque thankque

Frogs—twee twee twee gallump galllump

Rain—blip blip ... bop bop bop ... lick lick luk lyk ... whissssper ... dubbs dubbs ... shwashuuuu shwashuuuu

Can-openers—whirrrrrup

Blender—galimp gleurp whirrrrrrr

Boiling spaghetti—blup blupb bluppppppb-ppppbppp

Lemonade poured to glass—vooooruuuu-eeeeeeee

Soda—fizzzzzzzzzzzzzzzzzzzzzzzz

Airplanes—hmmmmmmmmm UMMMmm Ummmmmmmmmmmmmmmmmmmm

Windshield wipers, heaters, and turn signals—whr r r uh rrr sken waace F hh Fhh Fhh Fhh er rek click zreem zreem

Toilet flushing—ch ch ch swish sh sh sh oooooo mmmmmmmm eeeeeeee

Sneeze—aaaaaaaa chooooooooooooo

Motor scooter—pa pa pa pa pa t t t t t t t t t t t

One class of first-graders was especially proud of its *Book of Outdoor and Indoor Sounds* which they had made. They had found the sounds, made the sounds, illustrated the book and pasted it all together so that it could fold up. This group was elated with its joint accomplishment and wanted to dance the story of sounds—the children felt that the only way their dance would communicate their findings was to reproduce the sounds they had discovered.

Outdoor Book of Sounds

Dogs— arffffyarl

Cats—meeeeou ouuuuu

Rooster—cockadoodle doooooo

Helicopter—roooooooom mum

Fire-engine siren—zrellmmm pprum

Birds—twerpppee ... chirrrrrip

Book of Indoor Sounds

People—yayaya yakyak tatatuetue

Baby—wha ar ar ah wah

Mother sweeping—swish ... shiwhie

Garbage in can—oooom mmmflip

Clock—tick toc tictic tic

Telephone—zwingggggle zwigggggggg

With experience it is amazing how much of our world can be heard as children become adept in hearing sound and responding to it sensitively.

Some different approaches to exploring sound follow:

"In groups of threes or fours, let's try to make some sound patterns. Let's have one group make a series of patterns just using their mouths; two groups make patterns just using hands; two other groups use just their feet; three groups patterns with feet, hands, and another part; and these last two groups use any parts of you but make your series of patterns hold together."

Claudia told about her adventure trying to actually follow the sound of the frogs in the pond behind her house. "Each time I would get to where I thought the frog was, I would hear the sound somewhere else!" There must be many, many frogs in the pond and they were developing a sound composition.

Spring sounds always bring forth gems which we try to capture and extend. Illustrations of sounds of spring follow:

The buzz of the hustling bees in the pink-rosy flowers.

The swishing of the catfish cruising in the lake.

The grunting of muddy pigs and the mewing of baby "kits."
The clucking of mother hens rounding up their babies.
The clicking of reels at the lazy old pond.
The whistle of the ferry boats sauntering up the river, followed by the flap, flap, flipping of wild ducks keeping time with the put put put of the new red tractor.

After reading a book, one fourth grade made a list of picture words and made poems to match the words. A high, shrill sound was pictured as a "zazzagy" line—yellow or orange. A heavy noise was seen as a very black or brown color. Then the class made stories or poems about sounds and moods. One poem had a smooth mood.

> One day I saw a boat
> On the river afloat
> Softly it did glide
> On the silent tide
> Silently it went
> Going where it went
> by Mia.

Gilbert made a rough stormy poem.

Noisy stormy night
Monotonous continuous rain
The booming of lightning
The crashing of thunder
The continuous beating of rain on the roof
The noisy excitement of people, running in the rain
Noisy stormy night
Monotonous continuous rain

It is interesting to note the relationship of identifying and reproducing sounds to language development and clarification of speech. The descriptive language of children becomes a useful medium for expressive communication.

Sound can become so much a part of us that we find it fun to imagine with sound. Have you ever thought about the following? Well, we have actually accompanied our sound conversations with dancing.

Samples of Different Sound Conversations

Said the Bubble Gum to the Jelly Beans ... said the Gumdrops to the Licorice Stick ... said the Cotton Candy to the Lollipop ... Let's All Talk   talk   talk talk.

Birds talk ... yes, they do. They speak to each other. They talk about grain and berries and birds high up in trees. Want to hear us "bird talk"?

Our masks become real and make conversation with sound. (In art class this group had just made primitive masks to go with a study of pyramids. The masks provided an important incentive for much imaginative language.)

Because we are so soft, did you ever think that we could make up a dance with our sound— O talk of Jell-O, marshmallOws, meltaway chOcOlates, and ice cream—Orange?

Did you know that color has sound? We found that soft green, gay yellow, perky pink, bossy purple, naughty brown, and just O.K. blue enhance language and communication with sound.

Graphic Representations of Sounds

When we get pretty good at sound we find that we can graphically represent our sounds individually and in groups. We even made a mural from graphic representations of our favorite sounds and then we put them into dance.

PERCUSSION

Percussion is making sound vibrations by tapping, hitting, and shaking an object. The have opportunities to work with sound. Percussion provides for an expanding of creative abilities; it is an outlet for release of tension, and can be controlled and directed toward children's best interests and development of the moment.

Rather than buying expensive or elaborate percussion instruments, boys and girls can construct their own. This is a creative endeavor and an important part of the program of children's dance. Teachers need not feel handicapped when a piano is not available, for children's dance is often facilitated by percussion planned and used by children.

Finding Sound Items

Before we make percussion instruments with young children we often find simple devices to gain percussive effects. By striking two sticks, pencils, rolls from paper toweling, by tapping on desks, floors, and waste paper baskets, we are making percussion noises. We hear different sounds as we hit them against different surfaces. Children make games out of producing sounds by jingling keys, shaking all kinds of things in tin cans, rattling bottle caps, and stones in boxes, and bouncing balls. Young children also use available materials such as milk cartons, cereal and salt boxes, paper plates, shoe boxes, paper bags, shells, bells, and various plastic bottles and containers. Many

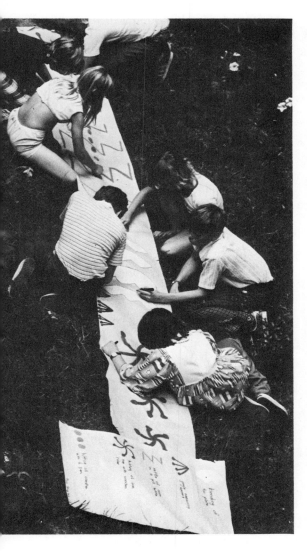

drum is the most common percussion instrument, but we are also including things we blow on or into and things with strings which we pluck. We classify our sound instruments as drums, wood, shakers, metal, blowers, strings, and miscellaneous others.

Children love to make sounds. It is amazing how readily boys and girls will discriminate between *noise* and a *sound* when they of these can be found in the classroom; sometimes we hunt for *something* that makes sound and use this as an initial percussion experience. It is fun, too, to bring something from home that makes a sound —then we can find out about all of the different kinds of things we can shake, tap, and hit.

Older children study about and then make percussion instruments to supplement social studies and language arts. Study of other cultures has included research on their percussion instruments. While engaged in a social studies unit on China, one group of fifth-graders reproduced several crude Chinese instruments which they used to accompany a dance composition of rice planting for a "sound happening." Science has much to teach about sound; in some schools, boys and girls have made instruments as a part of their science study. For one group of boys and girls science and social studies were combined and percussion instruments were the culminating experience. Camps also provide a splendid place for making and trying out percussion instruments. An Indian pow-wow, a campfire evening, or a carnival become adventurous when they have been motivated by an experience with percussion. The ingenuity which children display when given an opportunity to discover materials, construct instruments, and work out stories and designs is satisfying and vital to creative growth. Some of their creations become beautiful objects with the addition of color and design.

Making Percussion Instruments

Older boys and girls, as well as parents and student teachers, have made percussion instruments for kindergarten and some first grades. But the instruments most cherished are those the boys and girls plan and make themselves and then use in many ways for unanticipated purposes.

Helpful hints. Although the decorating of various instruments is important, the decorating must not detract from the sound. Color dynamics have a powerful effect on children. Instruments should look cheerful and colorful. Detergents added to paint makes it more adhesive and will prevent peeling. Finger paint is also useful but is best preserved with shallac. Mystic or masking tape is inexpensive and practical for securing objects onto or into instruments. Contact paper can also be used. Sticks, wooden or metal spoons, dowels, etc. can be used as beaters.

There are many things with which to fill shakers: sunflower seeds, acorns, nuts, spaghetti, beans, rice, and rocks. Different sizes and shapes create different sounds. Tape softens the sound of tin cans; care must be taken not to deaden the instrument. Dowels for handles must be secured firmly in the shakers. Rough edges can be covered with tape.

In making wood instruments, the harder the wood, the sharper the tone. Rough wood should be sanded to prevent splinters. Watch for rough edges. Make sure that wire ends are not exposed. They can be wrapped in yarn to prevent scratching.

Delicate glassware should not be used for children's instruments because of safety factors.

Drums

Drums may be constructed in any size or shape to produce a variety of tones. A drum consists of a *frame* over which is firmly stretched a thin material called the *head*. Some materials that have been used for the frame are barrels, kegs, buckets, tree trunks, wastepaper baskets, flower pots, coconuts, and boxes and cans of different types. The head material may be rubber tubing, shellacked muslin, rawhide (wet before stretching over frame), heavy paper (such as parchment or cardboard), linen, canvas, oilcloth, parachute nylon, or thin plastics. Edges of the frame need to be smooth in order not to cut through the drum head. The head should be pulled *tightly* and laced, nailed, or cemented to hold securely.

The sound of the drum depends upon how tightly the material is stretched. Drums, especially the bongo, should be open and free for maximum sound. When making drums or bongos, if screws are used, they should be around the edges so that the skin may be tightened or loosened. Avoid using sharp instruments to strike a drum, for these could injure the skin head. It is best not to paint the head because it takes away from the tone produced.

Cereal box drum—decorate paper cut to size of frame. Staple around frame and shellac to preserve. Use lid and staple shellacked paper or plastic over top and bottom. Bind with tape. Ends over drum head may also be thumbtacked before being bound with tape.

Tin can drum—remove top and bottom of any size cans (fruit, coffee, etc). Pull cover tight over ends. Punch holes in material (using gummed notebook rings for reinforcement) and lace firmly with string, carpet yarn, or nylon cord. Decorate. Bells may be added for sound.

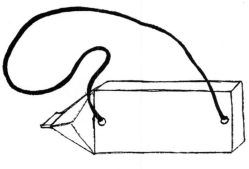

Dum de drum or carton drum—fold in top of milk carton and tape. Cut holes at each end, put cord through holes. Cord should be long enough to go around the neck and so that the arm doing the beating will not be restricted. Cover carton with sturdy paper and decorate.

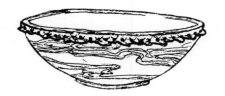

Salad bowl drum—large wooden salad bowl painted with bright colors. Cover top with plastic held in place with thumtacks.

Earthenware drum—Hide or skin stretched tightly across flower pot and bound securely with elastic and gummed tape or with hide straps.

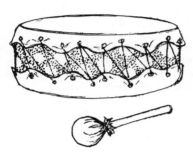

Indian drum—round metal frame or cylinder with hide, plastic, or rubber tubing stretched firmly across ends. Holes punched and reinforced in hide. Lace through holes with rawhide strips or heavy string.

Clorox bottle drum—screw top on bottle and secure with masking tape or glue. Decorate. Hit with dowel stick, spoon, etc.

Waste basket or keg bongo—cut hide or similiar material in a circle for head of drum. Make holes every two inches in the hide and insert metal eyelets. After the eyelets are in place put the hide on top of basket or keg, wetting hide so that it can be pulled tight. Weave hide string through holes, pulling tightly and securely. For added tightness the hide may also be secured by winding the lacing around basket or keg.

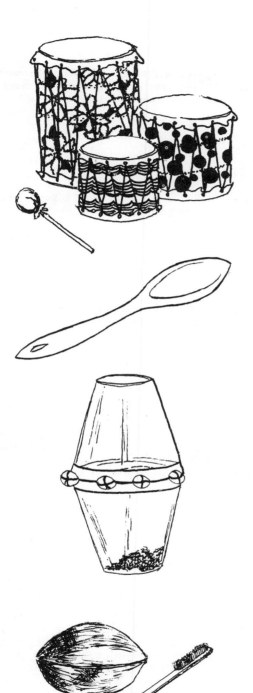

The 1, 2, 3 Bongo—cut off ends and cover cans with bright contact paper. Stretch rubber tubing or hide across bottom and top and lace firmly with rawhide cord or heavy string. Attach the drums together with heavy cord or attach with screws to small pieces of wood. Use a dowel stick covered with leftover pieces of skin and colored tape as a beater.

Drumsticks (beaters)—handles made of wood, dowelling, whittled sticks, cocktail muddlers, broom handles, and pencils. Knobs, or drumstick heads, have been made of cotton, twine, elastic, and so on. Spoons and shoe-horns make convenient beaters.

Shakers

Cup-a-tune—two plastic or paper cups taped or glued together, filled with grain (peas, barley, rice). Bells around outside of cup for added sound and decoration.

Coconut shaker-drum—dry whole coconut in oven for about 15 minutes. Cut in half. Hollow out. With coarse sandpaper smooth and clean inside and outside. Fill with coins, beads, or grain and tape or glue two halves together. Brush with turpentine for shine and to increase sound. Use as shaker, a scraper using metal brush, or as a drum by hitting with spoon or stick.

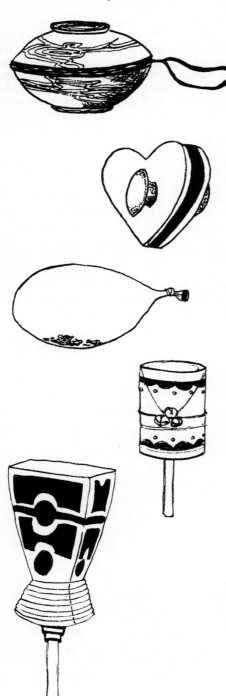

Two wooden nut bowls—fill two bowls with nails, buttons, and bells. Insert handle firmly and tape bowls together securely.

Two cookie cutters—join with colored tape. Fill with split peas for sound.

Balloons—fill with sand, rice, beans, or a combination. Blow a little air inside, tie end.

Tin can, plastic, or carton shakers—cover two cans with decorated paper and tape together. Fill with grain or stones. If a handle is desired put a wooden dowel or pencil through a hole in bottom and firmly secure.

Rattle head—place grains or stones into decorated plastic liquid soap bottle. Put dowel in opening for handle, seal with tape.

Pie pan shaker—place dried beans in aluminum pie pan, another pie pan on top. Staple firmly together. Around the outer diameter of the tins punch ten to twelve holes. Using a nail, punch holes into bottle caps so they may be strung. String bottle caps in pairs so that two will hit against each other between each hole. Decorate.

Shaker bells—punch holes in tops of different-sized cans. Thread heavy string though holes and put a fishing weight on end of the largest can and bells on the smaller cans. Hold string and shake. Different sounds are produced from each can.

Light bulb maraca—make water and flour paste. Dip newspaper strips into paste and cover large-necked lightbulb with many layers. Let dry. Hit bulb to break, decorate. May be coated with plastic or shellac.

Chinese doll—blow up balloon to desired size and knot. Cover with many layers of newspaper strips dipped in flour and water paste. (Do not cover neck of balloon). Dry, break balloon and pull out knot, putting rice through hole. Insert ice cream stick or tongue depressor in hole and secure firmly with glue and tape. Decorate with face.

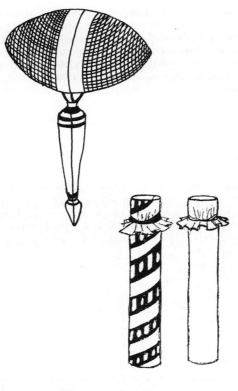

Tin "Can-Can" shaker—Two strainers put together with adhesive tape. Marbles inside.

Mr. and Mrs. Rhythm—fill paper towel tubes with stones. Cover ends, decorate.

Thunder-makers—hold and shake long sheets of aluminum or poster board. If edges are sharp, tape around edges.

Make a shell—string shells on a heavy cord and shake, or hit with wooden dowel or spoon.

Wood Instruments

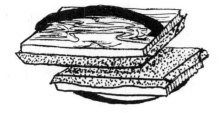

Wood blocks—cut wood to desired size. Tack or glue sandpaper on bottoms and sides. Tack on ribbon loose enough so that children can put hands through them to grasp blocks.

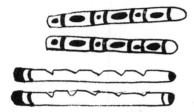

Rhythm sticks—sandpaper slender dowels or broom handles. Round ends with sandpaper. Sticks should be at least 10 inches in length for a good sound. Bamboo poles make great rhythm sticks. (Diagonal V's can also be cut out of bamboo to make notches for blowing.)

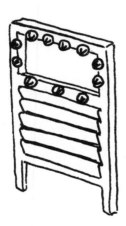

Musical washboards—different boards make different tones, depending on the material from which they are made (such as plastic or metal.) Board can be played with thimbles, tin spoons, or metal. Bells, nails, bottle tops, etc., may be attached for extra sounds.

Picket fence—flat board with eight clothespins nailed on upside down. Piece of wooden dowel or pencil used to play up and down the "fence."

Clackers or hand puppets—bore holes in one end of two pieces of board cut the same size. Decorate. Secure clackers together with wire or strong string. For the younger child a sock can be added on the end with the ties and made into a clacker puppet.

Clogs or jingle blocks—loosely nail three or four soda-pop tops into thin wood. Tap them against palms for clanging sound. Handles can be made if desired.

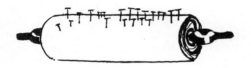

Roller nail—drive large-headed nails at equal spaces but different heights into large rolling pin or any club-shape piece of wood. Hard round stick skimmed along nails for sound (also used to beat the roller).

Sounds Made by Hitting or Blowing

Large sea shells—can be used as trumpets when blown into or can be hit with another shell.

Bamboo flute—cut a piece of bamboo (flute-sized) and with a wood-burning set, burn six small holes for the fingers and one larger one on the end. Blow over the large hole, using fingers to cover some of the smaller holes.

Glasses and bottles—blow across water-filled heavy glasses. The more water in the glass or bottle, the higher the tone.

Tin can sounder—three cans hung by wire on board. Marbles or bells inside cans. Wooden stick beater.

Pie tin cymbals—nail wooden blocks, for handles, to two pie tins. Decorate.

Tambourine—made from the top of round cardboard covers, particularly those coming from cereal boxes, pie plates, foil plates, tin can covers with edges tapped or hammered down, and paper plates. Shells, buttons, bells, bottle tops can be attached.

Pie plate tambourine—punch holes around edge of rims of two paper pie plates. Insert metal open-hole rivets. Bind with yarn. Small bells attached close to rim. Bottle tops or sea shells may be used instead of bells. Paper plates painted with design in center. Or fill pie plates with nuts, paper clips, and sew together with ribbon, yarn, or string.

Capbello—holes punched into bottle caps and strung on wire coat hanger. Twist wire together again; bottle caps move easily back and forth. Bells can be placed alternately between bottle caps. Wool over wire ends to prevent scratching.

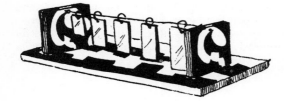

Metal sounders—cut metal into ten pieces of varying lengths. Suspend pieces from top of wooden frame at 1-inch intervals. Bore holes in ends of metal pieces and use wire to suspend them from top cross-piece of frame.

Belperin—bell percussion instrument made by securing bells with thread or string to long piece of scrap leather, ribbon, or elastic with ties at both ends. Make ties long enough so that instrument can be tied around waist, arm, ankle, neck, etc.

Gong—spray surface of the top of a heavy industrial cleaner container with aluminum rust-o-leum to prevent rusting and to make it shiny. Drill two holes in metal, fasten heavy wire through holes to a 4-foot broomstick. Gong can be struck with a rubber-headed mallet.

Chimes—cut galvanized pipe into 5 or more different lengths. Drill holes at top of each pipe. Use piece of wood as a crossbar. Drive 5 nails into crossbar spaced 5 inches apart where the pipes will hang. Fish casting line is good to use to hang the pipes to the crossbar. To keep pipes from moving a lot while being played, cut holes in a piece of wood a little larger than the pipes to allow movement. Striking the top part of the pipe produces different sounds. The longer the pipe, the lower the pitch. The striker should be a dowel or a metal bar.

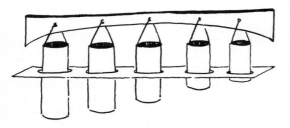

Ol' bones—shank bones can be boiled and strung, then hit or scraped against each other.

Strings and Things

Box strings—stretch strings or rubber bands over a small box, across a forked branch of a tree, or over a covered container on a bridge to make various tone qualities.

Gut bucket or one-man band—turn tub or bucket upside down and drill small hole in middle of bottom. Tie a knot in end of heavy string and run through hole and attach to end of broom handle or dowel. Notch end of broomstick to fit over edge of tub and attach to side of tub. Adjust tones by stretching string and stroking it. Wax string or cat gut also used.

Cigarango—made from cigar box or similar wooden box. Oval hole cut in lid. Wooden board inserted at one end for handle. Handle and lid held in place with adhesive tape or small nails. Strings are cat gut, raised by pencil or small dowelling, and held in place with glued tape. Strings tightened by screw eyes.

Egg-slice pick—use egg slicer as strumming-percussion instrument, making handles for each side with rope, or fasten slicer to slab of wood to make lap instrument. Instrument may be picked with guitar pick, nut picker, etc., for a variety of sound.

Rubber band harp—two sticks of wood about 12 to 15 inches long joined together at top and bottom by cross-pieces fastened by small nails. String the harp by stretching a number of rubber bands. Arrange bands so that they will play a scale. An old tooth brush can be rubbed across them or they can be plucked with fingers.

Zither—cut small circle in box top. Insert three pairs of screw eyes at both ends of box, lengthwise. Attach piano or guitar wire, or nylon fishing line for strings. Decorate. Tune by turning the screw eyes.

Xylophones and Other Tone Instruments

Musical bottles—take eight super-large soda bottles. Put 8 oz. of water into first bottle, increase by 8 oz. in each succeeding bottle until last bottle has 64 oz. Line bottles up in graduated order of tones and strike with spoon or wire brush. Make each bottle a different color by adding food color to water. (Remind children not to strike bottles too hard.)

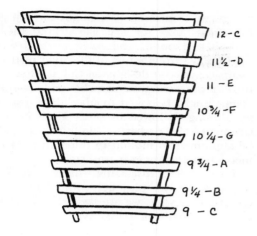

12 – C
11½ – D
11 – E
10¾ – F
10¼ – G
9¾ – A
9¼ – B
9 – C

Wood marimba—cut a 7-foot length of wood (thickness 1″ by 1⅓″), into lengths. Frame is made from narrow strips (½″ × ½″). Space individual strips 1 inch apart; attach them with strong tape—make sure it is loose enough to vibrate. (Nailing strips doesn't work because tone and vibration are lost.) Use wooden dowels for strikers.

Using Percussion

After proudly making and displaying their instruments, experimenting with them, and listening to the sounds made, children want to hear sounds they can make. Working together in groups is a valuable and necessary experience for children. Percussion instruments provide an opportunity for almost immediate cooperation in working and playing with others.

When first bringing children and instruments (or adults and instruments) together, bedlam often ensues. This is a new activity, and children are fascinated with the many sounds their instruments can produce. Experimentation will be noisy. However, if this is an introduction to percussion, the girls and boys need to become familiar with the instruments, and are encouraged to beat, hit, shake, and blow them to explore the many kinds of sounds the different instruments make. It is important that each child have something in his hand to play so that all feel that they are participating and contributing. A few key questions have been helpful:

How many ways can we find to play our instrument?

Can we find a way to make two or three different sounds?

What is the very lightest sound we can make?

Can we start with soft sounds and get louder and louder?

Who has the highest sound? the lowest sound?

What different kinds of sounds do you suppose we can make? (sharp, ringing, blowing, shaking, thumping, continuous)

Where are all the drum sounds? the shaker sounds?

Do we have any sounds that play a tune or have a tone?

In the very beginning it is necessary to set up some controls—this is a good time to talk about the conductor of an orchestra and why he or she needs to have some signals for starting and stopping. Together signals can be worked out for each particular group. In the beginning the children become so absorbed in their instruments and the sounds coming from them that they forget about stopping and starting signals agreed upon. With time and reminders, they are able to handle themselves and their instruments.

While playing, children need to relax, use arms and wrists freely, and play the instruments with various parts of their hands and arms. A tightly clenched fist around a beater or shaker will greatly hamper a child in his use of movement and will affect the sound he produces. He also needs room in which to swing his beater up and down, out and around.

Children enjoy discovering different ways they can play their instruments. They find that drums are not simply "banged," but that a technique may be developed in playing them. The sound will be *drawn out* rather than *beaten* into the instrument. Tones may be altered by playing on different surface areas: top, bottom, sides, rim; by varying the section of the beater used; or by hitting the drum with the knuckles, fingers, fingertips, or fist.

Many kinds of drums need to be held away from the body to get good sound. Holding the instrument between the knees or under arms produces a better sound.

The following illustrations are some ways of exploring with percussion.

"Let's hear all the drums playing together. Suppose we have one drummer start and then the others join in—who will start? Let's see what the other groups of instruments sound like—shakers … blowers … strings … bells … cymbals. From all these groupings, what kind of sounds did we hear? Are there any that seem to go together? Are some better than others?

"What are some of your favorite songs? What are some of the songs you sing in music or in assembly that you like?" (The response depends upon the season, current and catchy music from radio or TV, and some old-time favorites.) "Can we all start to sing 'It's a Small, Small World'? Just sing without any instruments this first time. Now sing and play your instruments, but be careful that you do not drown out your singing."

At first there may be a collection of disorderly sounds, so try to listen to *how* the group is playing. We might have just the drums play (or first the drums, then shakers, bell sounds, and so on) or the drum might play throughout and the other instruments come in at designated times. Then, a little more structure can be added—the drums might be asked to play alone while we all sing, followed by other kinds of instruments. An orchestra conductor should be appointed to motion to different instruments when to come in and stop.

Time is spent discussing what we are doing, how we can play better, and how we can listen to what we are trying to do. We get better with practice! We continue to work on singing and playing our instruments—finding that we have to be very careful with the drums because they can drown us out—or the shakers can go on too long and become monotonous. Some individuals listen as an audience and then give advice.

Often a decision is made to group by instruments. We all start playing together very softly to louder and louder, and then stop, then just the opposite.

"Does anyone know the musical term for what we have just done? Yes, with *crescendo* we start low or soft and build up, getting louder and louder; and with *decrescendo* or *diminuendo* we start loud and gradually get softer. Could we hear you play the rhythmic pattern of these words, and include the accent? In small groups, can you put these three words into a series so that they make a pleasing sound pattern?"

If a piano is available, it can start, and the percussion leader can cue the other groups. Children feel that the piano helps to keep them together. The piano might be alternated with the percussion, but in so doing care needs to be taken not to lose a beat on the change. If we have a piano, we might have the piano take the first phrase, the tambourines and bells take the second, the shakers the third, and the drums the fourth phrase. (This depends on the former experience of the group; it ties in well when there is understanding of rhythmic elements.) If there is no piano, this can be done with a harmonica or an accordion.

We find that we can play the beat of any song. We can listen to a song played on the piano (or on a record) and then play along. Part of the group may play the fundamental beat, while the others play the rhythmic pattern. We clap the rhythmic pattern, while some of the instruments keep the underlying beat. Some groups have called playing the underlying beat the *whole* and those playing the rhythmic pattern, the *parts*. More than one third-grader has asked, "Why don't you play the *whole* and we'll play the *parts?*" This is when we find that different instruments get different effects. When we do have a piano to help us, we find it interesting to play songs in different styles. We can play the same song and make it sound Japanese, Hawaiian, Mexican, Russian, and even "country music," by the kinds of instruments we play and how we play them.

Familiar songs like "Old MacDonald Had a Farm," provide opportunities to play underlying beats and rhythmic patterns, and to invent many interesting effects of animal sounds. We experiment with which instruments seem to sound like certain animals.

Soon we find that we are no longer producing just noise by merely banging drums, shaking rattles, and beating gongs. We find ways of getting variations of sound. We learn to improve on the playing of "Jingle Bells" by hitting the gongs a new way, realize that there is an appropriate time to use the washboard, and know that drums are most effective if played for a desired sound—some experiences require *heavy* drums, while others need the drums only to keep a steady, underlying beat throughout.

Older boys and girls have made this particular venture even more complicated by adding movement for the measure lines, with students taking the part of phrasing "moving" the phrase symbol. Children are often capable of more than we expect, and amaze us with their ability to make up mixed rhythms and create interesting rhythms with different placements of accents.

Percussion Accompaniment for Movement

To help us keep a steady pulse, we often move some part of us with the beat. We keep our heads going while we play. Sometimes in order to gain a better awareness of the beat, part of the group walks out the rhythm while others play the accompaniment. We review with our instruments the many kinds of locomotor movements and try to play slow walk, turns, fast leaps, and mazurkas. We hear the locomotor movements with only one sound, which is even and steady. The combinations—skip, gallop, slide, and polka—all have more sounds, and these particular ones are *uneven* sounds and we hear uneven sounds as we play.

We achieve interesting effects by moving some part of our bodies while sitting on the floor and playing our instruments. Part of the group may *clap* a movement while the other part plays its instruments.

Here are some patterns that have come from a class of eleven- and twelve-year-olds:

This class is working in groups with a leader for each group. Howard's group moves on the floor doing their galloping steps while one part of the group accompanies with some kind of mouth percussion. Another part makes an orchestra with several percussion instruments. Laurie's group, divided into fours, moves with a run and short swings for underlying beat. Another group moves to a rhythmic pattern that will fit the underlying beat. A third carries the already established underlying beat on the drums. The last carries a rhythmic pattern with other instruments. Stephen's group moves with a leader, slowly, increasing and decreasing the tempo. Another group follows with percussion accompaniment. Mary's group does a variety of hard and soft, heavy and light, fast and slow movement improvisations. The entire group concentrates on the movement and accompanies with percussion instruments that seem to fit Mary's improvisation.

One of the best ways to become aware of patterns is to *move* to them first, and then to accompany them with some kind of percussion.

A rhythmic pattern of gallop, gallop, run run run, leap can be accompanied by shakers on the gallops and by drums on the runs and leaps. For example,

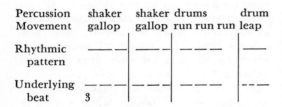

To sharpen awareness of the rhythmic elements of accent, underlying beat, rhythmic pattern tempo, measure, and phrase, we worked on each part separately. The group took four measures of underlying beats (sixteen sounds), then we walked to these sixteen steady beats. We decided that it might be interesting to add accents and put one at the beginning of each measure. This divided up the beats into four measures of four beats each, giving four accents. We then jumped on the accent. As the group became familiar with the separate elements, they decided to divide into smaller groups, with each taking a part: one group moving with the accent, and others moving with

the underlying beat. (We could have stopped there and worked out percussion accompaniment, but this particular group was capable of adding more parts.) Another group was formed and added a rhythmic pattern of hops, jumps, and runs.

Accent	JUMP	JUMP
Movement	hop hop jump	hop hop jump
Rhythmic pattern	— — —	— — —
Underlying beat	4 — — — —	— — — —

Accent	JUMP	JUMP
Movement	run run run run	hop hop jump
Rhythmic pattern	— — — —	— — —
Underlying beat	4 — — — —	— — — —

One twelve-year-old suggested that it might be easy to practice this in one spot, so we faced each other and tried the movements in place. This particular exploration ended with a circle formation with four groups working on the four parts: (1) underlying beat, (2) accent, (3) rhythmic pattern, and (4) percussion. The underlying beat moved about the circle. The accent faced center and on the first jump landed with feet apart. On the second accent they landed with feet together, which faced out from the center and repeated the pattern. The rhythmic pattern faced center except on the runs, which were done in individual circles. When this movement exploration was completely worked out, percussion was added and this fourth group was in the center of the circle and accompanied the movement with appropriate instruments playing underlying beats and rhythmic patterns. This group decided that their efforts would make a good dance, so they added levels and range of movement to their patterns, making them as elaborate as they could, and used percussion to accompany their dance. (Ventures of this type call for guidance from the teacher in helping to keep the activity within the capacities of the group.)

Percussion is Fun

Children never seem to tire of the rhythmic pattern of names. We can start with one name, such as Susy Brown, repeat this name, clap "Susy Brown," and then play the rhythm on our instruments. We find that when we say it one way it has one group of sounds, and when we say it another way, it has a different group of sounds. But whether we say it fast or slowly, evenly or unevenly, there is a pattern to "Susy Brown." It is interesting to see how many different patterns we can play for a name.

A name sound game can be played after each child has found the way he wants to play the accent and rhythmic pattern in his own name. We go around the circle taking turns, each playing his own name three times. This can be done without losing a beat between names.

Children have enjoyed working with codes, radio dispatches, Indian signals, and other communication systems. This is done by having one group start to play a series of beats and the answer coming from a second group. *Codes* and their *answers* are another source. One group may be asked to send the dispatch and another group to answer; or the class may be divided into groups, and each group in turn answer the message:

Code
Rhythmic pattern   — — — —   — — — —
Underlying beat   3 __ __ __ __   __ __ __
               — — — —   — —
               3 __ __ __   — — —

Answer
               — — —   — — — —
               3 __ __ __   __ __ __
               — — — —   — —
               3 __ __ __   — — —

Another way percussion has been used successfully is by having a child go to the window and "tell" with his instrument what he sees. Christine saw a taxi starting. The effect she gave of slamming the door was fun for the class to guess. She used a beater on a pie tin symbol to produce her effect. Quite different was Clayton's percussion "takeoff" of the garbage collector he saw. His sounds came from two tin can shakers. Still other percussion interpretations have been used for bird calls, sirens, traffic, and street repair.

Radio commercials are a source of many percussion patterns. Children from the fourth grade up add movement to the patterns and ask their classmates to guess the commercial. Even though many of the same commercials have been used over and over again, no two have ever been presented in exactly the same manner. Some of the radio commercials or advertising slogans which children called out (when asked to think of a few) can be listed on the floor or board. They talk about them, say them over and over, and clap the rhythmic patterns. When they seem to understand the process, the groups can be given the problem to agree on a commercial or slogan which they can play on their instruments, and then to put movement to the pattern. Sometimes this takes the form of abstraction and at other times, an interpretation of the idea but the rhythmic pattern continues throughout.

Other interpretations for percussion patterns have been furnished by rounds and nursery rhymes, rope-jumping verses, peddlers' calls, slogans, quotations, and work songs. Sport cheers, chants, materials from language arts and social studies also afford many opportunities for work with percussion.

Open-ended experiences can be modified in terms of particular interests, seasonal factors, weather conditions, or unique situational factors. These offer important extensions. In a way these are projective devices which give maximum opportunity to children to make the adaptations and extensions by means of using their percussion. Illustrations have included such ideas as the following:

The haunted house in ghost town is_____.
One page in the Dictionary is about_____.
If we had to live in outer space_____.
Pirates shipwrecked_____.
The road map says_____.
Merry merry Christmas, everyone_____.
Math problems for class included_____.
Lists of consonants blends _____.
Lists of words beginning with S_____.
We've got spring fever because_____.

Percussion is an exciting and stimulating activity, and some groups cannot "take" as much as others. It is a good way to begin a period, especially because it gives older children a better review of the elements of tempo, intensity, rhythmic pattern, underlying beat, measure, phrase, and accent.

Percussion has led to composing songs, stories, and dance interpretations. Classroom units have grown from such incidences as the second-grader's discovery that the playing of the wood block sounded like a clock. Older children have formed themselves into a band and accompanied some of their folk dances. One group with two guitars and percussion called and played for square dancing. This group was able to write and follow its own scores.

Creating stories has resulted with percussion used to accompany stories, incidents, or characters in stories. The story of milk includes the progressive of the following incidents:

Growing grass
to
Cows grazing
to

Milking machines
to
Trucks to dairy
to
Filling cartons
to
Store delivery
to
You

The children entitled this percussive story "From Moo to You."

We were fortunate to have a college Afro-Dance Group visit us. The drummers, particularly, interested us. We knew a lot about the African culture because we had been studying it in social studies and language arts. We learned that African dance was accompanied by drums. It was wonderful for us to see the "real thing." The colorful costumes also intrigued us because they were so full of intricate designs. As a result of this experience, the class worked out a dance of their interpretations of the patterns in the costumes with percussion accompaniment.

One of the greatest features of percussion is that boys and girls enjoy it so much. Schools can reap countless valuable learning adventures by providing opportunities for using percussion.

RESOURCES

A Helpful Piano Accompanist

The accompanist is an important member of the group. He or she understands and enjoys children and respects and helps them with their creations. He or she is enthusiastic and encouraging and regards creative efforts as important. The accompanist is keenly alert to the ways in which children

move and appreciative of the way they use their imaginations to respond to sound. Piano music is a vital and valuable part of the creative rhythm experience when the accompanist adjusts the playing to the mood and tempo of the group, watching and getting the feel of their gallops, skips and polkas.

So much depends upon the accompanist's being able to "feel movement." There is a personal involvement between children and their movement and the accompanist. There are times when the music is used to keep a group going, particularly when basic movement is being developed. The accompanist along with the teacher is an encourager and expediter.

Skill in playing is less important than understanding people. We receive little help for creative work from a person whose only interest is in the music before her. If she usually follows definite pieces of music, giving her attention to the page before her rather than having her attention on the children, she cannot be fully aware of what is happening to them. The accompaniment should be distinct, captivating, and well accented and hold the tempo established by the class. A confident accompanist can be of great help to the children.

Movement is clarified by providing a strong supporting rhythmical beat and controlling tempo. As the children become more and more confident and excited, their tempo tends to quicken; as they get tired, tempo tends to lag. Accompanying movement is something one develops. The more one works with children the freer and richer the facility at the keyboard will become and the more meaningful the music. Ability to improvise, imagination, spontaneity, and sensitivity to the children are of primary concern. Even an accompanist with a fairly extensive repertoire cannot always summon the appropriate music to fit the children's movements. Frequently, she needs to improvise to maintain the spirit and catch the idea of the group. The "right music" at the "right time" can add meaning and depth to the children's creations.

If a regular accompanist is not available we have had assistance from classroom teachers, the music teacher, parents, student teachers, and boys and girls. Anyone who has just a little skill on the piano can do acceptable jobs for dance, if she will watch the children and take her cues from them. A few simple chords are often adequate and may be just what is needed; the piano can be played high for light movements of high levels, low for low levels, loud for heavy, and soft for light movements. The piano assumes the same importance as a percussion instrument. In this respect it can be played in the following ways: by increasing or decreasing the tempo and intensity, raising and lowering the pitch to indicate levels, or by taking the underlying beat or rhythmic pattern. *Music* as we know it may not necessarily come out of the piano, but *sound* does. It is a fine experience for a teacher or a child to feel the movement, watch others move, and then reproduce it in sound. The accompanists literally feel the movement in their fingers, responding on the piano as boys and girls respond with moving.

One third-grade class always seemed to enter the room skipping. One day they were asked to clap the rhythm of the skip, and then to skip again. The accompanist, taking her cue from the children, accompanied the skip with a lilting rhythm. As she changed the tune, Bobby asked if the same music could be played again, because it made him "skip all over." She recalled it as best she could and so that it would not be forgotten roughly jotted it down in a book we kept at the piano for just that purpose. To the delight of the third-graders, when they came to dance the next day, "their skip" was played. This shows how simple music can be enjoyed and appreciated by children when it is created for them with their movement patterns in mind.

The music that has been included in this book is the result of simple piano improvisations, spontaneously played and recorded to fit particular movement experiences. With repetition, these improvisations took on definite form, and were recorded and used with different groups of children.

The song "Balloons for Sale" came about in the following way. There had been a fair in town, and the children were excited about having their own fair. After much discussion, they divided into groups to work out their program. The balloon man must

SKIP

Lightly, with marked rhythm

Nina Coffing

have fascinated this group, because two groups decided to work out their interpretation of him. As they worked on movements, they made a "patter" of their words. Mrs. Burns was listening intently and as they worked, she recorded what they were saying. She drew their attention to the fact that they had written a verse, and made it into a song for them.

Records

There are times when we need to listen to records to help us become more aware of

BALLOONS FOR SALE

Well marked

Florence Burns

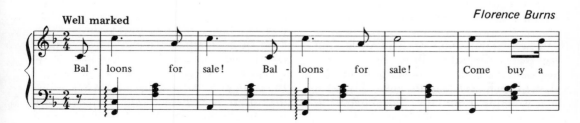

Bal - loons   for   sale!   Bal - loons   for   sale!   Come   buy   a

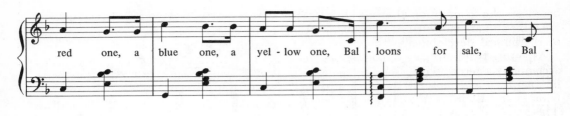

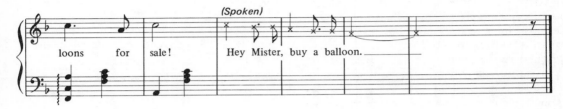

rhythmic elements or to see if we can get the "feel" of the music. When this happens we talk about the kind of movement that we may use with that music. There are times when we listen to music and then use if for improvisation because sometimes it is fun to do just whatever we want to music we like. This is most fruitful when boys and girls are comfortable with movement. There is *no* one correct movement because children hear the music in their own way. There are times when we move to *specific* music which the accompanist plays for us or which we hear on the record player. For this, we need to listen first to get the rhythm and then to adjust the dance to the recording. This type of dancing comes *after* we can move freely, distinguish rhythm, and adjust our own rhythm to whatever we hear. To improve our square-dance calling, we study the work of professional callers on records, noting their style. However, much of our square dancing is done to music with *our own calls.*

There is an abundance of good music suitable for children. Boys and girls enjoy responding to music appropriate for their dance capabilities and interests. Recordings are valuable when they are purposefully used; recordings should be selected so that they will serve specific purposes for specific groups of children at certain times. The purpose may be:

Music listening
Movement accompaniment
Intensifying rhythmic understanding
Improvisation
Percussion accompaniment
Setting a mood
Providing ideas or a theme for folk dancing
Accompanying calling for square dancing
Stimulating social dancing

In other words, recordings should enhance what we are trying to achieve at a particular time; they should *assist* rather than *dictate.* A problem sometimes arises when using recordings with young children because the tempo of young children is usually much faster than that set by many records. There are times when records become a crutch and dictate what to do and how to do it rather than being used as stimulators or aids to creativeness for children. The teacher on the spot *is the key* and can never be replaced by an impersonal voice on a record giving directions to a group of children he or she does not know. Too many records are made based on the assumption that all children are alike and are currently at the same level of rhythmical development.

As young children have opportunities to accompany a record with sticks, percussion, or singing, it adds not only variety but contributes to their rhythmic development. There are many records that are useful in giving young children marked contrasts in qualities, moods, melodies, and dramatic effects. Such records may be used to stimulate children to move at will, expressing themselves in their own way. The teacher plays an important role in challenging children to exaggerate their movements, project themselves, and extend their ways of moving. After children and teachers have developed background in dance and are proficient in areas such as square dance, then there is a purposeful reason for using the record with a good caller. We are now ready for him and can follow his calls, and the record extends our competencies.

Children are encouraged to bring in records which they particularly like and which are rhythmically stimulating to them. Sometimes they are "just right" for a mood we are trying to create. Other times the children call their folk dances to a record of their choice, or we respond to their current popular record with our latest fad step.

When selecting music for children's dance, the following questions may be helpful:

Is it childlike?

Does the record have a strong recognizable beat?

Does it have rhythmic buoyancy and simplicity in rhythmic structure and form?

Is the music long enough in duration to be used as an aid to teaching?

Does it have appeal for children and is it capable of heightening their responses and imagination?

Does it have interesting melody and quality?

Is the music peppy, spirited, catchy, and pleasing in melody and mood?

Is the tempo appropriate for the particular group of children and is there interesting variation in the tempo?

Does the music have identifiable melodic phrases, accent, and strong rhythmic power?

If it has a theme, is it recognizable?

Is it in good taste for children?

Does it add to the range of material in the class record collection?

Tape Recorder

The teacher who has a tape recorder or a casette handy has a most valuable aid to her teaching; just the right kind of music for the specific moment can be stored away. Catching tunes of children as they are originating them, and having them refined and then taped for future use is helpful. Taping someone playing the piano when you are working with children provides music for later use. Many creative gems can be recorded for future use. The tape recorder helps us to preserve material that is meaningful and adds to our collections of resources.

After children have had a variety of experiences with records, teachers can introduce the tape recorder, making it possible for them to make their own modifications to their songs, chants, and dance accompaniments.

Sound may be used as a creative activity within itself. It is an important partner of movement because it not only accompanies and intensifies movement, but it also helps to sharpen perception. The extensive area of sound is invaluable to any teacher as she facilitates the growth of children through creativity, rhythm, and movement.

V

Boys and Girls Dancing

14

Fun with Folk and Social Dance

Dancing is fun! There is a spirit of exhilaration and spontaneity in the air when we dance. Sometimes boys and girls stop, exhausted, only to say "Let's do it again!"; usually they participate wholeheartedly in such activities. *Folk and social dancing* is meaningful, because it represents a natural and a progressive development from more fundamental movement experiences to various more structured movements.

Dance experiences progress from the learning of combinations of basic movements and their interrelatedness with elements or space, time, and force, to specific folk and social dance forms. If children have acquired a fundamental movement vocabulary through a program in creative rhythmic movement, and if they are helped to enjoy movement, they will already have experienced many of the basic dance step patterns. They will also have experienced moving according to different floor patterns and directions, as well as responding to tempo, pulse, and phrasing in music. Participating in a specific dance with a particular movement will simply mean a review, and it will be unnecessary to spend several periods trying to teach specific step patterns.

Boys and girls also need to have acquired the skill of listening and following directions. They need to be able to work easily in group situations and to feel comfortable with themselves and the group. Now it is a matter of putting together so much of what they already know to extend their experiences. To put it another way, this type of activity is an extension of movement and rhythmic experiences into an organized whole—a dance. The dance has a beginning and certain sequences of combinations of movements (dance steps) and a specific melody or chant, and it communicates feelings or stories.

FOLK DANCING

We have observed that as older boys and girls develop movement competencies they are not hesitant to engage in various *folk dance forms* nor are they embarrassed by boy-girl combinations, and they readily participate in the real fun that comes from moving rhythmically as a part of a group.

Folk dancing is a group activity that fits into the developmental pattern of older childhood. Its contribution begins as boys and girls desire to associate with their own group and peers. Folk dance provides a feeling of accomplishment for all those par-

ticipating. Moving together, responding, communicating, and being an essential part of a rhythmic experience is valuable to children.

This chapter addresses itself to children and folk and social dancing. In these areas of dance people can speak with their whole bodies—communicating, moving, singing, or chanting rhythmically. In the AAHPER publication *Children's Dance* in a section on "Ethnic and Folk Dance," Gertrude Blanchard says, "one part of ethnic dance is folk dance. It is the fun part where the reason for dancing is personal pleasure. ... Folk dance is that part of ethnic which they (people) do for fun, for the joy of moving, for personal pleasure of inter-relating with others in rhythmic patterns....We are concerned with children's dance and the area of ethnic in which most children participate is folk dance. Whether Mexican, African, Finnish or Korean, it is that part of the dance culture which is done for fun, and, as such, should be presented to give pleasure to the participant." [1]

In the beginning, fun must be stressed. The children need to get the feel of the rhythm, which will start them moving and give them the opportunity to have a pleasurable experience. If the emphasis is on fun and group activity, all the children can enter into the activity wholeheartedly, with little embarrassment or self-consciousness. Lengthy and involved descriptions, slow tempo, or practicing a set pattern over and over tends to kill any approach to folk dancing. Mistakes can be overlooked, for it is the spirit, tempo, and meaning of the dance that needs to be encouraged with children, rather than the style.

When dancing, spontaneous fingersnaps, claps, heel clicks, hip bumps, or stamps are injected by some, reflective of their mores or cultural mannerisms, they need not detract from the spirit or character of the dance.

However there is a time for boys and girls

to perfect a dance after they have had some experience. This is often done in a specific style for a specific purpose. Patterns become automatic as they catch the spirit of dancing together and associate it with something that is within their own experience. Later they become aware of style and spirit and of why the dance is performed in a particular manner. Gaining folk dance experience, they realize that some steps are basically similar, but that it is the manner in which they are danced and the positions that vary. In the beginning, fun must be the result of children's participation, as well as better understanding of self and others.

In a national status report of dance in the elementary school, it was stated that "by far the greatest number of respondents perceives the elementary school dance program as the *teaching of dances*, and the dances taught as folk dances, singing games and square dances." [2] This opinion implied that dances were taught to boys and girls in "units." When this "unit" type of teaching is employed, too often boys and girls have not had previous developmental movement experiences which help them to discover movement skills and dance patterns, nor have they had previous progressive rhythmical experiences. The idea that there is a certain time that boys and girls may be brought together to learn a specific dance prescribed or presented by the teacher is wrong—children must be given opportunities to *participate* in dance experiences rather than merely being taught specific dances.

Problems are bound to occur if boys and girls are brought together infrequently to learn a specific dance, which is often out of context with other school experiences; this often happens because of a need to present something for an assembly or special program. This is the best way to turn many boys and girls away from folk dancing. It

---

[1] AAHPER, *Children's Dance*, p. 57.

[2] "Status," *Journal of Health, Physical Education and Recreation*, AAHPER (June 1971), p. 140.

seems it is just like saying, skate around the rink with a partner in a circle to music, when they have had little background if any in skating. Many teachers have had unhappy experiences themselves in folk dancing or feel a rhythmical lack in their background. This is understandable and we hope that by sharing in some of the experiences we have presented in this book a new attempt at folk dancing will be forthcoming and that teachers, boys and girls will have fun and joy in all dancing together.

Both *folk and social dancing* are meaningful and important when they are considered as a part of the school program. Whether the dances emerge from children or are purposefully selected and presented, they may be used as an aid to learning, when boys and girls become interested in historical events and life in other lands, and when their interests extend from their immediate surroundings to the world outside.

Folk dance comes from people. From the beginning of time, people have participated in dance activities. Boys and girls can create their own folk dances, as well as participate in dances of other cultures, places, and times. The fun comes in the active participation, in the involvement of dancing together.

Dancing, particularly folk dancing, is a form of communication, an expression and communication of human feelings participated in by people the world over. Through their dancing people tell us much about their needs, their aspirations, and the times in which they live. Folk dances are stories—happenings of people here and now and of people of long ago from faraway places. Folk dances concern sad and happy experiences, rituals, ceremonies, traditions, and worship. They often relate to nature and to challenges and feats of skill and bravery.

As cultures change, so do some of their dances. Boys and girls are very much a part of current world happenings, a fact that can highlight and bring into focus folk stories and dances. Also, they are often intrigued with the idea that dances have been handed down from generation to generation and have persisted because of their meaning to those who participated.

Some of our happiest times have been when a visitor from another part of the world, or from a culture different from ours, joined us and shared their songs and dances. For instance, when we were studying about the Orient and Clarabelle's mother helped us to dance some of her stories, the group had a great time dancing about Chinese New Year. What an important way for us to find out about people as people when we dance some of their dances. Grass skirts and leis, feathers, scarves, characteristic hats, wooden shoes, boots, sticks, drums, shakers, tambourines, bagpipes, kalimbos and steel drums take on new and exciting meanings for us. We also begin to understand more about people and their need for water, sun, rain, food and friendship—all of which we are prone to take for granted.

Folk dancing provides many purposes for boys and girls as they participate enthusiastically in the spirit of dancing. This approach to dancing from about the fourth grade up is quite different from the status report of folk dancing found in many schools across the country.

Illustrations of Folk-Dance Forms for Young Children

Singing Games for Young Children

Singing games may be thought of as an initial form of folk dance. All over the world children have inherited singing games. They are deeply rooted in the heritage of families of people. They have been and continue to be used, played, or danced by generation after generation. There is a relationship between the dance songs illustrated in Chapter 8 and singing games in that the melody and lyrics are short, repetitive, and we move and sing at the same time for specific purposes. However, *dance songs have been created by us and may apply to any age, whereas singing games for the most part are traditional and are applicable to very young children.* Also, singing games consist of a structured form and because of the folk quality it seems natural to refer to them in this chapter on folk and social dance forms.

Frequently, singing games call for individual action within a group setting. The repetition in the rhythmic pattern and the sing-song melody indicates at least in our culture that they are danced by young children. However, this is not to say that the form of singing games for young children is simple; we presuppose that they are able to respond to spatial elements of floor patterns, make a circle or stay in lines, or assume a place in a scattered situation. We assume that they have developed enough control to take turns or to take their place within a group, that they can follow directions and sing as they move. We also assume that they have had some movement experiences, that they can move in different directions rhythmically with the group. Many kindergarten children are not ready, others are.

Singing games have a beginning and ending, have definite rhythmic and spatial elements to be followed, and communicate a story, idea, or a feeling. This may be real or nonsensical; children like nonsense. But even though some singing games may seem nonsensical, they may have real meaning in terms of the culture in which they originated. Or it may be that in translation or handing it down from generation to generation the true meaning was lost. At any rate, there is no doubt that some singing games are useful.

There are many singing games which have lived for generations and offer rich learning experiences for children. There is a place for singing games when children can handle them, because of their rhythmical contribution and the opportunity to help children make associations. Singing games become meaningful to children as we help them to understand what they are dancing and singing about. For instance, we can share information with young children about the origin of some of our singing games, such as the "Muffin Man" and what this song means to boys and girls in England (a far-off country) and what we have that is comparable in this country such as "Ice Cream Man" instead of the "Muffin Man." Then meaning and identification are involved. Samples of other associations which we have made include:

Did You Ever See a Lassie? (name—Susie or Phillip)

London Bridge Is Falling Down—Old, Old Bridge Falling Down ... Careful not to be caught.

Not only do we need to help to preserve this type of folk music for children, but many of the tunes are ones children love and repeat over and over. As a group of young children are participating in a singing game, they often seem to say by their faces, "isn't it fun just to be me and you singing, moving, and dancing together." Our emphasis is on feeling satisfaction and being involved in participating in the spirit of the song rather than being on a left or right foot.

Sometimes we talk about how much we are like all other boys and girls, and that the only thing that might make us seem different is where we live. We know that China is a long way away, but we can sing and dance Ching Loo's Folk Song and we have even made up additional verses.

When visiting our school, Abdul Razak, from Iraq, shared some of his songs with us. The following was too difficult for us to learn in his native language, so he translated the song and taught it to us. It is a follow-the-leader type of singing game, with the group following whatever two or more leaders do.

NEVER MIND

Chinese Folk Song

1. Ching loo, Chi-na boy, flew his pa-per kite, Came a gust of wind and blew it out of sight.
2. Ching loo, Chi-na boy, tried to sing a song, Sang it high and low and al-ways sang it wrong.
3. Ching loo, Chi-na boy, went to buy some rice, Wan-dered up and down but couldn't pay the price.

"Ting-a - ling, ting- a-ling" said Ching loo, Nev-er mind I've an-oth - er kite.
Nev-er mind I've an-oth - er song.
Nev-er mind I___ need no rice.

WE ARE THE LEADERS

Abdul Rasak

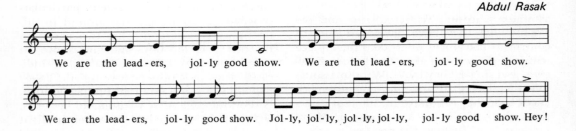

We are the lead-ers, jol-ly good show. We are the lead-ers, jol-ly good show.

We are the lead-ers, jol-ly good show. Jol-ly, jol-ly, jol-ly, jol-ly, jol-ly good show. Hey!

Norman's father had been in Ghana for two years, and finally Norman and his mother were going to join him. His third grade was curious about the new place Norman was going to live and were pleased to find out that boys and girls there were a bit like them. We had fun with a folk song called "Che Che Kole," which was found in the *Hi Neighbor* series, Book Two.[3] This is one of our finest sources for folk material for young children.

As children get older and have more experience moving, they often make up dances to various singing game songs. Our "Skipping Song" is an illustration. It was first originated to encourage children to skip together and to explore a variety of movement. It was adapted to "Sing a Song of Sixpence," but has been sung to a number of other tunes of $\frac{4}{4}$ time.

[3] U.S. Committee to UNICEF. United Nations, New York.

Skipping Song

We'll skip and skip and skip and skip and skip
    around the room
First I skip alone but I need a partner soon.
    I skip here and choose one; and you skip over
        there

Come along and have some fun and skip 'most anywhere.

Sing a song of skipping
A pocket full of things
  Four and twenty [or "many many"] children
    skipping in a ring
When the music stops, then Johnny says "Watch me—
  "Can you do the things I do, they're simple as can be."

This song not only provides an opportunity for children to skip together while singing and to introduce them to folk dancing but also allows for creative individual action—one child can set the pattern for the others to follow. In this way, a variety of movements may be quickly reviewed. The "Skipping Song" has also served as a mixer activity for children and parents together, or for different age groups dancing together.

One day while working in small groups on combinations of movements, one group made up a similar type of folk dance to the tune of "Skip to My Lou," which they called "Choose a Movement."

Choose a Movement

(All slide in a circle floor pattern while singing the first part.)

Choose a movement, that's what we'll do
Choose a movement, that's what we'll do
I have a movement, how about you?
What's your movement, Randy?

(Randy goes to center of the circle and does his movement, the rest following while singing the second part)

Here's my movement, you can do it too!
Here's Randy's movement, we can do it too
Here's Randy's movement, we can do it too.
Choose another movement, Jackie.

(The dance continues with each person choosing another to start a new movement.)

Folk Dancing for Older Boys and Girls

Many of the singing games can be enlarged and extended into folk-type dances. For instance, the song "Sometimes Fast, Sometimes Slow" was adapted for young children from the song "That's What Makes the World Go 'Round." With older groups, circles of six or eight are formed and boys and girls find different ways they can go around in a circle—or "Make the World Go 'Round." After a short time for experimenting, each group decides on one particular way, which they do as they sing the chorus part. Much ingenuity is evident, particularly when circles are moving around in different ways. The dance has two parts—to the first part the boys and girls move all together according to the body part indicated. During chorus ("move a little") they move the way the small group has decided.

Working with Miss Watson and her class, we created a folk dance based on a chant from names of class members. We started putting names together and chanting the sounds of them. We moved to these names and liked the sound of Justus, Ernestine, and Renee. We found that different names made us use different kinds of movements. We decided to take just first letters of names and see how many we could put together in chant form. The song on page 282 resulted from the first letters of several names, and the class also developed movements to dance.

When the class was asked to dance for a teachers' conference, they wanted to do their "Jemba" and to teach it to the teachers. After much discussion, they decided that they needed to add another part which would give them time to go to the audience and invite teachers to dance with them.

THAT'S WHAT MAKES THE WORLD GO ROUND

Lively

We have heads, now let them go! We have heads, now let them go!

Move them up and move them down. That's what makes the world go 'round!

Move a lit-tle, move a lit-tle, move some more, Move a lit-tle, move a lit-tle, on the floor.

Move a lit-tle, move a lit-tle, move some more. That's what makes the world go 'round.

JEMBA KAMBA RAE

Jem-ba, Jem-ba, Jem-ba, Jem-ba Kam-ba Rae. Jem-ba, Jem-ba, Jem-ba, We'll Let's

1. do it our own way. 2. do an-oth-er way. Oh I need you and you need me.

You need me and I need you, We can dance most an-y way do-ing Jem-ba, Kam-ba Rae.

Jemba	Justus	Ernestine	Mike	Barry	Andra
			Mike		
Kamba	Karen	Andra	Mike	Barry	Andra
	Kirk		Mike		
Rae	Randy	Andra	Ernestine		
	Randy				
	Ronnie				
	Ricky				
	Renee				
	Royal				

They wanted to keep the chant a secret and agreed not to tell anyone what their chant meant. To their "Jemba" song and dance they now added (as they danced toward the teachers):

> Oh, I need you and you need me.
> You need me and I need you.
> Come along and move with me
> To Jemba Kamba Rae.

Many of the teachers had asked them what Jemba meant, and the children were bursting to tell their secret. They were very smug as they pointed to their chart (above), which was displayed around the room. Each child stood in front of the word containing the initial of his or her name.

The Polka

A class of fourth-graders was experimenting with combinations of skips, gallops, and slides; several were doing a type of polka without realizing it. They were intrigued with their new-found pattern and started exaggerating, adding or accenting with different body parts and spatial elements. As they stopped to rest, Felicia was asked to show her combination. The class was asked to follow her movements and to try to find a part of it which they had used before. They did not want to watch, they wanted to try! Attention was called to the fact that the boys and girls they had observed were doing a *polka*.

We worked on the step pattern and Winfred asked, "How do you spell that?" Their teacher, Miss Garber, picked up the cue and talked with the class about the *polka*. When they returned to their classroom, she used the word in her spelling list. The next time we met, they wanted to start out with the polka. When asked if they had learned how to spell polka, there was a spelling chorus in response to "What does it start with?" "P." "How does it end?" "A." The following folk dance and song developed as the class started polkaing through space, spelling and chanting—

> The polka—the polka—P-O-L-K-A [Spelling]
> The polka—the polka—P-O-L-K-A
> It starts with a "P" and ends with "A"
> The polka—the polka—P-O-L-K-A.

Their music teacher was with them that day, so she picked up their chanting on the piano and added melody. Individually they added many variations to their polka pattern, some doing it in partners and others following each other within small groups, singing as they moved. They wanted to make a polka dance and add more to what they were doing. Again, Miss Garber used this opportunity to develop a language chart of their polka song which they added as a second part. Each student handed me his part in writing including movements, floor patterns, and the composition of the group. Together in groups they worked out their movements, floor patterns, and the composition of the group. The next time we met they had another chart with a series of leaders of small groups listed. The small groups responded with their dance pattern when their leader was called, i.e.:

Richard, Richard, tell us what to do
Richard, Richard, tell us what to do
Richard, Richard, tell us what to do
Richard, Richard, tell us what to do!

Between each sequence of group patterns, they went back to singing and dancing the polka. There were seven groups and the group movements were as varied as the boys and girls in the class. Because they had a background in movement, there was no problem in adapting their group movements to the dance.

This was not the end of their polka dance. One day the principal told the group that a large group of college students who were going to do student teaching were visiting their school the next day. She asked if they would like to dance for the students. They accepted the invitation and worked out what they would like to do. They decided that they would like to teach the "older people" their polka. Again, with Miss Garber's help, another chart was added as an introduction:

THE POLKA

Arr. *Elizabeth Sutherland*

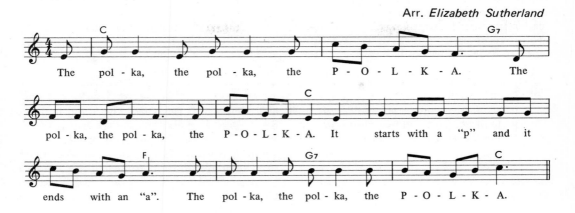

The pol - ka, the pol - ka, the P - O - L - K - A. The
pol - ka, the pol - ka, the P - O - L - K - A. It starts with a "p" and it
ends with an "a". The pol - ka, the pol - ka, the P - O - L - K - A.

The Polka, the polka is fun to do—
Why not come and join us too?
The Polka, the polka is fun to do—
Come on—join us—polka too.

Children have used Walt Disney's songs, books, and records to motivate or enhance movement and percussion experiences. The following is a sample of one of their folk dances.

It's a Small World

First verse: Circle—hands joined.

Start walking sideward with *left* foot, cross right foot over in front of left. Continue until the 15th walk and hold (*on left*).

Start walking sideward with *right* foot, cross left foot over in front of right. Continue until the 15th walk and hold (*on right*).

Chorus: Partners face each other

4 schottisches

Circle—hands joining—face center.

Go forward with 4 walk-hop combinations, go backward with 3 walk-hops, one accented walk or stamp (*hold*).

Second verse: Repeat movements of first verse, circling left and right

Chorus: Repeat chorus—jump on last movement.

The Calypso

A group of fifth-graders was studying about the islands in the Caribbean. Many of the calypso songs were actually a means of communication among the island people. The boys and girls discovered a basic calypso dance-step pattern of walk, walk, walk, heel. They turned this pattern into a dance form having two parts.

A popular student teacher in the school dropped by as this same group was dancing their calypso. He watched for a while and then asked how they would like to learn a dance his older brother had taught him when he was their age. He had two people hold a pole and continue to lower it two to three inches each time. Then he showed them how he could limbo.

CALYPSO

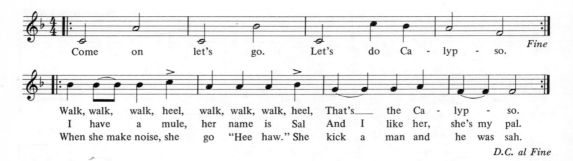

Walk, walk, walk, heel, walk, walk, walk, heel, That's___ the Ca - lyp - so.
I have a mule, her name is Sal And I like her, she's my pal.
When she make noise, she go "Hee haw." She kick a man and he was sah.

D.C. al Fine

LIMBO

Arr. *Richard Bull*

1. Can you Lim - bo, Lim-bo like me, Lim - bo, Lim - bo like me?
2. I can Lim - bo, Lim-bo like you, Lim - bo, Lim - bo like you?

The class was anxious to learn. Alan suggested that we put our feet about a foot apart and that we try to keep our shoulders level. Then, with a sort of shuffle step forward, with shoulders swinging from side to side, the head back, the trunk also twists to get under the pole without touching it. The song above was developed to be played for the limbo.

Boys and girls readily identify with songs and tales of American origin. It seems appropriate at the beginning to introduce children to American forms so that they can experience some of the American folk dances. Dances such as "Pop Goes the Weasel," "Shoo Fly," "Bingo," "Salty Dog Rag," "Red River Gal," etc., have been particular favorites in the past. Boys and girls can carry the tune of the dance and provide their own accompaniment. Also, they find that they can adapt steps and create extensions of their own. The "Hokie Kokie" and "Pawpaw Patch" are included here as samples. The "Hokie Kokie" is called by various names in different parts of the country, but regardless of the name, it is the kind of folk dance that appeals to children.

Hokie Kokie

The "Hokie Kokie" is an illustration of a spirited tune with lively tempo. The emphasis is placed on dancing and singing together as a group, rather than on just exactly what the words say. In this dance it does not matter which arm or foot is used (right or left). The important thing is that children participate, enjoy it, and ask for more. Variations have been worked out on the chorus—"and you do the Hokie Kokie." Some of the variations are: all children clapping first to one side and then the other; shagging around in individual circles, skipping, schottisching, individually doing the lindy hop; or in couples, doing creative movement patterns; or one couple going into the center, with others following their movements—taking turns, with one

HOKIE KOKIE

Arr. *Alonah Stith*

1. Put your one arm in,_____ Put your one arm out,_____
Put your one arm in,_____ And shake it all a - bout._____ You do the
Ho - kie Ko-kie,_____ You do it O - key do-key,_____ You do the
Ho - kie Ko-kie,_____ And that's what it's all___ a - bout! Hey! Hey!

2. Put your other arm in . . . .
3. Put your one leg in . . . .
4. Put your head . . . .
5. Put your whole self . . . .

couple and then another going in on each chorus; and taking turns going around the circle, following first the pattern of one couple and then the next.

Pawpaw Patch

"Pawpaw Patch" has more structure in floor pattern, movement design, and alternating roles of leadership, compared with some of the other dances. This song provides for following directions as children sing and dance. It serves as a fine introduction to American line and square dances.

The sound of the word "pawpaw" seems to amuse youngsters—therefore it is easy to encourage them to go to the dictionary or encyclopedia to find information. Pawpaw —sometimes called *papaw*—is the name of a small tree or large shrub having purple flowers. The fruit has a rind, and is similar in shape to a small flattened baked potato, oblong, or egg-shaped.

Traditionally, there are three verses to the song:

1. Where, oh where, is pretty little Nellie
2. Come on, boys, let's go find her
3. Picking up pawpaws put 'em in your pocket

Boys and girls of nine and ten years old are beginning to be sensitive about appearance and sometimes the connotation of "pretty" does not seem to fit. We adapt words and prefer to sing the first verse.

"Where, oh where, is that girl, Cindy, or Valerie," or whoever the girl dancing happens to be. If it happens to be a boy, we sing "Where, oh where, is that boy, Kevin or Bernie." The second verse often becomes, "Come on, let's go find her (or him) or the name of the person."

Even though the dance calls for partners of boys and girls, this is not necessary as long as all children enthusiastically join in the dance. Partners might in some cases be of the same sex. This is bound to happen if we have extra boys or girls; this way, all are included and we adapt the song to fit the situation. However, as mentioned earlier, if boys and girls have had progressive movement and dance experience they don't seem to mind boy-girl partners.

The dance starts with two lines of partners standing side by side facing in the same direction, toward the front of the

PAW PAW PATCH

Arr. *Judy Hogan*

1. Where oh where is that girl Cin - dy? Where oh where is that girl Cin - dy?

Where oh where is that girl Cin - dy? Way down yon-der in the paw- paw patch.

2. Come on ____ let's go find her, Come on ____ let's go find her.

Come on ____ let's go find her, Way down yon-der in the paw - paw patch.

3. Picking up pawpaws, putting in our pocket.
   Picking up pawpaws, putting in our pocket.
   Picking up pawpaws, putting in our pocket.
   Way down yonder in the pawpaw patch.

room. The lines are designated as having a front and back with the head couple at the front of the lines. When there are boy-girl partners, the girls are always on the boys' right.

On the first verse, "Where, oh where is that girl Cindy?," Cindy skips across in front of Kevin and around his line to the back and then down through the middle of the two lines back to her place. All continue singing until she is back.

In the second verse, "Come on, let's go find her," all in Kevin's line follow him around Cindy's line and back to their own places.

On the third verse, "Picking up paw-paws, putting in our pockets," all in the two lines in partners follow Cindy and Kevin, taking the same path taken during the second verse, with motions of bending down to pick pawpaws and put them in their pocket. When Cindy and Kevin reach the back of the lines they make an arch and the other couples move through, with a new head couple at the front of the line. The dance begins again. Cindy and Kevin have sketched their floor pattern. In this dance, the activity and the singing are continuous. The tempo is rapid and movement is strenuous.

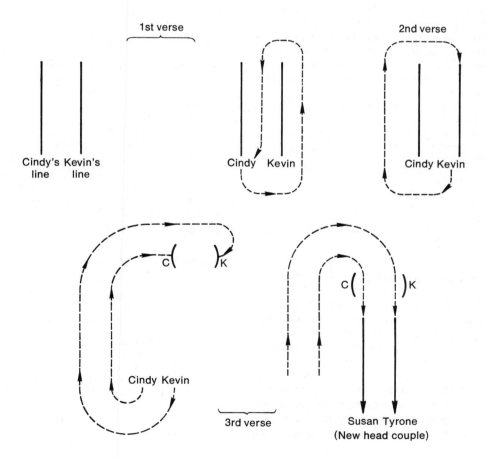

1st verse

Cindy's line   Kevin's line

2nd verse

Cindy   Kevin

Cindy Kevin

C   K

Cindy Kevin

C   K

3rd verse

Susan Tyrone
(New head couple)

The Virginia Reel

The Virginia Reel has been around for a long time. The original dance came to this country from England; American colonists changed the style and the name. This folk dance seems to be a natural progression from a dance such as "Pawpaw Patch." No matter the size of the class, all can actively participate as they recognize movements or learn new figures. Again the emphasis is on having fun dancing together in partners, rather than on boy-girl couples. Usually when the Virginia Reel is first danced, the students are in two long parallel lines, with partners facing each other. The front and back (end) as well as the center and the outside of the lines are identified with partners at the front of the line as the head couple. Traditionally, this dance has been presented to groups by figures and the group memorizes the figures. Because of the learnings involved we have a "chanter" or "caller."

The music starts and the boys and girls listen and get into the swing of the rhythm and then respond to this introductory call.

Everybody ready!
>Everyone forward
>Everyone back to place
>And listen to the call.
>
>Everyone forward again
>Everyone back to place.

If children have had previous work with directions in space and responding to rhythm of music, they can get into action immediately. The only caution is to listen to the caller, therefore, the injection of *listen to the call*. With the above introduction and with the group moving together, the boys and girls are ready to dance the Virginia Reel, using the following calls, but not necessarily in sequence; the sequence depends upon the response of the group. Often as new figures are learned the calls

are repeated to give everyone more time to think out the call and "get with the music."

Everyone ready for the Virginia Reel!

First part: Everyone

Everyone forward and back
Everyone forward and back again
Forward with a right-arm swing
Forward with a left-arm swing
Forward again with a two-hand swing
Forward again around back to back
Forward again with a back to back or do-si-do

(Do-si-do or do-sa-do is a folk-dance term associated with the movement of passing one's partner back to back.)

Second part: Head couple

>Head couple ready with a slide
>Head couple slide on down to the end
>Slide on down through the center
>Slide on down to the end
>Slide all of the way down
>And slide or sashay back
>Slide or sashay back to your place.

(Sashay is another folk dance term associated with sliding. The slide or sashay call is repeated until the head couple is back in place.)

Third part: Everyone ready!

>Head couple leads off
>Everyone follows up
>Lead off to the outside
>Go 'way down to the end.
>
>Head couple leads off
>And goes to the end
>Everyone follows up
>Head couple makes an arch
>And all follow through
>Follow on down to the front
>With a new head couple
>And we start all over again.

(If the head couple hesitates, the caller simply motions the direction and usually the idea is caught immediately.) The head couple partners turn away from each other and lead their lines around the outside to the other end of the line. An arch is formed by the head couple and the rest of the partners pass under, leading down to the front with a new head couple. The entire dance is repeated and continued indefinitely.

When the boys and girls become adept at responding to the calls and can all dance together, keeping a peppy tempo, many parallel lines of partners are formed, each with a head couple. This way the *reel*—another figure—is added to the second part of the dance. The reel consists of swinging one's partner and then an opposite person, and then going back to swinging the partner. The head couple must swing once and a half around in order to be facing their opposites. After the beginning, there is just one swing each time. Then the head couple dances the reel all the way down to the end of the lines. This is continued until all have been swung.

Again, with boys and girls we do not make a point of the kind of swing used. This is dependent upon the experience and maturity of the group. At the outset, for some it may mean a two-hand swing because at the moment this is most comfortable. Other groups immediately start with a right-arm swing with their partner and a left-arm swing with the opposite. The caller adjusts his call to the group.

New second part: Everyone ready for the reel!

> Head couple reel
> Right-arm swing with partner
> Once and a half around
> Left-arm swing with opposite
> Once around
> Back to your own and it's
> Right to your own and left to the next
> All the way down

Swing with your own
Swing with your opposite
All the way to the end
Right-arm swing with your partner
Once and a half around
And slide on back to place.

(When the head couple reaches the end, they swing once and a half around and then slide down through the center of the line back to their own place. The second part of the dance is now danced with the reel figure in the place of sliding down through the center of the line to the end. However, the reel figure is followed by sliding back to the front to original place of the head couple.)

The Virginia Reel now becomes a folk dance with three key parts.

First part:

> Everyone forward and back.

Second part:

> Head couples reel
> Head couples slide on back.

Third part:

> Head couples lead off
> Everyone follow up
> Head couples arch
> All follow through.

…and start the dance all over again with new head couples.

Shortly, children join in on the calls. Soon they are calling for the entire group. As they become familiar with the Virginia Reel, classes have made many variations and adaptations. On one occasion for an all-school Jamboree, one-sixth grade taught its version of the Virginia Reel to the whole school, including parents and teachers. Others have used their form of the Virginia Reel for a party at Christmas time to Christmas music and for Open School Night to involve teachers and parents. One group was particularly pleased with its adaptation of the Virginia Reel—it became the Virginia Reel in "rock" style.

American Folk Dancing

Boys and girls who have had happy experiences in folk dancing ask for more. As they have a taste of success chanting or singing calls such as in "Paw paw Patch" or "Virginia Reel" they desire to know more about calling. When helping older children learn more about American dancing we start in a large single circle with all moving together while working on calling. It is important that the boys and girls *think* through dance patterns. They have already experienced dancing in two lines in the Virginia Reel. Now they progress to dancing in a single circle, to double circle, and to sets or squares. Progression is gradual, responding to calls and dancing as a large group with a partner in a single circle, to working in small groups of two couples in a double circle to groups of four couples in squares. By the time they are ready for squares many students can call, and all have experienced folk-dance ingredients. For instance, a dance in a square, usually referred to as a square dance, has three parts: an *introductory* call, a *main* call, and an *ending* call. As we dance in a single circle we learn introductory and ending calls; in a double circle we become familiar with main calls, and then when we get into squares we are ready to respond to the calls of the square. Having already experienced a variety of calls and their ingredients, and having had previous experiences with spatial elements of direction and floor designs, the children can now enjoy the square dances.

Dancing and Learning "Calls" in a Single Circle

In a single circle all can participate actively and at the same time learn a few simple calls as we dance. As stated previously, calling is like chanting. Calling really consists of chanting or singing to a melody. At the outset, "calls" need to be *simple* and *repetitive* so that children may become readily familiar with them and follow them easily. As they experience dancing and calling, they realize more and more that the *call* really gives them *direction* and tells them what to do. Children can think through *key* calls from the very first time they dance them. The following is an example:

All *join* hands and *circle left*
And circle left, circle left
Yes, join hands and circle left
Circle left, circle left.

Into the *center* and *back again*
Back again, back again
Into the center and back again
And *listen to the call.*

This time *circle to the right*
To the right, to the right
This time circle to the right
And listen to the call.

Back to the left and don't get lost
Don't get lost, don't get lost
Circle left and don't get lost
That's all to the call.

Children figure out the key calls of *circle left, into the center,* and *circle right.*
Other key calls which boys and girls readily identify are:

Swing your partner
Swing your corner
Promenade

Do-si-do your corner
Do-si-do your corner
Honor your partner
Honor your corner.

These key calls are used over and over in a variety of patterns.

In the beginning we are not too concerned with the positions children take to swing. Whether it is an elbow swing, two-hand swing, or social dance position is dependent upon their social maturity. The important thing is that we learn to listen to the call, get moving, and swing in some manner to a good folk-dance tune. Often we explore as many ways as we can find to swing a partner. As we get the "feel" of the rhythm and become acquainted with calls and gain in experience, good swinging comes naturally.

In a like manner, we handle the question of partners, taking for granted that this is a wholesome form of boy-girl relationship. For children who have had happy, meaningful creative rhythmic movement experiences throughout the grades, there is little problem. While figuring out the calls we talk about partners, because the calls ask for them. If we decide on boy-girl couples, the girl is on the boy's right. If we do not have enough boys or girls to go around, or for some reason we do have a partner problem, we pair those remaining without making a point of it, or *without eliminating anyone.*

While we are discussing partners we also identify the call about *corners.* If partners turn away from each other they are facing another person, and this person is called the *corner.* As for "honor your partner" or "honor your corner," these actually are greetings—children express them as a "Hi or a Hello." We avoid putting emphasis on bowing or curtsying, which are difficult and unnatural for many children, because this form of greeting is not usually a part of experiences of boys and girls. Instead we get them into action immediately. If they use their own form of greeting first, then as they understand more and more about folk dancing and its implications, the idea of formalized bowing and curtsying makes sense to them. We are concerned with quality and excellence and work toward that end. But for the present our emphasis is on helping them become involved in enjoyable and meaningful movement experiences.

Promenade is another key call which boys and girls perfect in time. If they do not happen to know the term "promenade," we talk about it and decide it is like a walk around a ring or circle, going back to where we started. In the beginning some may skip rather than walk—as long as they are responding to the rhythm of the call and the music, this is all right. If some partners prefer one position to another, such as joining with one hand, we treat this in a similar manner as we did the swing. The swing and the promenade are two of the most fundamental calls used; they usually complete a call. Children readily identify them and can respond immediately to them. We have substituted the *swing* and *promenade* calls for the more complicated calls of "grand right and left," the "allemandes," and other difficult beginning and ending calls.

Some of the calls which we have simplified by using the swing and promenade and adapted to use in single circles include: "Little Old Cabin in the Lane," "O Susanna," "Shoo Fly Swing," and "Do-si-Do or Do-si-do Your Corner." The more involved calls such as "allemandes" come later when the boys and girls are more proficient and ready for them.

There is a wealth of good American folk tunes available for piano or on record. (If records are used they should be without calls.) Feeling the underlying pulse and the accent, the dancers form a large single circle, with the girls on the boys' right, and start moving, picking out the calls as they dance. An introductory call that can be given over and over again so children get used to listening, following the call, and responding by dancing is:

> All jump up 'til you come down
> Swing your partner 'round and 'round
> 'Til that foot of yours
> Makes a sound on the floor
> And promenade your partner 'round.

Key words are given on the accent—these are the words that contain pertinent instructions, such as "jump up," "swing your partner," and "promenade." The other phrases, such as " 'til you come down," are identified as "patter." The *patter* can be discussed so that children see that it helps to keep the rhythm and to provide time to complete the movements, but they are of no particular meaning to the call. The boys and girls can call together, giving accent to the key words. The call must be distinct and accented. As they start to work with the entire call, including using the *patter,* the children realize the importance of sensing the phrasing of the music and of coordinating the call and the music. They must also learn to allow time for a group to complete the motions involved in the key call before giving another call.

Some additional examples of calls include:

Introductory Calls:

> All *join hands* and *circle left*
> Circle left around the floor
> Take your *partner*—give her a swing.
> And *promenade* her around the ring.

> Everyone here let's go
> Turn to your *partner* and *do-si-so*
> Now to your *corner* and do the same
> Back to your *partner* and right *promenade.*

> Swing your partner
> Watch her fly
> Swing her low

> And swing her high
> Now *stop* where you are and
> *Promenade* oh *promenade.*

> Swing swing everyone swing
> Swing your corner
> Now your own
> And promenade, oh promenade.

Ending Calls:

> Promenade in single file
> Girl in *front,* boy in *back*
> Promenade in *single file*
> And just let me remind you
> *Boys turn back* in the same old track
> And *swing* the *new girl behind* you.

(This call is repeated many times until the call is given: "And promenade the girl you just swung.")

Boys and girls are ingenious when they have opportunities to make up their own calls. Illustrations of some original introductory and ending calls include the following:

Turn to your partner and stamp, stamp, stamp
Turn to your corner and clap, clap, clap
Back to your partner with a swing
Now take her for a promenade spin.

Face your partner and say hello
Face your corner and do-si-do
All join hands and circle right
Break and swing and promenade.

Everybody jump up high
Everybody swing
Everybody whoop and holler
As you promenade the ring.

Everyone ready for a hotcha swing
Wow wow—watch 'em go
Wow wow—watch 'em go
Hotcha hotcha
Stop where you are and promenade.

Swing that girl
'Round 'n 'round
'Til she swings right off the ground

Stamp your feet right on the floor
Now start to swing and swing some more.

Girls to the center and back again
Boys to the center and do the same
Everybody home, let's swing your own
And promenade, yes promenade.

Dancing in Double Circle Formation— Two Couples

When the children are familiar with a few of the basic introductory and ending calls and can respond readily to changes in tempo and in phrasing, they can think through more complicated calls, referred to as *main* calls. For this they form a double circle in groups of fours—two couples facing each other. Many of the main calls in simplified and adapted form include such phrases as "Step right back and watch her smile," "I'll swing your gal," "Take a little peek," "Star by the right," and "Dive for the oyster." All couples facing clockwise are head couples. An example of a main call is:

Step right back and watch her smile
Step right up and swing her awhile
Step right back and watch her grin
Step right up and swing her agin.

The call is then given: "Head couples swing your own and take her to the next." All of the head couples then take their partner and promenade clockwise to the next couple. All now have a new couple with whom to dance. The children are now working with an opposite couple—responding to three people rather than one.

Dancing this way, everyone learns at once, and this avoids having children standing around waiting for their turns to dance. As children become familiar with a wide variety of calls, they can take faster tempos. This is the time they also begin to acquire style, so that more complicated calls may

be successfully given, such as the allemandes and grand right and left. It is like any other learning experience within the school program, for as addition comes before long division, simple, repetitive calls come before the complicated ones.

In a short time many main calls are thought through as children are actively involved in the process of listening, thinking, and responding. Here are some more examples of main calls:

Around that couple and take a peek
Back to the center and swing your gal
Around that couple and peek once more
Back to the center and swing all four.

I'll swing your girl, you swing mine
By golly, ain't that fine
An even swap, an even trade
Your little squaw for my old maid.

Girl 'round the girl
Boy 'round the boy
Boy 'round the girl
Girl 'round the boy.

Make a star with right-hand cross
The right-hand cross, the right-hand cross
Back with the left and don't get lost
Don't get lost, don't get lost
Swing your opposite, now your own.

Often several calls are put together before a couple moves on to the next couple. Introductory calls can also be combined with a main call, finishing a sequence with an ending call.

With our understanding and repertoire of calls increasing and with ease in responding and dancing with others to music and to the calls, we are soon ready for dancing in a square for square dancing.

Dancing in Squares

Squares are designs in space. In our earlier work with space, we explored shapes, including squares. We now recognize that the folk-dance figures include changes in direction and changing designs in a square. A square is made up of four couples with girls still on the right of boys. The head couple in each square is identified, as well as second, third, and fourth couples. The dancing is now a matter of interaction among four couples. A square dance usually consists of three parts—introductory call, main call, and ending call. Every boy and girl should be familiar with these calls, so now it is a matter of enjoying them by dancing with seven other people in a square formation. The main call is given first for the head couple to dance according to the direction of the caller. After the head couple completes the call, each of the other couples in succession respond to the caller and executes the dance figures. This is different from what has been experienced before, because now partners have to wait their turn to dance. However, response to a caller now comes easily, and the tempo of dancing has increased so that the children do not require explanations and demonstrations; they are simply applying what they have experienced earlier.

When children become skilled in folk dancing in squares, many find that they can dance and call at the same time. Soon some of the boys and girls begin to emerge as callers. It is difficult being the caller for square dancing because of the specific number of couples involved; it is necessary to be concerned with all the squares on the floor. Remembering sequence in calls,

watching four or five squares, and remembering where couples are in the call is difficult. But a fifth- or sixth-grader feels a great sense of accomplishment when he can not only move to and create square dance patterns but also call them.

Original Calls from Boys and Girls

Children enjoy writing and directing their own square dance calls. Many of these are composed with current country music, popular music, folk tunes, or favorite songs. Here are examples of original square dances and calls.

Hoedown

Circle to the left and away we go
Don't you step on my gal's toe
Move along with hands held tight
Now the other way, to the right.

Keep on going with a grin
Ready for the set that you'll be in
Swing your partner and swing some more
Swing her again and circle four.

Swing the gal on your left, small or big
And let's all go for the hoedown jig
Boys in the center and the gals all 'round
See the boys they're a bunch of clowns.

Boys step out to the left-hand gal
Swing her around and swing like mad
Circle to the left and listen to the call
Of the hoedown jig, one and all.

HOE DOWN

Arr. *Alonah Stith*

Gail's Group—Comin 'Round the Mountain

Beginning Call: Honor your partner,
Honor your corner,
Circle left,
Circle right, 'till you reach home.

Main Call: First couple out to the right of the ring.

When you get there *all four swing.*

Swing 'em high, swing 'em low,
Then let's see you *do-si-do.*

When you're through, let's *circle* four,
Now *grab your partner* and *swing* some more.

Now on to the next to the right of the ring
(Repeat call with 3rd, 4th couple and go home)

Second couple out to the right of the ring.

Third couple repeat
Fourth couple repeat

End Call: Everybody swing and promenade.

Lois' and Agnes' Call to "MacNamara's Band"

Oh, the head and foot go forward,
And then go back to place
The side two couples do the same,
And then go back to place.
Now swing your corner gal,
Swing her fast and strong.
Go back and swing your own,
And don't you do it wrong.
Girls in the center,
Now back and face your friend
Take him round the outside and
Make him glad he went.
Keep on promenading
Until you get him home.
Now swing your partner round and round,
And don't let him go.

Opportunities for success are abundant in the area of folk dance, as are opportunities to feel good about self and others. The above illustrations are simple accounts that have been meaningful to particular groups of boys, girls, and teachers at particular times. Communities, current music, and events of the time provide situations for students to create new dances. Even though a folk dance is structured, it does provide marked experiences for children to use the movement and rhythmic elements of time, force, sound, and space which they have learned earlier in exploratory form. Opportunities for creative expression are limitless.

SOCIAL DANCE

For the present it seems that social dance forms such as the fox trot, tango, rhumba, and mambo, have been temporarily put on the shelf in favor of youth's current popular "fad" dancing. It is important that young people have their social dance forms in which they can readily become involved with their peers. This is as it should be. What the next few years will bring is any-ones' guess. No doubt, dances will change. There seems to be slight indication that the lindy, Charleston, cha-cha, and a rejuve-nated form of the fox trot may be returning. The Charleston, Lindy, Susie Q, jitterbug, and twist were originated in their times by young people in their attempt to break away from the established formality of such forms as the two step and waltz.

Regardless of the nature of the popular social dance forms of the future—a return to revised versions of the dances of yester-year or new forms—boys and girls with a sound background in movement and rhythm will become active participants rather than sideline sitters.

Social dance, currently termed "fad" dance, has an important place in school programs. Social dance goes hand in hand with folk dance. Some of the current social forms may well be folk dances of the future.

Even though a class of children may have been together for six or seven years, some-thing magical seems to happen when boys and girls become eleven or twelve. This is the time when it seems as though they first begin to notice each other as individuals. We do not have to put on our bifocals, turn up our hearing aids, or heighten our antennae to recognize this discovery. At this time teachers may play an important role by providing wholesome experiences for them to be together in the social set-ting of social dance experiences. An offer-ing of meaningful experiences in which their older brothers and sisters participate and which they see daily on television may contribute to social development. True, the varying stages of development and maturity in any one class must be taken into consideration when instigating a pro-gram in social dance, but the current form of today's fad dancing seems to have posi-tive features for all children. There is not a specific set pattern for girls to follow as far as couples are concerned—the girl having to follow a specific lead of a partner. A boy or girl can even be com-fortable with or without a partner moving and responding to the music.

The music of today—jazz, rock and roll, soul, swinging country, ragtime—invites boys and girls to draw from their move-ment background and spontaneously re-spond to the beat, giving them an oppor-tunity to use movement and creativity in purposeful ways. The more extensive their movement and rhythmic background, the more readily they can express themselves. For the most part, fad dancing seems to be characterized by isolation of various body parts, and using combinations of movement in expressive ways. For instance, the "swim" isolates the shoulders and arms, and then uses a variety of combinations of movement using the specific body parts. The character of the movement changes by the very com-bination of movements used in exaggerated ways affected by time and spatial elements. We might say that fad dancing is using movement combinations purposefully, and giving them a specific name. Isolating the neck and the head and then uniquely expressing through a combination of head and neck movements makes up the dance called a "chicken." The name of a dance may come from the music or from the combination of movements, or may be merely a nonsense name.

We start working with groups of chil-dren by inviting them to bring in current records which they enjoy or use records which they suggest. We listen to the

melody, sometimes complex because of the polyrhythmic structure, and then select a record with a strong beat to which we can respond. We listen, trying to feel and respond to the beat.

Some boys and girls immediately relate naturally and intuitively to the rhythm, but for many it is more difficult to handle the different rhythmic combinations. Sometimes students can divide into couples or groups and set out to find combinations of movements that can be executed with isolated body parts. Differences in expressive qualities of movements are recognized as they are related to different types of

popular music. Boys and girls with a good rhythmic and creative movement background realize that the majority of movements involving the use of feet have some form of a walk, or a slight hop. What makes the locomotion seem different is the effect of elements of time and space.

Feeling Groovy

A popular record was playing when a group came into the playroom. Some listened and others started moving. Upon stopping the record, we asked the question, "When you hear the word *groovy*, what does it say to you? How does it make you feel? Rather than tell us, can you show us, by yourself or with others?"

There were wide variations of movement interpretations. Variations ranged from two youngsters who happened to be by a column in the room sitting and standing against it slowly pushing themselves lazily up and down the column, to two boys jazzing it up; to a group of girls exaggerating the skipping movement with jerks and shoulder and hip swings; to two boys chasing each other all over the room; to Kirk just lying down, moving first one body part and then another; to small groups mimicking foolish, funny, clownish, silly movements. This improvisation was too good to pass up. We asked that they work longer on exactly what they were doing and try to exaggerate their movements toward more projection. We took time out to discuss the idea of projection. In a short time the group was invited to listen to the record "Feeling Groovy." Spontaneously, they started to respond to the music. They were asked to try their movements to the music and see if they could find a certain part of the music which seemed to fit. Some adaptations were made and a dance was developed. Floor patterns of each individual part were charted and finally a new dance called *Feeling Groovy* emerged. Popular music contributes to a spur-of-the-moment experience, as an occasional stimulus for a dance, as well as for improvisation.

One class decided that they could create their own fad form. They knew that there had once been a dance called the "monkey"; they decided that they would work out other dances using animals. This proved to be a hilarious day. After listening to a rock and roll, fast tempo record with a pronounced beat and trying to feel the beat, they spontaneously started to improvise giraffe-like movements, emphasizing various moving parts of the giraffe and try-

ing to relate these movements to the beat of the record. Here was involvement, fun in expressing ideas, and much social interaction. This idea caught the fancy of this group and they requested several periods of time so that they could originate a new dance which they later called "slamina" ("animals" spelled backward). In different groups they went to work experimenting, giving and taking from each other, and then selecting movement qualities and patterns which best expressed their version of their specific animals—the zebra, peacock, elephant, donkey, and chimpanzee. Their manifestations of animal movements were expressive and fit the music. "Slamina" spread through the school and even on the playground—individuals or groups could be seen showing others, even without records.

Never to be forgotten is one experience that resulted from working with electronic music. Selecting a record that we could handle, we improvised moving different parts—eyes, head, shoulder, feet. The movements seemed extremely rigid, slow, and directed. As we shared several of our improvisations, the group was reminded of robots. We decided that the boys had the best movements and we could learn from them. Patterns were put together and a new dance emerged—what a surprise for this group to observe on TV a few months later a new fad dance called the "Robot."

Over the years the social dance in this country has periodically been influenced by other cultures and reflected in such dances as the tango, rhumba, mambo, samba, and calypso. Currently, the influence of Africa and American black culture is being reflected in some of our social dance. This contribution is presently seen in terms of bringing joy and social involvement in dancing and exposure to unexpected and different-sounding rhythms in music. Many children in schools identify culturally to soul music—their expressive movements and mannerisms are unique and exciting. There seems to be a total relationship between themselves (their bodies in movement) and the rhythm, and there is a rhythmic vitality which is contagious. We marvel at their performance. Try as we do, some of us realize that we can never catch on to the *Soul Train,* but we can appreciate and be grateful that boys and girls from the black experience have so much to share through dance. As boys and girls and teachers daily find social camaraderie in recognizing and sharing differences, we learn to genuinely appreciate other cultures and one another as we dance and sing together. As Rita said, "Gee, I can't make my feet go the way Curtis can." "Nope," said Curtis,

"Cause you're you and I'm me." This was overheard as they were involved in a group, making up their own social dance.

Selection of music for social dancing is made in terms of meaningfulness for specific groups of children and in terms of the children's movement and rhythmical readiness competencies. Introducing children to other ideas and cultures of the world by sharing their songs and dances may well be a beginning in helping them find out about customs, mannerisms, and languages of people different from themselves. For instance, the American Indian, the Puerto Rican, Hawaiians, and the American black culture have deep roots and traditions and we need to help boys and girls respect and appreciate differences.

15

Putting It All Together: Making Dances

Children's *dances* are made by children. Throughout the elementary school years teachers working with children in creative rhythmic movement—with dance—are working toward helping children portray their feelings, ideas, and movement skills in organized ways as a major form of communication. Such activities take many forms, some highly casual or spontaneous, others more sophisticated. Some are studies in progress; others are compositions worthy of performance.

Throughout this book we have been working toward those factors which appear to be central in making dances. Exploring movement, using space, understanding aspects of rhythm, working alone and in groups, and releasing creative ideas and responses are all basic. We are able to help children of any age make their dances. There is an obvious progression of maturity and quality as elements of dance are developed and perfected.

This is to introduce a variety of dance compositions described in detail in the latter part of this chapter. These are creative dance compositions. Each dance has its unique name and is presented to show the *process* involved in its development. Throughout this book care has been taken to develop dance elements separately.

When "we put it all together" we have a meaningful process and a wholeness.

Dance that makes a difference in the lives of boys and girls is dance *conceived and performed by them in their own way.* Although difficult to define, the essential quality must reflect the child's world. His ideas, feelings, learnings, needs, fantasies, and questions are evident as he responds to movement; dance is an outward sensitivity that calls for a response to something real within a child. At times a dance may seem important only for a moment and may be appreciated only by him at a specific time because he has been its conceiver, producer, and performer. At other times the individual wants his dance shared with others. Whether the performance is for self or for an audience, the experience can be so intense and the work of launching can be so potent that its effect remains with children for a lifetime.

Many adults have difficulty in recognizing, clarifying, and extending children's thoughts and feelings and channeling them in the form of dance. Children have plenty to dance about or to dance out! The role of teachers is to encourage and to help children begin. We must learn to listen and to look—to see and to feel what the children want to communicate through movement.

DANCE IS MORE THAN MOVEMENT

When we listen to children express themselves about dance, we find that they have diversified and mature conceptions of dance; they seem to recognize that dance is expressive and does not rely on movement alone. The following ideas about dance come from children:

A five-year-old child says, "A dance is not talking or listening, just looking at me—that's a dance."

An eight-year-old girl says, "We don't all do the same thing at the same time, but it all goes together; we have the same idea and are dancing out the same story."

An inner-city school boy says, "Dance is feeling something. like feeling happy, and wanting you to feel the same way as you look at me. A dance must use movement. We must feel the movement and we want you to feel the movement too. The movements have to say something to you."

Members of a group of eleven- and twelve-year-olds say, "If I wanted to dance you a scary story, I wouldn't use swingy, skippy, happy music. I would use scary, stop and start music. Then you would know what my dance is about."

"If you have a story you want to tell, you have to be able to make your body do with movement what you make your pencil do on paper. You have to think out what you want to say so that it makes sense to someone watching."

"A dance is in my heart; I think about it with my head; I talk to myself about it and when it sounds like I think I want it to be, I start to dance it by trying all kinds of movement. I keep this up until I think I am dancing out what I have inside."

Movement is not dance, but *all dance involves movement.* Children must be able to move easily and readily in order to compose effective dances. They require time to perfect movement skills necessary to make their bodies do what their emotions dictate. Boys and girls become secure in movement as they have opportunities to understand and to analyze movement and to use it to express themselves.

Movement experiences can be initiated and presented in such a way that children are anxious to respond to new and more complex situations. Dance is not concerned with developing movement in a vacuum but rather with developing, inventing, and controlling movement *simultaneously with thinking, inquiring, sensing, responding, and feeling.* Dance is moving through, with, and in dimensions of space, and moving with various degrees of speed and intensity

to communicate one's ideas. It is moving to control and to change oneself at will, by going through space in time. The development of the imagination is ignited and creativity is uncorked as children become inventive and selective of movement.

A comprehensive and developmental analysis of the nature of children's dance is found in Chapter 4.

The Teacher as Guide

The teacher is essential in fostering dance for children. He lets children be themselves and express themselves through their movement repertoire. He helps them establish feelings and ideas to be communicated by talking with the children, raising questions, providing varied and meaningful movement opportunities, and helping to clarify that which children themselves want to communicate. Without this clarity of feelings and ideas and without a child *wanting* to design and to build, there can be little meaning in dance for children.

Teachers listen to and take many leads from children's responses. We give children ample time to allow their perceptions to take shape. This requires patience and high-level human relations factors. In other words, teachers assist children rather than try to fashion them in an adult image. Owing to time factors, some adults show a lack of appreciation for children's concentration on finding ways of moving their bodies, at times trying to superimpose on children their own form or system of techniques, or patterns of dictated movement. This is not the way to assist children to realize their own potential of quality in movement. Instead, teachers should help children plan to dance *what they most want to dance,* rather than *what we think they should dance.*

The teacher's role as a guide remains constant. It is essential that we not rush the process of composing dances with children before they have:

A small repertoire of their own movements

Some awareness of the great phenomenon of space and rhythm and the ability to respond rhythmically

Control to some degree of the human communication system

A willingness to invent and to take chances

Extensive exploration and the ability to use their discoveries in improvisations and dance studies

Opportunities spontaneously to improvise, to solve sensory and movement problems, to figure out sequences, to combine elements, and to use expressive movements

Ability to work with others

THE NATURE OF DANCE STUDIES AND COMPOSITIONS

When ideas and feelings are used to stimulate movement, a variety of studies and compositions can result. A young child hears the ticking of a clock and translates this into a swinging movement. He wants to *be* a clock. He begins with a floor pattern of the outline of a clock, adding movement. He starts his movement according to the way the sound of saying "ah-tick-ah-tock" makes him feel.

In this instance, the idea of the clock stimulated the different movement expressions; experiences modified these expressions. This is how a study starts and develops into a composition.

The artist who does a charcoal sketch of a tree begins with the idea of the tree. He may work first with the parts of the tree—the trunk, branches, the leaves. Each part might be a study in itself, but the picture in its entirety is a composition. Like the artist's creation, the child's movement composition expresses an idea or feeling. Movement should become an automatic tool, leaving the child free to concentrate on the idea. Dance studies may be very simple which even the youngest children may complete in a short time.

A combination of studies, or a variety of experiences (feelings or ideas) in sequence, with definite form, unity, and organization, is a composition. *A composition has a beginning and an end and a feeling of wholeness.* Compositions require careful planning as groups deal with spatial factors, rhythmic elements, and effective movement factors. They may be created in one period or extended over several.

We plan with boys and girls ways of developing dance studies and compositions which emerge naturally from chants, dance songs, movement discoveries, spatial designs, rhythmic responses, and everyday experiences. Through dance boys and girls are invited to reveal themselves as they are in their environment, or the environment in which they would like to be. Care must be taken continually that this invitation is not withdrawn. If this happens, they then only dance *what they think adults want to see or hear or know about them.* However, stories or ideas cannot be translated into dance experiences before children have sensory experience and before they are comfortable with their movement ventures. This is quite different from presenting a dance because it is expected, rather than because children have completed meaningful compositions which they cherish.

Children have shown that, regardless of age, they are able to handle details in sequential and organized ways. They can see relationships and make associations. There are many levels of maturity for dance composition among children in a given school. The younger they are, the simpler the statement and the more clearly related to their particular world at the moment. As youngsters mature, the quality of experiences can yield dance compositions of a more sophisticated nature.

A teacher must be prepared to accept from children what emerges when they are involved in improvising, inventing, discovering, and selecting movement or thematic material. This is true of any age

group. In the beginning, what occurs may appear to be brash or trite. In time, with enriching and appropriate experiences, quality will be developed. Care must be exerted to keep the compositions short and to the point of communicating the central statement. Children need help in not cluttering their compositions with extraneous substatements which go on and on.

In the process of helping, we need to be watchful that children do not get in over their heads. We make it possible for the compositions to grow by helping children clarify what they are trying to say, keeping the ideas simple, and helping them build their ideas. Care should be taken to prevent children from taking on too much at once. For example, a sixth-grade group wanted to portray its conceptions of Thanksgiving in a dance. They began with explorations which came from the pumpkin. This led to more involved ideas about harvest and terminated in a larger piece which they refined and perfected into their dance of "Thanksgiving Proclamation." Ultimately, they asked to share it with the entire school. The planning was a progressive step-by-step procedure. Another group, third-graders, was able to translate their skipping activities into a dance that had the recognizable elements of composition: various groupings and regroupings of children, and interesting spatial designs they charted graphically so they could more effectively remember the sequence. Variety was achieved not only by the accompaniment to their arrangements of high and low, fast and slow variations of the skip but also in the quality and style of skipping. In composing this dance, the children were helped to develop a strong feeling for unity and organization. Before the year was over, this group had opportunities to compose many effective dances on various subjects.

While working on dance studies and compositions, children and teachers together can learn, have fun, penetrate realms of curiosity, tackle problems, and experience achievement. This positive type of activity does not occur when a teacher only watches, tells, and manipulates.

Giving and Receiving Dance

As children have opportunities to become skilled in dance they need to experience sharing their studies or dances with others. There are times when a group (or individual) needs to perform. This calls for awareness of factors involved in communicating with others, projecting oneself, and for refining elements in the particular dances to be shared. It requires that the children work toward quality in their compositional work. When they decide to perform, this calls for practice, perfecting certain sequences of movement, and provision for transitions. At this time, the teacher's role becomes one of critic and guide. She must help children to understand the refinement necessary to reach a desired and appropriate performance level.

When children become the performers they become *givers*. Performing dance is an important experience for children when they have dances to share. But care must be taken to keep the material within the realm of childhood. We want children not to be afraid of an audience. The scary feelings are natural and must be recognized as such; the good feelings of accomplishment and adulation will follow. When children want to perform they realize that this is not a time to "show off," but a time to give something. Teachers must not rush children into a performance. There is a readiness which takes the form of being confident, assured, and eager. As this occurs and children are successful, they are delighted with their giving.

We need to provide opportunities for children to experience dance performance. Older boys and girls can perform for younger children, and vice versa. Often high school and college dance groups have performed and the children have then performed for the older group. On some occasions, they have all danced together. This is how we help children to both *give* and *receive* dance and to understand the nature of performing.

Children should also be helped to *receive* dance in a gracious and supportive manner, as an audience. This again is started in their earliest explorations of movement within a group. Helping children become an audience is a developmental process and its origins are in classroom operations, rather than in large, all-school assemblies. For dance, this is a continuous occurrence. We help children develop tolerance, acceptance, and the ability to sharpen perceptions. We also help boys and girls find ways of giving constructive criticism and praise. All of this takes time and contributes to enjoyment.

On Stage: A Special Place

We like to regard the stage *as a place where something special happens*. We respect this area and have excitement for its use. A stage may be thought of as the usual permanent auditorium raised platform or a temporary area set aside on the floor of the classroom, gymnasium, playroom, or out of doors. We can be either givers or receivers of something special within this area.

From the outset in teaching creative rhythmic movement, we begin introducing the idea of the significance of the stage. For example, following a period of movement exploration, we want to help the children see or listen to our discoveries. We designate a spot or area where this can happen and label it "our stage."

Both givers and receivers have a responsibility to listen to, watch, and respond to the participants with respect and encouragement. Children are helpful in building their own rules or reminders of what it means to be "on stage."

The auditorium, with its colorful and mysterious curtains, is also a place to respect

and appreciate as we both give and receive. Often the only available work space for dance is on the auditorium stage. When this is the case, it is assumed that it is like any other work area. However, the teacher must help children get over their natural inclination to take this area lightly. Such attitudes about "on stage" as a special place can be extended as children go to assemblies, to concerts, and to other kinds of performances.

Props and Costumes

Teachers find that props and costumes have a natural place in the performance of children's dance. For the most part the orientation in children's dance is educational and creative expression rather than performance. The dance is the focus and the costumes and props must add, rather than detract. On the other hand, there are unlimited opportunities for simple props and costumes to extend, dramatize, and add zest to children's work.

When working with children, it is difficult to predict what might be needed at a particular time to facilitate the movement or the dance experience. Therefore, teachers need to be alert to ways of securing and using such items quickly.

Props include a variety of objects which help to stimulate or communicate a dance. They not only add to the setting but are also essential to some dances.

A group of older boys and girls were completing a dance composition which they called "Aeroaquaterra." It had to do with the visit of a leprechaun who needed to go from place to place on land, sea, and in the air. This composition could not have been carried out in a meaningful manner for children without props, in this case *cartons*. The group needed a contraption for the leprechaun's transportation from place to place, so the children designed and constructed from cartons an *aeroaquaterra*—shaped like a ship with airplane tail. A hat box was turned into a paddle wheel, the top of a carton was used for a big pinwheel propeller. Their creativity did not end here—the group attached this to the side of a child's wagon so it could move across the stage.

In addition to the materials mentioned above, many others can be used for props: ropes, clothes-lines, nylon, string, elastic, nets, packing barrels, transparent plastic, furniture, benches, bleachers, chairs, balloons, hoops, balls, sacks, newspapers and portable screens, etc. Probably our most essential props include raw materials such as brown wrapping paper, newsprint, chalk, magic markers, and construction paper from which particular props are made.

Charts. In order to help children remember, or to extend their dance experience, we like to have large charts available. These are usually made out of newsprint and attached to a piece of cardboard.

Charts have many different functions: they show

Sequence of ideas in a dance

Sequence of people in groupings

Sequence of percussion accompaniment

Sequence of dance in a performance

Orientation to spatial relationships

Cues of a story or poem

Aids in square dance calls

Floor patterns of individuals and their particular role in the dance

Floor pattern of entire dance

Words of a song being used

Murals are visual resources that intensify children's work by portraying some of their dances in chalk or paint in picture form. These have been used as backdrops or settings to accompany dances.

Graphically represented sound compositions, such as enlarged scores, have been helpful. All of the visual resources have been large and colorful so that they can be seen from a distance.

People probably represent our greatest props! The following illustrations suggest the various ways in which they help:

Reading a poem, story, or words to accompany a dance. The reading and dance must be synchronized.

Helping children orient themselves to and in new space.

Arranging for young children to have a place to start and a place to return.

Keeping a book in which the children's ideas, parts of dances as they are completed, floor patterns, rhythmic patterns, or any new ideas are recorded.

Helping the children write out their parts or sequences in dances, or notating their dances in their own way.

Costumes that enhance, dramatize, extend, or directly contribute to the message of the dance can provide an additional significant experience for children. If the costume gets in the way of movement, causes discomfort, becomes worrisome, or overpowers the dance, however, it becomes a deterrent. The dance should stand on its own merit. Costumes may be considered as trimming, giving the dance an extra "something." Many children love to dress up, and when they have worked hard on a dance they love to give it that extra flair or to *color it up*. Children's dances are usually so vital that costuming per se is relatively unimportant except as children themselves want it.

When children feel comfortable in creatively and esthetically communicating the essence of the dance, this is a time to consider costumes, rather than before the dance has been designed. Many children's dances are more beautiful without the trimmings. Costumes should be simple, appropriate, imaginative, and created by the children themselves. This adds another dimension to planning which is a creative activity within itself.

There are times when we use costumes to induce a spontaneous dance-like happening or as a motivation for improvisation. It is important that the children themselves decide on how to use their costumes. Masks and costumes may change the personality of a boy or girl, as well as create opportunities for a dance to evolve. Those that add to dances have included hats, gloves, patches over the eye, towels, men's shirts, scarves, netting or gauze, feathers, balloons, flowers, curtain materials, wrist and ankle bells, ribbons, multicolored pieces of cloth and bags (fruit, onion, gauze, burlap, and large paper grocery and cleaning bags). The best costumes are those which the children create themselves.

The following is an example of how a chant emerges from children as they work in the classroom.

It was almost Halloween, and the boys and girls were excited about the kind of costumes they would make. The idea came to them from an experience they had had in art class with large cardboard cartons. One child put a carton over him and said "Look, I'm a space man on my way to Mars." The group was ignited, and with the help of the classroom teacher, art teacher, aides, and parents, they became involved in all kinds of constructions. This was particularly important to this group because on Halloween they had a special assembly to which everyone wore costumes and as a part of the program they had a parade.

There were as many as two and three boys and girls in some of their constructed costumes and this posed another problem. The group was concerned because their kinds of costumes did not permit them to sit down.

We discussed how different it would be to move within a box, to move connected to other boys and girls in other constructions, to move in their creations with ease. They had not thought about this before.

"Suppose you think about your costume for a few minutes; if more than one of you are involved in making an outfit, then you get together! How do you get into your costume? How do you think it will feel to move when you are all covered up? How do you think it will feel if you cannot see your feet? What will you do with your arms? How will two or three of you move together so that you will not be walking all over each other? What will happen if you cannot bend any of your parts? Will you be able to run or move quickly?

"Now is a good time to experiment without your constructions and find answers to your problems. When your costumes are finished we will try again." There was intense concentration, trying out, trying to manipulate each other, because of the new restrictions. There was much questioning and much projecting. Because this group moved freely it was quite a different experience for this class to move with constrictions and particularly to move and try to represent themselves in their arrangement without the costume. This was a satisfying experience and paid off for the group two days later when they were ready to try out their costume constructions.

DANCE COMPOSITIONS

Sources for dance compositions are multitudinous. Children do not have to resort to fads, clichés, or unrelated elements because their world is full of ideas to be expressed. Their sources have to do with age, activities, surroundings, and feelings. They are different for each group and each child within a group. Angelo, a four-year-old whose whole world has been one block long, dances about that which he knows. This is quite different from the world of four-year-old Pete, who travels the township with his dad on his garbage truck. Sara, who lives in the middle of the ghetto, and Jeff, who travels with his dad, a diplomatic attaché, are also different. All have different sources on which they can draw for their dance ideas. Compositional sources are also suggested from the outer world of space, children's literature, history, folk songs, field trips to the country, the city, the mountains, the ocean, holidays, mechanical and electrical wonders, science, seasons, pets, museums, the customs, traditions, and lives of people, and the exciting world of sound and color.

Who is to prescribe what a dance for children shall be? Such decisions should rely on maximum involvement of the children themselves. However, as we fulfill our role as guides, expeditors, and leaders we must be alert to the numerous sources for dance studies and compositions. There must be vitality and relevance.

Illustrations of Dance Compositions

"Not for Me"—Horse Dance

"What can we do with one foot? Now, what can we do with two feet? Find different ways of moving with your feet." These were the initial questions which led to the horse dance. The response to the suggestion that the group find different ways led predominantly to gallops. The question was posed, "What gallops?" "Horses!" "What kind?" "Ponies, circus horses, race horses, police horses, stallions, cowboy horses, quarter horses." "Where do you see or find horses? When you come back tomorrow, we will try some of your horses."

We suggested that they work alone or with others on a special kind of horse. Danny's perplexed us, since we thought it was a bucking bronco or a trick riding horse. "No," said Danny, "I'm Wild Bill Hickup!" We all wanted to be wild horses and bucking broncos, but we could not exaggerate our movements as Danny did. His title stuck.

The group was interested in being different horses and finding other ways to gallop. When asked if they would like to make up a dance which would tell a story about their horses, some of them immediately started to find a stall (their spot from which to work). We called them back and said we meant a dance in which the whole class would be a part. This was a new experience and they were sure that they could.

They selected six different kinds of horses that they wanted in their dance: ponies, circus horses, work horses, police horses, race horses, and of course, Wild Bill Hickup. With some help, they decided on the horses, and each person made his selection. A place was suggested for them to work which later would become their stalls, or a place to come from and return to. They started working out ideas of what they wanted their horses to do.

There was much to do in finding the movements that would express what we wanted our horses to do and how it would be done. Again we looked at what we had done and how we could put this into a dance. They made suggestions for starting and developed the following plan:

Sequence of Studies in Horse Dance Composition

Introduction
  Two little ponies gallop in the field.
  Ponies talk ("Wonder what it would be like to be in the circus?").

1. *Circus Horse*

    Ponies as circus horses.
    Ponies talk ("Not for me")
  Ponies back to field galloping.
  Ponies talk ("Wonder what it would be like to be a farm horse?").

2. *Farmer John's Work Horses*

    Ponies join work horses

Ponies talk ("He's too old for me").
Ponies back to field galloping.
Ponies talk ("Wonder what it would be like to be a police horse?").

3. *Police Horses*

    Ponies follow police horses.
    Ponies talk ("He's too big for me").
  Ponies back to field galloping.
  Ponies talk ("How about being a race horse?").

4. *Race Horse*

    Race around track.
    Ponies to race horse gate
    Ponies talk ("Too fast for me").
  Ponies back to field galloping.
  Ponies talk ("Look out for old Wild Bill Hick up!").

5. *Wild Bill Hickup*

    Ponies as wild horses.
    Ponies talk ("He's too wild for me").

Ending—Two ponies gallop slower and slower into middle of field. Ponies talk ("Guess I just want to be my own self.")

HORSE DANCE

Clark W. Graves

Work Horses

Police Horses

Race Horses Fast — *Repeat as long as necessary*

Wild Bill Very fast — *Repeat as long as necessary*

D.C. al Fine (Repeat "pony" music when necessary.)

When the story and dance had been worked out, music was composed. The sequence of the final product is included on the next page to show how a second grade group planned a specific story that became a dance.

Things Are Swinging All Over Town

The dance "Things Are Swinging All Over Town" developed from young children's discovering the swinging movement as they were finding out how they could move different parts of themselves. We invented various swinging patterns and worked on "feeling" swinging movements. Miss Woolard extended the swinging experience in the classroom. The class listed and discussed many things that swing and then developed vocabulary and reading

charts from these listings of associations. From this eventually came the song, which stimulated additional movement exploration, and when a variety of swinging movements had been discovered, it was turned into a dance. On the first and last verse all children participated and devised movements that made one feel as though it were a swinging world. On certain parts small groups participated.

The Dancing Elephant and his Friends

Often young children delight in responding to older children's creations. For example, when Alice's Elephant was displayed in the hall, it delighted a group of young children. Three first graders were intrigued and said they wanted to dance with the elephant. Their interest was com-

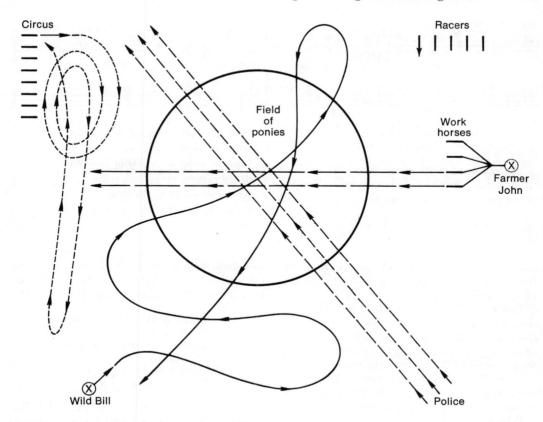

municated to the class, who also wanted to dance with the elephant.

Marty and Dave went to the sixth grade room, with a note in hand, to get Alice to bring her elephant to their room. In the meantime the floor was cleared and the group was ready to receive Alice's Elephant.

Upon observing the picture of the elephant the group felt that he was "dancing all over." This became a challenge for the group to explore ways of "dancing all over" if they were elephants.

The group also wanted the elephant to have friends dancing. This led to the nosy,

THINGS ARE SWINGING ALL OVER TOWN

Arr. *Clark W. Graves*

1. Things are swing - ing all o - ver town. Things are swing - ing all o - ver town.

This is what we all can see, Things are swing-ing all o-ver town.

2. *Skinny monkey* swings on a tree.
   Skinny monkey swings on a tree.
   This is what we all can see.
   Skinny monkey swings on a tree.
3. You can *Swing* on a *swing* with me!
4. *Elephant* can swing his big trunk.

5. *Little boys* can swing off their bunks.
6. *Kites* can swing in the sky so high.
7. *Branches* swing in the bright blue sky.
8. *Happy puppies* swing their tails.
9. *Oppossum* swings upside down.
10. Things are *swinging* all over town!

stretchy giraffe, the prickly porcupine, the funny naughty monkey, and the bouncing baby bear.

Pictures were requested. This made it desirable for other sixth graders to watch the animals dancing and to make large chalk drawings. The drawings depicted various ways the children as animals moved.

The sixth graders also seemed to benefit from the work. They took pride in their creations as well as in pleasing the young children.

Good Morning

For the past several mornings a class of young children had been out of doors looking for signs of spring. They watched for colors, for leaves starting to push out; they looked to see what was inside some of the little buds and "bumps" popping out of trees and bushes. They cracked open some of the buds they found. They listened to the birds talking and singing to each other. Squirrels seemed to be playing busy games. How important the children felt when they discovered a flower just popping through the ground.

Spring was different from winter—it was a happy time. It was like Patti's dress—all rainbowy colors and lots of greens.

Spring made them feel like dancing. They

spontaneously made their dance and it all seemed to fit together. The group said they were dancing the following story:

> Spring is like the morning
> When all the world wakes up.
> Tiny plants inside the seeds
> Wake to feel the sun.
> Flowers dance and sing,
> Good morning world!

This dance "study" illustrates the importance of the subtle listening to children and allowing them to express their observations, words, and movement rather than to follow a pattern of seeds slowly growing into plants and having flowers in spring.

One particular third-grade group had been studying poetry—their teacher tried to help them get the "feel" of the poems they read and wrote. She also suggested appropriate poems to use in movements because these children were becoming more skillful in handling their bodies rhythmically and in using elements of space. Without an accompanist, the class resorted to chanting some of the poetry as accompaniment to our movements.

Jump or Jiggle

The poem "Jump or Jiggle" by Evelyn Beyer provided motivation for movement

JUMP OR JIGGLE

Jump and jig - gle,   Jump and jig - gle,   Jump and jig - gle,   Jig-gle,jig-gle,jig-glejig-gle,   Jiggle.

exploration and improvisation and making a dance. The boys and girls discussed movements of various animals and portrayed their ideas of those which are big and small, high and low, fat and skinny, slow and fast. This experience was the background for the "Jump or Jiggle" dance.

The classroom teacher wrote the poem on a large chart so that the children could see its contents from some distance. They were asked to read the poem by themselves and select a part of it that they would like to express. Almost immediately they drew attention to the fact that rabbits jump—and wanted to change the rabbit to jump rather than hop as indicated in the poem. They also wanted to change the horse movements to gallop. We were pleased with this application of movement symbols and thought that it would not do injustice to the poem.

There were thirteen different animals, which meant thirteen different parts. Each child wanted to participate in two different groups so he or she could be two animals. After the groups were ready to show their parts, "feeling" and exaggerating the movements of each animal, we discussed with the individual groups ways of getting more variety by giving attention to spatial elements, direction, levels, and range.

The parts of "Jump and Jiggle" went together readily and there was expressive movement and interesting variety in spatial elements, but there seemed to be something wrong rhythmically. Our chanting of the poem as it was written was too short to give us time to perform our movements. This was resolved by repeating each part (or line

of the poem); to illustrate, using the first line, the rhythmic pattern became:

> Frogs jump
> Frogs jump
> Frogs jump
> Jump jump jump jump *jump*

This gave us time to express our animals and the chanting seemed natural.

We introduced the dance with everyone moving at once, expressing the words "jump" or "jiggle" with exaggerated movements to a verse which we added. We were ready to work on the ending—"But—I walk." It was decided that each group would work out their own way of walking, and that they would go in order of their appearance, verbally chanting their way of walking. Also, they would all go to a designated place and sit down. At a later date, music was composed for the dance.

The World Is Made of Many Things

Children wanted to know more about the world. Probing their questions about the world revealed that they had limited understanding not only of the world but of where they lived and the forces that affected them.

A sensitive teacher attempted to help the group start with themselves in their present setting and to specify those things in their own world; this experience was the impetus for the following dance "The World Is Made of Many Things." Here the children's concepts of small and big, heavy and light were broadened and intensified as they expressed concepts and related associations through movement. The concept *big* revealed associations of anything from mountains to elephants to airplanes and skyscrapers. Their explanations of natural and mechanical phenomena were fascinating, with robots and machines comprehended as mechanical and animals and trees as natural. The class was divided into groups, each of which selected a certain concept, such as small, and expressed it through movement. Each group was given an opportunity to express what it was in the world. Extending the dance in this manner, two parts were developed. Part one included all dancing and interpreting concepts through feelings, and part two included interpreting with an idea. Each group had opportunities to interpret its selected concept of what it represented in the world.

OUR WORLD IS MADE OF MANY THINGS

Arr. *Clark W. Graves*

This dance has been used with many groups in many ways; with older groups, it has been used as a folk-type dance.

Hats Hats Hats

Hats as props have triggered ingenuity, imagination, and creativity. There are times when teachers want to work with children on an idea of short duration in a fun way. Hats are readily available with diversity and with a flair of humor and novelty. The hats themselves are so communicative that they provide a colorful way of helping boys and girls make a dance with ease. This is a good prop for very large groups.

Two sixth-grade groups were asked to bring hats to school. It was suggested that

they bring one that they liked, which was different or which interested them. How the character of these groups was changed by the hats as they sauntered into the gymnasium! Humor was generated as the crew assembled.

The group was fascinated by the variety of hats. They fell automatically into several categories. These included work hats, sun hats, ceremonial hats, sports hats, military hats, and hats of other cultures.

With this group it was suggested that they become one mass of hats, sitting on the floor or on knees with hats dominating. What a colorful conglomeration of texture, size, and shapes. A chant was introduced using only the word *hat*. The group was guided into chanting softly in low tones "hat, hat" and gradually increasing the tempo and intensity as they slowly rose to a standing position. The inflection, tempo, and intensity of the chant became a fascinating group experience.

Groups were formed of similar types of hats present. No attempt was made to equalize members in each group. There were:

Ladies' fashion hats

Politicians' hats

Cowboy hats

Motorcycle helmets

Beach hats

Religious hats

Rain hats

Farmers' hats

Sun bonnets

Construction workers' helmets

Service personnel (taxi, chauffeur) hats

Others (Mexican, Hawaiian hats)

Groups were guided into planning movements which characterized their hats. They were to use the one word *hat* chanted to the rhythm which symbolized their activity. When movements were worked out, individuals within a small group started their chant and performed their study, as was carried out in the total group. To illustrate: the group with dress-up hats started from their knees repeatedly chanting "hats" and rose, walking as if in a fashion show. Their chants reflected formality, "Southern Belles," parties, teas, and funerals!

The cowboys' hats represented riding horses and ponies and were accompanied by "Ahat Ahat Ahat" in a galloping rhythmic pattern.

The motorcycle hats group expressed the hard, loud, intense start and the rapid take-off as they chanted "hats"——

The hats representing the military chanted in military cadence with marked accent on the first "hat" in the "*hat* hat hat hat."

The composition closed with spontaneously chanting:

> Hats hats hats—
> Hats for show, hats to wear,
> Hats from here, hats from there,
> Hats for me, hats for you,
> Hats for summer, hats for fall,
> Hats are big, hats are small—
> Hats hats hats!

It's Cold

It was in the month of February.
It was *co-oo-ld*.
Rita went to look for Valerie.
It is cold—it is icy and cold,
It is cold—it is icy and cold,
It is breezy—oh so breezy.
It is breezy—oh so breezy.
Take it easy.
It's shh-iv-erry—very shh-iv-erry
It's shh-iv-erry—very shh-iv-erry.
It's fun!
It's slip-pery—slippery.
It's slip-pery—slippery.
Take it easy.
It's freezing—really freezing.
It's freezing—really freezing.
You're sneezing!
Huh! Look at Curtis ...
He looks like a penguin!
It's frosty—cold and frosty
It's frosty—cold and frosty
It is chilly. Cold and chilly.
It is chilly. Cold and chilly.
All in the month of February.

A study of weather was generated on one extremely cold day in February. Miss Gar-

It was in the month of February.
It was CO-OO-LD.
Rita went to look for Valarie.
It is cold - it is -icy- and cold.
It is cold - it is -icy- and cold.
It is breezy - -oh-so breezy.
It is breezy - -oh-so breezy.
Take it easy.
It's shh-iv-erry-very shh-iv-erry.
It's shh-iv-erry- very shh-iv-erry.
It's fun !!
It's slip-pery - slippery.

It's slip-pery - slippery.
Take it easy.
It's freeezing-really freeezing.
It's freeezing - really freeezing.
You're sneezing !!
Huh! Look at Curtis...
They look like penguins.
It's frosty - cold and frosty.
It's frosty - cold and frosty.
It is chilly. Cold and chilly.
It is chilly. Cold and chilly.
All in the month of February.

ber, the teacher, asked her class to talk about how they felt when it was so cold. On the board she recorded some of their expressions, listing descriptive words. They talked about what cold weather meant to them and what they thought made cold weather. Vocabulary charts of association with cold weather were developed, stories and poems about winter were written, and pictures were painted. As the children responded to words such as *freezing, shivery,* and *breezy,* they said it was like dancing and asked if they could make a dance showing how they felt when it was cold.

In responding with movement to "cold" words, the boys and girls expressed feelings which came from deep inside ... they were cold! This was movement magic expressed before their eyes. Here was dance that seemed to happen naturally. Each boy and girl became completely involved and yet there were a group unity, interesting spatial relationships, and dramatic rhythmic qualities. Something important had happened. If we had purposely choreographed a dance, we could not have improved upon our communication.

Capturing the spirit of the movement, Miss Garber and the class caught the expression in story form. She arranged it in a chart form for use the next time we worked on the dance. She also asked each person to think about what they had done and when they returned to the class to write out the words they had worked with and a description of what they had done. Curtis' description is an illustration:

Breezy—I turn blowing around Vernon.

Easy—I almost fall down backwards.

Shivery—I shiver fast from feet to head—every part.

Slippery—I slide on my knees and hands.

Freezing—I freeze stiff, one part and another and another.

Sneezing—I sneeze, a big one!

Penguins—I tap my feet, turn around, and feel like a penguin leading some of the kids.

Frosty—I move my hands around and blow myself.

Chilly—I lean on Vernon's back and freeze stiff like an icicle.

The class discussed the need for a beginning for their dance and five of the group said they would work it out and write it for us to try. Here is what they wrote:

Rita runs out fast going in a circle. She is so cold her shoulders are up to her ears. She meets Valerie and they jump up and down. They are cold. Then they call their friends and we all come fast moving around each other making circles. Then we all spread our arms out because we are breezy cold turning around each other backwards slipping and sliding.

This was a good beginning. The class decided that Deborah would read the poem. The class then worked on the ending to

show that they had frozen into a shape and stayed that way. The class danced the story in different ways; Deborah read the poem and they danced without any sound except a sneeze. This became one of this group's favorite dances. It was important enough to them to have them request to make a similar type of dance when spring came.

The Dummy Line

Miss Watson's class in Memphis became intrigued with the song "The Dummy Line" and wanted to turn it into a dance. This is an illustration of how a song from a standard music book can be extended to enhance many aspects of the curriculum including dance.

The group was asked to sing the song for us. They said it was about a slow, slow train which went from St. Louis to Memphis. They were impressed that "kids" got on the train and did not have the fare. The conductor scolded them, chased them, and threw them off. The kids walked to Memphis and beat the train! We suggested that they find out all they could about the route the train took and any other information about the train so that we could start making their dance.

The next day with maps and much shared information on the board, the class was helped to sketch the route of the Dummy Line. They showed St. Louis in relation to Memphis, the Mississippi River in relation to the train route, the need for the bridge just before Cairo, the downhill grade just before Reelfoot, and the need for a tunnel. The children found that the route was not straight but had many curves and ups and downs.

Now we had information on which to help them build a dance. We started moving with spatial elements—the spatial design (floor pattern) that we thought the train would take and how up and down grades could be indicated. The route had been translated from the blackboard to a mural so we could check our path and directions and levels of movement. After much discussion we agreed upon the floor pattern we would use and became involved in making parts of the dance. In response to the question, "What do we need besides our route?" the children decided that two people should become the engine leading the train, while other people would make up the train, a conductor, and a caboose. They also needed two children to be thrown off the train and then walk to Memphis, as well as others to become the tunnel, bridge, and some tracks. In groups the children started planning to find movements to communicate their ideas. After a period of time we showed our explorations, discussed and received comments, and found that before we could try to put parts together there were some problems to be solved. The problems included what the walkers would do when the train went through the tunnel (it was decided that they could show going up and over the hill by leaping and cartwheeling while the train went down under); how they could show interesting rather than monotonous walking (they made exaggerated motions of sitting down, sleeping, and doing "funny things"); and how they could show being tracks at the beginning, at the end in Memphis, the tunnel or bridge.

Soon the essence of the Dummy Line was caught—expressive dance patterns started to emerge. Boys and girls were able to coordinate their efforts and capture the feeling of a long train on a bumpy, up and down track. With projection each part was recognizable:

The tracks
The conductor
The long train
Riders thrown off and becoming walkers
The bridge
The tunnel
Pulling into Memphis.

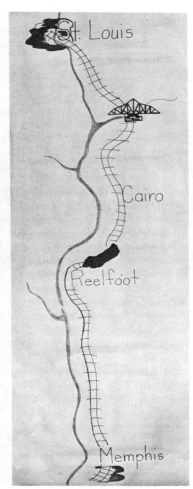

With their parts coordinated and transitions made, a beginning and ending were determined and the Dummy Line was danced.

The shuffle of their feet and the singing of the song with mouth sound effects, plus wood blocks, served as accompaniment. The varying tempo of the moving, stopping, and starting train was caught in their movements and voices. Their only costumes, made out of construction paper, were stovepipe hats for the engine or train leaders, conductor's hats, and a lantern shape for the side of the caboose. They worked hard on their dance and their interest continued in wanting to make it better.

Kite Weather

Space had been conquered by this class. They had discovered their powers to sustain themselves in space and defy gravity. They finally were gaining control of their human instruments. Leaping, running, jumping, and doing combinations of movements in

ments such as smoke rising or hats blowing away. This poem is full of contrasts because elements of time, force, and space abound.

Ten items were identified for relating to kite weather. Four of the most physical boys in the group became breezes. There were four children selected for each of the other nine parts of the dance. They arranged the sequence and planned ways of extending movements in expressive ways.

The dance was fast and rhythmical. The children seemed to be floating in the air. To contribute to the feeling tone, kites were made, flown, and discussed. A kite mural was made showing a variety of kites in strong blowing breezes. Large colorful kites were constructed as background scenery.

This dance was spectacular, especially in the dramatic way the children held their focus at the end so that the audience would "see children in the air."

the air, they could control their speed and stop at will—they had found how to command themselves moving.

It was spring and the idea of kites meant "taking off" and "up-in-the airness." Sensing their new-found powers and feelings in movement, Mrs. Judd, their classroom teacher, found a poem, "Kite Weather," which she thought appropriate for this group. It seemed to exemplify their movement status and provide for them to demonstrate their powers in space.

She knew that they needed much room to take off, out and around, because strong vigorous movements would be needed. The gymnasium was required for such spatial exploration.

The group worked with the various elements in the poem, inventing movement, feeling what it was like to hold onto a strong string, or engaging in contrasting move-

Kite Weather[1]
Ralph Bergengren

To the south the geese are going
Across the world a breeze is blowing—
Blowing leaves from every tree,
Blowing ships upon the sea,
Blowing hats off people's heads,
Blowing chimney smoke to threads.
Blowing 'till the curtain flutters,
Slamming doors, and shaking shutters.

Then's the time to fly your kite,
But you have to hold it tight.

Blow, breeze, blow!
And lift your kite along
Blow, breeze, blow!

The string is stout and strong.
Just a little harder blow,
Up and up, we too, would go.
People would look up and stare,
Seeing children in the air.

[1] From *Here and Now Storybook*, ed. Lucy Sprague Mitchell (New York: E. P. Dutton & Co., Inc., 1937).

KITE WEATHER

Alonah Stith

To the south, the geese are going, Across the world a breeze is blow - - - - -

- - - - - - - ing, Blowing leaves from every tree, Blowing ships upon the sea, Blowing hats off people's heads, Blowing chimney smoke to threads - - - -

gliss.　tr　tr　ff

Blowing till the curtain
flutters,

Slamming doors and
shutters.

Then's the time to
fly your kite.

But you have to hold it tight - - - - - - - - - - -

8va　gliss.　gliss.　*8va*　gliss.　gliss.

Blow, breeze, blow!

And lift your
kite along,

Blow, breeze,
blow!

The string is
stout and strong,

Just a little
harder blow.

Up and up we go.

People would look up and
stare,

Seeing
children
in the air.

Indians Are Real

One can never predict how vivid, intense, or lasting experience in dance can be with children. What began as a casual observation about a name developed into a study of Indians started by children in the second grade and continued by their request when they were in the fourth grade.

A second-grade group was on a field trip to a park at the outskirts of the city. During the course of the day the inscription *Powhatan* was discovered and the inquiry made of the meaning of that word. The answer was given directly. Powhatan was the big Indian Chief who had lived in this part of the country long, long ago. This park was named Powhatan Park. Then the questions came:

Did Powhatan live here in this park?
Was he fierce? Did he kill people?
Did he have a fast horse?
Why was he Chief?
Did Indians really live here? Are Indians real?

It was obvious from these questions that the children knew very little about Indians except for the information, much of it false, that they had gleaned from TV or Western movies.

The next day the teacher read them a story of Pocahontas, the daughter of Powhatan. This story led to the children's wanting to learn more about Powhatan, the Indians, and their tribes. From a variety of resources, they learned about Indians—that they were people just like us, only they lived differently because the country was different. They also found out about what they did, what they ate, and how they lived together.

They talked and read about what it might have been like to be a chief, or a brave, or a boy or girl at that time. They also found out that the Indians danced and this was their special way to express their feelings about what made them happy. They found that they danced when they had plenty of food—this was expressing gratitude. The children were impressed to learn that if Indians needed rain or help in growing their crops, they danced. They related this to prayer.

The second grade had gained many understandings to express through dance. They wanted to dance about proud Chief Powhatan. Then they decided that they wanted three dances—one which the braves would do, another that the squaws could do, and still a different dance showing other chiefs. They also worked on the Indian movement pattern of walk and hops, and

on other kinds of walks. They responded rhythmically to basic tom-tom beats. They sensed this rhythm through their body and responded with different parts.

In the classroom they worked out the essence of what they wanted to communicate in dance.

Once there was a proud chief named Powhatan. One day he called together all the braves, squaws and the chiefs from other tribes for a pow-wow. He asked them to dance, first the braves, then the squaws, and finally the chiefs. The squaws made bowls and gave them to Powhatan and the chiefs. All of the Indians came back together for the pow-wow. They raised their hands to the sky and gave thanks.

Their dance depicted how deeply involved they were in their respective roles. The feeling of pride was shown in the walk and stature of Chief Powhatan, a person very much in command when he listened for sounds and gave signals and showed thankfulness. He never lost his serious character from the moment he started calling his group. He looked to the north, south, east and west and called his braves from the waters, hills, or the woods, and his squaws from inside and outside the wigwams and the three chiefs from nearby tribes. The chiefs remained serious as they gave thanks for the tribal gathering.

The outward expressions of importance of the braves was shown. Their competitiveness in comparing their skills with the bow and arrow and stone throwing, and their swiftness in moving are portrayed in a dance in three parts. The "Squaws' Dance," in five parts, showed the girls' understandings of some of the roles of the Indian women and their respect for the chiefs. The children were depicting the lives of the Indians as they understood it. Later they added a tribal dance so that they all could participate.

Music was then prepared for the dance patterns, as well as a chant for Powhatan and the braves. These chants added to the dance and provided smooth transitions between sections.

The children showed in their final dance product that they had respect and appreciation for the Indian and that Powhatan was no longer an inscription to them but a chief, a leader, a man who really lived and was full of wonder for them.

Two Years Later

When this same group of boys and girls entered the fourth grade, during a class conference toward the end of the first week the teacher asked for things the children would most like to learn about during the year. Indians dominated the list. They wanted to know about Indian tribes other

INDIAN DANCE

Clark W. Graves

Enter Chief—Calls braves, squaws and other chiefs

Tribal Dance—Repeat 3 times—Ending: cross arms and slowly to floor.

Braves' Dance—Tempo is gradually faster, and tempo gets slower again.

Chiefs' Dance

than Powhatan's. They wanted to know about Indian language and communication. Did the Indians have a God or Gods or Great Spirits to listen to their prayers or were they all the same? Inquiring how they knew about the great Chief Powhatan and his child Pocahontas, this teacher was amazed to hear them tell of their extensive learnings and understandings of Indians. They remembered in great detail their dance, which they performed again. After they had danced, it was suggested that if they would teach the others some of their Indian dance patterns and help them discover other movements that seemed appro-

priate for Indians to use when they danced, perhaps they could plan another Indian dance.

As the group became involved in a further study of Indians and their life, they became interested in Indian symbols and what they meant. Rituals took on more meaning and they began to understand why Indians danced when it was necessary to destroy animals in order to secure food and clothing. They also began to recognize that dances served the same purpose for Indians that prayer or religious ceremonies served for them. They found stories, Indian tales, and songs about Indian dances which fascinated them. They compared the Indian way of life to their own.

As they worked on Indian dance patterns, they began to find more patterns and respond to more complicated rhythms on the tom-tom. A new Indian dance was composed. The children also recorded many of the new facts they had learned in mural form. They made a collection of Indian symbols found in pottery, jewelry, and art, and then compiled their own collections of stories about Indian life.

The following was transcribed on a scroll to introduce the five episodes in the new Indian dance.

Dance of the Blackfoot Indians

The chiefs of the Blackfoot Indian tribe welcome you.

(Study 1) An Indian brave is sounding out a message on the tom-tom. He is telling the surrounding tribes that the Blackfoot Indians have won the war. He is also sounding a prayer message to the gods to heal their chief, Big Foot, who was hurt in battle.

(Study 2) The Indian braves pray and dance for the life of their chief. The Medicine Man places a magic spell on Chief Big Foot. Slowly, the chief rises. He has been healed. The braves are happy and dance again.

(Study 3) Nature and all living things are sacred to the Blackfoot Indians. When it is necessary to destroy animals they pray to their god. To celebrate the healing of the Chief the braves decide to have a feast. After praying to their gods for a good hunt, they go out. They spot a buffalo. The braves aim, pull back their arrows, and shoot. The buffalo falls to the ground. The braves drag the buffalo back to their tribe, where they dance and prepare for a feast.

(Study 4) Now that their chief is well, the Blackfoot Indians begin to worry about the lack of rain for their crops. They pray to their Great Spirit for rain. They dance. Finally, the rain pours down upon the crops. Slowly the crops grow and the Indians dance for joy.

(Study 5) To thank their Great Spirit for their blessings—the winning of the war, the healing of their Chief, and for sending of the rain for their crops— the Blackfoot Indian Chiefs smoke the peace pipe and the braves dance. At last, peace has come to the Blackfoot Indians.

The dance was accompanied entirely by tom-tom and percussion scores. The children themselves developed the scores for each of their dances and played their own accompaniment.

Because of the insight of their teachers, this group of children was given opportunities to acquire *facts about a people rather than retain stereotyped myths.* Myths were replaced with facts and appreciations. They found out that *Indians did not dance slapping their mouths and making loud, wild sounds but that they danced to ask for*

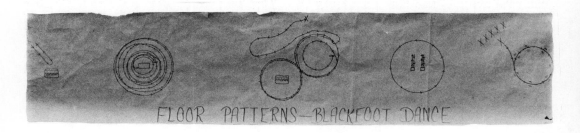

FLOOR PATTERNS—BLACKFOOT DANCE

help when they needed to worship and give *thanks, to make the sick well, to tell stories about animals, to have fun together.* Nor did the Indians say "How" when they greeted. As Deborah said, "Indians are people—like us. We should thank them for what they did to keep our country beautiful." So these children did not simply learn a dance; they were also provided an opportunity for a continuing study of an important culture. This contributed not only to creative rhythmic movement but also to their comprehension of other traditions and ways of living and communicating, culminating in their own creative efforts.

Fun in the Sun

The dance *Fun in the Sun* came about following a series of good feelings of accomplishment as performers in dance studies. This third grade had been received well that spring, performing some of their dances for a number of interested audiences. They had worked for two years on what it meant to be a *good audience* and recently they knew what it meant to work *to perfect dances* that *they wanted to share.* Now they were asking for another dance. It was late spring and the class had the problem of having too many ideas they wanted to make into dances. There was only enough time before vacation to make either one dance to involve the whole class or several shorter dances with small groups. Their decision was one with the class.

The teacher suggested that they write letters telling what they would most like to do at vacation time, or about a place they had been that they had liked most and why. We read their letters to determine the ideas or feelings expressed, hoping that this way we could find the basis for a dance. The prevailing subjects of their letters consisted of:

Transportation ideas and experiences

Fairs and parks

Zoos

Camp

Beach, the sea and the ocean.

By far the largest number related to the beach and the ocean. The letters about the ocean contained a variety of ideas which could be tied together into a dance. We shared this information with the class and asked those who had written about the beach, ocean, or sea to read their letters to the class. The class was to listen carefully for ideas that they liked and would be interested in making into a dance. Sandra's letter vividly related her time crabbing with her grandmother. Although most of us knew little about crabbing, some did not know what a crab looked like. By the time Sandra finished her letter, answered questions, and drew a crab cage on the board, we just had to have a dance about a little crab.

The substance of the letters provided the story for our dance. Donna, a third grader, grasped the ideas from the letters and from the conversation that followed, and included them in a story. She brought her story to class and wanted to read it to the group. They were proud and pleased with her story and there was no doubt about it— this was what they wanted to dance. Her story was called "Fun in the Sun" and it is presented here exactly the way it was written by Donna. We were all pleased that one of the best parts of the story included the little crab.

Every morning to the East the sun rises higher and higher. Patti and Paulette & Randal and Vernon ran out and danced around on the sand. They like to make tracks in the sand. They like to make their initials, P's, R's, V's. They also like to watch the waves come and wash their tracks away.

Patti and Paulette & and Randal and Vernon like to play tag with the waves. They would run up and run back. The waves brought friends, the waves brought shells. The children liked to listen to the sounds the shells make. The waves came again and again.

Vernon and the other children went to the pier. They liked to watch the men drop the cages down and wait for a crab to come along. Oh my! They caught a crab. They brought the cage over on the sand.

The waves came again and again. This time they brought a surfer. The children walked to see the surfer. The waves came again and again.

Then they saw beautiful sailboats. They were all different colors. They pretended they were sailboats. Then they saw motor boats. The motor boats were very fast indeed.

They all walked where men were fishing. Randal & Vernon fished too. They would cast their fishing rods way out and bring them back again. Then they cast them out again. They liked the fish and the colors too. They would look at the different shapes, too. One of their favorite fish is a flounder because it is flat.

Then the sun starts going to the West. The tide is beginning to go back. Patti and Paulette & Randal and Vernon went back and still played until their mother called them. They all said, "Wait a minute." But then the little crab got out and chased them all the way home. Then the sun sank away into the West.

The story was analyzed and ideas clarified. There was much sharing of information, and various resources sought to extend or varify content. The class determined that there were eleven different parts to be danced:

> Sun
> The four children
> Waves
> Shells
> Crabbers
> The little crab
> Surfer
> Sailboats
> Motor boats
> Fisherman
> Fish.

The class immediately decided that the sun would start their dance and the little crab would be the ending along with the sun. They liked the idea of Patti, Paulette, Randall and Vernon, the four children, tying

all their dance parts together. They agreed that there was so much to do. Parts were selected first according to their understandings of first-hand experience with waves, sailboats, or surfers. This proved valuable because some of our concerns were immediately alleviated with first-hand experiences. "How would we ever express a surf rider?" "Oh, that's easy," said Eddie. "With a long run he goes into a slide on his tummy and chest along the floor." The waves that came again and again tapped imagination and creativity, but they were magnificent and gave a special rhythmical quality which was sustained throughout the composition. Many of the parts called for large groupings, so the class was delighted that they had opportunities to dance many different parts. Floor patterns and sequences were recorded to help them remember. As work progressed, we continually assumed the role of *audience and critic*—telling and showing how we might do better, what we might change, what needed exaggeration.

The group insisted that the only way they could make or perform the dance was for Donna to accompany them by reading her story and that they would add sound effects. In time, their dance reached quality proportions and they wanted to share *Fun in the Sun* because they liked so much "watching" and dancing. They were getting ready to give a performance and decided that they would like to try to put their dance into color. They called for the art teacher to secure her help. Catching their enthusiasm, she had to dance with them in order to help them transform their dance into color in a huge wall-length mural. They were pleased with their mural, which made a good backdrop and became a part of their dance.

Gazinta Bird

Four boys stopped after class and said they had decided that they would like to make a dance of their own—just boys! Because they couldn't decide on what kind of a dance they wanted, we asked if they had ever heard the poem about the Gazinta Bird. Because they had been having trouble with division and fractions, it was felt that they might enjoy a sort of takeoff on one of these mathematical concepts.

"Have you ever heard of a Gazinta Bird?" "A *what?*" "If we said, *2 Gazinta 4,* would you know what this was?" The six-line poem was read and the boys were amused and pleased with the idea and immediately started making grotesque, exaggerated, bird-like movements. They asked what the word *absurd* meant. We talked about it, and then the spontaneous movements became even more expressive. One movement stimulated another, and the boys started communicating as though they were birds from outer space. Giving them time to wear themselves down movement-wise, we asked what they thought about the idea. They agreed that it would be fun to try and that they would create a Bird—really *absurd!*

As the boys developed bird movements, they started chanting—alternating 1 Gazinta, 2 Gazinta, 3 Gazinta, 4 Gazinta. They continued to move rhythmically, exaggerating their movements even more. Rereading the poem, they decided it wasn't long enough, so they added some of their chanting ("Gazinta Bird Absurd!"). They then planned their floor patterns for the dance.

Their problem became how many boys

to recruit—"If two Gazinta four two times, then how many more guys will we need?" It was decided that they needed twelve Gazinta Birds in all—eight in addition to the original four. The boys were recruited, given Gazinta Bird numbers (5–12), and shown the movements the four had worked out to represent the Bird. Thus, in working out their dance, they also worked on arithmetic concepts. The use of charts was helpful to them to figure out the necessary number of dancers, as well as working out the dance sequences.

The Gazinta Bird[2]

Eve Merriam

There's a strange sort of bird of a word
That abides near the Great Divide,
A Gazinta is this bird absurd.

And here is how it got its name:
Two Gazinta Four two times,
And Four Gazinta eight the same.

I Hear Bells

The children in a fourth grade were asked if they would like to dance in an all-school Christmas program for the community. They were requested to dance to the choir's singing of "I Hear Bells" by Marion Chaplin. The children were enthusiastic about the invitation.

There are times when teachers must give specific direction and immediate guidance because of the time factors and urgency for a program in some school situations. For example, space was limited and the situation was complicated because there was a nativity scene with fixed scenery. Then too, there were many other children participating in the nativity episode. Therefore, this particular dance had to be adjusted to space, people, a choir, and a particular piece of music. Hence the teacher's role became one

2 From Eve Merriam, *Doesn't Always Have to Rhyme* (New York: Atheneum Publishers, 1964).

of expediting and setting a framework for some structured exploration. Only sixteen children could be included on the stage. This posed a problem within the class. Choices had to be made and provision made for the others in the class since they all wanted to dance. It was necessary not to destroy the cohesive feeling of the group. Provision was made for two groups, one to work with "I Hear Bells" and a second to dance in another aspect of the program.

Listening to the music, the children said it made them think of happy swinging bells and of "slowly pulling bells." We found that the melody was in two parts; therefore, we could form two groups sometimes moving together and at other times in opposition. The groups moved in opposition to each other most of the time and developed their dance accordingly.

Feet Talk

Some of the fifth-grade boys had developed considerable dexterity doing cartwheels, standing on their heads, leaping through the air, and turning flips. They were highly skilled in walking on their hands. If space happened to be too crowded or if obstructions were in their way, they were more apt to cartwheel or flip over them rather than walk around. While they were in the process of trying to outdo one another one day, I said kiddingly, "If you boys aren't careful, you will be talking with your feet rather than with your mouths or hands." Giving me that "I'll betcha" look they started walking on hands down the auditorium steps and all the way up the aisles to the auditorium door. The next time I saw them Michael said he had written a story and Glen, Winfred, and Curtis wanted to dance it with him on their hands. They already had a name for their dance— "Feet Talk."

Time was planned for them to work on their dance idea. In the meantime we suggested that they practice walking on their

hands. They had figured out different ways of using their feet for conversation and they wanted to show that they could talk to one another with their feet instead of using their mouths. They had also decided that they would use a few cartwheels and flips to change directions.

They had thought through many of the mechanics. They wanted help on getting them into a dance. They also decided that they needed a girl from their class to add more to Michael's story and to read it as they danced so that people would know *what* they were saying. People would know that their feet were talking but they wanted people to know *what* they were *saying*. The dance took shape in one session. It was then a matter of perfecting their movements and getting the timing right. A chart follows showing their development of this dance.

FEET TALK
Michael Theirey
Read by Deborah

CONVERSATION WITH FEET	ACTION
Hey! "Here comes Glen walking down the street."	Comes down stage, walking on hands, turns around center.
Glen sees Michael. "Hello, Michael." "Hi Glen."	Face each other.
"What will we do?" "I don't know."	Still facing each other. Moving closer.
"Let's go this way." "No, let's go this way."	Cartwheels to right, back on hands. Cartwheels to left, back on hands.
"Hey wait for me! I know which way to go."	Enters from side going round and round. Others come to meet him.
"OK. But hurry up, slow poke."	Go round and round.
"I bet you can't do this!" said Glen.	All face each other. Glen pushes himself in the air from one hand, snapping fingers of other hand.
"I bet you we can."	Others follow.
"I bet you can't do this." "We can do anything."	Winfred jumps on hands. Others follow.

"Well, how about this?"	Going down to elbows on flat arms, back to hands. Several times.
"Sure, we can do it."	Others follow Michael.
"Look who's coming. Hi, Curtis. Bet you can't do this one."	Others go to meet him. All go back to center stage. Curtis stands on head and turns around slowly.
"Can't do it!"	Others follow but turn around standing on hands with feet saying "can't do it."
"Hey, I have to go home," said Glen. "My mother's calling," said Michael.	Glen exits going down auditorium steps and out aisle, still walking on hands. Turns around, goes backward to steps. Down steps on hands forward, exits.
"Come on home, Winfred." "See you."	Goes off to side on hands.
"No one left. I'll go, home, too."	Turns once around on head. Walks off on hands.

Pollution

The children in an entire school were concerned with pollution. They were anxious to do something about the pollution around their school. One group wanted to express its concern in dance, to show the accumulation of trash cans overflowing, and the presence of smoke in the air around the school, the growing amount of smog from cars, buses, and trucks in the area, and the increasing flow of trash into the streams and ponds, which made dirty water and almost killed the fish living in the ponds.

The teacher had the children in this group consolidate their observations and make a script to be used for their dance. Their script follows:

Part I

Randall loved his freedom of space. He could ride his horse, Thunder, for miles and miles and enjoy the open spaces.

Richard would spend his time at his pond playing and feeding his favorite fish. He would try to trick them. The fish would jump up high —out of the water.

Glen would play with his basketball. He would dribble all over the playground. As he dribbled, he tried to jump over the trash can. It was no problem. He could do that easily. There was plenty of open space, through which he could dribble his ball.

Part II

But one day, Glen dribbled all around and all of a sudden there were four trash cans and he tried to get over all four. He looked puzzled.

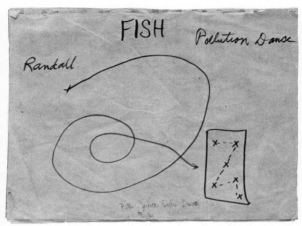

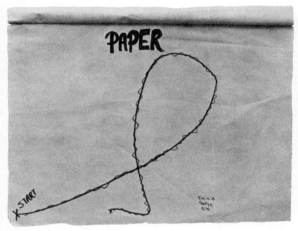

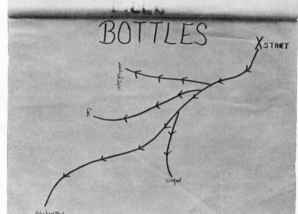

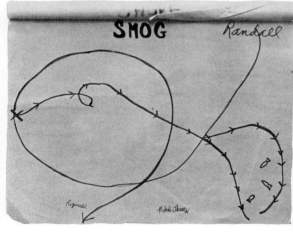

338

Something dreadful happened—more and more trash cans began to appear for Glen to go over and it took away his fun. Finally one day the trash cans became so full they exploded and Glen had to dribble around the trash. He had little space to dribble.

Later, newspapers began to blow on the playground. They got in the way. He could not get away from papers, no matter where he went.

After the papers, then bottles rolled onto the playground. Litter was all over the place. Glen had to jump over the litter. This was no fun!

Randall called his friends Richard and Glen to play. While they were trying to play, some clouds of smoke drifted in and settled all over the place. It got so bad they could not find the ball. Finally, they decided to go fishing. They had no place to play anymore. But while they were fishing along came the smog. THICK, HORRIBLE, UGLY, DIRTY smog. The smoke joined the smog. The boys began to cough. They could hardly breathe. The fish went back into the water.

Randall and his friends became discouraged. There was no place to ride his horse. Richard said there was no place to fish and Glen said, "That goes for basketball and baseball."

There was no place to play. Everywhere there was litter. There was trash, bottles, paper, smoke, and smog.

Part III

Glen said, "Here comes Curtis. Maybe he has an idea." Sure enough, Curtis did have an idea —to start a pollution campaign. They made huge posters they carried on sticks and lead a parade chanting, "Away With Pollution."

Later, after the Pollution Campaign, Randall and his friends decided to go fishing again. This time they found no trash, bottles, paper, smoke, or smog. After fishing, Randall began to ride his horse, Thunder. Once again he could gallop all around—up and down, for now the air had blown clean and free.

We discussed the script with the group as a basis for planning their dance. It was decided that individuals would become trash, paper, bottles, smoke, smog, fish, and also each of the boys would dance his part. The sequence of the dance was to follow the sequence of the three parts of the script.

After the boys and girls selected their respective parts and worked on the movement they were asked to explain their own parts. This is how some of them did it.

Tyrone: I am a third trash can. We spin round and round on our knees. Then Glen comes and jumps over us. We get bigger and bigger. Finally I explode and go all over the place.

Susan: I am one of the trash cans. I roll out and huddle up together moving with the other trash cans and we get fuller and fuller. I explode and splatter everywhere and stay.

Rita: I am a flying newspaper. I feel light and fly high in the air and get in Glen's way. All of the newspapers go round and round and up and up and down and try to stay in front or in back of him. Glen tries to push us away, but we just "freeze" like a newspaper and another group of newspapers fly in to do their parts and they "freeze" in newspaper shapes.

Michael: I am a bottle. Someone threw me into the playground and I whizz through the air and roll and roll, together with some of the other bottles. I get in Glen's way and he kicks me over and over and I stop.

Melody: I am smoke. I whirl around slower and slower around the paper and cover the litter so that the boys cannot find their ball.

Michael: I am dirty smog. I do high walk-leaps and turn round and round, slowly stretching out with the other smog. Then I dirty the water for the fish.

Eva Mae: My part is a fish. I swim through the water and jump up to tease Richard. Then I just wait while the litter and smoke and smog dance. I swim again and start playing with the fishing lines of the three boys. I hear the boys say, "let's go home" and all at once big black smog comes over me and I am almost dead.

All the boys and girls made large placards to be carried on sticks. In part III the four boys started parading with their placards, shouting the chant "Away With Pollution." As they paraded around the floor, each of the litter groups followed according to their chant (trash, paper, etc.). When Randall called "Pollution away" they froze and then dispersed. There were placards above the

POLLUTION

Alonah Stith

Randall loved his freedom of space. He could ride his horse, Thunder, up and down and around. He could ride for miles and miles and enjoyed the open spaces.

(Play section an octave higher
when repeating for the second time.)

Richard would spend his time at the fish pond playing and feeding his favorite fish.

He would try to trick them. The fish would jump up high out of the water. He would play with his fish for hours.

(Repeat section as needed according to movements.)

D.C. al Fine

fish pond which disappeared as they approached the pond. This left the boys to return to fishing in clean, clear water.

"Happiness Is—"

"Look! We want you to help us." So announced the fourth grade as they excitedly produced a huge chart. "Calm down and tell me about it." "You tell her, Miss Garber." "This morning I asked the boys and girls what makes them happy. Their ideas came fast as we talked about them and they thought we could make a *Happiness Is* Dance and a mural out of some of our feelings and ideas."

We moved for awhile to calm down and get in the mood to talk about their ideas. Some of their feelings and ideas had already "jelled." It was a matter of deciding which of the long list of ideas to select and how we would work out the ideas and which ideas

HAPPINESS IS

Arr. *Elizabeth Sutherland*

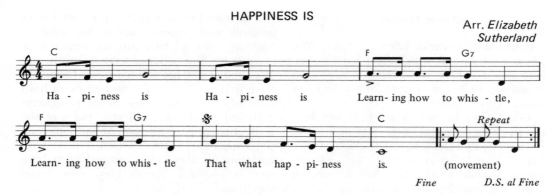

Ha - pi - ness   is   Ha - pi - ness   is   Learn- ing how   to whis - tle,

Learn- ing how   to whis - tle   That   what   hap - pi - ness   is.   (movement)

Fine   *D.S. al Fine*

they wanted to work on. It was suggested that they select the ideas that seemed to give variety and that would provide for small and large groupings. Six ideas were selected and then someone suggested that as long as Rita had just learned how to whistle that it would be funny if she would pretend to teach two boys. Everyone agreed that that would be a great way to start their dance. They were right! It proved to be whimsical and humorous and the boys fairly turned themselves inside out exaggerating learning to whistle.

There were now seven ideas to work out in groups. Selections were made and it was decided that they each would become a dance study to be included in a dance composition.

Mrs. Sutherland, the music teacher, was with us one day when we were developing our dance and asked if they would like to have some music (accompaniment had not even occurred to them up to this point).

They planned the order of dance study presentations. They had internalized feelings and expressed themselves in magical ways. There was silence during the study of finding something precious, and immediately the group wanted to know the secrets the boys were sharing. We discussed each study. Next we turned our attention to the sequence of the studies.

They also communicated their dance in a mural with each group putting their parts

on the mural. Often when they danced *Happiness Is* for an audience the mural added to background.

Happiness Is...

learning how to whistle, just horsing around, having a best friend, finding something precious, sharing a secret, having a fashion show, leaping over mud puddles, dancing and singing, dancing and singing for you!!

TOWARD QUALITY AND SELF-AWARENESS

Probably the most magnificent of all the world's wonders are children who open themselves to us and reveal in subtle but intimate ways their unique self. Such a self seeks opportunities to feel, to move, to dance, to be alive. To know such boys and girls over a period of time and to share in their world is a privilege; such opportunities are rare since there are so many children and we are apt to pass them by unknowingly. What a joy when we can pause long enough to extend opportunities to unleash latent talents. Such individuals often do not realize their own ability to move unafraid in expressing fantasy or stark realism. This is the child revealing himself in his own world.

The following example is presented as a kind of ultimate toward which teachers aspire.

Three Wishes

Patti asked to make her own dance. She wrote a paragraph which reflected her private world. There was such freshness and sensitivity in her statement. She called her dance "three wishes."

Essentially this was a story of her love for the charm of balloons! She had a sad friend who had lost a large colorful balloon. Patti's *first wish* was that her friend's balloon would come back. But it did not until she told her friend her secret. Her secret had to do with a very special way of making wishes. The magic way of wishing had to be repeated three times with closed eyes.

As this happened the balloon floated back. Patti and her friend were joyful and responded to the balloon with special care.

The friend suggested that they use Patti's magical wish again, hoping for another balloon. This was tried and the *second wish* came true. The balloons were so lovely and so prized that Patti wanted other friends to have balloons. After she wished extra hard (a *third wish*), four groups of five youngsters each appeared from different parts of the room, bringing a profusion of balloons coming with them. The children danced with balloons on their feet, around arms, and tied to all body parts. They were large, small, and many colors.

The movements for Patti, her friend, and the children were graceful, perceptive, and inventive. The pattern of movement for Patti's wishes was delicate, sensitive, thoughtful, and intense. Her entire body was rhythmically in tune. Her spatial designs were clear and yet diversified. The

dance was performed in silence, which added to its dramatic quality. As the *third wish* was granted music was added.

The end of the dance communicated happiness in the realization that *wishes do come true.*

In creative rhythmic movement—in dance —children are enabled to realize themselves as important somebodies with sensitivities and feelings. They can express their ideas by their most effective means of communication, which is movement, the universal language of all children. Self-awareness, creative power, and aesthetic understandings are enhanced as they dance. Their joy in sharing their dances indicates that they are realizing their Bill of Rights.

Children seek the continual help of adults who know them and respect them as people, who recognize their imperative need for activity, and who respond to their quest to discover and develop the uniqueness of self. We can make childhood a cherished time for all children by accepting *this challenge.*

You see *me*
Do you know me?

Deep down inside—
   yearning heart
   itching mind
   vibrating body
   creative spirit
Is the Real Me!

Give me the chance
   let me move
   help me dance

And I will give you
   the best
   that is *me*

Then you will know—
And see—
THE REAL ME!

Gladys Andrews Fleming

Creativity, rhythm, movement, and dance can make life fuller and richer for boys and girls!

344

Resources

Note the numerous references and resources used throughout this manuscript. In addition a selected list of references is given to assist those interested in various aspects of creative rhythmic movement and children's dance.

I. FLEMING, GLADYS ANDREWS, ed., *Children's Dance*. Washington, D.C.: AAHPER, 1973. Chapter 10 contains a comprehensive list of references: books, records, films.

II. Additional References

A. Art and Music

CARADENTE, GIOVANNI, *Calder, Mobiles and Stabiles*. New York: New American Library, 1968.

CARR, CONSTANCE, *Music for Children's Living*. Washington, D.C.: A.C.E.I., 1970.

FEZZI, ELDA, *Henry Moore*. New York: Hamlyn, 1972.

KLEE, PAUL, *Pedagogical Sketchbook*. New York: Frederick A. Praeger, Inc., 1953.

MILLER, CARL S., ed., *Sing, Children, Sing* (Songs, Dances and Singing Games of Many Lands and Peoples). New York: Chappell and Co., 1972.

MONTGOMERY, CHANDLER, *Art for Teachers of Children*. Columbus, Ohio: Charles E. Merrill, Co., 1968.

SHEEHY, EMMA D., *Children Discover Music and Dance*, Early Childhood Education Series. New York: Columbia Teachers' College Press, 1968.

SNOW, AIDA CANARRSA, *Growing With Children Through Art*. New York: Reinhold Book Corp., 1968.

STECHER, MIRIAM and HUGH MC-ELHENY, *Joy and Learning Through Music and Movement Improvisation*, N.Y.: The Macmillan Company, 1972.

United States Committee for UNICEF, *Hi Neighbor Series*. New York: United Nations.

B. Chants

BURROUGHS, MARGARET TAYLOR, *Did You Feed My Cow*. New York: Follett Publishing Co., 1969.

HUGILL, STAN, *Shanties and Sailor's Songs*. New York: Frederick A. Praeger, Inc., 1969.

TASHJIAN, VIRGINIA A., *Juba This and Juba That*. Boston: Little, Brown and Company, 1969.

C. Creativity

CARSON, RACHEL. *The Sense of Wonder*. New York: Harper & Row, 1956.

FLEMING, ROBERT S., ed., *Curriculum for Today's Boys and Girls*. Columbus, Ohio: Charles E. Merrill, 1963. See

Chapter 12 by Chandler, Montgomery, "Sensing and Responding to the World: Aesthetic Development," and Chapter 13 by Gladys Andrews, "Releasing Creativity—Extending Curriculum Opportunities."

JOSLIN, ROBERT O., and LARRY WEST, *Colors, Patterns and Textures.* Chicago: Henry Regnery Co., 1974.

The Journal of Creative Behavior, published by the Creative Education Foundation, Inc., Buffalo, N.Y.

METHENY, ELEANOR, ed., *People Make Ideas Happen.* Washington, D.C.: AAHPER, 1971.

McVICKAR, POLLY, *Imagination Key to Human Potential.* Washington, D.C.: National Association for the Education of Young Children, 1972.

MEARNS, HUGHES, *Creative Power: The Education of Youth in the Creative Arts,* N.Y.: Dover Publications, Inc., 1958.

MOUSTAKAS, CLARK, and CERETA PERRY, *Learning to be Free.* Englewood Cliffs, N.J.: Prentice-Hall, Inc., 1973.

Editors of *Outdoor World, The Splendor of the Seasons.* Waukesha. Wisconsin: Country Beautiful Corp., 1973.

SCHIFF, BENNETT, *Artists in the Schools.* Washington, D.C.: National Endowment for the Arts, U.S. Office of Education.

TAYLOR, JOSHUA C., *Learning to Look.* Chicago: University of Chicago Press, 1957.

YARDLEY, ALICE, *Reaching Out.* New York: Chilton Press, 1973.

D. Creative Rhythmic Movement: Dance

BARLIN, ANNE, *The Art of Learning Through Movement.* Los Angeles: Ward Ritchie, 1971.

BOORMAN, JOYCE, *Dance and Language Experiences with Children.* Don Mills, Ontario: Longman Canada Limited, 1973.

CARROLL, JEAN, and PETER LOFTHOUSE, *Creative Dance for Boys.* London: Macdonald and Evans, 1969.

CHERRY, CLAIRE, *Creative Movement for the Developing Child.* Palo Alto, California: Fearon Publishers, 1968.

DIMONDSTEIN, GERALDINE, *Children Dance in the Classroom.* New York: The Macmillan Company, 1971.

GRAY, VERA, and RACHEL PERCIVAL. *Music Movement and Mime for Children.* New York: Oxford University Press, 1963.

KRAUS, RICHARD, *Folk Dancing.* New York: The Macmillan Company, 1962.

METTLER, BARBARA, *Children's Creative Dance Book.* Tucson, Arizona: Mettler Studios, 1970.

MURRAY, RUTH, *Dance In Elementary Education. A Program for Boys and Girls,* 3rd ed. New York: Harper & Row, Publishers, 1974.

WAKEFIELD, ELEANOR ELY, *Folk Dancing in America.* New York: Pratt and Co., 1966.

E. Movement

ANDREWS, GLADYS, JEANETTE SAURBORN, and ELSA SCHNEIDER, *Physical Education for Today's Boys and Girls.* Boston: Allyn & Bacon, Inc. This book is being revised.

A.C.E.I., *Physical Education for Children's Healthful Living.* Washington, D.C., 1968.

BARRETT, KATE, *Exploration—A Method for Teaching Movement.* Madison, Wisconsin: College Printing and Typing Co., Inc., 1965.

BRINK, EDWARD, and ROGER RADA, *Experience in Movement.* Dubuque, Iowa: Kendall/Hunt Co., 1975.

CRATTY, BRYANT, *Active Learning.* Englewood Cliffs. N.J.: Prentice Hall, Inc., 1971.

DIEM, LISELOTT, *Who Can.* Frankfort, Germany: Wilhelm Limpert, 1967. (Available, Box 292, Trumbull, Conn.)

FLINCHUM, BETTY, *Motor Development in Early Childhood.* St. Louis, Mo.: The C. V. Mosby Co., 1975.

GERHARDT, LYDIA, *Moving and Knowing.* Englewood Cliffs, N.J.: Prentice Hall, Inc., 1973.

HALVERSON, LOLAS E., "Development of Motor Patterns in Young Children," *Quest*, Monograph VI (May 1969), 44–53.

HUNT, VALERIE, "Movement Behavior: A Model for Action," *Quest*, Monograph II (April 1964), 69–91.

NORTH, MARION, *Movement Education.* N.Y.: E. P. Dutton & Co., Inc., 1973.

PORTER, LORENA, *Movement Education for Children.* Washington, D.C.: A.E.K.N.E., 1969.

Quest, Monograph II, "The Art and Science of Human Movement" (April, 1964). Publication of the National Association for Physical Education of College Women and the National College Physical Education Association for Men. For subscription or single issues: Frances Bleick, 1419 9th Ave. South, St. Cloud, Minn. 56301.

————, Monograph XXIII, "The Language of Movement" (January, 1975).

SCHURR, EVELYN L., *Movement Experiences for Children*, 2nd ed., Englewood Cliffs, N.J.: Prentice-Hall, Inc., 1975.

SINCLAIR, CAROLINE B., *Movement of the Young Child.* Columbus, Ohio: Charles & Merrill Co., 1973.

SWEENEY, R. T., ed., *Selected Readings in Movement Education.* Reading, Mass.: Addison-Wesley Co., 1970.

F. Poetry and Stories

ARBUTHNOT, MAY HILL, *Time for Poetry.* N.Y.: Scott, Foresman Co., 1951.

COATSWORTH, ELIZABETH, *The Children Come Running.* New York: Golden Press (U.N. Children's Fund), 1960.

COURLANDER, HAROLD, ed., *Ride With the Sun: Folk Tales and Stories from all Countries of United Nations.* N.Y.: McGraw Hill Book Company, 1955.

DE REGNIERS, BEATRICE, *Something Special.* New York: Harcourt Brace Jovanovich, Inc., 1958.

HUBER, MIRIAM BLANTON, ed., *Story and Verse for Children.* New York: The Macmillan Company, 1955.

JACOBS, LELAND B., *Using Literature with Young Children.* New York: Teachers' College Press, 1965.

LATHEM, EDWARD CONNERY, ed. *The Poetry of Robert Frost*, New York: Holt, Rinehart and Winston, Inc., 1964.

National Geographic Society, *The World of the American Indian.* Washington, D.C.: National Geographical Society, 1974.

NICKERSON, BETTY, *Celebrate the Sun.* Philadelphia: J. B. Lippincott Co., 1969.

SANDBURG, CARL, *Complete Poems.* N.Y.: Harcourt Brace Jovanovich, Inc., 1950.

THOMPSON, BLANCHE JENNINGS, *Silver Pennies.* N.Y.: Macmillan Co., 1953.

G. Children's Books

GLADSTONE, GARY, *Hey Hey, Can't Catch Me!* New York: Van Nostrand Reinhold Company, n.d.

HOBAN, FARA, *Look Again.* New York: The Macmillan Company, 1971.

KEEN, MARTIN L., *How and Why Wonder Book of Sound.* New York: Grosset & Dunlap, Inc., 1970.

KLUGMAN, HERTHA, *Can You Swallow a Squiggle?* N.Y.: Wonder Books, 1971.

LEAR, EDWARD, *The Quangle Wangle's Hat.* N.Y.: Franklin Watts, Inc., 1970.

LIONNI, LEO, *Fish is Fish.* New York: Random House, Inc., 1970.

RUSSELL, SOLVEIG PAULSON, *Lines and Shapes: A First Look at Geometry.* New York: Henry Z. Walck, Inc., 1965.

SAMSON, ANN, *Lines and Spines and Porcupines.* N.Y.: Doubleday, 1969.

SCHLEIN, MIRIAM, *Fast Is Not a Ladybug*. N.Y.: William R. Scott, Inc., 1973.

SHOWERS, PAUL, *The Listening Walk*. New York: Thomas Y. Crowell Company, 1961.

SPIER, PETER, *Crash! Bang! Boom!* Garden City. N.Y.: Doubleday & Company, Inc., 1972.

TOBAN, JANA, *Shapes and Things*. New York: The Macmillan Company, 1970.

TISON, ANNETTE, and TALUS TAYLOR, *The Adventures of the Three Colors*. New York: World Publishing Co., 1971.

UBELL, EARL, *The World of Push and Pull*. New York: Atheneum, 1964.

VAVRE, ROBERT, *Tiger Flower*. New York: Reynal, 1968.

H.   Miscellaneous

A.C.E.I., *Children Are Centers for Understanding Media*. Washington, D.C., 1973.

GILLIES, EMILY, *Creative Dramatics for All Children*. Washington, D.C.: A.C.E.I., 1973.

LEISY, JAMES, *The Good Times Song Book*. Nashville, Tenn.: Abingdon Press, 1974.

McDERMOTT, GERALD, *Arrow to the Sun*. N.Y.: The Viking Press, Inc., 1974.

MARKIN, PATRICIA, and JOAN LANE, *Bibliography of Books for Children*. Washington, D.C.: A.C.E.I., 1974.

WERNER, PETER, and RICHARD SIMMONS, *Do It Yourself*. Dubuque, Iowa: Kendall/Hunt Co., 1973.

Index